CHIVALRY

CHIVALRY

Maurice Keen

Yale University Press
New Haven and London

Designed by Caroline Williamson.

Filmset by Clavier Phototypesetting, Southend-on-Sea, Essex
Printed in Great Britain at The Pitman Press, Bath

Library of Congress Cataloging in Publication Data

Keen, Maurice Hugh.
  Chivalry.

  Bibliography: p.
  Includes index.
  1. Chivalry. 2. Knights and knighthood — Europe. 3. Europe — Nobility
— History. 4. Heraldry — Europe. 5. Civilization, Medieval. I. Title.
CR4513.K44   1984   394'.7   83-23282

ISBN 0-300-03360-5 (pbk.)

CONTENTS

LIST OF ILLUSTRATIONS

Following Page 20

Following Page 84

Following Page 116

Following Page 180

Following Page 212

ACKNOWLEDGEMENTS

As a child, I was always fascinated by stories that were told me about 'knights in shining armour'. When I was older, I was very lucky in my teachers, two of whom turned my childish excitement over the idea of knights into a serious interest: Sir Walter Oakeshott, who taught me at Winchester, and Sir Richard Southern, who was my tutor at Balliol when I was an undergraduate. To each I owe a very profound debt, which I cannot attempt to put into words. I have a further particular debt of gratitude to Sir Richard, who read the typescript of this book and gave advice and criticism which was in every instance to the point.

I must specially mention how grateful I am to the Leverhulme Trust. In 1978 they made me a generous grant which enabled me to spend abroad a very substantial part of the academic year 1978–9, when my College kindly gave me sabbatical leave. Without this support, much of the research on which this book is based could not have been undertaken.

So many others have helped me that I think that I must mention now something that is usually mentioned later. All the mistakes, misprints and misunderstandings in this book are my responsibility. Perhaps I may illustrate. Shortly before I sent off the typescript I found that I had consistently referred to a knightly order of *la Dame Verte à l'Escu Blanc* – an order which, as I presented it, appears to be dedicated to some kind of Jumblie girl with sea green hair. It should of course be the order of *la Dame Blanche à l'Escu Vert*, the white lady with the green shield, and not *vice versa*. At an even later stage I found that I had, in recording a particular incident, transmogrified by mistranslation a female anchoress into a male hermit. These are the kind of mistakes that the kindest and most careful of advisers cannot spot. I expect that more of them will be found under the wainscotting in due course, and it is my fault that they are still lurking there.

Nevertheless I must still thank, and very warmly, those who have helped me. Three scholars gave me ideas and inspiration while I was writing: Dr J. D'Arcy Boulton, to whose distinguished thesis on the curial orders of chivalry I owe a great deal; Professor John Larner, who allowed me to see and study the typescript of his paper on chivalry in Italy in the time of Dante; and Dr Linda Paterson, who in a lecture to the Medieval Society in Oxford gave me a glimpse of the importance of Provencal epic, whose significance would otherwise have been a closed book to me, because of my linguistic shortcomings. I must also say how particularly grateful I am to Mr Karl Leyser, Mr Philippe Contamine, Mr Patrick Wormald, Mr Randall Rogers, Mr Michael Maclagan, Dr Martin Brett, and to Malcolm and Juliet Vale for their advice and guidance. I should also mention the help that I have received on particular points from Mr Simon Lloyd, Dr Christopher Tyerman and Mr T. D. Mathew. I must thank very warmly Mrs Juliet Barker for checking out many references and saving me from many errors; Mrs Mary Bugge, who typed the manuscript; John Nicoll and Caroline Williamson of Yale University Press, who were consistently helpful and patient; and the staff of the libraries that I have visited in the course of my work. I am most grateful to Elizabeth Eagleston and Damian Dewhirst for their help with the proofs, and to my wife Mary for help with the proofs and at every stage of the whole business of putting a book together.

There is one special debt that I must particularly acknowledge. Several of the chapters of this book found their first form in papers which were presented to audiences in Ireland, in the constituent colleges of the National University, and one at Trinity College, Dublin. Irish audiences are patient, courteous and generous in their criticism, and I am deeply grateful to those who were my hosts there, to Professor F. X. Martin and Professor John Barry and the members of their departments in Dublin and Cork, and to Dr Ian Robinson of Trinity College. Above all, I must acknowledge my debt to the late Mr Denis Bethell, Statutory Lecturer in medieval history in University College, Dublin, to whose hospitality and to whose ideas and counsel I owe more than I can say.

This long list reminds me of how many of my ideas I owe to others. I have doubtless too often garbled them, and the garblings, like the errors in this book, are mine.

CHAPTER I

Introduction: The Idea of Chivalry

'The age of chivalry is gone: that of sophisters, economists and calculators has succeeded: and the glory of Europe is extinguished for ever.'[1] It was the plight of Marie Antoinette that inspired Edmund Burke's indignant cry, and there is a certain appositeness about identifying the death of chivalry with the end of the French *ancien régime*. But most people, I imagine, would suppose that the age of chivalry had passed a good long time before 1791. If a genuine age of chivalry is to be sought, it is surely in the middle ages, and not the early modern age, that most would locate it, somewhere between, say, the year 1100 and the beginning of the sixteenth century: somewhere, that is to say, between the launching of the first crusade and the Reformation; between the composition of the Song of Roland and the death of Bayart; between the time when the triumph of the Norman horsemen at Hastings was recorded in the Bayeux tapestry and the triumph of artillery. But was there ever, really, an age of chivalry, even then? Was chivalry ever more than a polite veneer, a matter of forms rather than a social influence of any significance, let alone the 'glory of Europe'. And if it ever was more than a matter of forms and words, what was it? These are the questions which it is the object of this book to investigate, and they are not easy questions to answer.

Chivalry is an evocative word, conjuring up images in the mind – of the knight fully armed, perhaps with the crusaders' red cross sewn upon his surcoat; of martial adventures in strange lands; of castles with tall towers and of the fair women who dwelt in them. It is also, for that very reason, a word elusive of definition. One can define within reasonably close limits what is meant by the word knight, the French *chevalier*: it denotes a man of aristocratic standing and probably of noble ancestry, who is capable, if called upon, of equipping himself with a war horse and the arms of a heavy cavalryman, and who has been through certain rituals that make him what he is – who has been 'dubbed' to knighthood. But chivalry, the abstraction from *chevalier*, is not so easily pinned down. It is a word that was used in the middle ages with different meanings and shades of meaning by different writers and in different contexts. Sometimes, especially in early texts, it means no more than a body of heavily armed horsemen, a collective of *chevaliers*.[2] Sometimes chivalry is spoken of as an order, as if knighthood ought to be compared to an order of religion: sometimes it is spoken of as an estate, a social class – the warrior class whose martial function, according to medieval writers, was to defend the *patria* and the Church. Sometimes it is used to encapsulate a code of values apposite to this order or estate. Chivalry cannot be divorced from the martial world of the mounted warrior: it cannot be divorced from aristocracy, because knights commonly were men of high lineage: and from the middle of the twelfth century on it very frequently carries ethical or religious overtones. But it remains a word elusive of definition, tonal rather than precise in its implications. If we are to get any way towards deciding whether chivalry was, in the period bet-ween about 1100 and about 1500, a social influence of any significance, we shall need at the outset to find sources that give some reasonably extended account of what the word could and should mean, since it is plainly not a word that can be pinned down clearly and succinctly in a dictionary definition.

There are various different kinds of sources to which we can turn for guidance at this point. Among the most obvious are the courtly romances, since the authors and redactors of medieval romance were enthusiastic in explaining that the stories of their heroes presented a model of true chivalry. 'In this book you will learn of things delectable and worthy to be remembered for the exaltation of *noblesse* and chivalry, and to the edification and example of all men; and above all of those whose will it is to achieve in arms the highest honour.'[3] So runs the introduction to the romance of *Lancelot* published in 1488. And the romances do indeed help, in one obvious way, toward a definition of chivalry's elusive ethical implica-tions. From a very early stage we find the romantic authors habitually associating together certain qualities which they clearly regarded as the classic virtues of good knighthood: *prouesse*, *loyauté*, *largesse* (generosity), *courtoisie*, and *franchise* (the free and frank bearing that is visible testimony to the combination of good birth with virtue).[4] The association of these qualities in chivalry is already established in the romances of Chrétien de Troyes (written *c.*1165–*c.*1185), and from his time on to the end of the middle ages their combination remains the stereotype of chivalrous distinc-tion.

For the historian, however, there is a real difficulty about the application to his purposes of this stereotype. How is he to set about relating a model drawn from a world of fiction and fantasy to the real world which is his business? The pages of romance plunge him immediately into realms unfamiliar to history: where victories are won single handed over odds that are incredible; where rivers flow that can only be traversed by bridges fashioned from glass or from the blades of swords; where in the boundless forest a rider may stumble upon a hermitage where Christ's passion is visibly re-enacted at the Mass – or upon a Questing Beast.[5] The romance story-tellers are quite open in their admission that their matter is 'outrageous'. The wind that sighs over their enchanted ground blows away the humdrum limitations of the stage on which real life is enacted. An ideal of knighthood culled from what appears so often to be essentially a literature of escape is scarcely a promising model for a social historian to make much of.

We shall in fact need to return to the romances, many times, but for the moment their evidence is too obviously open to the charge that, outside literature, chivalry really was no more than a polite veneer, a thing of forms and words and ceremonies which provided a means whereby the well-born could relieve the bloodiness of life by decking their activities with a tinsel gloss borrowed from romance. Many historians, among them the great Huizinga whose *Waning of the Middle Ages* contains what has become the classic account of later medieval chivalry, have argued that this was indeed the case.[6] The imitative propensities of late medieval court culture, which in the fifteenth century led to the staging of tournaments in Arthurian dress and to the re-enactment at banquests of scenes and ceremonies modelled upon romance, lend weight to their argument. If I agreed with their view I would not be writing this book, but it is not a view which can be rebutted simply; and this means that we cannot, at the outset, accept the literary model of the knight of sovereign prowess as a basis of definition, in an inquiry into the social significance of chivalry.

Another type of source material is less vulnerable than the romances are to the charge that, being founded in a world of illusion, they explain only the posturings of men in the real world. The great churchmen of the middle ages, in their treatises upon government and upon the right ordering of Christian society and in their sermons, had much to say about how knights ought to conduct themselves in real life and especially about the function of knighthood in the Christian world. Very important in this last respect were the writings of those authors who treated of the three orders or estates in Christian society: the clergy, whose business is with prayer and with pastoral ministration to society's spiritual needs; the warriors, whose business it is with their swords to uphold justice, protect the weak, and defend the Church; and the labourers, by whose toil the land is tilled and whose work provides for the physical needs both of themselves and of the other two estates.[7] This idea of the tripartite ordering of society appears very early, indeed long before any such word as chivalry had been coined. King Alfred gave it clear expression in his translation of Boethius, written in the 890s, and its origins are undoubtedly older still.[8] This is one of the limitations upon its usefulness in our quest for a definition of chivalry; the idea of the warriors as a separate order with a distinct function antedates, by an easy margin, the use of the word chivalry. Even in the eleventh century, writers like Adalbero of Laon and Gerard of Cambrai, in discussing the threefold ordering of society, use to denote the secular martial class words better translated as the 'warriors' rather than the 'knights', such as *bellatores* or *pugnatores*, – words which lack specifically chivalrous overtones.[9] Another and perhaps more obvious limitation upon the usefulness of this idea of the special function of the warrior for our purposes is the fact that the idea of the threefold ordering of society, while it became a commonplace of social commentary, never adequately corresponded with the facts of social life, even in the very early middle ages. It represents an ideal vision, more useful to contemporaries who wished to measure and impugn the actual shortcomings of society than to the historian who wishes to know things as they once were.

Nevertheless it is an important idea, and one which had profound influence in the process of establishing a definition of chivalry, as we shall see in due course. We can observe its influence in this direction clearly in the *Livre des manières* of Etienne de Fougères, Bishop of Lisieux, who wrote in the 1170s (and in the vernacular, the language of knights), and whose work has at least a claim to contain the first systematic treatment of chivalry. The threefold order of society provided the basis for his work, and for him, significantly, the warrior estate was, quite simply, the *chevalerie*. Because this identification seemed to him self-evident, his treatment of chivalry carries us beyond the question of functions into the fringes of the social and ritual world of knighthood, through its emphasis, for instance, on the association of the knight's social standing and his lineage (he should be a free man, *de franche mere né*) and its references to the oath that the knight should make when he receives the 'order' of chivalry and takes his sword 'from the altar'. But Etienne's definition of chivalry as an 'order' affords us only a glimpse of something more lying behind that important word, which may suggest something of the cult of the cavalier specifically and of an independent culture of chivalry, yet remains a suggestion to that effect, and no more. His lengthy critique of the shortcomings of the knights who were his contemporaries reveals his real concern, which is not with what knighthood is so much as with what it is not. It also reveals another limitation upon the usefulness of a professional ecclesiastic's point of view with reference to the definition of chivalry. As a good churchman, he sees it as the knight's business to be the strong right arm of the Church, which should do the bidding of the superior clerical order – and without too much questioning.[10] It is doubtful whether many knights would have seen their duty here in such clear-cut terms as he did.

Looking at matters through priestly eyes, as they naturally most often did, ecclesiastical authors showed a very general tendency to portray chivalry in terms of priestly priorities which most knights either did not fully understand or felt justified in ignoring. This comes out particularly clearly in the writings of the great clerical champions of the church reform movement of the eleventh and twelfth centuries. Bonizo of Sutri, for instance, in his *Liber de vita Christiana* (*c.* 1090) has much that is very interesting to say about the function of the warrior in Christian society, but his Gregorian prejudices are exposed when he remarks that 'if Kings and magnates and knights were not to be summoned to *persecute schismatics and heretics and excommunicates* . . . the order of warriors would seem superfluous in the Christian legion.'[11] For St Bernard, contrasting in his *De laude novae militiae* the effete and luxurious secular knighthood with the Templars 'who deck themselves not in gold and silver, but with faith within and mail without, to strike terror, not avarice, into the hearts of their enemies',[12] the crusader becomes virtually the exclusive type of true chivalry, and the crusader at that who is fired by singleminded religious zeal – 'you who have truly confessed *from the heart*'. Even among crusaders, those whom he regarded as the only true knights can never have been more than a handful. We begin to see that the high ecclesiastical idea of chivalry suffers from a limitation ultimately very similar to that which inhibits the usefulness of the romances for purposes of definition: it is too idealistic. Where the romances offer a reflection of life that is too superb, it makes reality look mean by contrasting it with an inaccessible measure of dedication.

This does not of course mean that the views of the great churchmen did not profoundly influence the knighthood's idea of its purpose and place in society: they did. The learning of churchmen certainly enlarged the view of what chivalry meant, and brought home effectively the lesson that *chevalerie* without *clergie* (learning) was nothing worth, that they were twin pillars of society.[13] John of Salisbury's idea of chivalry, as a profession that had been instituted by God and that was in its own right necessary to human well-being,[14] clearly also had considerable influence in the long run, though largely indirectly: his clear and elegant Latin was not immediately penetrable by secular men, and his ideas percolated only gradually to their circles. Nevertheless, we can glimpse reflections of his and similar ideas in their attitudes, particularly, in the light of his paean of praise in the *Policraticus* for the discipline of the Romans and the rigorous training of their martial youth, in the later enthusiasm for 'Books of Chivalry' which turn out to be translations of the Roman writer on military tactics and training, Vegetius.[15] Didactic works in the vernacular, like Thomas of Zerclaire's great treatise on virtue in the active life, *Der wälsche Gast* (1216), had a still more direct impact. That particular work, which drew its teaching ultimately from the schools but used extensively examples of virtue drawn from knightly romance, continued to be read by knights down to the end of the middle ages.[16] Without clerical learning in the background, chivalry could scarcely have progressed far beyond a kind of hereditary military professionalism, occasionally heroic but essentially crude.

To try to follow up the line of inquiry suggested here would, however, at this present stage, lead us far away from our immediate purpose, the quest for some sort of working model of what chivalry once meant. With that end in view, a third type of source, which bears the imprint of the influence both of the romances and of ecclesiastical opinion, but which is different from either, will prove much more useful. A considerable number of treatises on chivalry have survived, written specifically for the instruction of knighthood and for the most part in the vernacular language that secular men such as knights could understand. Few if any of these treatises are completely free of the charge that they paint a picture either too rosy or too lofty, and a good many of them were written by authors who had an axe of some sort to grind. Some of them are too romantic, many mere applications of the commonplaces of the pulpit or of moral theology to the knightly way of life. Some however do make an attempt to treat of chivalry as a way of life in its own right, and to offer instruction to that end. Let us concentrate our attention for the moment on three works which fall into this latter class: the anonymous poem called the *Ordene de chevalerie*; the *Book of the Ordre of Chyvalry (Libre del ordre de cavayleria)* of the great Majorcan mystic, Ramon Lull; and the *Book of Chivalry (Libre de chevalerie)* written by the fourteenth-century French knight Geoffrey de Charny. All three of these works date from a period when the ideas of the great church reformers of the Gregorian period had been absorbed into the mainstream of medieval culture: this makes it all the more striking that, as we shall presently see, they seem to be so little touched by them.

★

No one knows who wrote the *Ordene de chevalerie*, or precisely when; but it is clearly Northern French, and was probably composed before 1250.[17] It achieved widespread popularity and men continued to refer to its authority even in the later fifteenth century. It was copied into numerous manuscripts, and appears often in company with other material interesting to knightly readers: here together with a treatise on hunting and an ordinance concerning tournaments; here in the company of a pilgrim guide to the Holy Land and a report by the Patriarch of Jerusalem on the state of Outremer; here again in the company of a little anonymous poem comparing Jesus to a knight, and some notes on falconry.[18] An abbreviated prose version was made of it, which was almost equally as popular as the original poem. The work takes the form of a little story of how Hugh, Count of Tiberias, was captured in battle by Saladin, who out of respect for his valour agreed to release him if he would fulfil one particular and peculiar request. This was that he should show the Sultan the manner by which knights are made under the Christian law. Faced with the alternative of an outrageous ransom, Hugh reluctantly agreed to make his captor a knight after the proper forms, and the poem focusses about this ritual, explaining at each step what it is that is symbolised by the ceremony.

First Hugh dressed Saladin's beard and hair, and then he brought him to a bath: this is a bath of courtesy and bounty, he said, and should recall to you the baptism of the child, for you must come out of it as clean of sin as the infant from the font. Then he brought him to a fair bed, to signify the repose of paradise, which is what every knight must strive to win by his 'chivalry'. Raising him, he dressed him first in a white robe, signifying the cleanness of the body; over that he threw a scarlet cloak, to remind him of the knight's duty to be ready to shed his blood at need in defence of God's church. Then he drew on brown stockings, to remind him of the earth in which he must lie in the end, and to prepare in life for death. After that he bound about Saladin's waist a belt of white, signifying virginity, and that he should hold back lust in his loins. Then came the gold spurs, to show that the knight must be as swift to follow God's commandments as the pricked charger. Last, he girded him with the sword, whose two sharp edges are to remind the new knight that justice and loyalty must go together, and that it is the knight's task to defend the poor from the strong oppressor. There should have followed one thing more, the *collée*, a light blow from the hand of him who had girded the new knight, but this Hugh, as Saladin's prisoner, would not give: he could not strike his 'master'. But he did give him four commandments to which a newly made knight must be bound for all his life following. He must not be consenting to any false judgement, or be a party in any way to treason; he must honour all women and damsels and be ready to aid them to the limit of his power; he must hear, when possible, a mass every day, and must fast every Friday in remembrance of Christ's passion.[19]

The *Ordene de chevalerie* is a very interesting poem. The fact that it is Saladin whom Hugh is taking through the steps of initiation into knighthood shows what a far cry there is from this piece, in spite of its crusading setting, to the militant crusading zeal of St Bernard's ideal of chivalry. Though the ritual is a specifically Christian ritual and chivalry is portrayed as a path towards Christian salvation in the repose of paradise, the making of a knight is portrayed as an entirely secular rite which has no need for a priest or for the church's altar for its accomplishment. The emphasis upon the discipline under which the knight must keep his body may echo distantly what John of Salisbury had to say about the rigour of the Romans, but the spirit of the poem is much closer to the chivalrous ideology of the romances. Two of their classic knightly virtues, loyalty and courtesy, are expressly stressed: hardiness and prowess are assumed (what has drawn

Saladin to Hugh is that he recognises him as a man of prowess, a
preudhomme). And the poem ends with a bow to *largesse*, as Saladin frees
Hugh and sends him home with the price of his ransom advanced from the
Sultan's own treasury. Of the four commandments that Hugh gives, the two
first, that the knight must eschew false judgement and treason and must
honour and aid womankind, recall two classic themes of romantic narrative. What we are hearing about, though, belongs to the world of reality, not
that of illusion: we know that countless men did go through ritual similar to
that the poem describes in order to become knights, and its popularity
attests that its interpretation of the symbolism of the rite must have been
widely understood. It offers an excellent introduction to what men understood chivalry to mean.

★

The *Ordene* is anonymous: by contrast we know a great deal about Ramon
Lull, the author of our second treatise on chivalry.[20] His father had been a
companion of King James of Aragon in the conquest of Majorca from the
Moors, and was rewarded by him with estates near Palma which his son
inherited. Young Ramon entered the royal service early; he became the
companion and later the seneschal of James, the younger son of his father's
patron James the Conqueror and the future King of Majorca. In his youth,
Ramon delighted in chivalrous accomplishments, wrote songs after the
manner of the troubadours, and led, it would seem, a fairly profligate life.
He married, and was unfaithful: 'the beauty of women, O Lord, has been a
plague and a tribulation to my eyes', he was to declare many years later.[21]
Then, one day, as he was struggling with the verses of a new amorous lay for
the current mistress of his affections, he looked up to see, on his right side,
'the Lord God Jesus hanging upon the Cross.'[22] He left his poetry and went
to rest: but a week later when he was wrestling again with the same poem his
vision re-appeared. After three more visitations, he surrendered himself
finally to the demands that this insistent visitation made on him, and
deserted his old ways. This was in 1263: the vocation that he found to be
revealed to him was nothing less than the conversion of Islam. He
immersed himself in the study both of Latin and Arabic, and in 1276 he
began to teach in the Franciscan College at Miramar, founded (no doubt at
his suggestion) by his old friend James of Majorca. The rest of his life is an
extraordinary story of endless journeys: of sojourns among the learned at
Paris, Montpellier, and further afield; of the prolific composition of the
books in which he sought to encapsulate a whole recondite philosophy. It
culminated in his martyrdom at Bougie in 1316, where he was stoned to
death by the Moslems whom he had come to convert. He was then more
than eighty years old.

Lull's *Libre del ordre de cavayleria* was clearly written after his renunciation of the ways of his early life, and bears many marks of his conversion: internal evidence suggests that it was written before the foundation of the College at Miramar.[23] It is a rambling work, and in its wanderings says more than can be condensed into a short space. Like the *Ordene de chevalerie*, it opens in the form of a narrative. A squire, riding through the forest on his way to the King's great court, where he is to be made a knight (along with many others), loses his way and comes to the cell of an aged hermit, who proves to be one who, after a long life spent in arms and chivalry, has retired to the wood to pass his last days in holy contemplation. Discovering the squire's purpose, the hermit finds him strangely ignorant of the obligations on which he is about, as a knight, to enter, and begins to read to him from a little book, which explains the meaning of chivalry. This little book he finally presents to the squire, so that he may carry it to the King's court and show it to all those who are to be made knights. The little book is, of course, Ramon Lull's work itself.

The book opens with an account of the origins of chivalry. When, after the fall of man, war and 'misprision' began to enter the world, and to disturb it, chivalry was instituted to restrain and defend the people. One man in every thousand *(ex mille electus)* 'the most loyal, most strong and of most noble courage', was chosen to be a knight *(miles)*.[24] This man was equipped with a horse, 'the most noble of beasts', and the best armour that could be had: he was given a squire to serve him, and the common people were set under him to till the land and sustain him and his beasts. From this beginning, Lull says, chivalry has endured continually down to his own day, and it is the duty of every knight to train up his son from childhood with a view to discharging those functions for which chivalry was originally instituted. This should not just mean a training in horsemanship and the martial arts: there is more to chivalry than that. Indeed, its ethics and science ought to be written in books, and there ought to be schools of instruction in chivalry just as there are schools in which clerks learn their doctrine.[25] This first glimpse of the potential of military colleges as the forcing grounds of a martial ethos is a vision worthy of the ambitious propagandist for missionary colleges, such as that at Miramar, that Lull was. The potential was not to be realised until the early Renaissance, for another two and a half centuries.

In the absence of schools, books are the best answer, and Lull goes on to discuss in detail the duties of a knight. His first duty, he says, is to defend the faith of Christ against unbelievers, which will win him honour both in this world and the next: here speaks the crusader's son. He must also defend his temporal lord, and protect the weak, women, widows and orphans. He should exercise his body continually, by hunting wild beasts – the hart, the boar and the wolf – and by seeking jousts and tournaments. Under the

King, he should judge the people and supervise their labours: indeed, it is from the knighthood that kings ought to choose their provosts and bailiffs and other secular officers. The knight must be ready to go out from his castle to defend the ways and to pursue robbers and malefactors.[26] He must also school himself in the virtues necessary to discharge these duties, in wisdom, charity and loyalty, above all in courage 'for chivalry abideth not so agreeably in no place as in *noblesse* of courage'.[27] He must prize honour before all, and eschew pride, false-swearing, idleness, lechery, and especially treason (we should note the strongly archaic flavour of Lull's conception of the ultimate treasons: to slay your lord, or to lie with his wife, or to surrender his castle). Towards the end of the book Lull sums up what sort of man this will make a knight to be. He will be a man courteous and nobly spoken, well clad, one who holds open house within the limit of his means.[29] Loyalty and truth, hardiness, *largesse* and humility will be the principal qualities of character that we ought to expect in him.

An important chapter describes the examination to which every squire seeking knighthood should be subjected, to ensure that he has the proper qualifications.[30] He must be able-bodied, and of sufficient age to discharge the tasks of knighthood. He should come of good lineage and must have sufficient wealth to support his rank. The knight who is examining him should also inquire into the manner of his life, looking for signs of the valour and nobility necessary to knighthood, and should ensure that he is without known 'reproach'. He should inquire also of the squire his motives for seeking knighthood: to acquire knighthood for the wrong reasons, for advantage and rank, is as bad as simony in a clerk. Here is an eminently sensible list of questions, which, with a change here and there of vocabulary, would do no discredit to a selection board for commissions in an armoured regiment today. When he has satisfied all these tests, the squire should be allowed to go forward to take the order of knighthood, (probably at some great feast of the Church, at Pentecost, Christmas or Easter). On the eve of his knighthood he ought to confess himself and to spend the night waking in prayer and contemplation. Next day he should attend mass along with all the others who are to be knighted with him, and there should be a sermon in which the meaning of the articles of faith, the ten commandments and the seven sacraments are explained by the preacher. Then before the altar the squire should receive knighthood from one who is already a knight. Lull goes on to explain at great length the symbolic significance of the various arms and articles of harness that are given to a knight (the symbolism of the sword and the spurs are precisely the same as in the *Ordene de chevalerie*). After this, his book is rounded off with a disquisition on the vices and virtues, and their application to the life of a knight, and a brief account of the honour which all men owe to chivalry.

Lull's *Libre del ordre de cavalayria* was immensely successful. It was translated into French and Castilian, into Middle Scots by Sir Gilbert of the Haye and into English by Caxton: three editions of the French version were published in the early sixteenth century.[31] In effect, it became the classic account of knighthood (outside Germany) and we should therefore be careful to note the salient features of the picture of chivalry that it offers. It is, as we should expect from Lull, somewhat more ecclesiastically oriented than the *Ordene de chevalerie*. The new knight will receive his knighthood in church, and the author of the book is at pains to make sure that he should be informed about the essentials of his faith and the nature of the Christian virtues. There is a crusading flavour to more than one passage. But we should be careful not to overstress this aspect of Lull's account. He stresses the harmony that there should be between the order of knighthood and the priestly order, but he seems to regard each as in its own sphere independent. His account of the origins of knighthood is given in terms that are entirely secular. He urges knights to exercise themselves at jousts and tournaments, which were banned by the church. Knighthood, moreover, is in his mind clearly very closely bound up with secular government: his knight is not only a nobly born warrior but also a lord of men, and much of his duty comes under the general heading of maintaining law and justice. Lull does underscore, and heavily, the need for the knight to observe discipline, of body and soul, which we are beginning to recognise as a recurrent theme: but there is to be relief to this disciplinary rigour, time for hunting and other sports, and he expects the knight to be wealthy, well clad and to keep a great household. And once again we find our attention focussed on the same list of specifically knightly qualities that we first heard of in the romances, and which do not seem to be in any direct way derivative from theological treatments of virtue (though of course, as Lull saw, they can be brought into line with them): courtesy, loyalty, hardiness, *largesse, franchise*.

The imprint of Lull's religious preoccupations is plain in his book, but the imprint of his own knightly experience is equally plain, and at times plainer. A number of passages suggest that, in fact, the prose romance of *Lancelot* was one important source that he used when putting it together.[32] His singling out of Alexander's liberality as an example of *largesse* suggests that he may have known the advice that Aristotle, in the *Romance of Alexander*, gave to that King, to win loyal service by giving generously. Ramon Lull was no doubt widely enough read in secular literature in his young days, when he was making poems after the manner of the troubadours. This helps to explain why his picture of chivalry, deeply Christian as it is, is so remarkably free of priestly overtones, so humane and in many ways so secular in its outlines. There can be little doubt that in this respect it was in tune with the general attitude of knightly circles.

★

Lull knew something of knighthood from his early years: Geoffrey de Charny, the author of our third treatise, lived and died in arms. Lord of Pierre Perthuis, Montfort, Savoisy and Licey, he first saw service in Gascony in 1337. In 1340 he defended Tournai against the English, and in 1341 he served in Brittany under the heir of France, John Duke of Normandy. In 1347 he was one of those who joined the unsuccessful crusade of Humbert, the last independent Dauphin of Vienne. In 1349 he was the leader of the band of Frenchmen who attempted to recover Calais by a surprise; the story of their repulse at the hands of Edward III and Walter Manny is recorded in some detail by the chronicler Froissart. When his old commander, Duke John, succeeded to the French throne he acquired new prominence; he was almost certainly a member of the chivalrous Order of the Star which John the Good created to rival Edward III's new Order of the Garter, and in 1355 he was appointed to be the bearer of the French King's royal standard, the miraculous Oriflamme of St Denis. He was guarding the King's standard when he was killed at the battle of Poitiers in 1356.[33]

Geoffrey de Charny was in fact the author not just of one but of three works on chivalry. Though they are very differently presented, the themes of all three are very similar. One takes the form of a series of questions about knotty points in chivalry, which Geoffrey put to the knights of the Order of the Star. There are three sets of questions, one concerning jousts (single encounters between knights in the lists); one concerning tournaments (encounters between teams of knights); and the third concerning war. Alas, no answers to them are recorded, and perhaps they never were answered. The other two are known as the *Livre* and the *Livre de chevalerie* of Geoffrey de Charny; the former is in verse and the latter in prose, but their content is almost identical, and there is the same progression as in the *Questions* from the subject of jousts to the subject of tournaments and so forward to war. The verse work brings out more clearly the wry humour of the author, with its warnings about the tumbles, discomforts and failures that the aspirant to chivalry may expect to encounter – including such ignominious mishaps as the sea-sickness which is likely to be the accompaniment of a voyage on crusade. The prose work is longer, more polished, and probably later; if the verse work was written, as seems likely, after Geoffrey had been sea-sick on the crusade of 1347, this probably belongs to the early 1350s, as the *Questions* clearly do. It is this work with which we shall be principally concerned.[34]

In all three works, Charny was much concerned with nice points about the scales of honour and achievement in chivalry. His guiding principle is that 'he who achieves more, is the more worthy.'[35] Young men at arms who

distinguish themselves in the joust deserve praise, he says, but those who
distinguish themselves in the tourney deserve higher praise (we should note
that he speaks throughout of men at arms, not of knights only: chivalry for
him extends beyond the circle of those who have been formally dubbed
knights). These in turn must give way before those who have won honour in
war, for war is a graver business and more honourable 'and passes all other
manner of arms'.[36] Those who have served with distinction in wars in their
own lands are to be honoured, but still more to be honoured are those who
have seen service in 'distant and strange countries', for instance those who
have sought the wars in Italy and have won fame there.[37] The best men of all
will be those who have advanced from one honour to the next: who in their
childhood have loved to hear stories of deeds of arms, who as soon as they
have reached sufficient age have armed themselves for jousts, and at the
first chance have entered on 'the great business of war'; men who, learning
with experience, have set themselves to study their profession, to know the
means of taking strong places by siege or by escalade, and have adventured
themselves in distant places.[38] But we must consider motives as well as
deeds. Those poor companions whose eagerness for booty carries them
always to the fore deserve praise, but not so much praise as the great man
who seeks the vanguard only to maintain the honour of his name.[39] Earthly
renown is of very significant value to Charny; and so is endeavour, for no
man should rest content with what he has achieved. That is why it is good
for a man at arms to be in love *par amours*, says Geoffrey: he will seek even
higher renown for the honour that it will do to his lady.[40] Think what her
feelings will be when the man whom she has chosen in her heart enters a
room, and she sees all men, knights, lords and esquires, pressing to honour
him on account of his *bonne renommée*, she knowing within herself that his
love is hers. Discretion, though, is important: the loyal lover keeps his love
secret, and does not bray his conquests. His joy of his love will be greater for
his loyalty, and his determination to be worthy of her no whit the less.

Geoffrey de Charny's view of chivalry is a thoroughly humane one, and
attractive for that reason. Dance and song are good for young men, and he
likes to see a cheerful spirit. You must not be cast down about the bumps
you receive; some are bound to come your way. You must discipline your
body and keep fit, but if good wine is offered to you there is no need to
eschew it, provided moderation is exercised. It is good to listen to old
soldiers and to their stories of campaigns in far places. For all this, though,
there can be no mistaking how deeply Christian religious feelings have
coloured his whole view of chivalry. The good, simple and bold are *preux*:
those who by their valour displayed in many places have risen to high rank
are *soulverain preux*: but you may tell those who are *plus soulvereinement
preux* by the wisdom with which they attribute all their glory and achievement to the grace of God and the Virgin. He who puts his trust in his own

strength will at the last be undone, says Geoffrey, as we can learn from the
stories of Samson and Absalom and Julius Caesar. For the perfect model of
knighthood one should look to Judas Maccabeus, the Old Testament
Jewish hero, who was *preux* and *hardi*, handsome but without pride, ever
honourable, a great fighter who died armed in God's causes. He who can be
likened to this noble knight will come to the highest honour in chivalry, for
he shall have honour in this world and the repose of paradise hereafter.[41]
Directed towards these twin ends, chivalry becomes a Christian discipline,
oriented toward man's highest goal, salvation.

   The parallel between the order of chivalry and a religious order is one
which Geoffrey is fond of recalling. No order of religion imposes heavier
rigours than chivalry does, and the regular observance of the points of
religion is as needful to the knight as it is to any religious, for there is no
order in which soul and body alike must be so continually prepared against
the hour of death. Chivalry is a means to salvation: he who takes arms for
just purpose will save his soul, be it in his lord's cause, or in defence of the
weak, or to save his own honour and heritage, or against the infidel.[42] Here
Geoffrey anticipates the eloquent cry of a later French captain in the wars
against the English, Jean de Bueil: 'we poor soldiers will save our souls by
arms, just as well as we would by living in contemplation upon a diet of
roots'.[43] The last words of his book are a combination of a prayer and a war
cry: 'Pray for him who made this book: Charny! Charny!'

   Geoffrey's description of the ritual of making a knight and its symbolism
is taken directly from the *Ordene de chevalerie*.[44] At a number of points, for
instance in his account of the origins of government and chivalry and in his
emphasis upon the propriety of Kings choosing their officers from among
the knighthood, he is very close to Ramon Lull, whom he had almost
certainly read. The general picture that he gives of chivalry is similar in
essentials to that given in these two earlier works, though the tone of his
book is in some ways obviously different. There seem to be three chief
respects in which his account differs from theirs and extends it. One is the
inclusion not only of knighthood in its strict sense but of the whole estate of
men at arms within the order of chivalry: it offers a way of life for the esquire
and the 'poor companions' just as much as for the knight proper. This is in
line with social developments of the fourteenth century – fewer men were
then seeking to be formally 'dubbed'[45] – but it does give a certain added
emphasis to the professional aspect of chivalry. The second is his treatment
of woman in the context of the chivalrous life, and of love as a human
passion which, rightly regulated, sharpens and refines the honourable
ambitions of martial men. The *Frauendienst* of courtly literature appears
here shorn of its exaggeration, in a form whose relevance to human activity
and endeavour most of us know something about from our own experience. The third is the dynamism which his scales of prowess and valour

introduce into knightly obligation. Chivalry involves a constant quest to improve on achievement and cannot rest satisfied.

The point here is not just a moral one: Geoffrey's method of judging prowess is firmly anchored to the appearances of this world. He is indeed concerned with the internal world, as we have seen, but the indices of chivalrous achievement that he suggests are external acts and the repute that has attached to them. In this way his book offers a kind of identikit picture which will assist us in recognising one who has achieved great things in chivalry by the pattern of his experience and its range, without having to probe for subjective reactions which are unverifiable. He will be a man who has been at jousts and tournaments and at war in other lands beside his own, who has served his lord in arms and has crossed the sea in quest of adventures and fame. This emphasis on *lointains voyages* offers another analogue in the real world to the world of romance, whose knights continuously ride out beyond the perimeter of civilisation into the endless forests in quest of adventure – an analogue, once again, from which the exaggerations of fiction have been shorn away. Altogether, what Geoffrey wrote carries us a long way forward in the quest for what should be understood by the word chivalry. We can see much more clearly what sort of activities we shall need to examine, what sort of competition we shall need to watch for, if we are to assess its significance as a social force. We should have expected the bearer of the Oriflamme to be a sound guide, and we are not disappointed.

Between the mid fourteenth century, when Geoffrey de Charny was writing, and the beginning of the sixteenth, a large number of treatises on chivalry, and of books which incorporated such treatises, were written. On the whole, they do not add a very great deal to the essentials of the picture offered in the three works which we have looked at in detail. Johannes Roth, in his *Ritterspiegel* (c. 1410) offers a series of symbolical interpretations of the ritual of making a knight which are different from those of either Lull or the *Ordene*, and a long disquisition on the hierarchy of the aristocratic ranks, from princes downwards, to whom knighthood in Germany was open (the German *Heerschild*), but in spirit his long work is in a familiar vein.[46] Ghillebert de Lannoy in his *Instruction d'un jeune prince* and the author of the *Enseignement de la vraye noblesse* (two interdependent works, written in the first half of the fifteenth century) knew the *Ordene*. Both used Lull extensively.[47] They, like Roth and like their contemporary, the much-travelled Castilian knight Diego de Valera who wrote a *Traictée de noblesse*,[48] included in their works a substantial and significant treatment of the origin and significance of armorial bearings, a subject now included almost

automatically in any serious discussion of chivalry. Both they and Valera
also have a great deal to say about the significance of the martial example of
the Romans as a model of true chivalry. This emphasis on classical example,
which served to strengthen the conception of chivalry as an essentially
secular institution, is a marked feature of later medieval treatments of the
subject. So also is the clearer and more explicit connection suggested
between chivalry, nobility of life and good lineage, with as a concomitant
the extension of the estate of chivalry to include the whole martial and
potentially armigerous aristocracy, esquires, gentlemen and men at arms as
well as knights.

But on the whole, new overtones are much less striking in these later
works than the themes that are familiar. We re-encounter repeatedly in
them the same account of the origins of knighthood that we found in
Ramon Lull. Over and over again chivalry is associated, as in his book, with
the art of government: indeed, it becomes clear that 'books of chivalry' and
'mirrors for princes' are associated *genres* of writing. The list of the knight's
obligations, to defend the Church and the people (that order tending more
and more often to be reversed), to protect the fatherless and the widow, and
to exercise himself continually in arms, becomes trite by repetition. Geoffrey de Charny would have approved wholeheartedly Ghillebert de
Lannoy's advice to his son, to busy himself with martial training, to go
jousting, and to read in chronicles of the doings of the valiant of ancient
times.[49] There is a very familiar ring too to the list of the qualities of the sort
of men whose company the young Lannoy is advised to seek, those who are
bons, saiges et cortois, preux et vaillans.[50] Men's conception of what was
essential to chivalry remained sufficiently unchanged, it would seem, from
the end of the twelfth century or thereabouts to the end of the fifteenth, to
give a study of the subject over that period a certain unity.

We set out at the beginning of this chapter in quest of a definition of
chivalry. While recognising that a word so tonal and imprecise can never be
pinned down within precise limits of meaning, we are now a great deal
nearer to being able to suggest lines of definition that will do for working
purposes. On the basis of the treatises that we have examined, chivalry may
be described as an ethos in which martial, aristocratic and Christian
elements were fused together. I say fused, partly because the compound
seems to be something new and whole in its own right, partly because it is
clearly so difficult to completely separate the elements in it. In a given
context, one facet may be to the fore, but it remains hard to exclude
overtones from elsewhere. Indeed, no one of the component elements in
the compound is in itself simple in structure. The military aspect of chivalry
is associated with skill in horsemanship specifically, a costly expertise
which could be hard to acquire, for one not born to a good heritage. The
aristocratic aspect is not just a matter of birth; it is connected with ideas of

the function of knighthood and with a scale of virtues which implies that aristocracy is a matter of worth as much as it is of lineage. The Christian aspect is presented surprisingly free of the imprint of ecclesiastical prejudice and priorities. Chivalry, as it is described in the treatises, is a way of life in which we can discern these three essential facets, the military, the noble, and the religious; but a way of life is a complex thing, like a living organism; we have only the beginnings of a definition, and there is plenty left to explore.

CHAPTER II

The Secular Origins of Chivalry

Geoffrey de Charny, in his *Livre de chevalerie*, offers us a model of the chivalrous man which we ought to be able to recognise from real life, without having to probe questions of internal motivation on which historical sources throw inadequate light. We shall not be disappointed in the historical quest for men of the right stamp, and we shall find that the artists who drew word portraits of them were clearly conscious of the existence of a conventional model of the *preux chevalier* to which the outlines of their picture should conform.

Let us take an example. In 1394–5 Thomas III, Marquis of Saluzzo, was whiling away the idle hours of his captivity in the hands of his family's ancestral enemy, the Count of Savoy, in the composition of a long allegorical work which he entitled the *Chevalier errant*.[1] In the course of the story his wandering knight (no doubt Thomas himself in a dreamland of his own making) found his way to the court of Lady Fortune, where he found encamped a number of prominent contemporaries who were also her suppliants. The Marquis describes each in turn. Most come in for somewhat critical appraisal – for instance Wenceslas, King of the Romans, who is depicted as a soft man in early middle age, inclined to lie in bed of a morning and already developing the taste for wine which was to be his undoing later. There are one or two, however, who fare more happily, among them a young knight of about thirty, *bel et joli et amoureux*, who turns out to be the Milanese *condottiero* Galeas of Mantua. This young man, says Thomas, was first armed at the siege of Saluzzo, where he fought bravely and was wounded. Later he distinguished himself in a joust at Fossano, where he delivered a German knight of a vow to achieve certain deeds of arms against whatever man of his own standing would take up his challenge to joust. This was for Galeas the first of many similar adventures which he undertook 'for the sake of a lady of high beauty, whom he loved *par amours*.'

Galeas went travelling, and was engaged in the wars of the French against
the English: it was on the day that he unhorsed in single combat an English
captain who had discomfited many Frenchmen that he was made a knight.
He crossed the Great Sea (the Mediterranean) on pilgrimage, visited the
monastery of St Catherine in Sinai, and was retained for a while in the
service of the King of Cyprus. After that he took part for the King of France
in his war against the Duke of Juliers, travelled in Germany and fought
against the Turks under the banner of the King of Hungary. 'Know that
whatever trial of arms is proposed to him, you will always find him ready: if
he lives long enough, he will be one to compare for his chivalry with the
good Sir Tristram of Lyonesse or with Sir Palamedes.'[3] These closing words
show how well aware Thomas was that the shape of the career he was
describing was related to a model, and could entitle Galeas to a place
among the *soulverein preux* – the men whom Geoffrey de Charny describes
as going from strength to strength in joust and war, loving loyally, and
travelling to far countries in quest of martial experience.

One of the most significant features of the model that Thomas of Saluzzo
judged to be realised in the career of Galeas of Mantua was that it was
already traditional long before his time, and long before that of Geoffrey de
Charny too. It was older, we shall find, than the days when the *Ordene de
chevalerie* was composed, as old at least as the time when Etienne de
Fougères was writing about chivalry in the later twelfth century. At just
about the same time that Etienne was at work, a young man called Arnold,
son and heir of Baldwin Count of Guines, was starting on his knightly
course. The outline of his career, as it is recounted by the family chronicler,
Lambert of Ardres, fits into an almost identical mould with that of Galeas,
as described by Thomas of Saluzzo.[4] There are lacking, perhaps, a few of
the touches of floridity that are typical of the later fourteenth century:
otherwise the differences of tone as well as of essentials are minimal.

Arnold of Ardres was born in the 1160s. He was placed as a youth in the
care of Philip of Flanders, 'to be brought up in good manners and instructed
in the office of knighthood.'[5] Philip was rich, a veteran of the crusades and a
patron of chivalrous letters whose *largesse* Chrétien de Troyes hailed in his
Perceval,[6] and at his court Arnold found himself among the flower of the
young nobility of Flanders. There he made his mark, says Lambert, 'by his
good looks and by his prowess in every martial exercise.'[7] In 1181, when he
was of age to be knighted, his father gathered a great assembly at Pentecost
in his own court: and Arnold, together with four of his fast friends, was
dubbed a knight. As soon as the ceremony was over, Lambert tells us,
Arnold, newly robed, dived into the crowd of servants, minstrels and
jesters who were present, on whom he showered gifts of money.[8] After this,
there was no keeping him at home: he was determined to make his début as
a knight in style: 'he did not wish to stay in his own country in idleness and

without martial diversion, but chose rather to travel far and wide in search of tournaments and glory, so as to learn to live amply and achieve worldly honour'.[9] He became enamoured of Ida, Countess of Boulogne, a lady of relaxed morals (and substantial inheritance), who had the experience of two unsuccessful marriages behind her: and many secret messages of love passed between them. When she was carried off by main force by another aspirant to her hand and riches, Arnold swore to come to her rescue, and for his pains was taken prisoner by his rival, an interlude which taught him a little wisdom. When he came home, having paid a ransom, he promised to follow his father's guidance. He served him in his wars; he accepted the bride of his choice, Beatrice, heiress of Bourbourg, who was wise, beautiful, and learned, says Lambert; and as Lord of Ardres he continued to live in style with her. He always delighted, we are told, to hear tales of the great champions of old and of later times, of Roland and Oliver, of Arthur, of the crusaders' capture of Antioch. One of the chronicler's most vivid pictures is of the young Arnold and his companions gathering on a winter's night about a roaring fire, with the winds howling outside, and prevailing on Walter of Cleves to tell the story of how Ardres was founded and of the origin of the family of its lords.[10]

Lambert's description of the young life of Arnold of Ardres is no isolated picture. The characteristic features of the description of the early career of his slightly older contemporary, William the Marshal, as the minstrel author of the *Histoire de Guillaume le Maréchal* describes it, are essentially similar.[11] William, it is true, was not so fortunate in his birth: he was not a count's heir, but the fourth son of John Fitzgilbert, an English baron who, though well connected, was himself only of middling rank. William as a youth was placed in the household of John's cousin, the Count of Tankarville, a powerful baron of the lower Seine and a great frequenter of tournaments. In 1167, when William was about eighteen, he was dubbed a knight by the count on the eve of a skirmish at Drincourt with the Count of Flanders and his men, in which he distinguished himself. That same year he was twice at tournaments in company with the Count of Tankarville, and acquitted himself with particular credit. His courageous conduct in the Poitou campaign a year later brought him to the attention of Eleanor of Aquitaine, Henry II's queen. It was through her favour that in 1169 the martial training of her son, the young King Henry, her husband's heir, was entrusted to his care.

This was William's first great step forward, the entry into one of the most prestigious knightly circles of his age. His new task had its dangers; as chief among the knights of the young Henry's household he must have played a part in the young King's revolt against his father in 1173, but we do not know much about it. His role as a 'tutor' in chivalry certainly had its attractions too; the author of his history next presents him as the leader of

1. The hermit instructs the squire in the order of knighthood, from Ramon Lull's *Book of the Order of Chivalry.* See p. 9.

2–3 (this page). Methods of handling the lance: thrown as a projectile, carried overarm, and couched. From the Bayeux Tapestry. See p. 24.

4 (facing page). Christian chivalry: St George and St Anthony, by Pisanello (National Gallery).

5. Charge with the couched lance. Enamel from the Stavelot altar, twelfth century (Pierpont Morgan Library). See p. 24.

7 (facing page). Charge with the couched lance, from twelfth-century *Book of St Edmund* (Pierpont Morgan Library). See p. 24.

6. The couched lance: Richard Marshal unhorses Baldwin of Guisnes, possibly at Monmouth in 1233 (Corpus Christi College). See p. 25.

8 (left). Knighthood and religion: the soul of Roland is carried to heaven. From *Les Grandes Chroniques de France* (Bibliothèque Nationale).

10 (facing page, above). The Mysteries of the Grail: Christ rises from the Grail at the mass of Bishop Josephe (Bibliothèque de l'Arsenal). See p. 60.

11 (facing page, centre). Girding with the sword (British Library). See pp. 71–3.

12 (facing page, below). Delivery of arms, from the Bayeux Tapestry: the usual interpretation is that William is giving Harold the *collée* of knighthood. See pp. 7, 66–7.

9 (left). The Swan Knight comes to Nijmegen (Bayerische Staatsbibliothek). See p. 58.

uiuxendentes. mestimabili gaudio perfusi   moliebatur eū filiis suis iuuenibs; duobs; ijde.

13. Girding at the altar: the dubbing of Galahad (Bibliothèque Nationale). See pp. 65, 75.

14. The Emperor Sigismund dubbing a knight in Rome (Österreichische Nationalbibliothek).

15 (left). The making of a knight in the field (College of Arms). See pp. 79–80.

Henry's knights in a series of great tournaments in northern France (including one held under the auspices of Philip of Flanders, the patron of Arnold of Ardres, at the time when the young Henry was staying as a guest at his court). William's achievements in these engagements steadily added to his rising reputation as a knight of mark, as the horses and prisoners which he took at them added to his wealth. His prowess was so widely known that when in 1182 he fell out simultaneously with young Henry and his father (rumours had been circulating of an affair between William and Queen Margaret of France) both the Count of Flanders and the Duke of Burgundy offered him lands and a pension if he would enter their service.[12] His fall from favour with the Angevins was short-lived, however, and he did not need to look for new masters. He was back in favour when the young Henry died at the castle of Martel on the Dordogne, and it was he who undertook to discharge the young King's unfulfilled crusading vow by going himself in arms to the Holy Land. There, says his biographer, he achieved more notable feats of arms against the Saracen in a year than another man could have done in seven.[13]

The details of William's subsequent career need not detain us: on his return from the Holy Land he was taken into the royal service, where his standing brought him marriage to Isabel de Clare, heiress to the earldom of Pembroke; under Richard Coeur de Lion and then John he played a part in high politics, and when he died he was virtually regent – rector regis et regni – for the young Henry III. Enough has been said to show how similar in its early outline it is to that of Arnold of Ardres, and how well both tally with Geoffrey de Charny's later model. If ever a knight lived up to Geoffrey's principle of chivalrous prowess, 'he who achieves more is the more worthy', it was surely William the Marshal. The two accounts of knightly careers in the second half of the twelfth century that we have been following make it clear, in fact, that already then a pattern of chivalrous living, with a defined style of its own, was well established. An adventurous youth, an apprenticeship in the tourney to the 'great business of war', the eschewing of idleness at home and seeking service in far-flung places, all these are already essential ingredients of a stylish opening in chivalry. Loyalty and prowess, hardiness and *courtoisie* are all qualities as firmly underlined by William's biographer as they are by later writers on chivalry: they are qualities instinctively associated with knightly living, not just with knightly fiction.

The courtly element in the twelfth-century image of knighthood is an aspect that requires emphasis. In a broad sense *courtoisie* implies manners fitting to a court, and it is striking how much William the Marshal's world is a world of the court as well as of the camp. His first real stride forward came when he caught the eye of Eleanor of Aquitaine, the famous patroness of the troubadours. The great tournament at Pleurs near Epernay in which he took part in 1177 was held under the auspices of Henry of Champagne;[14] it was at the command of Henry's countess Marie (Eleanor's daughter) that Chrétien de Troyes took up the story of Lancelot; and Andreas Capellanus made her the arbitress of the judgements of love in his *De arte honeste amandi*.[15] William was a guest too, as we have seen, at the court of Philip of Flanders, another great patron of chivalry and of courtly letters. Of the amorous aspects of courtliness there is not much hint in William's biography, it is true, though the Countess of Joigni and her ladies were singing and dancing with the knights when he came to the tournament at Joigni, and watched him be the first to unhorse an opponent.[16] Lambert of Ardres however shows that his hero knew well how to play the courtly game of love with Countess Ida. The riches and colour of court life are well brought out by both authors; by Lambert in his account of the feasting on the occasion of Arnold's knighthood, by William's biographer when he tells of the rich accoutrements of the knights who came to the tournament at Pleurs, and of their splendid chargers that had been bought as far afield as Spain and Sicily. Greater men than a Count of Guines or even of Champagne would be still more lavish. Frederic Barbarossa set up by Mainz on the banks of the Rhine what seemed to be a whole city of tents and pavilions to house the host that came to witness the knighting of his two sons in 1184 and to join in the tourneying there.[17] Heinrich von Veldeke compared the scene in his *Eneit* to the great feast in Virgil for the marriage of Lavinia and Aeneas: 'I never heard of such a festival, unless it was that at Mainz, when Kaiser Frederick knighted his sons.'[18]

Festivals and tournaments and the lustre of princely courts brought together men from afar; they also gathered together men of very varied standing in terms of wealth and birth. Arnold of Ardres was a Count's son, heir to an old name and fortune: William the Marshal's patron, the young Henry, was a greater man than he, heir to a throne. William himself though, when we first meet him, was a landless youth, with a fortune still to make, like those 'poor companions' whom Geoffrey de Charny includes in the brotherhood of chivalry, remarking on their eagerness in quest of booty; yet William mingled in this chivalrous society on equal terms. There were undoubtedly many companions poorer again than he, in terms of birth and prospects, among those young *chevaliers errans* whom William's biographer depicts as going from tourney to tourney in quest of praise and gain. Poor knights of small or no inheritance were also prominent among the troubadours who sought the patronage of such great ladies as Eleanor of Aquitaine. The picture given by Lambert of Ardres of Arnold leaping into the crowd of minstrels, pages, and jesters and distributing his *largesse* is a reminder that there could not be a courtly world without hangers on – some of them, no doubt, hanging on by their teeth. They were not all martial men: there were clerks and minstrels, men of letters too. This was a cultivated society as well as a wide-ranging one in terms of wealth and ancestry.

Orderic Vitalis, in his description of the household of William the Conqueror's companion, Hugh of Chester, describes a society in many ways similar to that in which Arnold of Ardres and William the Marshal grew up. Hugh, he says, was a lover of this world's pomp, a prodigal man who loved 'songs and games and horses and such vanities'.[19] There was always a great crowd of young men about him, of varied standing and both knights and clerks. Among the latter was one Gerold, who used to tell them all of the deeds of Maurice, George, Demetrius, and other martial saints, and who knew the story of William Court-Nez – that Count William of Orange who was the hero of a whole cycle of epic *chansons*. The difference between Orderic and Lambert that is here significant is of course that the former was describing a world a whole hundred years older. The world of Arnold of Ardres and of William the Marshal was not born overnight. If we are to understand how its chivalrous mode of living came into being, and how its norms of conduct came to be established, we shall have to look back over the developments of something like a preceding century and a half. These developments may for convenience be considered under three heads, military, social, and literary – the latter two, to some considerable extent, overlapping.

★

The eleventh century was a very important period in the military history of the middle ages, and in the history of cavalry tactics especially. The introduction into Europe of the stirrup (an Eastern invention) had since the early eighth century greatly enhanced the importance of cavalry. Stirrups gave the mounted warrior a far greater stability in the saddle and an altogether improved control of his horse. It would seem however that it was not until the eleventh century that, as a result of further technical advances, the tactic developed whereby, at a crucial point in battle, the charge of heavy cavalrymen holding their lances in the 'couched' position (tucked firmly under the right armpit and levelled at the enemy) could decide the day. It has been argued that this was an earlier development, almost coeval with the introduction of the stirrup, but the best evidence seems definitely to point to the period after the year 1000, and perhaps as late as the end of the eleventh century, as that in which this manner of fighting, which was to be long the classic cavalry tactic of medieval warfare, was first adopted.[20]

Without the stirrup, the shock charge with couched lance could not have been a possible manoeuvre, but the spear and the saddle were also important. There are basically four ways in which a spear may be used by a mounted warrior. It may be carried, gripped roughly at the point of balance, with the right arm extended, to deliver a blow under arm. It may be so carried as to deliver an over-arm thrust. Or it may be used as a projectile and thrown at the enemy from close quarters. For all these purposes a relatively light spear is required, which will be held at or near the point of balance. The fourth method of using the spear or lance on horseback is quite different. It is tucked tightly under the right armpit, so that it remains steady, and gripped further back, with the left arm left free to handle reins and shield. Horse, rider and lance are thus gathered together into what has been called a 'human projectile'. A body of horsemen thus armed can deliver at a massed enemy a hammer blow, whose effect depends on the momentum of the charge and the shock of impact. This was the famous cavalry charge of the Franks: as one contemporary put it, 'a Frank on horseback would drive a hole through the walls of Babylon'.[21] To make the manoeuvre effective, a heavier lance was needed: a light one would simply shatter on impact. It was also found that the rider who fought in this way could grip his lance somewhat further back from the natural point of balance and still hold it steady, and he could therefore use a longer lance, which was an obvious advantage in the situation that has been described. An improved saddle-bow at the rear, to prevent the rider being carried out of his seat by the shock of contact, was also useful.

Iconographic evidence suggests that the second half of the eleventh century was the key period in the development of this new method of cavalry warfare. Illustrations in ninth- and tenth-century manuscripts show the spear being used in the first three manners I have mentioned, but not the fourth: it is however illustrated in one or two eleventh-century manuscripts, for example in the Admont Bible (c. 1080). The most striking iconographic evidence, though, is that of the Bayeux tapestry (again, c. 1080).[22] This shows warriors using spears in all four of the ways mentioned. Most are thrusting overarm, or throwing or preparing to throw their spears. There are others who are carrying them in rest, apparently preparatory to charging in the couched position. Three knights who are getting ready to charge thus at the outset of the battle of Hastings are clearly depicted with heavier spears than most others, with pennons dependent from them which would surely have interfered with their trajectory if they had tried to throw them, as some of their comrades are doing. The saddlebows of the Bayeux horsemen also suggest development when they are compared with earlier illustrations. Since depictions of knights charging with the couched lance become quite common thirty years or so after the Bayeux tapestry was completed, the inference is that the tapestry has caught a significant moment in the development of the new arms, when they were first coming into more general use.

Iconographic evidence, for the medieval period, can be misleading: artists so often copied earlier models that the study of illustrations can easily lead to the postdating of technical advance. In this case, however, literary evidence supports the conclusion drawn from iconography. When the new method of holding the lance was used by horseman against horseman, the effect of impact was either the shattering of both lances, or that one horseman drove his lance into his opponent's body (in which case his lance very probably broke), or that one or other combatant was carried clean out of the saddle. These are the typical effects of encounter in the numberless accounts of tournaments and single combats in twelfth-century romance. The first work to describe a cavalry engagement in which one or other of these effects is the repeated consequence of the clash of individual combatants is the Oxford version of the *Chanson de Roland*, for the manuscript of which various dates between 1100 and 1130 have been suggested. Geoffrey Malaterra, writing nearer 1100, describes how Serlo, one of the Hauteville brothers, worsted a Breton knight who had repeatedly unhorsed a series of Norman challengers at the siege of Tillières in the 1040s.[23] This is not good testimony for such an early date, but it is good testimony for Geoffrey's own time, which is very close to that of the composition of the *Chanson*. Of similar date are the engagements on the first crusade, in which the shock charge was more than once the key to Frankish victory. Anna Comnena speaks of the 'irresistible first shock' of the Frankish charge (one of the disadvantages of the tactic was that it had to succeed at the first impact: the Franks had not learnt to reform sufficiently quickly for a second effort if the first misfired).[24] As earlier references to unhorsing and to the shock charge are lacking, the evidence points very strongly to a key development in the last half of the eleventh century.

This new tactic was not the only development in the art of war at the end of the eleventh century, and it can be argued that others – advances in castle building and in techniques of siege warfare – were equally or even more important. From our point of view, however, the new cavalry tactic has a special importance. It was not and could not be merely a military development. A new measure of skill and training was demanded of its practitioner, and in an age when there were no standing armies and when military training had not yet become institutionalised, that was bound to have social consequences. It can hardly be an accident that it is at the end of the eleventh century and at the beginning of the twelfth that we first begin to hear of tournaments, a kind of occasion that would in due course provide writers like the minstrel–author of the *Histoire de Guillaume le Maréchal* with unlimited opportunities to describe the skill of their heroes in unhorsing their opponents. The tournament, which at this early stage was a sort of general free-for-all for teams of mounted warriors, was a perfect training ground in the new techniques: at the same time, as we have seen, tournaments were great social and courtly gatherings. The risks involved in them were moreover economic as well as physical, since a defeated combatant could be taken prisoner, lose his horse, and have to pay a ransom.

The new method of fighting in any case of itself involved a rise in the cost of equipment. A shirt of mail became doubly essential to the horseman, to protect him against the lance thrust of a charging adversary. He needed a good horse, and remounts, and someone to help him to look after them and to bring them to an engagement.[25] Most knights had in the first instance to find their own equipment: to be a cavalryman began to imply substantial means or substantial patronage. Aristocratic associations of one kind or another therefore began to be more important to the aspirant knight.

Contemporary sources do not tell us as much as we could wish about the training and equipping of warriors in the eleventh century. With regard to the former, education in a lordly household was obviously an important factor, and this kind of fosterage was already a long established custom. Hrabanus Maurus, back in the ninth century, tells of how young men in his day were placed in noble households and brought up there to endure physical rigours and to acquire the arts of horsemanship:[26] we have seen how, later, both William the Marshal and Arnold of Ardres were placed in such households, to be instructed in good manners and in the martial arts. Many lords maintained a body of knights in their household, and these no doubt took their part in the training of the young men. These domestic knights were armed and equipped at the lord's expense, and he might also arm and mount a favoured *protégé*. If the *protégé*'s father were well off, though, the expense would naturally fall on him. A poor young man might be in serious difficulties. William the Marshal lost his horse in his first fight at Drincourt, and by pawning the mantle in which he had been knighted the day before, he could replace it only with an indifferent mount. The anxiety of combatants to capture horses in battle is a recurrent theme in the martial *chansons de geste*, and it can be no surprise that it should be, or that one of the signs of the true *largesse* that they hail in a leader should be his liberality in rewarding his loyal men with presents of arms and horses.

The developments that we have been tracing, in arms and fighting techniques, were such as would be bound to foster a sense of identity among those who, by one means or another, could manage to fit themselves out as mounted warriors. Their skills and their training set them apart from other men. Ties of upbringing are always a potent social force, and these were easily forged where, as in this case, training and fosterage were so closely linked. Upbringing in a household helped also to develop a common sense of style in living among those who experienced it. No doubt there were plenty of men who – by watching their masters, by exercising their horses and by learning from experience of service in an inferior rank – managed by their initiative to edge a way into the cavalier's world when opportunity offered. But every new development, in the greater defensive protection that armour could be designed to offer and the greater weight that a more expensive war horse had consequently to carry, made such advancement a

little harder. New tactics and improved technology at each step strengthened the aristocratic bias of recruitment into knighthood, and sharpened
in its ranks the awareness of a common bond, called chivalry, uniting all
who could aspire to ride to wars and tournaments.

★

Originally, the Latin word *miles*, which is the word that writers like Lambert
of Ardres used to signify a knight, simply meant a professional soldier. As
good a way as any of approaching closer to the social developments which,
in significant ways, paralleled the military developments with which we
have so far been concerned, will be to look at certain shifts of meaning
and emphasis in the use made of this word during the eleventh and twelfth
centuries.

In the first place we find the word *miles* being used with a more limited
military sense than it had in classical Latin, to denote now specifically a
mounted warrior. We find it used occasionally in this way by Richer, at the
beginning of the eleventh century; in the accounts of the first crusade at the
century's end it has become a normal meaning,[27] and the *milites* are distinguished clearly from the foot soldiers. Secondly, we find the *milites* being
distinguished from other sections of society by their martial function, as the
warrior group distinct from the clergy on the one hand and on the other the
imbelle vulgus – the common people and especially rustics. This way of using
the word *miles* is especially noticeable in texts which concern the Peace and
Truce of God.[28] (This was the ecclesiastical legislation promulgated by local
church councils with the aim of maintaining the peace and protecting
non-combatants from hostilities, which was sanctioned by ecclesiastical
censures and, on occasion, by the action of faithful knights acting on
ecclesiastical instruction. The rules which were usually laid down banned
hostilities from Friday to Monday and on feasts of the church, and guaran-
teed immunity from war to non-combatants – priests, merchants, and
labourers.) A third way in which the word *miles* is increasingly used in this
period is in charters (especially in their witness lists), as a word denoting the
standing of an individual. At first it is used in this way to distinguish men of
very moderate means, whose families might hold perhaps a very small
estate, from the greater men, counts and castellans who were recognised as
nobles. Later, however, and very widely in France by the early twelfth
century, we find these greater men also identifying themselves as *milites*,
indeed being careful to do so.[29] The implication of this extension of the use
of the word as a title would seem to be that the two groups, the lesser
knighthood (earlier often described as *vassi* or vassals) and the greater
nobility (the overlords of vassals) were drawing together in terms of social
cohesion (though not, of course, economically) and that the word *miles* itself

was acquiring more clearly honorific associations. As a designation, it had risen in the social scale.[30]

In the light of what has been said about the development of new techniques of fighting on horseback, the first of these ways of using the word *miles* – as meaning a mounted warrior specifically – does not call for further comment. The other two ways do, and it would seem that there is some kind of connection between them, since in both cases the effect is to separate the *milites* more distinctly from other kinds of people. The distinction between them and others in the canons of the councils which promulgated the Peace and later the Truce of God is essentially a functional one: it is parallel to the distinctions drawn by such ecclesiastical men of letters as Adalbero of Laon and Gerard of Cambrai between the three orders of men in Christian society, the clergy, the warriors and the workers. Though these writers usually use words other than *milites* to denote the warriors, what they say has this important point in common with the canons: that in both cases the distinction between the warriors and the workers is not just a functional one, but has social overtones. In the canons the secular nobility are clearly included in the fighting order[31] – it was, after all, the wars of the nobles that threatened the peace and led the French church to intervene where royal authority was seen to be powerless. Correspondingly, Adalbero of Laon clearly considered the principals in the warrior class, whose duty it was to protect the church and the poor, to be the nobles.[32] In the charters, the implication recurs that the distinction between the *milites* and others is a matter of social status. *Milites*, in the earlier French charters, which have been exhaustively studied by Professor Duby and his colleagues, attest after the nobles proper (the great men who came of families headed by counts or at least castellans) but before free men of humbler standing than themselves. One sign of their standing at this date (the mid eleventh century) seems to have been their freedom from seigneurial ('banal') exactions.[33] Thus in these early French charters the knighthood appears as a kind of petty nobility, whose military service to its lords was the *quid pro quo* for its freedom from other irksome liabilities, a freedom which marked it off from the tillers of the soil. Later, as has been said, we see the greater nobles adopting the same title as the lesser men, and thus the distinction between the great and petty nobility is blurred: not economically, it is true – there they remained far apart – but in style and title. So the two poles of aristocracy begin to be drawn together: and the 'nobility' which Adalbero associated with the great men who commanded fighting resources is extended to embrace the knighthood generally, mounted followers as well as leaders – the whole order of chivalry that Lull was later to describe as a 'noble' order.

So far we have been talking in terms of words, of problems of vocabulary. The real driving force drawing together those at the poles of aristocratic society in eleventh-century France was their mutual need of one another. The great territorial lords, many of them descended of noble stock going back to Carolingian times,[34] needed the service of the petty knights in their endless wars with one another, struggles such as that between the houses of Blois and of Anjou for a controlling interest in Touraine or between the Normans and the Capetians in the Vexin. They needed their help equally in their endeavours to control the powerful castellans of their own territories, robber barons like the ferocious Thomas of Marle whom Louis VI had to fight so long to master.[35] In struggles such as these, his knights provided the lord with a *corps d'élite* of horsemen; perhaps still more important, they were the only kind of 'officer' group to whom he could look to discharge essential responsibilities in the manning of his castles and the conduct of sieges. Those great lords who succeeded in consolidating their hold over their lands and extended them needed more men to serve them in these ways, and it paid them to use their increased wealth to emphasise the attraction and the dignity of their service. For in return for their services, the greater lords had much to offer the knighthood: rewards, whether in the form of arms, money or land; or a hand towards a good marriage; or a measure of security in the enjoyment of their estates; above all, perhaps, the protection of their privilege and fortunes against the competition for economic advantage of rich townsmen and prospering peasants.

The insecurity of the lesser knighthood greatly sharpened their appreciation of the rewards that the great could offer. Hence their eager appreciation of *largesse*, and their delight in seeing it lavishly and publicly dispensed, to which chivalrous literature bears vivid witness. The *chansons* show us William of Orange and Garin le Loherain winning the service of poor knights with the promise of lavish gifts.[36] Aristotle, in the twelfth-century *Romance of Alexander*, explains eloquently to the young king how *largesse* wins the hearts of men and will gain him faithful service.[37] Arthur again, in the early romances, is portrayed as a model of *largesse*, to the poor knights especially. 'He honoured the rich as his companions and the poor for their worth and prowess, and also so as to increase his own honour in this world and in the eye of God.'[38] Complementarily, the skinflint lords and those who, like Darius in the *Romance of Alexander*, have promoted low-born men, unnourished in the true traditions of service, are the butts of the *chansons* and the early romances.[39] Here literature accurately mirrors the aspirations of real-life knightly society, in which the young bachelors, unmarried cadets with nothing to offer but their swords, their good birth and an upbringing which had taught them a taste for adventure, were the most numerous element crowding round the courts of the greater nobility. For such men, whose real social position was insecure, the service of the great had powerful psychological attractions as well as economic ones, because it associated them with the standing and reputation of the men and the lineages that they served. One literary function of Arthur's round table was clearly to be an emblem of the equal terms on which all knights, great and humble, mixed at his board once they had, by prowess or service, won their right to a place there.

★

The same pressures, and the same aspirations – those of young men on the fringes of aristocratic society, with careers to make or mar – are reflected in the amorous poetry of the Southern French troubadours. Some of these were of course great aristocrats, like the founding father of them all, Duke William IX of Aquitaine, who, we are told, had the image of his mistress painted on his shield, saying that 'it was his will to bear her in battle, as she had borne him in bed'.[40] But more, far more, were as Bezzola has described them: 'soudoiers et sirvens, guerroiers de fortune, promenant de château en château une vie aventureuse et libre'.[41] In the poems of such men, the adoration of a great lady, the wife of a count maybe or of a high baron, had more than simply erotic significance. Her acceptance of her admirer's love (which meant her acceptance of his amorous service, not admission to her bed) was the *laisser passer* into the rich, secure world of the court of which she was mistress. The courtly literature of the troubadours encapsulated thus an amorous ethic of service to a lady which was essentially comparable to the ethic of faithful service to a lord: indeed it borrowed not a little of its vocabulary from the legal vocabulary of lordship, fealty, and service. But there were, of course, important differences between amatory and feudal service, as well as similarities. Troubadour lyric, which was essentially introspective, sought to express the overwhelming force of adulatory passion, inspired by a beloved woman, which force it interpreted as the source of all excellence and endeavour in him whom it bound to her service. As Andreas the Chaplain put it, 'it is agreed that there is no good thing in the world, and no courtesy, that is not derived from love as from its fountain head'.[42] Thus in courtly love female approbation offered a new, secular and psychologically very powerful sanction to the secular conventions of the code of courtly virtue and martial honour. As Wolfram von Eschenbach's Willeham declared, in a great eve-of-battle speech to his knights, 'there are two rewards that await us, heaven and the recognition of noble women'.[43]

Simultaneously, this amatory ethic gave a stamp of social exclusiveness to a specifically courtly mode of loving. The poor knight's consciousness of the need for recognition of his amatory service is well reflected in the troubadours' often repeated claim that it is only the poor who understand true *courtoisie*: the rich seek in love the satisfaction of lust, but the poor knight labours and endures travails that refine his feelings and endow them with a special, courteous value.[44] Perhaps even more than the northern writers the troubadours were eager to denounce seigneurial avarice and to acclaim *largesse*: it was the southern knight Bertrand de Born who declared that he had no time for the lord who would not mortgage his estates so as to give prodigally;[45] and the first commandment of the God of Love in Andreas's treatise is to eschew avarice like the plague.[46] But at the same time, of course, courtly love presented an ideal of service in which a great lord could engage without thereby demeaning himself. Troubadour poetry, as eloquently as any northern *chanson* or romance, reflects the pressures which, in the twelfth century, were drawing the high nobility and the precarious professional knighthood together, and is courtly in the specific sense that the courts and castles of the great were the meeting ground for these two elements.

The greater seigneurial courts of twelfth-century France thus played a decisive part in finalising the shape of chivalrous modes and ideology, as we find them portrayed later in such works as those of Lull and Charny, and in the careers of such as Arnold of Ardres and William the Marshal. They were able to do so because they were, at the same time, a meeting ground for men drawn from different levels of aristocratic society, and the centres of a secular literary culture. In them gathered the audiences to whom the *chansons de geste* and the early Arthurian romances were addressed. The *chansons*, it should be stressed, represent a literature of some sophistication. Their authors were not, as was once supposed, ill-lettered minstrels who reworked popular stories: their versification shows the imprint of forms that originally belonged to Latin poetry, and many of their authors were undoubtedly themselves clerks, with some Latin learning of their own.[47] The authors of the early romances were some of them a good deal more learned again. They knew a good deal of classical literature, interest in which was stirring enthusiastically in the twelfth-century schools, and especially Virgil and Ovid. It is no accident that Chrétien de Troyes (who was steeped in Ovid) should quote Macrobius as his authority when he is describing the fairy robe, decorated with emblems of arithmetic, geometry, astronomy and music, which Erec wore at Arthur's court,[48] for Macrobius was one of the principal sources through which contemporary schoolmen were seeking to recover a deeper insight into classical philosophy. Elsewhere, Chrétien is emphatic in stressing the interconnection of chivalry and learning. Learning was appreciated in courtly writers, because their patrons – and indeed many of their patrons' clients – were often cultivated men too. They were not all tough military philistines (though some of them were). John of Marmoutier's encomiastic picture of Geoffrey the Handsome of Anjou takes care to depict him not only as a great military leader and a lover of chivalry and tournaments but also as a cultured prince, who had found tips for his siegecraft from the reading of Vegetius and was a connoisseur of vernacular poetry.[49] And we should not forget that Abelard was the son of a poor Breton knight who was anxious that his children should have a grounding in letters as well as in the military arts.[50] Knights and clerks sprang from the same stock and understood each other's worlds, better than is often allowed for.

Alongside the composition of the *chansons* and the romances we must set another literary activity which was a product too of the new learning of the courts and which also had an importance in giving chivalrous attitudes their classic shape. This was the writing of family histories, in which the high deeds of members of the lineage of the author's patron provided the theme.[51] The histories of Wace, of Benoit de Ste Maure, of Lambert of Ardres and of John of Marmoutier, different as they are, all broadly belong to this genre. It is not an entirely new genre of historical literature: we can see it foreshadowed in, for instance, Widukind's account of the origins of the Saxon royal house, written in the tenth century.[52] But it is new to find the lineages of noblemen who were not connected with a true royal line (or were only very tenuously so connected) being thus celebrated. Besides, these twelfth-century family histories are the products of the pen of a new kind of historian. The writing of history had for long ages been virtually the preserve of the monasteries, whose chronicles very naturally reflected the preoccupations and special interests of particular monastic houses. The authors of the family chronicles were more often secular clerks or chaplains attached to the household of the lord about whose line they wrote, and they brought a new angle of vision to their history. They were less interested in the alms that their patrons gave and in the churches that he and his ancestors had provided, and more interested in his genealogy and in the deeds that made him famous – in other words, in chivalrous topics.

The genealogy through which a lord traced his title to his patrimony was obviously critical to this kind of writer. It is the paternal line that is usually stressed, though any particularly dignified or territorially significant connections brought in by marriage will be carefully noted. The surname of the family, the cognomen usually derived from its chief territorial holding or castle, serves as the mark of the unity of the lineage (a little later, this will come to coincide with the armorial bearings of the family, which become the outward and visible symbol of the unity of a lineage). It is interesting to note that the chronicler even of a relatively modest family, such as Lambert of Wattrelos, who wrote in the late twelfth century and whose family came from the lesser knighthood of Flanders, was careful to single out those in his lineage who were knights – *milites*.[53] Here we see a formal association between lineage and knighthood in the process of formation, a foreshadowing of the later legal doctrine which would exclude from knighthood any who could not point to a knight in their paternal ancestry. Still more interesting, from our point of view, is what the family historians did when they found they had run out of accurate genealogical information. Over and again we find them tracing their lines finally back to a mythical Jesse figure, founder of the dynasty in the heroic past, with whose glory the whole line becomes associated. Thus Lambert of Ardres traces back the origins of Arnold's family to one Sifridus, a Scandinavian adventurer who seduced the daughter of a Count of Flanders (the origin of the line is thus linked to more dignified blood); the Angoulême history traces back the origin of its counts to one William Taillefer, a hero of Carolingian times; the dynasty of the counts of Anjou is traced back to one Tortulfus, a great warrior in the days of Charles the Bald, who married a daughter of the Duke of Burgundy. This Tortulfus is described as one skilled in war, proof against all its rigours, fearful of nothing save the loss of his honour. 'Thus', it is said, 'he brought nobility upon himself and all his race.'[54] The connection between ancestral deeds and the standing in dignity and honour of a lineage, which is the special contribution of this kind of literature to chivalrous ideology, could not be more clearly expressed.

By linking the lineages of their patrons' houses with the heroic past of which the *chansons* told, the family historians provided an emotive link with that past, and one which brought out its relevance to the present. This was a connection that had significance not only for their masters, but also for the clients of those masters. Honour was to be earned by serving those whose ancestors' deeds had rendered their lines illustrious, service which should be so loyally performed as to associate the servant in that reflected glory. Thus genealogical literature and epic *chanson*, in harness, underlined to the courtly world the contemporary relevance of the *chansons'* ethic of loyal service and generous patronage. In a similar way, in the vernacular verse histories that are closely related to the *chansons*, the heroic past became the stock historical foil to the present: the way to praise a man for valour is to say that he was a very Roland or Oliver in the fight. The romance writers, focussing on the Arthurian age which claimed equal historicity with that of Charlemagne, enlarged another dimension of the model of the ideal knight, his *courtoisie*, laying an emphasis on courtly and civilised behaviour worthy of a society that was becoming more refined and literate.

Perhaps the most remarkable feature of the chivalrous culture of twelfth-century France was the way in which its values and its models of knightly living were diffused so rapidly, and so far beyond their birthplace in French soil. One principal reason for this was no doubt the amazing *diaspora* of French knighthood that the later eleventh and twelfth centuries witnessed. Norman knights conquered England, southern Italy and Sicily; aided by knights from other parts of France, including the southern homelands of the troubadours, they took a prominent part in the wars against the Moors in Spain, and – still more dramatically – the leading role in the crusade to the Holy Land. Wherever they went, they took with them their customs, their culture, and their favourite stories. But the stories, and the values and the attitudes that they fostered, spread further afield than those lands which French arms colonised with French lordship and French culture. This was partly because the society of the twelfth century was very open, which made it a great time for travelling. Knights from the borders of the Empire came to France to take part in tournaments. Knights from Flanders crossed the sea to take service under the English king, as did some of Lambert of Wattrelos's relatives in the reign of King Henry I.[55] On the crusades, soldiers from all over Europe rubbed shoulders on campaign. The young clerks of the twelfth century were no less compulsive travellers than the knights, and their wandering too helped to make court culture, as well as the culture of the schools, international. But the French chivalric attitudes and values also spread to other lands because the themes of French literature reflected the aspirations of social groups in societies outside France, whose position was comparable with that of French knighthood, but whose history was different. Let us round off this survey of the social and military origins of chivalry by looking at two striking examples of this, the influence of French chivalry in the German empire and in Italy.

★

In the tenth century and through much of the eleventh, when the French monarchy was at its weakest, the German imperial monarchy was strong. It was able to prevent the rulers of the great 'stem-duchies' (Saxony, Bavaria, Swabia and Franconia) from consolidating their local power in the way that the Dukes and Counts of France did. Its strength was founded in its control of the imperial church, with its vast territorial wealth, and the effective control which successive emperors maintained in their own family lands. But in order to administer these estates effectively, the emperors needed reliable servants, and so did the bishops and abbots whom their influence had advanced. It is in this context that we begin to hear of the *ministeriales*, the 'serf knights' who were the ancestors of the castellans and simple knights of a later German age. They appear first in the empire as a privileged group among the unfree, whose obligations were closely associated with the household service of their lords, ecclesiastical or imperial. The marks of their unfreedom are clear: they had no right to alienate their lands to others beside fellow *ministeriales* of the lordship to which they belonged, or to acquire fiefs outside it except by permission of their lord, or to marry outside the lordship. These are limitations directly reminiscent of those of the labouring serf of France or England, and their rights and privileges, like those of serfs, were defined by the domanial law of a particular lordship: they had no common rights at law outside it. They are very unlike the rights and privileges of the free vassals of France. Nevertheless, the phrase 'serf-knights' is in one way rather misleading. Their obligations were anything but servile, in the ordinary sense; they included service in the lord's hall and in the supervision of his estates, and military service. The chief offices in his household, those of chamberlain, seneschal and marshal, were usually their exclusive preserve.[56] Their right to their own estates was, by the mid eleventh century, accepted in most places at least as being hereditary. Within their own native lordships, the *ministeriales* although technically unfree constituted a powerful and privileged group among the non-noble.

Their unfree status was indeed the key to their power and privilege. Because they were so dependent on their lord, and because of their close familial ties with him and his household, they were the natural men to whom he looked to man his castles and enforce his justice. Because of their general obligation to military service, they were a key element in his forces. As a consequence, many *ministeriales* were able to make themselves powerful. The confusion of the civil wars in Germany, that were sparked off by the quarrel between the empire and the papacy over ecclesiastical investitures in the later eleventh century, gave them a chance everywhere to consolidate their position. In the turbulence of the times their influence was often the only solid element of continuity in the government of a lordship (this was notably the case in the imperial lands themselves in the reign of Conrad III).[57] Their masters were now as visibly dependent on them as they on him, and their service was too valuable to permit attempts to enforce strictly the limitations of their position. Successful *ministeriales* began to acquire fiefs from lords other than their own domestic masters, for which they did homage (which symbolised free possession), and so the distinction between them and the lesser free nobility (the *Edelfreie*) began to be blurred. Werner von Bolanden, Frederic Barbarossa's *ministerialis*, was at the time of his death holding lands of no less than forty-six lords and had amassed a princely patrimony.[58] His success was exceptional: it was a much more modest but secure position that most aspired to. In a country where free landholding (*freies Eigen* under *Landrecht*) was a sign of nobility, the acquisition of fiefs was a key step in the rise of the *ministeriales* into the noble order, whose hierarchy was defined by tenure (*Lehnrecht*).[59]

It is not surprising, in these conditions, that we should find clear evidence that the *ministeriales* were becoming conscious of their social identity, and of the dignity of their service and privileges. They showed themselves capable of acting collectively: in the 1140s we hear of *ministeriales* holding assemblies (*colloquia*) without being summoned by their lords, and doing justice in them; in 1159 we find the *ministeriales* of Utrecht banding together to uphold their privileges.[60] The story told by the chronicler of the abbey of Ebersheimmunster in the 1160s gives a graphic indication of their self-awareness and their social aspirations in the mid twelfth century. Its story is that when Julius Caesar won over the Germans to his obedience, he made their princes senators and the lesser knights (that is to say the *ministeriales*)

Roman citizens. It goes on to tell how Caesar exhorted the princes to be good lords to their ministerial servants, to employ them in high offices, to protect them and to honour them with fiefs.[61] A distinction is maintained here, it is seen, between the ministeriality and the higher aristocracy. In Germany the distinction between the higher, lineal nobility *(frei geboren)* and the service nobility *(Dienstherren, Ritter)* was to endure long after the latter had established their hereditary noble status. What the chronicler's story makes clear is the sense that *ministeriales* had of themselves as standing apart from others of less dignified status (free or unfree), of belonging to the same 'Roman' world as the great nobles with whom they had so long enjoyed such close, but technically ignoble, association.

The German nobility remained peculiarly stratified, as the legists of the thirteenth century remind us. A prince who held his lands directly of the empire was higher in privilege and dignity (in the hierarchy of the *Heerschild*) than a count who held from a prince; below the counts stood the *Dienstherren*, who were many of them of ministerial origin; those who held of them stood formally one rung lower still. But as in France, we find all alike, high and low, beginning from some time in the twelfth century to call themselves *milites*. The signs of the rise of the *ministeriales* into the courtly and martial aristocracy are indeed similar to signs of the rise of the lesser French knighthood that we have observed (though they appear somewhat later). We find, for example, *ministeriales* using the title *miles* when they attest charters. We find them becoming conscious of their knightly lineage, being described as *de militari progenie* or *de militari sanguine* – of knightly descent or blood.[62] As in France, we find them crowding about the courts of great nobles who were also patrons of literature, like Henry the Lion of Saxony and the Landgraf Herman of Thuringia, not to mention the great Barbarossa himself. In legal terms it was the possession of fiefs that carried the *ministeriales* into the nobility – into the lower rungs of the *Heerschild* hierarchy. That is what, in legal texts, the word *Ritter* (the equivalent of the French *chevalier*) means: a member of a lesser aristocracy clearly defined apart from nobility's higher echelons. But the word *Ritter* and the derivative adjective *ritterlich* do not carry any such limitation in ethical treatises and romances. Here these words include the whole chivalrous society. Even of Barbarossa himself it could be said, in praise of his valour, that he had fought 'like a knight'.[63] As in France, a strong common bond was bringing high and low among the nobility closer to one another, the common bond of knighthood in which all alike shared.

Eilhart of Olberg, the author of the German *Tristan*, Walther von der Vogelweide, the greatest of the early *Minnesinger*, and Wolfram von Eschenbach who wrote the first German version of the Grail story, all came from ministerial backgrounds. That the *ministeriales* and their ilk should have embraced enthusiastically the French cult of chivalry should, in the light of what we have learnt about them, occasion no wonder. The world of the German *ministeriales* was like that of the French knights a world both of the court and the camp. For both alike, service provided a key to opportunity, and for both lordly *largesse* was the outward and visible sign of its just due. For the *ministeriales*, their knighthood and their cult of knighthood was the sign that, free or unfree, their servitude was an ennobling servitude. The culture, ethic and ideology of French chivalry chimed perfectly with their aspirations. So, in the late twelfth century, we find the German *Minnesinger* taking up the themes of the Provençal troubadours in their lyrics. We find other writers, such as Hartman von Aue and Wolfram von Eschenbach reworking and elaborating the material that they found in French texts to compose the first German versions of the Arthurian story. Although the Carolingian past was as much part of German as it was of French history, the influence of French models is clear also in the German versions of the stories of Charlemagne's time. France was, indeed, to the Germans the true land of knights – *das rehten ritterschefte Lant.*[64] There is much more here than a story of superficial borrowing from the literature of one country by writers in another who lacked a native and vernacular literary tradition of comparable sophistication. It is a very different story indeed, the story of the profound penetration of German aristocratic society by ideas and values which it first found expressed in French literature.

This is not to say that German chivalry was merely and simply a mirror image of that of France. Germany had her own native traditions, which were strong, and celebrated the fame of her own native champions of chivalry, such as Dietrich von Bern, Henry the Fowler, and the Emperor-Saint Henry II. In just the same way Spain, where too French ideas, conveyed largely through romantic narratives based on French originals, had a powerful influence, had her own knightly heroes, like the Cid Campeador. The rituals for making a knight differed in important details in the German lands from French practice; so did the rules for tournaments and, in due course, the legal tests of nobility. It means rather that it was under French influence that chivalrous ideas in Germany achieved definition, that the German cult of *Ritterschaft* and *Ere* was given shape by the French notions of *chevalerie* and *honeur*, just as the German ideals of *Manheit, Milte, Zuht* and *Trowve* are the direct analogues of the French *prouesse, largesse, courtoisie* and *loyauté*. In consequence, the conceptions of chivalry in the two lands (and elsewhere as well) were so close as to render the ideology of chivalry effectively international, in spite of the great differences in the political and economic preoccupations of knights and noblemen in the two countries.

★

The case of Italy mirrors that of Germany, and is at the same time distinctively different.[65] The obvious distinction is that the nobility of Italy, unlike
the aristocracy in Germany and France, was in many areas predominantly
urban. It is for this reason that it is often held that chivalry never really
struck root in Italy. Its ethos, so it is argued, was essentially alien in spirit to
the bourgeois patriciates whose commercial dominance meant that merchants, traders and bankers were the ruling class in the cities of northern
and central Italy. This is a false view. The men who controlled affairs in the
Italian cities of the twelfth and thirteenth centuries and after were not
bourgeois in the modern sense. As Philip Jones has put it, 'the towns of Italy
for all their growth in size and economic complexity retained the character,
in varying degrees, of communities of landowners. The urban communes
and *universitates*, founded in the eleventh and twelfth centuries, were the
creation not of merchants but of landlords; many urban immigrants were
or became land-holders; and land-ownership was the first ambition of all
urban classes.'[66] It is true, of course, that the better class of immigrants into
the cities in the eleventh and twelfth centuries – and the thirteenth century
too – were a very mixed bag. They included men who had bettered
themselves either as lawyers and notaries in the countryside communities
or by such devious means as money-lending, and who, having put together
a patrimony, hoped for richer pickings in the cities. It is also true that once
in the city all these sorts of men, those of seigneurial family and those of less
exalted ancestry alike, tended to be drawn to a greater or lesser degree into
urban commercial life. Their connections with the countryside remained
close, however. Most continued to own lands outside the city as well as
within the walls, and it was in land that the profits of commerce were most
often invested. In consequence there was no sharp distinction, in terms of
attitudes and aspirations, between families with a landed, aristocratic background and the 'plutocratic bourgeoisie' whose fortunes were founded in
commerce. The views of both alike had in many respects more in common
with what are usually regarded as the values natural to a seigneurial aristocracy rather than to a rising bourgeoisie.

The evidence of this was etched on the skyline of many a medieval
Italian city. That of Florence in the thirteenth century must, as Plesner puts
it, have presented the aspect of a 'forest of towers, more serried than the
chimneys of a modern industrial town'.[67] It is etched still more deeply on
the historical record, in the history of the tower societies of Florence, in the
sorry tale of clan vendetta which is such a feature of the history of the ruling
families of individual cities, and in the pride of men such as Dante that their
ancestors had been knights and crusaders. Memories of martial distinction
were sharp in Italy, and for good reason. In the effort first to shake off

episcopal control and later to limit the overlordship of the Empire, as in
their recurrent wars with one another, the Italian city communes had to rely
on their own military resources. It was not until the fourteenth century that
Italy became the classic battleground for wars fought by foreign mercenaries (and then only partially, and for a limited period). Like the lords of
northern Europe, the cities of Italy needed to be able to put into the field
their own vassal or subject forces, with their own horsemen, equipped and
accoutred as knights, and in order to do this they depended on the men of
well-off families, who could afford the relevant equipment and training. To
a certain extent, of course, they could rely on forces raised by the feudal
aristocracy of the *contado* (for there still was a rural aristocracy of lords, who
usually recognised their subjection to a city government), and taken into
their pay. Thus, according to Villani, the Guelf force that took the field
against Arezzo in 1288 included two hundred and fifty horsemen raised by
'the Guelf counts of Giudi, Mainardo da Susinana, Filipuccio of Jesi, Marquis Malaspina, the Judge of Gallura, the counts Alberti, and the other
minor barons of Tuscany'.[68] But long before that, true city-dwellers had
taken to knightly service. Writing of the mid twelfth century, Otto of
Freising tells us of the Italian cities that 'in order that they may not lack the
means of subduing their neighbours, they do not disdain to give the girdle
of knighthood or the grades of distinction to young men of inferior status,
and even to some workers of low mechanical crafts, whom other people bar
like the plague from the more respected and honourable pursuits'.[69] The
Genoese chronicler Caffaro tells how in 1173 the consuls 'despite the labour
and expense involved, created more than a hundred knights from within
Genoa and outside'.[70] In 1211 the same city created two hundred knights to
serve against the Malaspina. Villani tells us that in 1285 there were three
hundred dubbed knights in Florence.[71] The situation was similar in Lombardy. The men who led the Lombard communes to victory against the
Empire in the twelfth century came for the most part from that section of
the city populace that the chroniclers call the *milites*, that is to say from the
families who counted among their number men who called themselves
knights and who fought on horseback.

Azzo VIII of Este, at 'the great and honourable court of the peers of
Lombardy and his friends' that he held at Ferrara in 1294, first received
knighthood himself at the hands of Ghirardo da Cammino, Lord of Trev-
isa, and then with his own hand created fifty-two knights.[72] The genuine
ring of a great chivalrous ceremony echoes from the chroniclers' account of
this occasion. It is, in fact, quite clear that the spirit of chivalry was anything
but alien to communal Italy in the thirteenth century. The *Ordene de
chevalerie* and its explanation of the symbolism of the dubbing rite was
known well enough in Italy, and the dubbed knights of her cities had gone
through the same kind of rituals as their northern compeers.[73] Having done

so, they displayed a similar, elitist martial spirit. Rolandino of Parma, writing in the 1260s, tells how Tisolino da Camposanpiero, surrounded by his enemies in the field, refused to surrender to any but one of knightly blood: 'when none was found there they killed his good *destrier*, and then, alas, he himself was slain'.[74] Salimbene tells how, when the newly knighted Enrico da Pagani was slain, his father's comment was 'I care not; for my son was made a knight and died fighting like a man.'[75] The martial element in the society of the communal world needed a sustaining ethic, asserting its own value and values, just as much as the noble society of the lands north of the Alps did. Chivalry, for the Italians as for the Germans and the French, provided just that.

It is therefore no surprise to find the chivalric literary culture that was born in France being adopted and adapted in Italy with the same readiness as in Germany. The impact of troubadour lyric is clear very early; from the 1170s on we know of Italians who were writing in Provençal – and a hundred years later Dante could turn faultlessly the eight lines of Occitan that he put into the mouth of the troubadour Arnaut Daniel.[76] Up to his time indeed, Provençal was the language of poetry in many Italian courts. No doubt the role that Charles of Anjou played as the leader of the Guelfs in the later thirteenth century helped to make the French influence stronger; many of his knights were from Provence, and it was under Amaury of Narbonne and under his war-cry of *Nerbona cavaliere* that Dante fought at Campaldino.[77] But it had been well and truly established long before that. The troubadours found themselves very much at home at the courts of the Marquises of Montferrat and Saluzzo around the year 1200; it was about that time that the Provençal Raimbaut de Vaqueiras encountered a warm welcome at the former.[78] It was almost certainly at the court of the Patriarch of Aquileia at the end of the twelfth century that Thomas of Zirclaire made contact with the chivalrous French culture that colours the great didactic poem that he later wrote in Germany, *Der wälsche Gast*. The Italians also adopted the stories of Arthur and Charlemagne and made them their own. The Arthurian story was clearly well known in Italy quite early in the twelfth century (witness the famous frieze on the archivolt of the cathedral of Modena), that of the Carolingian heroes from about the same time – at the latest. It is not until the later thirteenth century, it is true, that we have evidence of Italians themselves putting together versions of these stories (that is the date of Rusticiano da Pisa's Arthurian collection, and of the *Gesta Francor*, the Italian version of the Charlemagne story). Other evidence however makes clear how very much the Italians had by that time made these stories their own. Folgore di San Gimigniano found it natural to picture his companions in arms as the compeers of the great heroes of French chivalrous literature: 'if need called, they would come to the tournaments of Camelot lance in hand'.[79] And the Paduan judge Giovanni da

Nono could record how the Cattanei of Limena claimed that they were descended from one of the knights of the Paladin Renaud de Montauban, and the da Ronchi that their ancestor was that Desiderius 'Whom King Charlemagne besieged for seven years'. His own family, da Nono believed, were descended from Roland.[80] Here is eloquent testimony to the way in which the French chivalrous stories had taken root in Italian soil, and at the same time a striking Italian analogue to the mythical knightly genealogies which the family historians in France so often elaborated for their patrons, as we saw earlier in this chapter.

The French influence on Italian chivalry in the early days left its mark very clearly. The first Italian writers to treat of chivalrous topics wrote, almost to a man, either in French or Provençal, and the Italian vocabulary of chivalry derived from the French: *cavalerria, dama,* and *torneamento* are all borrowed words. The influence, nevertheless, was not just one way. As we shall see in due course, in a later age it was to the lawyers of Italy that the French looked for definitions of the concept of nobility, which they dutifully copied into their handbooks on knighthood. French and German sneers at Italian townsmen had probably helped to concentrate and clarify Italian minds on the subject. For the moment that part of the story must wait; the fact will serve in the meanwhile as a reminder that chivalry will not bear treatment as a merely local phenomenon.

The universal currency that was so rapidly and generally achieved by stories that were first told in the French language, and the way in which French conceptions informed the notions of chivalry of Germans and Italians, is in part, no doubt, to be explained in terms of that *diaspora* of French knighthood in the eleventh and twelfth centuries that I talked of earlier. It also almost certainly owed much to the dominant part that French lords and knights played in the first crusades. It probably owed something besides to a chance factor, that the heroes of whom the French authors of the *chansons de geste* and of the earliest Arthurian romances wrote were the first heroes of the middle ages to be renowned specifically as horsemen, as model cavaliers. None of these factors would have been of any account, however, had it not been for the truly international character both of the aristocratic society and of the culture – secular as well as ecclesiastical – of the eleventh and twelfth centuries. The cosmopolitan quality of the great empire over which the historical Charlemagne had briefly presided some two centuries before had given France, Germany, Italy and Spain a share in a common heritage which left an enduring mark, in spite of the dislocation that was the consequence of the invasions of Vikings, Hungarians, and Saracens in the later ninth century. That was why the influence of, for instance, a great monastery such as Cluny could in this age be felt in all these territories; and why secular ideas and ideals equally could permeate with remarkable rapidity through their length and breadth (the fact that the life of the secular nobility was so intimately bound up with that of the monasteries and churches was indeed one of the reasons why this was so). But for this international character of the society that in the eleventh and twelfth centuries was emerging from the chaos of the age of the invasions, there would have been no chivalry, and no crusades, and the courtly love of troubadour lyric would be a literary eccentricity of a forgotten and provincial Occitan history, not a European cultural phenomenon.

Chivalry was nurtured in France, but took its shape in a European context. It gained currency as the sustaining ethos of warrior groups, identified on the one hand by their martial skill as horsemen, on the other by a combination of pride in ancestry and status and in traditions of service. It distinguished itself from the Germanic warrior ethic of earlier times partly by its new elitist pride in the art of fighting on horseback, partly by the new measure of secular cultural independence that we see reflected, in differing moods, in the twelfth-century vogue of genealogical histories among great families and in the troubadours' concept of courtly love as an ennobling force at the secular level – as also in the virtuoso erudition in secular customary law that many of the authors of the *chansons* and of the earliest romances display. In sum, by somewhere around the mid twelfth century, shifting social and cultural forces – new military techniques, a new vocabulary of status, new literary themes – had given definition to a new kind of figure, called the knight, and to a way of life that was coming to be called chivalry. Here he is, as described in the Provençal epic of *Girart*, composed just about the middle of that century:

> Folcon was in the battle lines, with a fine hauberk, seated on an excellently trained horse, swift and fiery and tested. And he was most graciously armed . . . And when the king saw him he stopped, and went to join the Count of Auvergne, and said to the French: 'Lords, look at the best knight that you have ever seen . . . He is brave and courtly and skilful, and noble and of a good lineage and eloquent, handsomely experienced in hunting and falconry; he knows how to play chess and backgammon, gaming and dicing. And his wealth was never denied to any, but each has as much as he wants . . . And he has never been slow to perform honourable deeds. He dearly loves God and the Trinity. And since the day he was born he has never entered a court of law where any wrong was done or discussed without grieving if he could do nothing about it . . . And he always loved a good knight; he has honoured the poor and lowly; and he judges each according to his worth.'[81]

This is an ideal picture of a knight cast recognisably in the same sort of mould as an Arnold of Ardres or a William the Marshal. The description of him touches on a whole series of themes that have been discussed in this chapter: martial skill in the saddle, lineage and *largesse*, courtly cultivation. One of the most striking features of it is its essentially secular emphasis – that brief reference to Folcon's love of God and the Trinity apart. If it is a sure guide, then it is as an essentially secular figure that the chivalrous knight steps onto the stage of history.

CHAPTER III

Chivalry, the Church and the Crusade

So far, our exploration of the origins of chivalry has centred almost exclusively on the martial and aristocratic aspects of this knightly mode of life. Yet in the treatises on chivalry that we examined earlier, there was a third strand inextricably interwoven with these two, the religious and Christian, which in the writings of such as Lull and Charny has coloured the whole presentation of knighthood. It is high time, clearly, that more inquiry be made about the specifically Christian quality of chivalry, and the place of religion in this ethic for secular men.

The subject is one which raises great problems, and most of all with regard to the period in which chivalrous ideas and ideals were in the process of crystallising into that shape in which we find them established in the age of William the Marshal and Arnold of Ardres (and which they retained for so long thereafter) – the period, that is to say, from a little after the middle of the tenth century down to the beginning of the thirteenth. The second half of this formative period was of course the great age of the crusade – of the launching of the first crusade at Clermont in 1095, of the conquest of Jerusalem, and the establishment of a Christian Frankish kingdom in Syria.

Most historians' accounts of the religious attitudes of knights and of Christian attitudes towards martial activity in the period have in consequence been oriented towards the history of the crusade and of the development of the crusading ideal – and rightly so, for the impact of the crusades on medieval civilisation, and indeed on European attitudes and civilisation for long after the middle ages, was profound, almost incalculable. But crusading and chivalry were not precisely the same thing. Chivalry, as we have seen, was related to a whole range of martial and aristocratic activities which had no necessary connection with crusading. There developed, moreover, about crusading a whole body of church doctrine, canonical and theological, which centred ultimately on the indulgence, the formal remission, on papal authority, of the sins of those who took part in a crusade.[1] No comparable body of church law and doctrine grew up around chivalry as such. The influence of crusading ideology on the ethic of chivalry, in its formative period, was obviously powerful, but we must be careful, as we pursue the origins of the religious strand in chivalry, not to confuse the two or to conflate them.

The really central problem that arises here is how far the new ideas of the tenth and eleventh centuries, of which the crusade was born, were also those that shaped the distinctive Christian strand in chivalry. It has usually been argued that they were, but, as we shall see, there are grounds for suggesting that this argument may, in some respects, have been overstated. Our best way of examining the problem will be to look first at some of the ideas that prompted the crusade and that the crusades themselves prompted; then we can turn to the evidence that suggests that these promptings are not the whole story.

★

One aspect of the crusading ideal which is important to the historian of chivalry is the way in which it brought the church authorities, and in particular the reformed papacy of the late eleventh century, to terms with war and the warrior's place in society. Pope Urban II's crusading appeal of 1095 came as a climax at the end of a long period of development in the church's attitude on these matters.[2] There had always been a tension in Christian thought in this area, between the pacific and the militant strands in the Judaeo-Christian tradition. The tension is there in the Bible itself. The Old Testament reveals Jehovah, as often as not, as the God of battles: the New Testament tells the story of the coming of the Prince of Peace, who preached that the meek should inherit the earth, and bade Peter to put up his sword. In the early church the pacific tradition was strong; Origen, among the early fathers, was typical in regarding the violence of Roman wars as a violation of Christian charity. After the conversion of Constantine, though, this position had to be amended somewhat, for now Roman wars were waged by a Christian emperor and in defence of a commonwealth that was itself becoming predominantly Christian. Augustine, writing at the end of the Imperial age, sketched out what were to become the foundations of the later, medieval Christian theory of the just war. Wars are justified, he taught, when a city or people has deliberately breached the peace, and has refused to amend the injuries done by its subjects; he also argued that loving intention – the intention of correcting sin and bringing sinners back into the fold – could justify the use of force.[3] Although they were seminal, pointing forward towards the doctrines of the crusading age, Augustine's views did not however amount to a systematic or fully developed treatment of the problem of war. The early middle ages thus inherited a stock of ideas about the justification of war, or the lack of it (and hence of the warrior's role in society), that was thoroughly ambiguous.

In the centuries following the collapse of the Roman Empire, the pacific tradition remained strong in the Western church. In a time when that church was heavily influenced by monasticism, it was natural that it should do so. The ideal of flight from the world inevitably underlined the contrast between the *militia Christi*, the true cloistered service of God, and *militia secularis*, the activity of secular warriors whose feuds, prompted by temporal passion and greed, made violence endemic in the world outside the cloister. The strength of the pacific tradition was also mirrored in this period in the penitential literature which, down to the middle of the eleventh century, was such a powerful influence on church law. The pentitential books made no bones about the general force of the sixth commandment: 'Thou shalt not kill.' Most imposed a forty-day penance for killing in war.[4] But while the pacific tradition seemed strong in this period, there were also ecclesiastical thinkers who, looking back like Augustine to the militant tradition of the Old Testament, tended towards the opposite line. The threat to churches and churchmen that was posed by the incursions into the lands of the old Empire of new waves of barbarian invaders, encouraged their way of thinking, especially when, in the later ninth century, Carolingian Europe seemed to be assailed on all sides by pagan enemies: Vikings in the north, Hungarians in the East, Moslems in southern Italy and Spain and all along the Mediterranean shore. So, as time went by, the balance of ecclesiastical thought began to tip in favour of militancy, until in the end the crusading indulgence turned the teaching of the pentitentials upside down. 'Those who make this journey shall win remission of all penance,'[5] Urban promised at Clermont: to fight and to kill, in this new war to free the Holy Places, would not incur penance but absolve men of the need of it.

It is in terms of this shift in ecclesiastical attitudes to war, whose thumbnail outlines I have attempted to sketch as briefly as possible, that many historians have explained the development of the idea of knighthood as a Christian vocation. The wars against the heathen in the Carolingian and Ottonian periods are seen by them – no doubt rightly – as the impetus behind the shift of ideas: the invasions were what brought home to churchmen their dependence on the 'order' of warriors for physical security. Thus we can see already the germ of the idea of the crusading indulgence in Pope Leo IV's appeal for support in 853 when the Saracens were threatening Rome; 'he who dies in this battle will not be denied the heavenly kingdom, for the Almighty will know that he died for the truth of our faith, for the salvation of the *patria*, and the defence of Christianity'.[6] Liturgical texts give still more eloquent evidence of the growing consciousness of Christian purpose in warfare. Thus we find in pontificals of the tenth century special prayers for the blessing of banners that might be borne against the heathen: 'bless and sanctify this banner that is borne for the protection of Holy Church against hostile fury, so that the faithful and the defenders of God's people who follow it may obtain triumph and victory over the enemy in your name and by the strength of the cross'.[7] A liturgy for the blessing of the warrior's sword, which is seen by many as anticipating the later liturgical rite for the making of a new knight, appears about the same time.[8] And in this same invasion period we also perceive the beginnings, in the west, of the cults of the military saints, especially of St Michael, the leader of God's heavenly host. The banner that the German kings Henry the Fowler and Otto I carried against the Hungarians bore the image of the archangel, and the great victory over them at the Lech in 955 was attributed to his aid.[9] A St Michael's mass in his honour was often recited as a thanksgiving for victory. The cult of St George seems to have been becoming widespread a little later, in the second half of the eleventh century, at the very eve of the crusades.[10] One of the earliest references to him as a patron of warriors in the west is Geoffrey Malaterra's story of his miraculous appearance, mounted on a white horse, to aid the Normans against the Saracens at Cerami in 1063.[11] His reputation was most likely spread by mercenaries returning from the Byzantine service, for in the east his cult had for some time been associated with wars against the heathen. That cause is thus the common factor behind a whole series of canonical, liturgical and hagiological developments.

There is another factor, too, besides the wars against the heathen, that has been linked by historians with the shift in ecclesiastical attitudes that we are considering. That is the growing concern of the church, in the governmental chaos that the heathen invasions of the ninth century brought in their wake, over the maintenance of peace and order in Christendom, which a depleted royal authority was unable to enforce locally. Particular significance is associated with the ecclesiastical legislation which sought to impose the Peace and Truce of God. Here the church hierarchy for the first time appears to have taken a real and important initiative towards the regulation and limitation of martial activity, and in doing so, to have gone over the head of formally constituted secular authority to deal directly itself with the knighthood. The peace movement had a positive and active side, for the peace councils sought to do more than merely restrict violence.[12] The bishop of Le Puy gathered a host and forced those knights who were unwilling to accept the canons of the council of Le Puy (990) to swear to observe them. Bishop Aimo of Bourges enforced the canons of his council in 1038 in the same way.[13] From here it can be seen as a short step to the canalisation of martial energy into a real war of which the church at large could approve, which indeed it would seek to direct, such as the crusade. The connection of ideas is seen very clearly at Clermont in 1095 where, in the same gathering in which he preached the crusade, Pope Urban II proclaimed the Truce of God and ordered it to be observed throughout the Roman obedience.[14]

There were other signs as well that, in the eleventh century, the church authorities were becoming more concerned with the direction and limitation – and in due course with the canalisation – of martial energies. When the Pisans were preparing their expedition to recover Sardinia from the Moslems, the Pope gave them a banner of St Peter to be their standard, thus placing the expedition in a degree under his auspices. Roger Guiscard was given a similar banner by Pope Alexander II, to carry in his war for the conquest of Arab Sicily.[15] Pope Gregory VII took things much further. Early in his pontificate he had plans for putting himself at the head of a great expedition to aid Jerusalem and the Christians of the East. The great quarrel over investitures that broke out between him and the Emperor Henry IV put paid to that idea, but in this new struggle he now called, without hesitation, on secular knighthood to come to the aid of St Peter's Vicar, as a Christian duty.[16] His disciple Anselm of Lucca looked back to St Augustine to justify such military action as loving persecution (*beata perse-cutio*), necessary for the purifying of the church.[17] Bonizo of Sutri, another of his apologists, made crystal clear the church's right to direct military action: clerks should themselves abstain from the shedding of blood, he wrote, 'but that is not to say that the faithful, and especially kings, magnates and knights, should not be summoned to persecute schismatics and heretics and excommunicates with their arms. For if this were so the order of warriors would seem superfluous in the Christian legion.'[18] The idea of knighthood as an order with a Christian vocation in the church's service is quite explicit here, and it clearly does not take much alteration of the spirit of Bonizo's view to throw in heathens and Moslems along with schismatics and heretics as enemies of the church against whom the knight's sword is meritoriously drawn. Gregory's plans for an expedition to aid Jerusalem, together with his promise of forgiveness of sins to those who fought against the Emperor in St Peter's cause – the *militia Sancti Petri* as he occasionally called them – bring us indeed to the very brink of the idea of crusade.[19]

In the preaching and propaganda of the crusade itself the concept of the Christian mission of knighthood as an order emerges with absolute clarity. The crusade is presented, indeed, in terms of a positive transformation of the knightly way of life. 'Let those who have been robbers now be soldiers of Christ . . . let those who have been hirelings for a few pieces of silver now attain an eternal reward,' said Urban II.[20] 'In our own time,' wrote Guibert de Nogent, 'God has instituted a Holy War, so that the order of knights and the unstable multitude who used to engage in mutual slaughter in the manner of ancient paganism may find a new way of gaining salvation: so that now they may seek God's grace in their wonted habit, and in the discharge of their own office, and no longer need to be drawn to seek salvation by utterly renouncing the world in the profession of the monk.'[21] There was of course much else in the propaganda of the first crusade besides this recurrent theme of a new potential suddenly opened to men previously wholly secular and godless in their conduct. There was the powerful appeal to the idea of pilgrimage, and the biblical resonances of the summons to make the journey to Jerusalem stirred all sorts of apocalyptic hopes and impulses. But in terms of the idea of knighthood as a Christian vocation, the new significance and purpose opened to the martial order by the crusade is very apparent. In the history of ecclesiastical thinking about war, the launching of the crusade marks a decisive point, setting a seal on a trend toward militancy which had been making progress over a long period.

The question we want to answer, however, is whether the launching of the crusade also marks a decisive point in the history of chivalry, and here the position is not so clear. The warning given at the beginning of this chapter, that we must be on our guard against conflating the idea of the crusade and the idea of Christian knighthood, becomes relevant. For it is one particular form of martial activity, not the whole range of the activities of secular knighthood, that has been brought by the crusade into a new framework of Christian vocation. In part, no doubt, the idea of the new way to salvation now offered to the knight is a rhetorical device, but it is one that is repeatedly and emphatically employed and its implication is clear. Baudry de Dol brings its point out very clearly, actually bidding men to 'lay aside the belt of secular knighthood' in favour of crusading.[22] St Bernard makes the same point later in his *De laude novae militiae templi*, where he contrasts the Christian devotion of the Templar who fights 'with pure mind for the supreme and true king' with the profligacy of secular knighthood.[23] We have seen a new way to salvation opened to knights, but it is narrow as well as new, clean different from the ordinary way of knighthood.

There has indeed been a great shift in ecclesiastical attitudes, at any rate if we look back far enough; one which has left way behind the spirit of the penitentials with their unhesitating condemnation of homicide in war. But the shift has taken place, we now begin to see, within a deeply ecclesiastical and hierarchic framework of ideas. The episcopal organisation of military forces to uphold the Peace of God and Gregory's appeal to the *militia Sancti Petri* point towards a knighthood which shall be the strong right arm of the priesthood and which shall be subject to its direct behest. In the clerical propaganda of the crusade, that is what has opened the 'new way' for knights. In the crusading context, the military orders – the Temple, the Hospital, and the Teutonic and Spanish orders – came to be just that, the strong right arm of the militant church. Their organisation, as reflected in their rules of life, represented a real fusion of ecclesiastical (as opposed to simply Christian) and martial ideals. The Templar's rule, granted at the council of Troyes in 1128, bound the Knights Templar to the ascetic obligations of obedience and chastity, and to a strict round of religious observance, modelled upon the monastic way of life.[24] It freed them from all secular allegiance and bound them to the authorities of the order, to its Grand Master and to its Chapter, who were themselves ultimately subject to higher ecclesiastical authority. The rule also provided for the organisation of the order and laid down for it the code of military discipline which made the Templars, with the Hospitallers whose rule was modelled on theirs, the elite forces of Christian Syria. The Templars' rule, and the subsequent rules of the other military orders, thus really did set them apart from the ordinary knighthood. But they represented an idea too coloured by the monastic ideal, and too coloured also by the passions engendered in the bitter quarrel of the papacy with the empire, to be offered, even in modified form, to the knighthood at large. Their dedication, as religious orders, cut them off from too much, from the courts, from the troubadour cult of love and the new models of knighthood that the secular romances presented, and from the tourneying field. These were the areas where dynamic new ideas were being forged in the twelfth century. In generalising the idea of knighthood as an order, with obligations separable from those of vassal to lord and of more general application, it seems likely that the example of the military orders was significant. In other respects the claims that their rules enshrined were too exclusive to permit them to exercise a decisive influence on knighthood generally; and the same was true of the teaching of Gregory VII and his apologists.

Indeed, what was really new about the church's teaching at the end of the eleventh century was not the sanctification that it gave to the calling of arms (in which regard the church hierarchy was, as we shall see, largely preaching to the converted), but the claim of the church authorities to direct martial energy, as of right. Significantly, the call to crusade evoked an immediate, indeed an amazingly general response, but the claim to authority did not. This was because the former played on ideas that had strong independent roots, whereas the latter proposed ideas that were not securely rooted at all. Church rites, such as the blessing of banners and swords, together with the cult of the military saints did help to remind knights, through symbolism and ritual, that as Christians they should view their calling in Christian terms. The crusade gave Jerusalem and the defence of the Holy Places a unique position of significance in the mental world of knighthood. But the Christian strand in chivalry had origins that were not only older than the eleventh century church reform movement but were rooted in a different soil.

★

So far, we have been pursuing our inquiry largely through ecclesiastical sources, and have found them to reflect views whose limitation seems often to be that they are too exclusively ecclesiastical. If we now turn to look at more secular and more specifically chivalrous material, we shall find our range of vision immediately extended, and our picture altered in a significant way.

The earliest sources that can fully and properly be called 'chivalrous' are the *chansons de geste*, and in them the wars against the heathen in the Carolingian age – the wars which we have seen as the first impetus in the story of shifting ecclesiastical attitudes – hold the centre of the stage again. From the start they also attest the profound impact of Christianity upon knighthood. The war in the *Chanson de Roland* is not just an earthly struggle: Gabriel stands guard beside the sleeping Charlemagne and is by him in his great struggle with the Emir; Gabriel was at Roland's side too, as he lay dying, and heard his prayer: 'Father, who raised Lazarus and who brought Daniel out of the lion's den, save my soul from danger and despair, and forgive me my sins.'[25] The prayers in *Guillaume d'Orange* are still more eloquent of real religious feeling, as for instance Vivien's stern reproach to himself for having prayed to the Virgin to save him from death: 'Truly, that was a foolish thought, to seek to save myself from death, when the Lord God himself did not, when He suffered death upon the cross to save us from our deadly foe.'[26] From the same poem we may place alongside this the touching scene where William kneels by the dying Vivien, with the consecrated host in his wallet with which he will shrive him, and hears Vivien recite his belief: 'I truly know that God is life and truth, who came to save His people. He was born in Bethlehem of the Virgin. He let Himself be hanged on the cross and was pierced by the spear of Longinus, so that blood and water flowed from His side.'[27] Here, in the context of heroic struggles with the heathen, we are brought face to face with the strong religious emotions of truly Christian soldiers. We are also brought up against their complete lack of self-consciousness about their role as Christian warriors. They are soldiers at once of God and of their earthly lords. Christ's example on the cross is an inspiration to their courage; but to fight courageously is also their secular duty. They are 'Christian soldiers' because they are both Christians and knights, and not because of any special commission that the authority of the church has given them.

What we see here is what the German historian Waas has christened *Ritterfrömmigkeit* – a specifically knightly brand of piety.[28] The *chansons de geste* give us our first direct taste of it, but in them it is already something naturally assumed, clearly in no sense novel, as the *chansons* themselves were at the end of the eleventh century. Obviously it bears witness to the effective teaching of the priesthood, and it owes much, no doubt, to the monasteries, with which the secular nobility who listened to the *chansons* had such close connections. The secular nobles were the men whose families had endowed the monasteries with their lands, who as their advocates took up the duty of defending their rights and as such often bore their banners in war, and whose names were written in the monasteries' necrologies to be specially mentioned in their prayers, and in the *libri memoriales* that were laid on the church's altar, so that those mentioned in them might benefit from the monks' intercession. For most of them, in these early days, the regional monastery was a far more significant religious institution than the papacy in far off Rome was – or ever could be. The monasteries in their turn were concerned with the martial activities of the nobles, as well as with their spiritual life, and had long been so. It was at Cluny, that grandest and noblest of churches which with her daughter-houses strove more than any other, perhaps, to influence the ways of the nobility, that the first life was written of a saint who had spent part of his life as a secular 'warrior in God's cause' – the life of St Gerard of Aurillac by Odo of Cluny.[29] Ralph Glaber tells us of how a group of Burgundian knights, going to fight in Spain, promised to St Odilo of Cluny all the plunder in gold and silver that they might win, and he placed it in the church there.[30] Here we see knightly piety in action, bringing its trophies as a tribute to a great regional monastery. The richness of the Cluniac ritual and of monastic vestments and ceremony plainly had a powerful impact on the imagination of the secular nobles, and has much to do with their fascinated interest in rich robes and ritual, which is reflected so clearly both in the Arthurian romances and in the efforts of the nobility to enrich with splendid ritual the secular life of their courts. Nevertheless, monastic influence alone will not totally explain the nature of the *Ritterfrömmigkeit* of eleventh- and twelfth-century knighthood. The contemplative ideal, which flees a violent world to seek the peace of the cloister, has clearly had little impact on it, as we meet it in the *chansons*. It is the piety of active men who have no qualms about the standing in God's eyes of their active, martial calling.

Passages and incidents in the *chansons de geste* suggest strongly, in fact, that we need to look further back than the age of Cluny for the origins of this knightly piety, just as we have to look back to an earlier age for the origins of their secular ethos. In the *chansons*, as we have seen earlier, such 'chivalrous' virtues as *largesse, prouesse* and loyalty are already established as the stereotypes of noble behaviour. These secular qualities – or at any rate qualities hardly distinguishable from them – are already the marks of the hero in the older Germanic literature which precedes the *chansons* and whose roots stretch back into the pre-Christian past. Liberality, loyalty and courage are the principal virtues in the warrior society depicted in the Anglo-Saxon epic of *Beowulf* (which may have been written as early as the eighth century).[31] Already present too in that poem is the view of youth as a testing time, in which the young warrior seeks to prove himself in the service of foreign lords and far from home; that is what the first part of the epic, in which the young Beowulf takes service under King Hrothgar and delivers his land from the monster Grendel and Grendel's still more monstrous mother, is about. When he returns triumphant as a proven hero, the time is ripe for his lord and kinsman Hygelac to honour him with great estates and to put the sword of Hrethel into his hands. This theme, of the testing of the young hero, reappears in the German Latin epics of the tenth and eleventh centuries, such as *Ruodlieb* and *Waltharius*[32]; it is also, of course, an endlessly repeated theme later, in chivalrous romance, where we meet again and again the figure of the young knight leaving home (or it may be Arthur's court), to prove himself in strange adventures. *Beowulf*, it is true, has nothing to do with fighting the heathen: his enemies were monsters and dragons, and the poem, though written in Christian times, appears to be describing events pictured as taking place in a pre-Christian era.[33] But this does not mean that the men of the age in which *Beowulf* was composed viewed the heroic virtues and Christian teaching as matters essentially separate. The truth is indeed almost the converse of that.

This is apparent when we turn from secular to Christian Germanic poetry: their terms are so nearly the same, often, as to be virtually interchangeable. The Old German *Heliand* describes Christ and His apostles in terms of a warrior band gathered about their noble leader. The Anglo-Saxon *Genesis* waxes eloquent over Abraham's war with the Elamites: 'then I heard that heroes ventured into battle at night: clashing of shields and spears arose in the camp . . . Abraham gave battle as ransom for his nephew, and not twisted gold: the Lord of Heaven struck to aid him.'[34] Here the narrative of the Christian Bible is translated directly into the language of secular epic, and religious virtues and heroic ones are assimilated into one another. As we read that the Lord struck to aid Abraham, we really get to grips with the reason why the German Kings Henry and Otto chose to display upon their banner the image of St Michael, the captain of the Lord's host; it symbolised their faith that their war with a heathen enemy mirrored and paralleled another war, Michael's struggle with the powers of darkness, and that he would strike to aid them. We can also see that it is no accident that, in the later liturgies for the blessing of swords and banners, the example of the Lord's warrior Abraham is invoked, along with that of other Old Testament heroes of the Jewish wars, Gideon, David and the Maccabees.[35] It is well to remember here that sacral swords have a history that stretches back into the pre-Christian past. Roland's Durendaal has its counterpart in *Waldhere* in the sword Mimming, which was forged by the great smith of the Teutonic pantheon, Weland:[36] as the relics in Durendaal's hilt (St Peter's tooth, a hair of St Denis, a fragment of the Virgin's robe) have their counterpart in Norse descriptions of magic 'life stones' set in the pommel of heathen swords.[37]

If we are to understand the knightly piety of the crusading age it is to this interpenetration of biblical and heroic traditions in the period following the adoption of Christianity by such Teutonic peoples as the Franks and the Anglo-Saxons that we have ultimately to look back. Only by doing so can we understand how it is that the piety of the heroes of the *chansons de geste* is so firmly set in an active, non-contemplative tradition. Here we should remember that in the newly converted Teutonic world the traditional values of the martial aristocracy naturally infected the attitudes of priests and even monks as well as laymen. Alcuin disapproved of monks who enjoyed secular lays, but the manuscript of *Beowulf* was preserved in a monastery and almost certainly written down in one.[38] Widukind of Corvey, though a monk, saw nothing amiss in recalling the fame and deeds of Hathagut, the warrior leader of pre-Christian Saxon history, and his description of the feuds in the Liudolfing house in his own time is close in spirit to the world of *Beowulf* and of the *Hildebranslied*.[39] Given that the great men of the ecclesiastical world, the bishops and abbots, were almost exclusively men of noble birth, drawn from the same families that led men in war (whether against the heathen or against each other), it was natural that an ecclesiastic like Widukind (who was himself related to the Liudolfing house) should write in this way.

Monasteries – whose monks prayed for the victories of the people – often became, indeed, the repositories of the martial as well as the religious tradition of the folk, and centres of the cult of the lineage of warrior leaders. Bede tells us that King Oswald's banner of purple and gold was hung above his tomb in the seventh-century church of Bardney, which had been founded by his niece, Queen Osthryd of Mercia.[40] So it should really come as no surprise later when we hear that there was a cult of William of Orange at the church of Gellone, which he had himself founded and where he ended his life as a monk, and that the church of St Juliet at Brioude proudly displayed his shield; that the churches of St Honorat des Aliscamps and of Notre Dame des Martres Tolosans disputed the title to the tomb of Vivien; and that those of Vienne and St Jean des Sorde both claimed to be the burial place of Archbishop Turpin.[41] These cults of the heroes of the *chansons* who died in war against the heathen are striking testimony to the way in which the twin goals of the active chivalrous life, fame in this world and salvation in the next, had begun to become entwined in the structure of eleventh-century piety.

The simultaneous pursuit of both these goals was at the heart of chivalry, of its very essence, and this is one of the surest signs that, in the end, what Waas has called *Ritterfrömmigkeit*, the knight's sense of Christian commitment, owes more to the Christian penetration of the old, once autonomous heroic ethic, infusing it with a new religious colour, than to later ecclesiastical prompting. Fame was alike the highest reward of the Teutonic warrior and the just meed of chivalrous prowess. 'Thou hast brought it to pass that thy fame shall live for ever': that is what Hrothgar said to Beowulf when he had slain Grendel.[42] Roland, dying at Roncesvalles, turned his face towards the Paynim, 'for he was fain that they should say he had died a conqueror'.[43] 'Right there let us try our strength', said Bamborough to Beaumanoir, when they had fixed the ground for the combat of the Thirty (1350), 'and do so much that people will speak of it in future times in halls, in palaces, in public places, and elsewhere throughout the world.'[44] What more can a knight ask, queried Geoffrey de Charny, than that which Judas Maccabaeus, the Lord's warrior, achieved, honour in this world and salvation in the next?[45] It was because of its antique root in the warrior's desire for praise and recognition that no preaching or teaching could shake the bellicosity out of the ideal of knighthood, for as Tacitus put it, writing of the ancient Germans and their lust for battle, 'renown is easiest won among perils'.[46] Christianity and bellicosity were woven together inseparably in the structure of chivalry from its beginning, as combined elements in its heritage from the past.

This same interweaving of Christian with heroic and secular motifs becomes characteristic of the treatment of the crusade in chivalrous narrative and poetry. Villehardouin's account of the fourth crusade is a good example. He is fully conscious of the significance of the crusading indulgence: his crusaders are pilgrims; their aim is to 'avenge the outrage suffered by Our Lord, and, if God so wills, to recapture Jerusalem'.[47] But his story, prose chronicle though it is, speaks the language of the epic *chansons*, and the classic chivalrous qualities of the warrior are what he really understands. Loyalty, for example: 'God forbid that I should ever be reproached with flying from the field and abandoning my emperor,' cries the wounded Louis de Béthune.[48] Or liberality: 'the Marquis [of Montferrat] was one of the most highly esteemed knights in all the world . . . for no one was more open-handed and generous than he'.[49] And of course Villehardouin put a special price upon individual valour, of which he picks out countless examples. The whole tone of his chronicle is well summed up in the words that he puts into the mouth of the Doge of Venice: 'Sirs, you are associated with the best and bravest people in all the world, in the highest enterprise anyone has undertaken.'[50] The crusade has become a great chivalrous adventure, in which the service of God and the quest for earthly renown and reward have become so interlaced that it is no longer practical to seek to unravel the strands.

We have seen how the idea of youth as a testing time for the young warrior, in which he seeks to establish his standing by adventuring far afield, was deeply embedded in the Teutonic heroic ethos. The crusade offered a means by which this aspect too of the heroic ethic could be drawn into a specifically Christian context. 'Blind is he who does not make once in his life an expedition to succour God and who for so little loses the praise

of the world'[51]: so wrote the crusader poet Theobald of Champagne. Here
we see the crusade being drawn into a structure of activities with a quasi-
ritual significance in that proving time of youth, the age for going to
tournies, for dedication to the service of a beloved woman – and for the
crusade. Because of its special religious significance its place in this
framework is that of the supreme proof of knightly quality, but from an
early point it is too firmly woven into a broader chivalrous context for the
secular, courtly and heroic to be set on one side, and the religious on the
other. 'There [in Syria] shall the knights great and small do deeds of
chivalry,' Conon de Béthune wrote on the eve of the third crusade. 'Thus a
man shall win paradise and honour, and the love and praise of his beloved.'
His contemporary Guy, *châtelain* of Coucy, was a little more frankly sensual: 'May God raise me to that honour, that I may hold her, in whom dwell
all my heart and thought, naked in my arms once before I cross the sea to
Outremer.'[52] Baudouin de Condé, who wrote late in the true crusading era,
at the end of the thirteenth century, is on the other hand less sensual but
more systematic and more militarily minded. The young bachelor should
throw all he has into it when he begins to tourney, he says, heart and soul
and his wealth as well; but if he would be considered a perfect knight the
time must come to take leave of the tourney and take the cross, for none can
call himself a true *preudhomme* until his sword has struck a blow against
God's enemies. 'Thus', his *Dit dou Baceller* concludes, 'it behoves the
bachelor to mount step by step in price and prowess.'[53] In this poem the idea
of a progress through scales of worth to the sovereign prowess, which is so
central to Geoffrey de Charny's account of chivalry, can be seen taking
shape.

Christian rituals and church law did much to underscore the special
significance of crusading in the chivalric scales of value. The crusader took
his vow in church, in the presence of a priest; he sewed onto his garment the
emblem of the cross. This served as a symbol, like the pilgrim's staff, of his
privileged and protected position under church law which secured to him
special advantages (some of which, such as freedom from legal pursuit for
debt, had nothing directly to do with chivalric values). Jerusalem did
acquire, in the eyes of knighthood, a significance that no other earthly city
could possess, and its conquest did open new horizons, the chance to
participate in a war that was significantly different from other wars. But
Theobald of Champagne's words, 'blind is he who has not once in his life
crossed the sea to succour God', made it clear that he was thinking in terms
other than those of the original ecclesiastical ideal of total dedication to
Holy War. He was not thinking in terms of a lifetime to be spent in the Holy
Land, as were the first Templars and the barons and knights who settled in
Outremer (and who were always too few for the defence of their conquest),
but in terms of a journey from which a man hoped to return. His was the

normal chivalrous conception of the crusade, that held by the great majority of knights who, after the triumph of the first crusade and the initial settlement, went to Palestine or thought of doing so. It was a conception that added an extra dimension to *Ritterfrömmigkeit*, to active knightly piety, and it was a dramatic and psychologically powerful addition thereto. But it served mostly to thicken the Christian veneer with which the old heroic values (and the new courtly ones too) were already deeply encrusted: it did not, as some ecclesiastics hoped it would, substitute for them something altogether different.

★

The same familiar theme of the interpenetration of Christian and secular values is reflected in some of the principal additions that the crusading age made to what may be called the literary mythology of chivalry. Two sets of stories illustrate this in a particularly illuminating way: the story of the *Chevalier au Cygne* (the romanticised version of the story of the first crusade), and the group of Arthurian romances that centre round the quest for the Holy Grail. A brief consideration of their matter and their manner of treating it will help to give a further dimension to the picture of the religious mentality of knighthood that this chapter has been seeking to define. Both illustrate the way in which secular aristocratic ideals, heroic and courtly, which had nothing to do with ecclesiastical ideology, remained basic to chivalry even in its most deliberate mood of religious commitment. Significantly, both sets of stories begin to take a definite shape in the late twelfth century and the early years of the thirteenth, in the very same period, that is to say, in which in the last chapter we found that social and military developments were defining, in their purely secular terms, a pattern of chivalrous living, and which were also the heyday of the crusade.

In the group of stories brought together in the romance of the *Chevalier au Cygne* the oldest is that originally and independently known as the *Chanson d'Antioche*.[54] In the form in which it survives this poem is the work of Greindor de Douai, who wrote a little before the year 1200, but it is a reworking of an older poem by one Richard the Pilgrim, whom some believe to have been an eyewitness of the events of the first crusade, and whose account of it tallies well with what the most respectable chroniclers tell us. It offers a basically accurate history of the crusade down to the taking of Antioch in 1098. Its tone is different from that of the Latin chronicles of the expedition: the debates and quarrels of the leaders of the crusade are put into direct speech, and much more is made, as we should expect, of individual acts of heroism; but it may still be described as essentially a verse chronicle. Greindor de Douai however also reworked another *chanson*, the *Chanson de Jerusalem*, which carried the story of the crusade on to the taking of Jerusalem and down to the Battle of Ascalon (1099), and this was a poem of a distinctly different quality. Its author was certainly not an eyewitness of events and he did not follow any reliable chronicle. Like the earlier work of Richard the Pilgrim, this *chanson* is full of battles and of the details of personal martial feats, but basically its content is fiction based on historical material, not history. This does not of course detract from its drama. Here are the splendid stories of how Cornumarant, son of the infidel king Cordabas, managed to slip out through the crusaders' besieging lines before Jerusalem, sounding his horn on the hills beyond to tell the defenders that he was safely away to seek relief: and of how, when Baldwin of Edessa came on him by surprise in the desert, he fled on his swift horse, Plantamor. Here too is the story of the miraculous events which took place when the crusader barons met to elect a King, and which signified to them that God's choice for the first Advocate of the Holy Sepulchre had fallen on Godfrey of Lorraine.[55] He and Cornumarant, the valiant Moslem, have become the central figures in a story which has more of the flavour of a true *chanson de geste* than of a verse chronicle.

Into this story, a little after Greindor's time, a third strand was woven, the story of Godfrey's ancestry (the legend concerning which, as we learn from other sources, was circulating already in the late twelfth century). The story is one whose outlines most will find familiar. Lost in the forest, Lothar, son of a King Philip, laid himself down to sleep by a clear spring. He was woken by the fair Elioxe, whose father's castle was close by; looking on her, he fell in love instantly and offered her his hand.[56] She consented to be his but warned him that it would cost her her life: she would bear him a son from whom would spring the race of the future conqueror of Jerusalem, and would die in doing so. So it fell out: while he was at the wars she bore him seven children, six boys and a girl, and died in childbirth. Each child, when it was born, had a gold chain about its neck. The old Queen, their grandmother, had hated Elioxe and looked askance at the children, whom she ordered to be abandoned in the forest, telling Lothar on his return that his wife had died giving birth to a monster. In the woods, the children were succoured by an old hermit, but news of it came to the Queen, and she sent a servant to steal their gold chains: he succeeded in stealing those of the six boys, who were instantly transformed into swans and flew away over the forest. The lonely girl wandered seeking them, till she came at last to her father's palace and was recognised: the brothers were found on a nearby lake, and regained their shape when the chains were restored – all save one, whose chain was lost. Four of the brothers now disappear from view: the fifth, the Swan Knight, having grown to knighthood, set out in a bark drawn by his swan brother. After forty days, they came to the Emperor Otto's palace at Nijmegen; here the Swan Knight stepped forward to champion the Duchess of Bouillon and her daughter Beatrice against the Duke of

Saxony who was challenging their inheritance. In a judicial duel he slew the Duke, and afterwards married Beatrice. When she asked him the question he had forbidden, what his birth was, the swan returned with the bark and took him away, sorrowing, never to be heard of again. But Beatrice still had their daughter Ida, and in due course she married Count Eustace of Boulogne, bearing him three sons, Eustace, Baldwin, and the conqueror Godfrey. Thus the familiar fairy story, better known as that of *Lohengrin*, was tacked as a prologue onto the cycle of stories that grew up around the song of Richard the Pilgrim. Its significance in the framework of the cycle is clear: it singles out the lineage of the future conqueror by associating with it a train of miraculous and prophetic events.

In the legendary material incorporated into the crusading cycle of the *Chevalier au Cygne* religious and secular themes are very closely interwoven. The story of Christ's prophecy on the cross to the good thief, in the *Chanson d'Antioche*, reveals God's purpose in the crusade, but colours it with overtones of the secular vendetta: 'Friend, in time a new people will come from beyond the sea who will exact vengeance for this death: so that no pagan shall remain, from here to the uttermost East.'[57] The fairy legend of the Swan Knight's appearance, at Nijmegen, becomes a heavenly sign in its new context. Its magic again reveals the divine purpose, but through a story on which the secular and aristocratic conception of lineage has left a profound mark, and in which crucial incidents, such as the encounter between Elioxe and Lothar and the Swan Knight's championship of Beatrice and her mother, have courtly, even amorous, overtones. The effect is to infuse the history of the recovery of the Holy Places, which is the focal centre of the narrative, with the colour of the secular chivalrous ethos.

In the Arthurian legend, the story of the quest for the Holy Grail plays what is almost precisely a reverse role. Sandwiched, in the Vulgate Cycle of stories about Arthur (and so in Malory), between the romance of *Lancelot* and the final drama of the *Mort Artu*, it infuses the whole chivalrous history of the company of the Round Table with religious significance. There are other striking analogies between the two stories, as we shall see, especially in their treatment of lineage. As we should expect, there are also strong crusading undertones in some versions of the Grail legend. In Wolfram von Eschenbach's *Parzival* we find the Grail castle of Munsalvaesche guarded by Templars,[58] and the opening of the French romance of *Perlesvaus* avows that its intent is that 'by writing and testimony the truth may be known of how knights and worthy men were willing to suffer toil and hardship to exalt the law of Jesus Christ'. Its author's proud genealogical claim for Perceval's line is that his father and all his uncles 'died in battle in the service of the Holy Prophet who renewed the law by His death and crucifixion.'[59] The Grail romances in addition offer some of the most striking examples of the juxtaposition of the themes of bellicosity and piety in the whole of chivalrous literature, and thus link back to another matter discussed earlier in this chapter.

Let us look a little closer at the story. Two narrative strands go into the making of the Grail legend. The story that Chrétien de Troyes told in his unfinished *Perceval* and that Wolfram followed and carried to a conclusion in his *Parzival* seems to have its origin in a Celtic heroic myth about the horn or dish of plenty (though the tale is already, in their poems, overlaid with Christian significance). The other strand we first pick up in Robert de Boron's romance, *Joseph of Arimathie*, and derives ultimately from the *Gospel of Nicodemus*, a fourth-century fabrication which forms part of the New Testament apocrypha.[60] Robert tells how Joseph, whom he calls the 'good soldier', obtained from Pilate not only the body of Jesus, but also the cup which was used at the Last Supper. Imprisoned by the Jews, he was miraculously released by the risen Christ (this from the *Gospel of Nicodemus*), who appeared bearing the holy cup and entrusted it to him (this is Robert's addition, or that of an intermediate source). Later Joseph and his brother-in-law Bron, the Rich Fisher, together with their company were fed in their wanderings by the Grail (the themes of the dish of plenty and of eucharistic sustenance are here intertwining). At the end of the story Bron and his son Alain depart for the farthest west, to await in the vales of Avalon the coming of a scion of their lineage who will be the new guardian of the Grail. In the *Didot Perceval* and in *Perlesvaus* (both romances of the early thirteenth century) the Celtic and the Christian apocryphal are brought together; Perceval, Alain's son and knight of the Round Table, achieves the quest for the Grail, heals the maimed Fisher King, and enters into his inheritance as the new keeper of the Grail.[61] The classic version of the story, given in the *Queste del Saint Graal* (the version incorporated in the Vulgate cycle) differs in that it is not Perceval, but Lancelot's son by Elaine, Galahad, who is the central figure; he too, however, is of Joseph's lineage. Brought up by his mother, he is led into Arthur's hall by an aged man in a white robe, and passes the test of the *Siege Perilous*. It is he who, in the company of Perceval and Bohort, achieves the Grail Quest when they come together to the Maimed King's castle of Corbenic, where the Grail is. At the mass of Bishop Josephé, the son of Joseph of Arimathea, the crucified Christ rises from the Grail and administers the sacrament. Galahad takes the Lance of Longinus and heals the Maimed King by anointing him with the blood that drops from it. Afterwards, in the land of Sarras, Galahad, having seen openly the mystery in the Holy Vessel, dies in ecstasy, and the Grail vanishes from the world. Perceval follows him to the tomb a year later, and Bohort returns alone to tell the story.

The chief difference between the stories in which Perceval is the central figure and the *Queste* in which Galahad takes over the role of the Grail Knight is that in the former more space is taken up with martial adventures, while in the latter religious allegory is more skilfully developed and theological preoccupations are more obvious. Correspondence between the doctrines expounded in the *Queste* and the mystical doctrines of St Bernard, together with smaller details (such as the white garb of its holy men, resembling the habits of white monks) betray that this version of the legend has a Cistercian origin.[62] Chivalrous adventure and religious preoccupations are however both crucial elements in both versions of the story. Both devote much space to the adventures of other knights besides Galahad and Perceval, and to those of Lancelot and Gawain in particular, and use their imperfections to set off the perfection of the Grail knight. But the aim is not, in either version, to present such a sharp dichotomy as we find in Bernard between the profligacy of worldly knighthood and the religious commitment of true Christian chivalry; rather it is to distinguish between degrees of virtue in knighthood, in the same way as Baudouin de Condé and Geoffrey de Charny seek to distinguish scales of chivalrous achievement and virtue. Lancelot may be tainted by his adulterous love for Guinevere, but he is a great Christian knight and in the *Queste* has his glimpse of the Grail, even though he does not see it openly. His wars against the heathen King Madaglan of Oriande, in *Perlesvaus*, exalt the crusading ideal. The significance of the Grail legends lies not in any contrasting of worldly with religious chivalry, but in the way in which they carry us, through stories of martial adventure, on to something beyond. The quest that they describe is not just for the Grail, as an object, but for what it symbolises: eucharistic grace and communion in ecstasy with God. The distinctive feature of the stories centring round it is that these spiritual things are presented as the ultimate goal and prize of the elite of knighthood: the idea of the knight errant seeking adventure and the quest for union with God are as it were fused together. As Frappier has put it, what the Grail romances express is not so much an ideal of knighthood in the service of religion but of knighthood as a religious service in itself.[63] Herein lies their special significance for the historian of the chivalrous mentality. In this group of stories *Ritterfrömmigkeit* has been translated into a religious exercise culminating in the mystical vision of the Truth.

The church authorities were consistently cautious in their approach to the story of the Holy Grail, neither accepting nor condemning it, leaving the whole matter in the limbo of legend. Their caution is not surprising. Despite the profoundly religious spirit of the Grail romances, they reflect attitudes that are strikingly non-sacerdotal. The liturgy of the Grail is given the setting not of a great church but of the hall of a feudal castle. In *Perlesvaus*, it is not by prayer but in arms and by storm that Perceval wrests back his inheritance from the King of Castle Mortal, and restores the service of the Grail. Among the clergy of the stories, the figures whom we most often encounter are hermits, solitaries whose way of life is just about as divorced as may be from the world of the organised ecclesiastical hierarchy, and most of them prove to be men who, until they felt the strength to bear arms ebbing from them in the autumn of life, had followed the vocation of knighthood. The commission of the 'good knight' Joseph of Arimathea comes to him not through the apostolate of the genuine gospels, which in the middle ages was commonly taken to prefigure the Christian priesthood, but from Christ himself, directly. Secular ideas about lineage have moreover made a deep impression on the manner in which Joseph's office and that of his descendants as guardians of the Grail is treated. Indeed, the whole Grail story is in one sense the history of a knightly lineage, just as the Swan Knight story is also the history of a lineage – in both cases of a line pre-elected by God to fulfil a special mission.

A very remarkable conception is at work here, one which suggests direct links between the goal of contemplative mysticism and the hyper-active way of life of the adventuring man at arms, of the knight errant. Such a conception was perhaps a natural if somewhat radical development from the analogy that, long ago, the heroic age had perceived between the terrestrial clash of arms of Christian and pagan (or in the Old Testament of Israel with her foes) and the supernatural struggle of the powers of good and evil. The idea cannot in the end find a place in a coherent mystical theology, but that does not detract from its significance, especially when it is remembered that to many knightly listeners and readers the more radical of its potential implications must have been opaque.

To the historian of the chivalrous mentality, the importance of the Grail romances and also of the story of the *Chevalier au Cygne* is the way in which they reflect accurately the confidence of Christian knighthood that its way of life was one pleasing to God and chivalry an order instituted directly by Him. The Grail romances have a particular importance in this context because the incidental adventures that crowd their pages remind us that this was not an idea confined to the narrow frame of reference of the crusade but one to which all chivalrous activity was seen equally as relevant: the loyal service of an honoured lord or beloved lady, the succour of the unjustly oppressed, the hardships of the knight errant on his travels, and even endurance of the trials of joust and tourney, as well as the defence of the Holy Places. These Christian knightly stories, at once romances of chivalry and of religion, thus extend our insight into the mental attitude behind that truculent cry of the crusader poet Aymer de Pegulhan: 'Behold, without renouncing our rich garments, our station in life, all that pleases and charms, we can obtain honour down here and joy in paradise.'[64] What Aymer in his eloquence is implicitly claiming here is that there is no need to try to prise apart the goals of worldly honour and of service acceptable to God, that the knightly life, with all its violence and with all the richness and decor of its aristocratic trappings, is within its own terms a road to salvation.

The idea here is one that looks back, through the colour and overlay of the fashions, phrases and moods of the late twelfth and early thirteenth centuries, to the conception of the religious worth that kingship (modelled on Christ's kingship) confers on service rendered to it, rather than to any ideal of knighthood serving the *sacerdotium*. This is typical of the attitude that underpinned the conception of chivalry as a Christian vocation. It was an attitude that was ultimately the fruit of the ancient marriage of Teutonic heroic values with the militant tradition of the Old Testament, rather than of later developments in ecclesiastical thinking – an attitude with a royal, not a priestly genealogy.

CHAPTER IV

The Ceremony of Dubbing to Knighthood

I have left one very important aspect of the early history of knighthood undiscussed up to this point, the ceremony of dubbing to knighthood. This is the ceremony that the *Ordene de chevalerie* and Ramon Lull describe so carefully, explaining in detail the Christian symbolism that informs each movement of its ritual – the bath recalling baptism and signifying cleansing from sin, the white belt signifying chastity that is girded on the new knight's loins, the sword placed in his hand whose sharp edges remind him of his duty to protect the weak and uphold justice. Given this sort of interpretation of its ritual, it is not surprising that the ceremony is usually accepted as particularly significant for its religious implications, and as being the outward and visible sign of the new direction that the reforming church of the eleventh and early twelfth centuries gave to secular knighthood. Léon Gautier, the great French historian of chivalry in the nineteenth century, treated it almost as if it had been for the medieval church an eighth sacrament.[1] It becomes very important, therefore – and especially in the light of the suggestions of the last chapter – to examine how far this view of the ceremony is justified. May we really call it an eighth sacrament, or are its religious implications somewhat less dramatic, just another sign of the way in which Christian ideals and Germanic practices became interwoven with one another – another part of the same history that was traced in the last chapter?

Certainly, there are some signs that here again there are at least two strands to the story. What sort of strands they seem to be can perhaps best be explained by illustration. That will help to explain why what looks like their original separation poses a problem for the historian of chivalry. Let us look first at what is probably the earliest detailed description of the making of a knight in a narrative historical source. This is John of Marmoutier's account of the knighting of Geoffrey the Fair of Anjou, which took place in

1128 at Rouen, on the eve of his marriage to Matilda, daughter of King Henry I of England. The young man took a ritual bath, we are told. He was then dressed in a tunic of cloth of gold and a purple cloak and was led before the King. Gold spurs were affixed to his heels, a shield decorated with painted lions was hung about his neck, and a sword, said to have been forged by Weland, was girded on him by the King. All this is very reminiscent of what Lull and the *Ordene* describe. Thirty young men who had accompanied Geoffrey were made knights at the same time, and to them King Henry distributed gifts of horses and arms. A week of feasting and tourneying followed, to celebrate the great occasion.[2]

There is no reference anywhere in this account to the church or to churchmen having any part in the ceremony (no more is there in the *Ordene de chevalerie*, it will be remembered). If, however, we look forward to the early fourteenth-century Roman Pontifical, another side to the picture emerges, for there we shall find a liturgical order for the making of a knight in St Peter's church which is very like this secular ceremony in its ritual, but in which churchmen play the central role. On the eve of his knighthood the aspirant shall be bathed in rose water: after that he shall spend the night in vigil in the church. Next morning he shall hear mass; a series of antiphons shall be sung and after that he shall come forward before the priest or prior. The priest shall give him the *collée* (or *paumée*: a light blow with the hand) and shall pray for God's blessing on his knighthood.[3] A sword shall be brought from the altar, which the priest shall bless and gird about him. After this, one of the noblemen present shall affix upon his heels gold spurs – the one office, in this *ordo*, to be performed by a layman. An alternative ecclesiastical ritual for the making of a knight is to be found in the late thirteenth-century pontifical of William Durandus of Mende. Here again it is the priest who girds the aspirant with his sword, who admonishes him in his duties, and who administers the *collée*.[4] The echoes of the description given by John of Marmoutier are not quite so clear and direct as they are in the Roman Pontifical, though they are there plainly enough. There are however other echoes which are very significant, of older ecclesiastical texts. Durandus's prayer for the blessing of the sword derives directly from a Mainz Pontifical of the mid *tenth* century[5] – which therefore long antedates John of Marmoutier's description of the ceremony which took place in 1128 at Rouen, but which has no clear and explicit connection with dubbing to knighthood. We are thus warned of problems in the way of the simple explanation of the relation between the ceremonies, that John on the one hand and the Pontificals on the other describe, which is that, sometime between 1128 and the end of the thirteenth century, John's purely secular rite had been 'ecclesiasticised'. It seems rather, as has been said, that there are two strands in the story, one ecclesiastical, the other secular.

That there is a relation between them is, however, clear enough. Our problem is to try to discern what that relation is, and if possible to decide which presentation offers the more significant and illuminating insight into the concept of knighthood, that of the Pontificals, which will square easily enough with Gautier's description of the dubbing rite as the 'eighth sacrament', or John of Marmoutier's, which will not. Since there seem to be difficulties in the way of explaining their relation in simple terms of the derivation of the one from the other, the best way forward will be to try initially to trace independently the origin and development first of the purely secular rite, and secondly of the ecclesiastical version. In the process, the way in which we need to view their connections may become rather clearer.

★

So let us try to trace back the secular strand first. Here we may start by looking a little more closely at something that John of Marmoutier tells us about the knighting of Geoffrey of Anjou: that Henry I distributed gifts of horses and arms to the young men who were knighted with him. In fact, the simple phrase 'he gave him arms' is often, in early texts, a way of describing the conferring of knighthood. Thus Orderic Vitalis puts into the mouth of William the Conqueror the bitter complaint against his rebellious son Robert that he had lured away 'the young men whom I brought up and to whom I gave the arms of knighthood'.[6] Elsewhere he tells how Robert of Grantmesnil served William when he was Duke of Normandy as a squire for five years: 'then the said duke armed him honourably, and now that he was a knight, rewarded him with rich gifts'.[7] The ceremony that here seems to be indicated, the delivery of arms to a young warrior, is one with a pedigree of great antiquity. Paul the Deacon describes how it was the custom of the early Lombard kings to send their sons to the court of a foreign lord, to be brought up and subsequently to be armed by him.[8] Wiglaf, in *Beowulf*, tells how the hero gave arms – helmets, corselets and swords – to those who were admitted to his war band.[9] These references take us back deep into the pre-chivalric past, but the pedigree goes back further still. Tacitus, in his *Germania*, describes how, among the Germans, the delivery of arms marked a young man's achievement of his majority. 'When that time comes, one of the chiefs or the father or a kinsman equips the young warrior with shield and spear in the public council. This with the Germans is the equivalent of our *toga*, the first public distinction of youth.'[10] The quest for the ultimate ancestry of the ceremonial delivery of arms thus takes us right back into the barbarian Teutonic world of the second century AD.

The old German ceremony of the delivery of arms and the ceremony of dubbing to knighthood must not be brought too close together; there does seem, though, to be a connection.[11] The word *adouber*, to dub, when it first appears often means simply to equip a man with martial arms.[12] But it is also used to describe the making of a knight, and this use is early; as time goes by it becomes the most common meaning of the word. Moreover, delivery of arms, which is what dubbing seems originally to mean, is commonly associated, in the early 'pre-chivalric' texts, with one or other of two occasions, with coming of age or with entry into a war band, just as it is in Tacitus in the one case and in Beowulf in the other. Knighthood, in the twelfth and early thirteenth centuries, was similarly often conferred when a young man came of age, and seems sometimes to have had associations with entry into a military following or vassal-group – the equivalent of a war-band. Thus in the twelfth century we are told how Frederick, son of the dead Count Palatine of Saxony, was brought up under the guardianship of one Count Ludwig 'until the time when he was girded with arms', and of how Count Raymond Berengar of Barcelona directed in his will that his younger son Peter should be under the guardianship of his other son Raymond 'until Peter shall be of age and made a knight'.[13] Ghiselbert of Mons in one passage suggests that in the Angevin lands, when an heir was under age and his lands in wardship, he would be made a knight at the same time that he did homage to his lord and entered on his inheritance.[14] Here the other connection, with entry into a war band, begins to come into view alongside the attainment of a young man's majority; for there are obvious links between the former and the ceremony of homage, when the vassal swore (among other things) to aid his lord in battle. Originally, indeed, the word vassal meant no more than a military companion or follower, a member of a war band who might hope for an estate as the reward for his service but was by no means sure of it. Significantly, the word *vassus* and the word *miles* are used interchangeably in some early texts.[15] So, when we find in the *chanson* William of Orange calling on the 'tattered young squires' to join his expedition to Spain, and promising to reward them richly and to dub them knights,[16] do we say that he was recruiting knights or vassals? It is really not possible to give a definite answer: the distinction is too nice in the context. It is however clear enough what he was doing, recruiting young men into a war band, and promising to give them arms.

Delivery of arms and knighthood thus seem to be linked by common connections both with the achievement of a majority and admission into a war band or military following – and to be linked also with the idea of vassalage. They are linked also in another way, in that both carry connotations of status. Carolingian texts make it clear that a vassal's possession of 'complete arms' (which arms, or their equivalent, were expected to be returned to his lord at his death as a 'heriot' so that the lord might 'deliver' them to another) distinguished him from the ordinary freeman who was only expected to possess a spear and shield.[17] The distinction here is perhaps better defined in professional than in social or hereditary terms, but these three in the middle ages were never very far apart. Vassalage and the possession of vassal estates or fiefs tended to become hereditary, and admission to a military following could easily be a way toward advancement in blood as well as riches. Orderic tells of how King Henry I of England gave great rewards to 'his young men, and especially to the knights who had faithfully endured hardship in his service', including 'the wives and daughters of those who had died together with their patrimonies, and so by his liberality raised them up beyond what they had dared to hope for'.[18] We are reminded here of the care taken by the genealogical historian Lambert of Wattrelos, both to distinguish all those in his paternal line who had been knights, and to single out for mention any connections of distinction that the maternal line had introduced into his lineage.[19] It is not until the twelfth century, it is true, that we find the rule first beginning to be mentioned, in the Assizes of Roger II of Sicily and in two constitutions of Frederick Barbarossa, that he who aspires to knighthood must be able to point to knights among his ancestors.[20] But the connection of knighthood – as of vassalage with which it was so closely linked – with lineage and so with hereditary standing goes back at least into the preceding century. Way back in the middle of the eleventh century we are told of how the Abbot of Bourgueil took pity on a poor young man of Touraine, Girard Borrel, and brought him up to be a knight, 'because he was a knight's son, descended from a long line of nobles'.[21]

In the early middle ages a man's standing might be judged partly by his blood; but the standing of the lord whom he served was at least equally important, and arguably more so. There is a similarity again between these two relationships. It is a commonplace that admission into a Germanic war band established between its leader and its members an association analogous to that of kinship. The companions who entered the war band espoused the feuds of their leader as if he were their kinsman; and he likewise espoused the feuds of those that he armed and fed, and claimed blood money from their slayers on a tariff that reflected his standing, not theirs – again as if they were his kin. We re-encounter a similar sense, of a close association between the man armed and the man who armed him, in knighthood. 'I hold no land of Charlemagne,' says Renaud de Montauban in the *chanson*.[22] 'No,' replies Ogier, 'but remember that it was he who armed you as a knight.' Similarly also, we encounter the idea that to receive knighthood from a lord of particular standing associated the recipient with that lord's honour and dignity. That is the idea that informs the repeated anxiety of the young aspirants of romance to receive knighthood at the hands of King Arthur, or of one of his great knights, such as Lancelot. Not in romance only: in history also we find, for instance, Henry II of England seeking the honour of knighthood from the King of Scots,[23] and St Bernard despatching letters to the Greek emperor, Manuel Comnenus, explaining that he is sending to him Henry, son of the Count of Champagne, so that he may be girded a knight of Christ by the emperor himself.[24] The twelfth century's understanding of this conception of associative honour is beautifully encapsulated in the words of the German ministerial poet Milo von Sevelingen: *'das Wurde werdens wirdet mir'* – the worth of the worthy makes me worthy.[25] The long ancestry of the idea is witnessed by Paul the Deacon's story, of how the Lombard kings, in a much earlier age, used to send their sons to be brought up in the court of some great foreign lord and to receive their arms from him, thus associating themselves with the honour and dignity of a great stranger.[26]

The significance of the delivery of arms and the idea of associative honour are combined in the accounts that we possess of mass promotions to knighthood, which from the beginning of the twelfth century start to be common. We are told, for instance, that in 1099 Ladislas of Poland, returning victorious from a campaign, held a great feast at the Assumption and knighted his son Boleslav: and not him only, says the chronicle, 'since for love of the young man and to honour him he bestowed arms on a host of other young men of his own age'.[27] Thirty of his young companions, John of Marmoutier says, were knighted at the same time as Geoffrey the Fair; Roger of Sicily, to honour his two sons, made forty other young men knights at the same time as them in 1135.[28] In the later twelfth century and after, references to mass knightings like these become legion, especially in the literary sources. They are not just a ritual development: they offered a means of solidifying, through the impact of ample and striking ceremony, ties based in fosterage in the same household, and of laying the foundations at the same time for the future war band of a lord's heir. Mass promotions, being in their nature great occasions, are also a sign that the ceremony of the giving of arms was by this time becoming richer and more elaborate. Here they should be set alongside references such as those in John of Marmoutier to the dress of aspirant knights, to cloth of gold and painted shields and to the ritual bath of knighthood.

Mass promotions suggest something else of importance too. Most of the earliest references to the ceremony of making a knight that are known concern very great men and their sons. When in these very early days we hear of lesser men who had been 'dubbed' knights, it is hard to know whether we should think of this as implying any ceremony that was at all elaborate, anything more than the presentation of the necessary equipment (or perhaps even their simple appearance properly equipped in a host). No doubt most of those who were made knights at mass promotions were rich young men of good birth who had been nourished at court together with the principal who was to be knighted. Even so, they show how the courtly circle was beginning to widen, and hint towards another way in which, as we saw in an earlier chapter, the higher and lower echelons of the aristocracy were drawn together through knighthood. They also give a hint as to how a ceremony a little more elaborate and definite than the mere delivery of arms may have spread laterally, in geographical terms, as well as vertically in social ones. It is quite clear that ceremonious knighting took hold, as a fashion, at different times in different places, and sometimes we can glimpse a particular reason: in Brabant, for instance, nobles begin to use the title 'knight' *(miles)* at just the same time when the knights of the Temple and the Hospital began to acquire lands there.[29] But the anxiety in one lord's court that ceremony and dignity should not be behind the peak of fashion, as observed elsewhere, was almost certainly the most potent factor. Between the aristocratic courts of the twelfth century there was much coming and going, of envoys, of adventurers, of minstrels, of clients seeking knightly or scholarly patronage; and reports of impressive ceremonies, actual or literary, fed the instincts for emulation and imitation.

When in the twelfth century we enter into the world of mass knightings, of more elaborate ceremony, and of a more sophisticated and ornate courtly literature – as we leave the obscurities of the age of the war band behind us – a clearer distinction between knighthood and vassalage at last begins to emerge. We can see as it were how the two branches have bifurcated from the ancient trunk. Now, when we hear of a vassal we expect surely to hear also of his fief, the estate with which he has been endowed; and we hear less and less of the landless, unhoused vassal, essentially a figure of the military household. The obligations of the vassal have become more definite and particular, and are more firmly connected with the possession of a particular fief or fiefs, with which his specific obligations to a particular lord are associated. As these developments of vassalage clarify the particularity of vassal obligations, so the more general and universal obligations of knighthood, conferred by a rite distinct from that of homage and more ceremonious than the old delivery of arms, are thrown into relief. References to knighthood at large as an 'order' become common. Etienne de Fougères writes of the 'order' of chivalry, and so does Chrétien de Troyes: Gornemant, knighting Perceval, confers upon him 'the highest order God has willed and made'.[30] And the instructions that he gives him – to spare his foe if he cries mercy, to keep counsel, to aid women in distress, to go to church and pray – have general, not particular reference. As other contemporary references show, these are by no means a sign that older and more particular associations of knighthood – with a young warrior's coming of age, with his obligation, as a knight, to serve his lord and to give his life for him if need be, with his ability to serve with what was defined as the full equipment of a heavy cavalryman – have been left behind. But a new slant has been added to his obligations, both to himself and others. The very word 'order' of knighthood implies duties with a wider frame of reference than those imposed by entry into a war band or a vassal-group.

'The word order explains itself: it means to say that those who are in the order must live by its rule.'[31] This is the comment of a late medieval treatise on chivalry. Of course chivalry never had a defined rule, in the sense that the monastic orders or the Templars did. John of Salisbury and Helinandus of Froidmont, however, are both speaking, in the twelfth century, of an oath which a knight should make on taking up knighthood,[32] and later texts have substantial lists of sworn obligations of knighthood.[33] The word 'order', moreover, especially when used in connection with obligations of a general nature, has a distinctly ecclesiastical flavour. It is reminiscent, in particular, of the distinction that eleventh-century ecclesiastical writers like Adalbero of Laon and Gerard of Cambrai drew between the three orders of Christian society and their functions. So far, all the associations that we have found that seem to throw light on the origin of knighthood – with the delivery of arms, with vassalage, with standing and lineage and honorific association, with coming of age – have been essentially secular in their implications. It is clearly time to look more closely at the ecclesiastical influences whose relevance to the rite of conferring knighthood is attested by the liturgies of the Roman Pontifical and of William Durandus, which were mentioned at the beginning of this chapter.

★

It is not at all clear that the rite for the blessing of the sword in the tenth-century Mainz Pontifical, which is the *ur*-text of all the liturgies for the making of a knight, was originally connected with a dubbing ceremony. The early Pontificals and sacramentaries contain blessings for all sorts of objects in everyday use, and there is no reason to suppose that the blessing of a sword – an object very much in everyday use in the tenth century – was dramatically different in kind from these. It is however clear with what sort of background we should associate the formal Mainz rite. Its background is that of the age of the heathen invasions, of the struggles against Vikings, Saracens and Hungarians in the post-Carolingian era, as its key words bear witness: 'Bless this sword . . . so that it may be a defence for churches, widows and orphans, and for all servants of God against the fury of the heathen.'[34] The rite belongs therefore to a period when Christianity seemed to be struggling for survival, and in which we hear of other similar rites, for the blessing of banners and of the army, and of new prayers of thanksgiving for victory. It is not surprising that in this age warriors whose role was compared to that of the Old Testament heroes who led the forces of Israel in the Lord's wars should have sought the church's blessing for their weapons, or that priests should have been ready to give it.

One of the most striking features of the early rites for the blessing of the

sword is that there is a direct relation between them and the earliest coronation rites, as is clear when the texts are placed side by side. This is in context
not surprising, since the kings of the age were the captains of the wars
against the heathen. What makes it significant is that the fact that the
earliest descriptions of coronation *ordines* are older than the Mainz rite: and
this significance is enhanced when we find that not only are the injunctions
to defend the widow and orphan and the blessing of a sword common to
both rites, but also that prayers for victory, which in early texts implore
God's blessing on the king, in later texts invoke the same blessing in
virtually the same words upon the knighthood at large.[35] There are other
signs of connections between the two rites as well. The girding of the
aspirant with his sword was clearly a very central element in the secular
ritual for making a knight, older and more basic to it than the *collée* or
paumée (which indeed remained unknown in Germany for a long period),
and it remains central in the dubbing rites of the later Pontificals, such as
that of William Durandus. But the earliest references that offer any details
of an elaborate girding ceremony – something more than the mere delivery
of arms – concern not knights, but kings. Thus we are told that when
Charlemagne made Louis the Pious King of Aquitaine in 791 he girded him
with a sword, and Louis did the same for Charles the Bald when he made
him a King in 838;[36] later girding was incorporated into the liturgical
coronation rite. The liturgy for making a knight seems therefore to have a
whole series of very close connections with the coronation rite.

The association is in many ways a very natural one. In early days
kingship, in the eyes of many, was probably better understood as an exalted
rank or degree rather than as an exalted office, as the highest rank in a
hierarchy of secular lordship that included dukes, margraves, counts and
other powerful lords. Dignity, however, carried with it authority, and the
girding ceremony symbolised this. All power derived from God, and the
sword of justice merited His blessing whether it was put into royal hands or
into those of some other great man. Indeed, many counts in the eleventh
century called themselves 'count by the grace of God' in the same way as
kings did. Significantly, a very high proportion of the early references to
knighting which mention girding with the sword concern very great men or
their sons, men who – like counts – exercised or might come to exercise a
jurisdiction less than that of a king but comparable with his. In fact it is not
clear that the Mainz rite (or the other similar rites which we encounter in
other early pontificals from the same Rhenish area) was intended for the
blessing of the sword of just any knight; it seems more likely that it was
originally only used when a sword was to be put in the hand of some great
man, and that a later age extended its application to others of lesser
standing. Flori has indeed argued, and trenchantly, that the moment at
which the old ceremony of delivering arms becomes identifiable with a rite

of initiation into knighthood is that at which a ritual girding becomes associated with it: as a result of which such girding, hitherto associated with the commission of authority (a significance retained in the coronation rite), becomes a sign of admission into an elevated status-group, that of the knight.[37] The fact that the eleventh century saw new developments in cavalry tactics and that in consequence equestrian groups became a more important and numerous element in hosts that were themselves becoming numerically larger, suggests a reason why more and humbler men came in this period to aspire to be girded with a measure of ceremony hitherto reserved to the powerful – with a resulting shift of emphasis in the significance of the ceremony in question. In the context of such development, the Mainz Pontifical with its rite for the blessing of a sword helps to remind us that knighthood, even in later days when men of the lesser nobility were often girded with elaborate ceremony, never divested itself entirely of connections with lordship and its magisterial function. Ramon Lull tells us so explicitly: 'therefore for to govern all the peoples that there be in the world God wills that there be many knights'.[38] Just as the palpable difference of rank between a king and a knight could, in a hierarchical and martially oriented feudal world, be viewed as a difference essentially of degree, so that between their functions could be viewed as a difference essentially of scale. An analogy between their initiation rites is therefore in no way surprising.

From our present point of view, the most important aspect of the analogy between coronation and the dubbing ceremony is that it may suggest how the delivery of arms, originally a purely secular occasion, came, like coronation, to be associated with an ecclesiastical rite. The earliest occasion on which we hear of a church rite for the consecration of a king is the coronation of Pepin as King of the Franks in 753. It is however clear that before Pepin's day the making of a king had involved a ritual process, originally entirely secular (or at any rate non-Christian), which formally empowered the leader chosen by the people to act as king.[39] As late as the tenth century Widukind, in his description of the crowning of Otto I, could distinguish between the secular ceremony of installing the King which took place in the *atrium* at the entrance to the church and the ecclesiastical rite of coronation which followed.[40] Here therefore are two strands, one secular and one ecclesiastical, in the history of the coronation ceremony, which were ultimately conflated in a single rite. There appear to be two strands similarly in the history of dubbing to knighthood: that which looks back to the old Germanic custom of delivery of arms, which is in origin secular, and that which looks back to the rite for the blessing of a warrior's sword, which is ecclesiastical. The liturgies in the Pontifical of William Durandus and in the Roman Pontifical marry the two together, thus endowing the ceremony with Christian and religious as well as secular and social significance.

There is, nevertheless, a great difference between the history of the coronation rite and the history of dubbing. The church succeeded in establishing for itself and its rites a virtual monopoly of a key role in the making of a king: as we shall see presently, it never achieved such a monopoly over any part of the process of conferring knighthood.

That there were those in high ecclesiastical circles in the eleventh and twelfth centuries who would have liked to see the church establish such a monopoly is virtually certain. From the point of view of the ecclesiastical authorities, the borrowings in the dubbing rite from the liturgy of king-making implied, as the great German historian Erdmann has put it, 'a transfer to individual knights of the ethical conceptions that the church had formerly applied to the ruler alone'.[41] As he and others have pointed out, we can see a similar transfer implied in the eleventh-century discussions of the functions of the three orders in Christian society: the duty of the warriors is to defend the people and uphold the peace among them, which is precisely the duty to which the coronation *ordo* dedicates a king. At the same time, in the Peace of God legislation, the church authorities can be seen intervening to impose directly upon warriors oaths whose purpose is to uphold peace and restrain martial violence. In the Gregorian period, the more extreme ecclesiastical hierocrats clearly wished to see all secular magistracy, not just the royal magistracy, exercised under the direction of ecclesiastical author-ity – and all the ethical associations of magistracy and of force associated with obligations to the church. Gregory VII, we know, did not hesitate to go over the heads of secular rulers in his summons to secular knighthood, as the *militia Sancti Petri*, to come to the aid of Peter's Vicar.[42] Urban II's summons to crusade was a call to knighthood at large to dedicate itself in a new way to the service of God and the church. His call was to the knight-hood direct, acknowledging no intermediary between himself, as Peter's Vicar, and them. Potentially, the church liturgies for the making of knights could symbolise, powerfully, this primary obligation of knighthood to the ecclesiastical order and its authority. The rite in the Roman Pontifical actually echoes Gregory VII's own phraseology, in its prayer that the newly dubbed warrior shall be a good knight of Christ and of St Peter.[43] There was every reason, it is plain, why the church authorities should encourage the association of a liturgical rite with the ceremony of dubbing, should wish to make it essential thereto, and should seek also to arrogate to the priesthood the central actions in the ceremony, the girding with the sword and the administration of the *collée*.

This is why it is so important to stress that these aims were never realised, that the church never achieved such a monopoly over making knights as it did over making kings. In the end the evidence of the Pontificals, impor-tant as it is as an indication of ecclesiastical ideas of what knighthood ought to imply, proves to be tangential to the history of dubbing. History does record occasions on which it can be shown that an ecclesiastic performed the central office of girding a new knight, but nearly all of them (though not quite all) involve princely bishops who were in their own right great secular lords.[44] Among the exceptions perhaps the most memorable is the knighting, at Castelnaudry on St John's day in 1214, of Amaury, son of Simon de Montfort, the leader of the Albigensian crusade. At the request of the Count, the Bishop of Orleans girded the young man at a mass held in a tent outside the town, which had been ravaged by two stormings. But the wholly exceptional nature of the ceremony is given away by the words of Pierre de Vaux de Cernay, the chronicler who describes it: 'O new and unheard of custom of chivalry.'[45] It was a deviation from the norm, and its unusually strong ecclesiastical tone was probably a consequence of Simon's anxiety, as leader of the Albigensian crusade, to emphasise publicly the role he and his house were playing as the church's champions in Cathar Languedoc. Though other thirteenth-century sources are full of accounts of knighting ceremonies conducted in churches, and though mass knightings came normally to be conducted in church and at one of the great church festivals, the accounts of these ceremonies, when they are specific, virtually always show that it was a layman who conferred knighthood on the aspirants. And even in the thirteenth century, in which the practice of making knights in church seems to have been more common and more generally customary than at any other time, there are quite as many occasions recorded on which men were knighted outside church and without ecclesiastics playing any part in the ceremony as there are accounts of knightings in churches.

It is not surprising that this should be the case, and that in spite of ecclesiastical influence a necessary connection between church ritual and knighting should have failed to develop. There were so many knights. It was one thing to associate solemn ritual with the making of a king or even the arming of a great lord's son, which were major occasions, another to associate it with the commencement of the martial careers of men many of whom were of very little account in terms of landed wealth or influence. This would perhaps have been no obstacle, if knights generally had been persuaded that church ritual was absolutely necessary to elevation to knightly status, but they were not, and it is easy to see why. Knighthood still carried too many associations that had little or no religious significance: with the achievement of a young man's legal majority, for instance; with the possession of secular weapons; with elevated status and ancestry. Besides, the warrior estate had, as we saw in the last chapter, already established its own interpretation of its Christian role long before the days of Gregory VII; and its ideas of what that meant had taken shape too firmly to be malleable into conformity with the Gregorian reformers' different and more exclusively ecclesiastical design. The warriors' magisterial functions, of protecting the church, defending the weak and maintaining justice, had been discharged, time out of mind, within the framework of the superior authority of kings and great secular lords, to whom warriors were bound by solemn oaths, often sworn upon a holy book or relic. In practical and legal terms it was immensely difficult to interpose other obligations overriding those so created; and in psychological terms it was even harder to modify the strength of the bond between the knight and his lord, who was so often the very man who had girded him with the sword of knighthood. Roland, in the *chanson*, does not think of himself as the church's soldier but as Charlemagne's; Christ is his heavenly lord, but his lord in the war that he is fighting against the Saracens is Charles, who put Durandaal into his hands.[46] In the *Kaiserrecht*, it is from the faithful servants of the emperor, who aided him against his rebels, that the origin of knighthood as an institution is derived.[47] Faithful secular service was an ideal too deeply rooted in the Germanic world in which the origins of the ceremony of making a knight were embedded for any other obligation ultimately to challenge its priority. Church ceremony and ecclesiastical teaching could enlarge and refine ideas of the range and meaning of knighthood's functions and could add a measure of general obligation to their original particularity; but they could never, even in the age of the crusade, effectively shake the hold of the principle of loyalty to secular lordship by interposing the church's own authority between the knight and his lord. No more could they displace secular authority from the chief role in the ceremony of conferring knighthood.

To say this does not mean that we should try to divest ourselves of the idea of medieval knighthood as, in its own eyes, an essentially Christian institution, or that we should regard the development of liturgies for the making of new knights as an irrelevance. The fact that so often knights were dubbed in church impressed on all minds that knighthood was a Christian calling, imposing broad obligations of Christian observance and morality, whether it was given in a church or not. Under the church's influence, crusading, the martial pilgrimage, established itself firmly as the highest mode of expression of the chivalric virtues of courage and endurance. Ecclesiastical teaching also gave definition to the idea of chivalry as an order, possessing, as every order should, its rule of life, and instructed the knight about how he should view his individual discharge of his office as a Christian duty. What it does mean is that when we speak of the Christian strand in chivalry we are speaking of something that had to find its expression within a framework of secular ideology and secular ceremony, which sacerdotal teaching could only modify, not transform. The reservation to secular men of the central role in the conferring of knighthood is a reminder of this, and a reminder too of chivalry's independence, not indeed of religious values, but of sacerdotal priorities.

The French scholar Ritter gets to the heart of the matter when he writes that the underlying assumptions of chivalry had less in common with the ecclesiasticism of Gregory VII or Bernard than they had with the views of those apologists of imperial power who saw the two great luminaries, the universal secular and ecclesiastical authorities, as each working in its own sphere for God's purpose,[48] in harmony but not in either case in subjection to the other. For it was the encomiasts of royal and especially of imperial power who, among the learned, first succeeded in inculcating the idea of the God-given role of kingship, and so defined the model from which such seminal texts as the old rite for the blessing of the sword derive their conception of knighthood. Even the idea of the warrior group as one of the three orders of Christian society, which was the element in ecclesiastical teaching which did most to modify the old heroic ideology of martial service to a particular lord, when it first appears (in King Alfred's translation of Boethius and in a slightly later Frankish text)[49] does not suggest any intermediary role for the clergy between the warrior and God's design for him. Later chivalrous writers did not see any occasion to modify the picture in that respect. The order of chivalry, says Chrétien de Troyes, is the highest order God has willed and made:[50] he says nothing of the church instituting its commission, but implies that it comes direct from God. All knights should be obedient to the emperor, and to the kings and barons who are under him, says Ramon Lull, echoing, perhaps rather distantly, the imperialist tradition:[51] he says nothing of obeying Peter's Vicar. From first to last, knighthood, even when conceived as an order, remains true to its ultimately secular origins; and its apostolic succession, in the dubbing ceremony, is perpetuated by a secular laying on of hands.

★

The later middle ages witnessed the development of a number of further variations of the ceremony of dubbing. These do not much alter the essential picture of the conceptions underlying it that we have traced so far. In so far as they do, this is principally in connection with the decline, from the later thirteenth century on, in the number of people taking up knighthood, a subject that we shall have to look at in a later chapter. Some of them, however, are interesting in themselves, and a brief account will help to round out a number of the points that have already concerned us.

We have noticed in many early texts the anxiety of aspirant knights to receive knighthood at the hands of some lord of particular distinction or repute. In the later middle ages a still more particular dignity was associated with receiving knighthood at the hands of one who had established a name for himself as a knight of prowess by deeds recognised as outstanding. Thus Peter Suchenwirt celebrated in verse the story of the knighting on crusade of his hero, Albert III of Austria, by the veteran crusader Count Herman;[52] and Ghillebert de Lannoy recounted proudly to his son how he had been knighted by the Teutonic Knight Ruffe von Pallen during a campaign in Poland.[53] Francis I chose to receive knighthood at the hands of Bayart, he who was known as the *chevalier sans reproche*.[54] The relation was considered to reflect honour on both parties, as is aptly illustrated by Zurara's story of the knighting of Suerio da Costa on one of Henry the Navigator's expeditions to West Africa. He insisted that he must have the honour from the hand of his comrade Alvaro de Freitas, 'since he knew him to be such a knight that his own knighthood would be beyond reproach'. So, the chronicler continues, 'that noble man was made a knight . . . and surely I believe that though Alvaro de Freitas was such a noble knight and it had befallen him to create others like him, yet never had his sword touched the head of so great a man, nor was he a little favoured that Suerio da Costa sought to be knighted at his hand, when he could have obtained the same from very honourable kings and great princes'.[55] These stories show how conscious chivalry was, in the late middle ages, of possessing what I have called its own apostolic succession, and illustrate its confidence in its own, independent secular ethic.

Others sought their accolade at times or in places which would give their knighthood special associations. On the occasion of their journeys to Rome for their imperial coronations, Charles IV, Sigismund and Frederic III made many knights on the banks of the Tiber. 'On the bridge over the river Tiber the Emperor displayed the banners of the Empire and of St George, and beneath them he dubbed many,' says the account of the *Romfahrt* of Sigismund.[56] Here part of the object was to exploit the shared associations of both chivalry and the empire with the antique glories of Rome – whose knighthood had once conquered the world. Similar ideas no doubt informed the splendid ritual devised for his own knighthood by Cola di Rienzo[57] (though it was to the glories of the Republic rather than of the Empire that he wished to look back). In England those who had taken their knighthood on certain special ceremonious occasions, on which a particular and elaborate ritual was followed (which is described in several fifteenth-century manuscripts),[58] were distinguished as Knights of the Bath. They were sometimes spoken of as having been initiated into the Order of the Bath; this was not an institutionalised, corporate order, such as the Order of the Garter or the Burgundian Order of the Golden Fleece were, but the phrase suggests nevertheless that some kind of association in secular honour was felt to exist among those who had thus been initiated into knighthood.

Those who, in the later middle ages, were initiated in another way were also sometimes spoken of as an 'order'. These were they who had taken their knighthood on pilgrimage at the Holy Sepulchre in Jerusalem.[59] There were clearly strong religious overtones to taking knighthood here, at the scene of Christ's passion and of the triumphs of the first crusade. Until the end of the fifteenth century, when Pope Alexander VI reserved the privilege of giving knighthood at the Sepulchre to the guardian of the Franciscan church there, the ceremony of dubbing seems, however, usually to have been performed by a layman. It is not possible, therefore, to connect this way of taking knighthood, which became popular in the fourteenth century, with the ecclesiastical dubbing rites of the Pontificals. The practice seems to have been particularly popular among the knighthood of Germany and part of its particular attraction may have been that by this means a 'free' imperial knight could avoid the suggestion of subordination and dependence that might be involved in accepting knighthood at the hands of a local lord or prince. The appearance on some German knightly tombs and memorials of a badge of the arms of the kingdom of Jerusalem seems often to have denoted that the knight remembered thereby had taken his knighthood at the Sepulchre, or that he had at least made the pilgrimage there – so gaining the right to call himself a knight of the 'order of the Sepulchre'.[60] The idea of taking knighthood in this way may originally have been suggested by certain passages in literary sources – there is a significant reference to dubbing at the Sepulchre in the twelfth-century *Chanson d'Antioche*.[61] This is a useful reminder of how important a part literature could play in spreading new chivalrous customs and rituals. Literary descriptions of dubbings that took place in church almost certainly played a more important part in popularising that practice in the twelfth and thirteenth centuries and after than did any of the liturgical texts (the history and scale of whose diffusion is in any case somewhat obscure).

A number of late medieval sources mention three normal occasions for receiving knighthood.[62] It may be given, they say, when the emperor or a king holds a solemn court, or at his coronation; usually the ceremony will take place in a church, after the bath and vigil, and the prince himself 'or some other lord who is a knight' will gird the aspirants. That is the first kind of occasion that these texts mention – and it fits well into the picture we have been given of great knighting ceremonies when the emperors came to Rome, or when the English kings made knights of the Bath. The second occasion for taking knighthood that they mention is on pilgrimage to the Holy Sepulchre, the rise of which practice we have also traced. The third occasion for taking knighthood that they all mention is on the eve of battle, or of the storming of a city, when men seek knighthood 'in order that their strength and virtue may be the greater'. From the latter part of the thirteenth century on, this became a very common occasion for the taking of knighthood. We hear, for instance, of Ottokar of Bohemia conducting a mass knighting in his host on the eve of doing battle with the Hungarians in 1260,[63] and of Simon de Montfort (the younger, the great Earl of Leicester)

making the young Earl of Gloucester and a number of other young noblemen knights on the eve of the battle of Lewes in 1264.[64] The practice was
not then new, and though earlier references are rarer they take us right back
into the eleventh century. Robert of Bellème was girded by William the
Conqueror at the siege of Fresnai le Vicomte in 1073.[65] In the Holy Land a
number of new knights were created on the eve of the battle of Ramleh in
1101, and Orderic describes how Cicely, wife of Tancred of Antioch,
knighted Gervase Brito, Haimo the Vicomte of Dol and 'a number of other
squires' on the eve of a battle in 1119.[66] In the fourteenth and fifteenth
centuries the making of knights became almost a regular feature of the eve
of battle, and the pages of such chroniclers as Froissart are in consequence
full of references to such creations.

Occasionally we hear something of the way in which knights newly
created on the eve of battle were instructed by those who dubbed them. Let
us set alongside one another two descriptions of such occasions, one from a
literary source and one from a chronicle. The consistency between the two
is striking, and they will give good insights into how men viewed the
significance of such creations. The late thirteenth-century romance of
Durmart le Galois describes how the hero knighted twenty of the noble
squires who were holding a mill outside Limerick on behalf of his love, the
Queen of Ireland, against the usurping high King Nogans. 'My lords,'
Durmart told them,

> now you are knights: and it is fitting that I should tell you something of
> what appertains to chivalry. A knight must be hardy, courteous, gen-
> erous, loyal and of fair speech: ferocious to his foe, frank and debonair to
> his friend. And lest anyone tell you that he who has not borne his shield or
> struck his blow in battle or tournament is not by rights a knight, see to it
> that you so conduct yourselves that you have a good right to the name. He
> has a right to the title of knighthood who has proved himself in arms and
> thereby won the praise of men. Seek therefore this day to do deeds that
> will deserve to be remembered, for every new knight should make a good
> beginning.[67]

With this fictional speech may be compared Froissart's account of that
made by King James of Portugal, when, on the eve of his victory over the
Castilians at Aljubarotta in 1385, he made knights of sixty Portuguese and
English squires. 'Good my lords,' he said,

> this order of chivalry is so high and so noble, that he who is a knight
> should have no dealing with anything that is low, with vile things or with
> cowardice, but he should be as hardy and as proud as a lion is in pursuit of
> his prey. And therefore it is my wish that this day you shall show such
> prowess as it befits you to show: that is why I have set you in the van of the

battle. There so do that you may win honour; otherwise your spurs are not well set upon you.[68]

King James, says Froissart, made knights of these men whom he set in the vanguard 'in the name of God and of St George'. The obligations of chivalry about which both he and Durmart in the romance chose to remind their new knights were however predominantly secular. The virtues that both stress are those that the *chansons* and romances had early forged into stereotypes of chivalrous quality; *hardiesse, loyaulté, prouesse*. Courage, the performance of good service, and the maintenance of the honour of knighthood are the key notes of their instruction. Courage and prowess are, of course, qualities which may be displayed (and with added honour) in a religious context, as on crusade against the heathen, but they are qualities which quintessentially have martial associations rather than religious ones, and their display is calculated to win the reward of secular honour. There is very little in the standards that these authorities propose, it is true, that cannot be reconciled with priestly teaching on the vices and the virtues – though perhaps the suggestion that it is the business of a knight to win a name that will be remembered has just a hint in it of the vainglory which so many preachers identified as the archetypal failing of the knighthood and nobility. On the other hand – as that significant exception forcibly reminds us – there is a very great deal that does not derive from sacerdotal teaching, and never did derive from it. It derived rather from heroic ideas which had been an essential element in the idea of knighthood, from the very beginning. The imprint of the legacy of the age of the war band, admission to which was marked by the delivery of arms, is still very clear in the late middle ages, and perhaps above all in the descriptions of the making of knights on the eve of battle, which was then so common a practice.

There *was* a specifically religious strand in the history of dubbing, and it was important; but when we speak of it we are speaking of something that had to find its expression within the framework of a secular ideology that was founded in a Christianised version of heroic traditions, and that sacerdotal teaching and sacerdotal priorities could only modify, not transform. The right perspective on it is given in the wonderful passage in the romance of *Lancelot* in which the Lady of the Lake instructs her charge in the duties of knighthood and the significance of the knight's arms.[69] All that she has to say is permeated with religious significance and symbolism. As we listen to her explaining the Christian and ethical signification of sword and shield, lance and hauberk, we are reminded that we are in a world in which a purely secular ethic, divorced from a religious framework of value, was almost impossible to conceive of. But we have to remember too who is giving these instructions to young Lancelot – a great lady of regal family and endowed with magical powers, not a priest. The virtues that Lancelot was to display in his life, as the romance recorded it were, moreover, the secular virtues of hardiness, prowess and loyalty. What the Lady does is to enshrine the martial calling and its code of honour into a Christian setting. The ceremony of dubbing, when it took place in church with elaborate ceremony (as in the late medieval English ceremony of the Bath), did likewise. It did not subordinate martial energy to ecclesiastical rule, and dubbing never was and never became an eighth sacrament.

CHAPTER V

The Rise of the Tournament

The same romantic literature that teaches us so much about dubbing and about conceptions of knighthood in the twelfth and thirteenth centuries is also a principal source for the early history of the tournament. All the great heroes of Arthurian story were masters of the tourney – even, in spite of the church's disapproval, the spotless Galahad.[1] The space which the romances devote to accounts of them, which to a modern reader can only seem excessive, testifies to their importance to the knightly way of life. Because of their popularity, and because knights came together from far and wide to attend great tournaments, they were a powerful force towards generalising both the standards and the rituals of European chivalry. The fact that their popularity grew in the face of the church's consistent censure gives us, moreover, a further measure of the degree to which the development of chivalrous attitudes and values progressed independent of the official climate of ecclesiastical opinion. The story of the development of tourneying, as a specific knightly activity, forms an important chapter in the early history of chivalry.

The history of the tournament begins in that same period in which we have seen the concepts of knighthood and the ceremony of admission to the knightly order crystallising into recognisable shape, the hundred years or so between the middle of the eleventh and the middle of the twelfth century. Mock war and martial training are virtually inseparable from one another, and no doubt the tournament had a pre-history before that, but it is obscure. Though an uncertain tradition ascribes the 'invention' of tournaments to an Angevin knight, Geoffrey de Preuilly, who was killed in 1066,[2] we do not hear much about them until around the year 1100, and they are ignored in the earliest *chansons de geste*. The twelfth-century writers who first use the word seem, many of them, to recognise it as a neologism.[3] By the end of the first quarter of the century, however, tournaments were

clearly popular in France, and especially in northern France. In the reign of
Henry I of England, a charter of Osbert of Arden refers to the painted
lances that he carries when he goes overseas to tournaments.[4] Galbert of
Bruges tells us that Count Charles the Good of Flanders, who was murdered
in 1127, 'frequented the tournaments in Normandy and France, and
outside that Kingdom too, and so kept his knights exercised in time of
peace and extended thereby his fame and glory and that of his country'.
Otto of Freising mentions what he calls a tournament at Wurzburg in 1127.[5]
Then, in 1130, comes the condemnation by Pope Innocent II at the second
Council of Clermont of what he called 'those detestable markets and fairs,
vulgarly called tournaments, at which knights are wont to assemble, in
order to display their strength and their rash boldness', together with his
command that those who are slain in them shall in future be denied
Christian burial.[6] By that time, clearly, their popularity was beginning to be
sufficiently widespread to cause concern to at least one of the universal
authorities of Christendom.

    Over the next half century, references to tournaments are legion, and it is
abundantly clear that their popularity was becoming universal. France was
still recognised as the native home of the tournament, as the English
chroniclers' name for it – *conflictus Gallicus* – testifies.[7] Northern France and
Champagne, whose Count Henry was as great a patron of the tourney as he
was of courtly letters, were the scenes of most of the tournaments that
William the Marshal attended in the 1170s and 1180s; and it seemed
natural to Wolfram von Eschenbach, a couple of decades later, that
Gahmuret, the father of his hero Parzival and a great champion of the
tourney, should have been bred in Anjou. But the Low Countries were from
an early point almost as important a centre: Philip of Flanders, like Henry
of Champagne a patron of the great Arthurian writer Chrétien de Troyes,
was famous for his love of them, and so was Count Baldwin of Hainault.
They were popular much further afield as well. We hear in 1159 of a great
tournament held at Antioch in Syria, and a very great and ceremonious
affair it was, for the Byzantine Emperor, Manuel Comnenus, himself took
part in it.[8] In 1175 in Saxony we hear of how Archbishop Wichman of
Magdeburg, learning that within a year no less than sixteen knights had
been killed in tournaments, excommunicated all those who took part in
them.[9] Their vogue had spread throughout Christendom. But before we
forget their French birthplace, we must note one significant gloss on the
history of the diffusion of the vogue of tourneying, that we find there the
same names and families associated with the patronage both of tournaments and of chivalrous and courtly literature: not only those of Henry of
Champagne and Philip of Flanders, who have been mentioned, but also
those of Eleanor of Aquitaine, and her children Henry the Young King,
Geoffrey of Brittany and Richard I. And the same is true of course of the

16.   The bath of knighthood, from a seventeenth-century facsimile of Writhe's *Garter Book* (Northampton-shire County Record Office). See pp. 65, 79.

17. Single combat outside a castle: Count Friedrich von Leiningen, from the Manasseh Codex (Universitätsbibliothek, Heidelberg). Single combats were probably the origin of jousts arranged in campaign, described on p. 207.

18. Ulrich von Lichtenstein, from the Manasseh Codex (Universitätsbibliothek, Heidelberg). See pp. 92–3.

19. An Arthurian joust: Gueherset unhorses Agravains (Bibliothèque Nationale). See p. 83.

20. A tournament *mêlée*, showing identifiable shields (Bibliothèque Nationale). See pp. 85, 125–6.

21 (facing page). Richard, Earl of Warwick, jousting at Calais, January 1414, from the fifteenth-century Beauchamp Pageants (British Library). See p. 87.

Nowe Erle Richard the second day came into the felde that is to sey the morowe
after the vij day his vysar close a chaplet on his basnet and a tuffe of estrich
fethres alofte his hors trapped wt his armes of Hamslape silid j barryd of goldis
and then mette wt hym the blank knyght and then ran to gider and the
Erle smote vp his vys thries j brake his besagues and other harneys all
his apparaile subed and so wt the victory and hym self vnknowen rode to his
pavilioun ageyn and sent to this blank knyght Shugh Saruey a yard
counter.

22. The tournament and courtly love: a lady arms her knight for the tourney, from the Manasseh Codex (Universitätsbibliothek, Heidelberg). See pp. 91–2.

23. Charlemagne's host in Spain: the miracle of the lances (Aachen Cathedral). See p. 105.

24. Arthurian relief on the archivolt of Modena Cathedral: the King and his knights rescue Guinevere.

25. Sculptured figure of Roland, with Durendaal in his hand, from a doorway in Verona Cathedral. See p. 105.

great Frederick Barbarossa in Germany. As we shall see, there is a connection here that is probably of considerable significance.

Nearly all the early accounts of tournaments that offer any detail come in fact from literary sources, which are open to the suspicion of having glamourised unduly the picture that they give of them. If some allowance is made for literary romanticisation, however, the descriptions of tournaments in, for instance, the romances of Chrétien de Troyes tally reasonably well with historical accounts, say those in the verse biography of William the Marshal. Both alike make it clear that the tournaments of the twelfth century were very rough occasions, only just distinguishable from real battle. A day for the tournament was announced, perhaps two or three weeks beforehand (more in the case of a great tournament), and publicised by messengers. The site of the tournament was settled in advance, and would cover a wide area, permitting the fight to range over the countryside and into villages. The limits that we usually hear of are that the tourney shall take place between two townships, between Rougemont and Montbéliard, for instance, or between Warwick and Kenilworth (as in Richard I's ordinance for tournaments in England).[10] There were no lists, and the only places where the participants could be safe were the roped off 'refuges' where they were permitted to rest and disarm. Those taking part were usually divided into two teams, the Angevins and the French, as it might be, or in England Northerners and Southerners, and customs quickly developed as to which side knights from a given area or 'march' should join. The earliest accounts say nothing of judges or referees, and though the principal weapons were lance and sword, virtually no holds were barred (though the use of bolts and arrows seems to have been frowned on). Prisoners were taken and held to ransom, and their horses and armour were the legitimate spoil of their captors. Chrétien's description in *Erec et Enide* of the tourney in the plain below Tenebroc well conveys the confusion when the fighting began: 'On either side the ranks tremble and a roar rises from the fight. The shock of lances is very great. Lances break and shields are riddled, the hauberks receive bumps and are torn asunder, saddles go empty and horsemen tumble, while the horses sweat and foam. Swords are quickly drawn on those who fall noisily, and some run to receive the promise of a ransom, others to stave off this disgrace.'[11] The line could indeed be thin between mock war and the real thing.

If the literary sources give the most vivid descriptions of the hurly-burly of tournaments, the historical sources reveal what serious and dangerous affairs they were. When Baldwin, son of the Count of Hainault, chose contrary to custom to join the French against the Flemings (because the former were outnumbered) at the tourney between Gournay and Resson le Mals in 1169, Philip of Flanders was so angry that he attacked immediately with his horse and footmen drawn up 'as if for war'.[12] A year later, when Baldwin went to the tournament at Trazegnies, we are told that because he knew that another of his territorial neighbours, the Duke of Brabant, bore rancour towards him, he in his turn brought a large force of infantry 'so that he might be safer in the tournament'[13]. In these conditions tournies offered an easy cover for the pursuit of established rivalries, and in the fury of confrontation self-restraint was easily lost sight of. William de Valence, Henry III's Potevin cousin, was badly beaten up by the opponents' squires at Newbury in 1248, and so when he and his men got the upper hand at Brackley later in the year they took a measure of revenge, and ill-treated the 'bachelors' of the other side. Valence's aliens, in their turn, were once again beaten up when they were routed at Rochester in 1251.[14] In the tournament at Chalons in 1273 things got out of hand after the Count of Chalons had seized Edward I of England about the neck in his effort to unhorse him, in breach of what the King considered to be the conventions. The footmen joined in in earnest, and there were heavy casualties, both among participants and spectators. Afterwards the occasion was remembered not as the tournament, but as 'the little battle of Chalons'.[15]

The reduction of bloodshed and restraint upon the rancours which were so easily engendered in the heat of affray were clearly among the principal objects of the rules of tournaments which were drawn up by the English kings Richard I and Edward I. Richard's ordinance licensed tournaments at five identified fields in the open country, and imposed a fee on all those participating – 20 marks for an earl, 10 for a baron, 4 for a landed knight and 2 marks for a knight without estate. The earls of Warenne, Gloucester and Salisbury were to form a court of control, and all who wished to tourney had to pay their fees in advance and swear to keep the peace.[16] Edward I's 'statute' was more elaborate, limiting the number of followers that any knight or baron might bring with him, enforcing the use of blunted or bated weapons, insisting that grooms and footmen should be without offensive arms, and that, if there was a feast, only squires carving personally for their lords should be admitted along with the principals.[17] These royal regulations seem to be unique to England,[18] but the thirteenth century did see, generally, a gradual abatement of the ferocity of tournaments. Insistence on the use of bated weapons (arms à plaisance, in later phrase, as opposed to arms à outrance) became more and more common, and it is clear that at some engagements (especially those called behourds) tourneying armour of padded leather and non-metal weapons were used. We begin to hear of judges of the tournament or 'diseurs', and the area over which the fight should range was defined more sharply; the field had to be better defined if judges were to be able to view the whole affair and to award prizes to those who on either side had excelled in prowess. Jousts – individual encounters between two knights which in William the Marshal's day had in a disorganised way often preceded the charge of the two teams and the beginning of the tournament proper – became more popular and better regulated. The fashion for them probably owed much to the numerous descriptions in literature of judicial duels (usually between a hero and a villain), which were clearly much appreciated, for if the tournament is mock war, the joust is in its way a kind of mock duel. Jousts began now to develop into the familiar set-piece encounters between pairs of opponents, coming forward *seriatim* from opposite ends of the lists, and charging one another before the spectators. At the tournament of Chauvency in 1285 there were two days of jousting at the beginning of the week's festivities, before the great tournament on the Thursday which was the climax of the meeting.[19] The tournament was thus by the end of the thirteenth century becoming gradually more ceremonious, and a little more distinguishable from real war.

In the time of Chauvency and for long afterwards, however, the tournament proper remained a ferocious and thoroughly dangerous affair. Risks, of course, were part of the attraction of the sport (as they are nowadays in mountaineering or motor-racing), but in spite of efforts to make the 'course' safer they continued to be uncomfortably high. The thirteenth century's tale of fatal tourneying casualities is a long and melancholy one, and the names of the very great figure prominently among them. Geoffrey de Mandeville, Earl of Essex, was trampled to death at a tournament in 1216.[20] Florence Count of Holland was killed tourneying in 1223; his son Florence perished in the same way in 1234, as did William, this Florence's brother, in 1238.[21] In 1279 Robert of Clermont, the brother of Philip III of France, sustained in his very first tournament head injuries which left him largely incapacitated for the rest of his life.[22] These are a few only of the greater men who were killed or crippled, and their names do not give a full impression of the potential scale of casualties. At a tournament at Neuss in 1241 over eighty knights are said to have died, many of them, apparently, suffocated in their armour in the dust and heat.[23] Casualties were heavy again at the 'little battle of Chalons', as they had been at Hertford in 1241, where Gilbert the Marshal met his end.[24] Suspicions of foul play were easily generated in circumstances such as these, and the political consequences of mortalities were potentially explosive. Earl Gilbert's death and the manner in which King Henry III dealt with the question of his inheritance were an important factor in the degenerating relations between that King and his English baronage, which were to reach their climax later in the civil wars of Simon de Montfort's time.

Why then was it, we may legitimately ask, that the popularity of tournaments not only withstood the impact of the calamities and disorders to which they gave rise (to say nothing of the Church's condemnation), but if anything increased as time went on. In fact, there were a number of good reasons why it did so. First and foremost, tournaments were undeniably good training for war. Indeed, training may be the secret of the obscure question of their origin. Since they first come into our ken at just the time when the technique of charging with the couched lance was developing, and since the charge with the lance, the breaking of lances and the unhorsing of opponents are the salient features round which virtually every detailed account of them centres, both in literary and in historical sources, it seems natural to link the two together. Besides, since the teams into which tourneyers were divided usually reflected the feudal relations of lordship and allegiance as well as territorial origin, tournaments gave men who were likely to serve together on campaign useful practice in operating as a group. But whether or not it was the need for training that gave the tournament its original impetus, the value of the training that it offered, in horsemanship and the handling of knightly weapons, is quite clear. Roger of Hoveden describes how the sons of Henry II went to France to seek tournaments (which their father had forbidden in England), because they knew that skill at war can only be acquired by practice, that 'he is not fit for battle who has never seen his own blood flow, who has not heard his teeth crunch under the blow of an opponent, or felt the full weight of his adversary upon him'.[25] The reason why Richard I changed his father's policy and licensed tournaments, William of Newburgh tells us, was because he saw that the French 'were fiercer and better trained for war . . . and he did not wish to see the French reproach the knights of his kingdom for rudeness and lack of skill'.[26] In thirteenth-century France, Jean de Meun, translating the classical treatise on tactics of Vegetius, broke away from his text to explain that in these days the tournament offered to young men of lineage the kind of training that (as he wrongly believed) gladiatorial contests had supplied in the antique world.[27] His near contemporary Henri de Laon significantly thought that the tournaments of the age were becoming too soft and ceremonious. They needed to keep up their standard of toughness and ferocity, because their object should be to identify those 'who have the courage to endure bodily hardship, which is what marks out the man who is fit to lead a company . . . the man who can support the weight of his helmet and who does not pause for heat or breathlessness . . . to be soaked in one's own sweat and blood, that I call the true bath of honour'.[28] Tournaments indeed needed to be fierce, if they were to serve their purpose as the preparation for war.

Another of Henri de Laon's criticisms of late thirteenth-century tournaments is that men came to them not to prove their strength but to win booty. The prospects of enrichment, through the ransoms of prisoners and the capture of valuable war horses, were certainly another reason for the popularity of tournaments. 'It is not love that makes young knights brave, it is poverty':[29] that is Flora's taunt against Phyllis, in their debate as to which is the more to be treasured, a knight's love or that of a clerk. William the Marshal's early history is the story of a young man who made his fortune at the tournament, and it shows that he well understood its business side. In the spring of 1177 he and Roger de Gaugie, a fellow member of the young King Henry's household, decided that they would go into partnership and attend every tournament that they could, sharing the profits; and in the course of ten months they captured and put to ransom no less than one hundred and three knights.[30] The chances of the tourney could of course as easily be the road to ruin as the road to riches, but booty and ransoms were not the only prospects of betterment that they held out to the impoverished and the cadet. One who distinguished himself at tournies had a prospect of catching the eye of a patron, and so of putting himself in the way of sounder insurance against lack of means. When William the Marshal fell out of favour with the Angevins in 1180 he had already such a name for prowess, won in the tourneying field, that both the Count of Flanders and the Duke of Burgundy were ready to offer handsome pensions if he would enter their service.[31] William as we know in fact turned down their offers, trusting no doubt that he would soon recover favour with his old masters (as he did); but the incident remains none the less instructive for that.

Particularly illuminating in this story is the sidelight that it throws upon the quest for praise which in all sources, historical and literary, is so consistently associated with love of the tourney, indicating the more tangible motives that could lie beneath it. If you wish to go to the Holy Land, his squire advised the Chatelain de Coucy in the romance, go to the tournament which King Richard has proclaimed in England: you may catch his eye, and then perhaps he will take you into his company.[32] And so, in the romance, it fell out; the Chatelain, who was poor, went to the tournament, did well, and was duly taken into Richard's pay for the crusade. The story is true enough to life: great men were on the look out for talent at tournaments. When in 1183 Baldwin of Hainault saw that a war was looming with the Duke of Brabant, he went, we are told, 'unarmed to the tournament that was held between Braine and Soissons, and by his prayers and promises retained as many knights from both sides as he could'.[33] The way things could work out is well illustrated in the semi-historical *Romance of Fulk Fitzwarin*. As soon as Fulk and his brothers had been knighted, they 'crossed the sea to seek honour and distinction: and never did they hear of a tourney or joust at which they did not wish to be present'. Then when Fulk's father died, King Richard called him home, gave him his inheritance on easy terms and entrusted him with the keeping of the March of Wales, 'for the King favoured him much for his loyalty and for the great reputation *(grant renommee)* that he had'.[34] Reputation won on the tourneying field could, it is clear, mean much more than the mere sound of praise.

The sound of praise is of course in itself sweet, and pride is a human motive almost as strong as profit, especially in an aristocratic society. Here was another reason for the popularity of the tournament. Great lords might bring troops of footmen to the tourney 'in order to be more secure', as Baldwin of Hainault did, but the glory and the prizes (as also the major risks, especially the financial ones) were for the knights and the knights alone. The tournament was an exercise for the elite, and simply to appear there, armed and mounted and with his own squire or squires in attendance, was in itself a demonstration of a man's right to mingle in an elite society, of his social identity. Because the first steps towards the better regulation of tournaments seemed to be to try to clear the 'pitch' of the less reputable elements, the developments of the thirteenth century tended to enhance this aspect of the tourney – its specifically social lustre. The landless knight is significantly the humblest figure whose fee to enter Richard I saw fit to regulate. Not so long afterwards the idea begins to appear that only knights who could prove their ancestry should be admitted to tourney; and before the end of the thirteenth century heralds were beginning to make rolls of the hereditary arms of those who attended tournaments that they had witnessed, records of the aristocratic standing of the company there gathered. The way is here pointing forward towards the age in which, in Germany, it would be the rule that none should be admitted to a tournament unless he could show that his ancestors had frequented them over fifty years, and where Sicily Herald would insist that, in order to qualify for admission to a great tournament, a man must be able to prove his four lines of noble descent.[35]

This tendency no doubt reflects knighthood's growing awareness of the challenge of bourgeois wealth to aristocratic dominance, and its response to that challenge with efforts to entrench its influence and way of life through caste exclusiveness. Complementarily, the growing popularity among the rich town patriciates, especially in the Low Countries, of urban tournaments like the feast of the Espinette at Lille[36] or the tourney in Arthurian dress that was staged at Magdeburg in 1281 reflect the eagerness of the leaders of a rising bourgeoisie to demonstrate that they were not incapable of the knightly virtues or of appreciating the refinements of chivalry.[37] The powerful force of social competition was at work here; we should beware, however, of overstressing the element of class tension that was involved. The aristocratic heralds preserved rolls of the arms of those who had been prize-winners at the Feast of the Espinette, and told of how the kings of France and the Counts of Flanders had ennobled them for the prowess that they had displayed, so raising them from the bourgeoisie into the hereditary nobility and admitting them to the charmed chivalrous circle.[38] The caste exclusiveness of chivalry is easily exaggerated. The attraction of the social lustre that it built around its activities, on the other hand, is not, and it cast its spell far wider than the circle of those who were to the manner born.

What may have been the most powerful of all influences supporting the popularity of the tournament has not yet been mentioned, however. There is only one incident which sounds anything like a tournament in Geoffrey of Monmouth's *History of the Kings of Britain* – the first exposition of the great Arthurian story, which was written a little before 1140 – but it has one very significant feature. Geoffrey is describing Arthur's great court at Caerleon, at Whitsuntide, and tells how, after the feast was over, 'the knights planned a mock battle, and competed together on horseback, while their womenfolk watched from the city walls and aroused them to passionate excitement by their flirtatious behaviour'.[39] In Wace's vernacular translation of the same story, completed a couple of decades later, the overtones of courtly love have in this scene become much clearer.[40] There are hints of the same influence at work in at least one passage in the *Histoire de Guillaume le Maréchal*, the one where the Marshal and his companions meet the Countess of Joigni and her ladies at the opening of the tournament there, and while away the time until opponents arrive by dancing to a song sung by William: when the first opposing horseman appears, William unhorses him in the presence of the Countess and her ladies.[41] In Chrétien de Troyes' narratives (written earlier than the *History*, but fictional, a fact which may be significant), the theme is fully developed. The ladies of Noauz and of Pomelegloi were the patronesses of the great tournament in his *Lancelot*, Queen Guinevere was present, and the ladies of the court had resolved that they would give themselves in marriage to those who showed their prowess.[42] The scene is staged to show how Lancelot, the exemplary lover, was ready at the command of his mistress Guinevere even to disgrace himself before the knights and women (though in the end she bid him to do his best, and everyone agreed that he had excelled all others). After Chrétien, no literary description of a tournament would be complete without its word-picture of the watching ladies, and of the tokens from their dresses, the sleeves of their gowns or their hair, which the champions proudly bore. Their presence, in fact and in fancy, endowed the individual encounters of the knights with strong erotic undercurrents.

It now becomes apparent why it is so significant that so many of the great names connected with the patronage of tournaments in the twelfth century are also the names of the great patrons of courtly literature. Among the most important literary discoveries of the courtly storytellers of that age was the way in which the amorous culture of the troubadours and the traditional chivalrous narrative, which focussed on a succession of martial episodes, could be yoked together so that an old kind of story could be woven around a new axis of interest. Writing for an aristrocratic audience, the storytellers took care to paint their literary pictures of feasts and tournaments in the bright colours that the knightly world loved, dwelling on burnished hauberks, emblazoned shields and banners, rich mantles and costly furs.

Here they drew from the life. It was only natural that the knightly world which listened to their stories should seek in turn to infuse into its sport and ceremony some reflection at least of the romantic interest with which these were charged in fiction. To put it in this way is inevitably to oversimplify, for the interplay of life and romance is always a complex matter, but the importance of that interplay, for the history of tournaments, is not in doubt. From the point of view that we have been following until now, the hurly-burly of such engagements has presented a spectacle dominated by crude and sometimes extreme masculine violence. From the new angle of vision that the romance storytellers open for us, what we see now is a very different scene, in which colour and violence fuse together into the display of the male before the female.

This additional courtly and amorous appeal of the tournament was one that could co-exist without difficulty with the other attractions we have been considering: the tourney's value as a training ground for war, its significance as an exercise in which great prizes could be won, and as a social gathering of a certain kind of elite. But it was capable of more elaborate development than they were, and in particular directions – those of ceremony, of theatre, and of what anthropologists call play. Perhaps the best early examples of all three combined were the two great jousting tours of the Bavarian knight Ulrich von Lichtenstein, his *Venusfahrt* (1227) and his *Artusfahrt* (1240).[43] For the *Venusfahrt* he equipped himself for the role of Frau Venus with a magnificent costume (and a brace of long blond plaits); attired in it, he made his way from Italy to Bohemia, offering a general challenge to all comers to joust with him in honour of his lady. To each comer who broke three lances with him he promised to present a gold ring: but if the challenger was defeated, he was to bow to the four corners of the earth in honour of Ulrich's lady. Ulrich travelled magnificently attended, and broke three hundred spears in a month's jousting (or so he claimed). His disguise, according to his account of his journey, gave rise to much piquant fun, and the role had moments of burlesque, as when a basket, in which Ulrich in 'drag' was being hauled up to his lady's window, collapsed with the hero in it. In the *Artusfahrt* he set out accoutred as King Arthur, together with six companions, also in Arthurian disguise; those who broke lances with them successfully were admitted to their company of 'the Round Table'. How much of Ulrich's account of his adventures is really true is not entirely clear; as Ruth Harvey wrote, 'in his pseudo-autobiography . . . quixotic idealism and businesslike calculation, solemnity and ironic laughter, the world of fantasy and the world of fact are jumbled together in a single kaleidoscopic medley'.[44] There is certainly, however, a basic sub-stratum of fact underlying it. Ulrich, moreover, although extravagant, was no lunatic *poseur*, like Don Quixote: he was an able lord and warrior, who enjoyed a long and distinguished career in arms and politics, and has an honourable niche in the history of his native Styria.[45] His fantasies were more exaggerated than most, but they reflect something of the genuine spirit and the tastes of his age and class.

This is clear from other accounts of jousts and tournaments in the period. The earliest reference to tourneying in Arthurian dress is not Ulrich's *Artusfahrt*, but occurs in the *Mémoires* of the Syrian Frank, Philip of Novara, who describes a tournament in Arthurian dress held in Cyprus in 1223, on the occasion of the knighting of the son of the crusader Baron John of Ibelin, Lord of Beirut.[46] We know much more about the tournament of Hem, organised by the Lords Aubert de Longueval and Huart de Bazentin in 1278. As the poet Sarasin describes it, this was a marvellous piece of Arthurian theatre.[47] Jeanne, Longueval's sister, played the role of Guinevere; Count Robert of Artois, as Yvain (complete with the lion of Chrétien's romance), delivered four girls from the 'Knight of the White Tower', who had imprisoned them; Kay, as seneschal, kept up a string of caustic comment in the true vein of his legendary character. His best cut was his jibe over the *Pucelle flagellée*, who, when delivered from her master whose dwarf had whipped her before the stands, ran to embrace that same master: 'the more the blows you give them, the better they like you', declared Kay.[48] Another Arthurian tournament was staged by Edward I in 1299, at which the 'loathly Damsel' made her appearance in person, with a nose a foot long and fangs worthy of Dracula (she was really a young squire in disguise).[49] The 'Round Table' tournaments, of which we hear frequently in the thirteenth century, and from far and wide – from Spain, England and the Low Countries – do not usually seem to have been in Arthurian dress; but there were festivities, song, dance and procession, which sought to emulate those of romance, and the fighting was with bated weapons.[50] A hundred knights and their ladies rode into Kenilworth in procession, singing, for the start of Roger Mortimer's 'Round Table' there in 1279.[51] In 1284 Edward I held a 'Round Table' at Nefyn, to celebrate the conquest of Wales: the press was so great that the floor collapsed in an upper room that had been set aside for dancing.[52] No one, fortunately, seems to have been seriously injured. All this festivity and ceremony did not mean, though, that these encounters were disputed with any less determination than other tournies: 'Round Tables' had their tally of fatal incidents. Sarasin's comment on the Ham tournament is a good summing up of the situation: 'the jousts were a fair sight to see, but a dire business to endure'.[53]

The best of all descriptions of a thirteenth-century tournament is the minstrel Jacques Bretel's account of the tournament held at Chauvency in October 1285 under the auspices of Louis de Looz, Count of Chimy. Bretel, before he arrived at Chauvency, had resolved to make a record of the proceedings and he was at pains to do justice to them: getting Bruiant the herald to name and point out the principal personages present, watching the jousts keenly (especially if the combatants were important men), mingling with the crowd of heralds and minstrels and listening to their cries and conversation, noting with care the refrains of the songs (mostly of love) and the games and dances after supper. The result is a series of superb vignettes, not only of the jousts but also of the interludes of the festival: for instance the game of *robardel*, in which two girls, one dressed as a shepherd and the other as a shepherdess, mimed the story of the theft of a kiss; the gallant exchanges between a knight and a lady which he chanced to overhear on the third evening (discreetly, he gives no names); his own response to Henry de Brieys's call to him, 'upon the faith you owe to the wine of Arbois that you drink', to preach a sermon of 'love and arms'.[54] It is a very gay and colourful scene.

Bretel's eloquence is concentrated chiefly on two subjects: on love on the one hand, and especially on love's power to inspire its subjects to high deeds, and on the fighting. Here he shows himself a master at conveying the excitement and the noise – the cries of heralds, the clash of arms and armour, the anxiety among the spectators. We are left in no doubt about the ferocity of the occasion. There was a moment when everyone thought that Conradin Warnier, the son of Bretel's friend Conrad Warnier, had been killed:[55] and it was thought better after that to have no jousts on the Wednesday, in case any accident should make it difficult to go on with the tournament proper (as opposed to jousting) on the Thursday. At the end of that day there were plenty with wounds that were grim enough. The poem presents an extraordinary mingling of themes, good humour and ironic jest alongside flagrant social snobbery, amorous song and gallant exchange set alongside the fierce competition and crude excitement of the fighting. All were, in fact, part and parcel of the tournament in this age.

★

The church, at an early stage, set its face firmly against the tournament. Innocent II condemned them, as we have seen, in the ninth canon of the Council of Clermont in 1130, and ordered that those who fell in them should not be given Christian burial. The ban was repeated by his successors over and over again, with increasing vehemence – and notable lack of effect – down to Clement V.[56] Ultimately John XXII looked the facts in the face and lifted it, in 1316.[57] Papal disapprobation was echoed by the preachers, and a whole literature of pious commination upon the tournament grew up. Caesarius of Heisterbach tells the story of a servant of the Court of Loos who saw at Montenak, near the spot where a number of knights had fallen, 'a great tournament of demons' exulting over their spoils.[58] Demons were heard crying near the scene of the tournament at

Neuss, where so many knights died in 1241, and were seen, in the form of vultures and crows, circling over the spot.[59] Matthew Paris tells the story of Ralph de Thony, whose dead brother, sitting up from the bed on which he lay a corpse, told him in this moment of resuscitation that he had seen the tortures of the damned, and cried out: 'Alas, for those tournaments! Why did I take such joy in them?'[60] An endless supply of stories of this kind provided the preachers with a ready store of examples to illustrate their denunciations.

In the light of what we have already learnt, it is not difficult to see why the church disapproved of tournaments. Jacques de Vitry tells of how he undertook to demonstrate to a knight that tournaments encourage all seven of the deadly sins. They promote pride, he says, since it is for human praise and empty glory that the participants strive. They promote hate and anger, because men seek revenge for the strokes that they and theirs have received in them, and because fatal casualties are so common. They promote *accidie* and depression, because those who have failed in them or have been the cause of injury fall into depression. They promote avarice: men come to despoil each other, and when they have wasted their substance seek to recoup themselves by levying exactions on their defenceless tenants. The feasts which are held at them promote gluttony and are a waste of goods – not the goods of the hosts only but of the poor from whom they take them. They are an exercise in vanity, because those who put their hearts into them lose track of spiritual values in pursuit of vain and earthly ones. They promote lechery, since they are fought to please wanton women: indeed knights even adopt 'tokens' from their dresses for their standards.[61]

There is no doubt at all that there is substance in every one of these charges. The sort of facts that formed the basis for them have already been extensively rehearsed. The extent of the conspicuous waste involved in tournaments, and their capacity to bring ruin upon those addicted to them – and so upon their subjects and dependents – is perhaps the point that has been least stressed so far, but Jacques de Vitry is quite right about it. Few knights were as lucky as the Seigneur de Hemricourt, whose wife's good management saved him. Though he frequently mortgaged his lands and his plate to pay tourneying expenses, he always seemed somehow to be able to redeem them, his kinsman Jacques tells us, and he could never quite understand how. Until, that is, the day when he was returning from the tournament between Juliers and Adenhoven, unlucky as so often before and musing on his indebtedness. He was passing by the common at Orye and noticed a great flock of sheep, and when he asked whose they were the shepherd (who did not know him) told him that they belonged to the Lady of Hemricourt. A little further on there was another great flock, and asking the same question he was given the same answer – and it began to dawn on him how he had survived so long, by his wife's secret and careful husbandry.

There was a touching scene when he arrived home, and he could at last freely face his wife with his wasting, she him with her saving. After all, she told him as she forgave him and begged forgiveness, 'all the honour that you win in the world I share with you'[62]. He was clearly a very lucky man. The less fortunate – the men whose addiction to the tourney often cost them their entire patrimony – are stock figures of literature. Ulrich von Lichtenstein pictures those who had been captured at the tournament at Freisach hurrying to the Jews and pawning their belongings in order to raise their ransoms.[63] Liability to ransom was of course by no means the only heavy expense that the *habitués* of the tournament had to shoulder. Horses and armour too were very expensive, and the greater ceremoniousness of tournaments, as time went by, meant that there was a greater gathering of those from whom knights could not afford to withold the *largesse* that was expected of men of their status – heralds, minstrels, grooms, squires, armourers – to say nothing of the costs of food, lodging and festivity that fell principally on the hosts. It is no wonder that Henry de Laon should have complained that the cost of tourneying had risen to the point where even the rich were driven to borrow, and a poor knight simply could not afford to seek to prove his prowess and standing in such ruinous ventures.[64]

So Jacques de Vitry was thoroughly justified in his denunciation of the wastefulness of tournaments. The real bedrock basis of the church's condemnation of them, however, and the original mainspring of the papal prohibitions, was the encouragement that they gave to the turbulent spirit of secular knighthood, in which the ecclesiastical authorities had long seen a direct threat to the good ordering of Christendom, and which led to homicide, destruction, and disorder. The thinking behind Innocent II's ban of 1130 was of a piece with that which underlay the church legislation that promoted the Peace and Truce of God, and was clearly linked with it. Just as it had seemed useful to proclaim the Truce of God at the same time as the crusade,[65] so it seemed useful, when a crusade was in preparation, to reiterate the ban on tournaments, since, like the petty wars of the nobility, they deflected knightly attention and energy away from what in ecclesiastical eyes were their proper object, the defence of the church and the crusade. In short, in the church's eyes, tournaments were not only the cause of unnecessary bloodshed (out of which all sorts of rancours might arise), they positively fostered a cult of violence which was a stumbling block in the way of the mission which the Prince of Peace had entrusted to his vicars upon earth.

The same objection, that they were a source of turbulence and disorder, underlay the objection to tournaments of secular royal authorities, which parallel those of the church. The patronage of tournaments offered territorial lords, whose power and dignity their royal overlords wished to cut down to size, a means of solidifying the hold they had over their own men and of forging alliances with others, and so of maintaining their own disorderly independence. They also provided a cover behind which great men could concert plans between themselves and with their followers for organising resistance to unwelcome features of royal policy. Tournaments helped to reassemble the opponents of King John who had dispersed after the sealing of Magna Carta.[66] His son Henry III was consistently alarmed by the gatherings of his magnates for tournies, and sought ineffectively to forbid them: those held at Brackley in 1219, at Chepstow in 1227, and at Dunstable in 1244 were all associated with factious movements.[67] It was under cover of assemblies for tournaments that the great English lords gathered their forces in 1312 in order to pursue and capture Edward II's favourite, Piers Gaveston.[68] Sedition apart, tournaments could distract the attention of influential subjects from the priorities that kings wished to impose. Even such a great patron and champion of the tournament as Edward I was not going to tolerate his knights and barons running off in the hope of winning glory in the lists when he needed their service in Scotland.[69]

It would be wearisome to attempt to list all the prohibitions against tourneying that the Kings of France and England issued on what were clearly (from their point of view) unexceptionable grounds. They were no more successful in curbing the knightly vogue than were the thunders of popes and preachers. Besides, they were half-hearted, for kings could find it useful themselves to pose as patrons of the tourney; and then all they had to be concerned about was that the magnificence of their own tournaments should outshine that of any gathering that a subject of theirs might bring together. Not much was to be hoped for from royal prohibitions when Philip the Fair of France could, with typical cynicism, forbid all tournaments by an edict of 28 December 1312, simply because he wished to make sure that there were no counter-attractions to the great tournament with which he proposed to celebrate the knighting of his own eldest son.[70]

It is the failure of the church, therefore, even to dent the popularity of tournaments, in spite of nearly two centuries of denunciation, that is really striking. In view of what has been said about the reasons for that popularity, the failure is perhaps not wholly surprising. There is one more aspect of the development of the tournament, however, that needs a little exploration in conclusion, and which will help to explain a little further why the church's consistent and apparently justified teaching fell on deaf ears.

Innocent III and Innocent IV both explicitly linked their prohibitions on tourneying with the need to direct all martial energies toward the recovery of the Holy Land, and so did Clement V.[71] But, we must ask, was the assumption here implied, that the calls in question were conflicting, a valid one? If we turn from the canons to the chronicles there is evidence to suggest that it was not. Innocent III was much involved in the preparations and preaching of the fourth crusade, but the occasion that brought the future leaders together, according to Villehardouin, was a tournament held at Écry during Advent in 1199.[72] Other chronicle references suggest that tournaments were often closely and positively connected with the organisation and recruitment of crusades. Alberic des Trois Fontaines tells us of how, at the conclusion of the Round Table tournament at Hesdin in 1235, the leading men present resolved to take the cross.[73] William of Flanders, we are told, on coming back from the Holy Land in 1251, proclaimed a tournament at Trazegnies, 'so as to encourage the nobles to take the cross'; unfortunately, he himself was killed in it.[74] It is clear, in fact, that in chivalric circles the belief was widespread that tournaments, far from being a distraction from the crusade, were connected with its promotion. In the opening lines of his account of the tournament of Hem, when lamenting the consequences of the royal bans on tourneying, Sarasin includes prominently among these the decline of enthusiasm for the crusade.[75] Baudouin de Condé, in his *Dit dou Baceller*, explains how the young knight, after making his *début* in the proper way in the tournament, should seek to mount in prowess 'step by step'; he will not achieve the right to call himself a true *preudhomme*, though, until he has seen service against the enemies of the Cross.[76] The hero of the romance of the *Chatelain de Coucy*, as we have seen, attended Richard I's (fictional) tournament in the hope of being taken into his service for the crusade. In the Holy Land, he bore on his helmet tresses modelled in *fil d'or* upon those of his mistress, the Lady of Favel, whose *manche* he had borne for a token in an earlier tournament.[77] All these authors see the crusade and the tournament (and in the last case the demands of courtly love as well) in a single context of Christian knightly prowess, not in terms of conflicting ideals.

Jacques de Vitry explains that the knight to whom he expounded the ways in which tournaments serve the cause of the deadly sins had thought previously that there was no sin in them. Clearly this knight was no exception in not seeing any conflict between his Christian duty and his favourite sport. Both at Hem and at Chauvency the company is pictured going dutifully to Mass, before and after the jousting. The story had wide currency of the knight who, on his way to a tournament, stopped to pray to the Virgin and lingered over his prayers, and who afterwards, arriving too late at the tournament, found all full of his praises. While he prayed, the Virgin herself had jousted for him.[78] In Huon De Méry's *Le Tournoiement d'Antechrist* we find Satan, who bears as a token part of the chemise of Proserpine, Queen of the Underworld, challenged by Christ in full armour, His shield emblazoned with the cross and with a token woven by the Virgin, His mother. Among His heavenly host there ride not only the Archangels and the personified Christian virtues, Chastity, Justice and Mercy, but also the personified chivalrous virtues, *Prouesse, Courtoisie* and *Debonnaireté*, together with the whole force of Arthur's knights. Of course *Largesse* was of the force too, his arms quartered with those of Alexander, the great giver – that same *largesse* which was at the root of so much conspicuous waste, and at the root also of Jacques de Vitry's bitter attack upon the extravagance of tournaments.[79]

Huon de Méry's poem, with its personified values and allegorised blazonry, has brought us back toward those elements of theatre and spectacle that were associated with the tournament, which we have explored earlier as one of the sources of their appeal – and which are often castigated as symptoms of its decadent triviality. But theatre is a serious activity. The object of the best theatre is not only to entertain, but also to instruct and to uplift. In the context of the tournament, the element of theatre had a serious purpose beyond that of lending colour to the occasion. It was a way of bringing it home that what was going on was more than a great social gathering centred on an exciting sport: that it was at the same time a celebration of the values of chivalry. When Sarasin describes Aubert de Longueval and Huart de Bazentin planning their tourney, he lapses naturally into moralising allegory: they call *Dame Courtoisie* to their council.[80] Bretel similarly, at the opening of the *Tournoiement de Chauvency*, records the words of *Prouesse* to his son *Hardement* – for both were to him allegorically present at the occasion.[81] In a similar way, by parading in Arthurian or other romantic dress, the participants were reminding themselves of the example that the great figures of the chivalrous past had set.

Tournaments, Ralph Ferrers told the Court of the Constable of England, are 'where the school and study of arms is'.[82] Elsewhere they are referred to as *écoles de prouesse*.[83] The 'school and study of arms' did not just mean practice in the use of weapons, in other words; it meant an introduction to a whole scale of values. That is why Bretel, for instance, breaks off so often in his account of Chauvency to explain the moral of what he is witnessing, as when he declares that 'without giving, a tourney is not worth two *livres tournois*: for largesse is one of the robes of *prouesse*; courtesy is the second; the third is . . . honesty'.[84] The church's attack upon the tournament was thus a challenge which raised questions, not just about the worth of an expensive knightly pastime, but about the whole knightly scale of merit. By knighthood tournies were seen as having an integral function in the framework of chivalry's being as an order, as the Christian vocation that it proudly proclaimed itself to be. That is why it is important to stress the way in which the newly knighted sought – and were taught to seek – experience of them; why it is important not to miss the role that tournaments played in promoting crusading activity; why it is important to notice the way in which both Baudouin de Condé and Geoffrey de Charny present experience of the tourney as a step on the way to higher things in the *mestier d'armes* in which a knight fulfils the Christian purpose of his order.[85] The failure of the church to persuade knighthood that its vision here was inadequate and distorted is thus a demonstration of knighthood's confidence in its own ways, its own traditions, its own independent manner of serving God's purposes. On its own ground, chivalry felt no need of sacerdotal guidance.

That plenty of knights missed or misinterpreted the lessons that they ought to have picked up from the tournament, as from elsewhere, goes without saying. But we should not on that account overreach to the easy conclusion that they only tell us about aristocratic arrogance and extravagance. To do so is to underrate very seriously their influence upon the social *mores* and attitudes of the knightly world, and their development.

Because tournaments were public tests of individual prowess in which prizes and renown could be won, they helped to gain currency and respect for the role of the knight errant, the wanderer urged forward by love, enterprise and inherent virtue to seek the opportunity to win honour. Because they brought together, besides knights and ladies, a host of other people, in particular the heralds, minstrels and *jongleurs* whose business it was to record and judge the proceedings and who were versed in the lore and history of chivalry, they provided a crucial link between the literary expression of chivalrous values and the real world. Above all, because they drew men together from far afield, they served as points of diffusion for chivalrous culture and for chivalrous standards. Along with the literature which drew so much of its colour from their spectacle, they are the most important influence towards chivalry's definition as an international martial and aristocratic ideology, whose rules, attitudes and values transcended local boundaries. In this respect they were almost certainly a more powerful influence even than the crusades. Tournaments were easier to get to than the Holy Land; the risks that they involved, though serious, were infinitely less than those of Holy War; and more knights – many, many more – in consequence took part in them. Indeed the reputation gained at them was often more immediately significant than reputation won beyond the sea. This may be disappointing to relate, but it helps to remind us why their influence could not but be very powerful, and very pervasive.

Hence it is important to remember that the tournament, although it could be mistaken for an end in itself, was not so viewed by serious observers. They saw it as a preparation for something else, experience of it as a step on the scale of chivalrous perfection. This meant that the lessons taught within the confines of the lists were regarded as having – ideally – a wider application. For instance, although there was a difference between the rights that a captor acquired over a prisoner taken in a tournament and a prisoner taken in war, and although the scale of ransoms was better regulated in the former case, the experience of the relations of captor and prisoner on the tournament field clearly did have something to teach both parties about the sort of civilised conventions (they would have called them 'chivalrous') that they should observe towards each other in real hostilities. A whole series of conventions, whose purposes later generations would rationalise into the framework of a nascent international law of war, can be seen achieving a measure at least of recognition in the twelfth and thirteenth centuries, largely under the aegis of tourneying experience. It could indeed be argued that the relatively subtle influence of the tournament did more, in the long run, to promote standards of civilised behaviour between belligerent forces than papal prohibitions, issued in the name of restraining undisciplined violence, ever looked like doing.

That the tournament could have so many and such diverse influences was in a large degree owing to its ability to tap the didactic resources of the rich semi-historical mythology of chivalry – in part through theatre and pageantry. This made it possible to harmonise the physical teaching of the tilting ground with that of other instructresses, among them the force of sexual passion sublimated into the quest for virtue. The development of that mythology itself is the subject that we must turn to in the next chapter.

CHAPTER VI

The Historical Mythology of Chivalry

The *Chanson des Saisnes*, a late *chanson de geste* whose theme is the wars of Charlemagne against the Saxons, declares that there are three matters above all about which every man should know something: the matter of France, the matter of Britain, and the matter of Rome the Great.[1] These three matters – the stories of Charlemagne and his paladins, of Arthur and the Round Table, and the classical histories of Troy and Thebes, of Alexander and Caesar – do indeed form the subject matter of the best of chivalrous literature. In their time they did more than that for chivalry. In an age which looked instinctively to the past for examples of wisdom and of virtuous living, the literature which retailed these traditional stories underpinned the values of chivalry by providing them with a faultlessly antique and highly evocative pedigree. The development of a literature centring round these three 'matters' is therefore an important chapter in the emergence of chivalrous culture.

The matter of France was the first of the three great 'matters' of the *Chanson des Saisnes* to catch the fancy of the knightly world. The earliest manuscripts of the Carolingian epics that have survived date from the period *c*.1100 to *c*.1130, but it is probable that the subject began to be popular a little earlier.[2] After *c*.1130, in the middle of the twelfth century, their vogue was temporarily eclipsed by that of poems centred on the matter of Rome, especially in northern and western France and at the Angevin court, where historical interest was strong. In the later twelfth century, when Chrétien de Troyes was writing, the matter of Arthur's Britain became all the rage. The popularity of all three matters was however enduring: they remained the favourite secular themes for those who wrote for a knightly audience down to the end of the middle ages. The shifts in the comparative vogue of the three sets of stories in the early days, in the twelfth century, seems to be largely explicable in terms of their different literary origins, a subject which does not greatly concern us. It is worth just bearing in mind that, whereas the stories of Charlemagne and Arthur were traditional and seem to have had a literary pre-history before they were written down, the stories that form the matter of Rome were drawn from books that were written in the antique period itself; and their popularity is clearly related to the revivified interest in classical literature of the twelfth-century schools. Our chief concern, however, is not with where the stories came from, but with the mirror that the twelfth- and thirteenth-century versions of them held up to life, with what they had to tell the knightly world about itself, its history and values – in other words, how together they came to constitute its distinctive mythology.

★

Two very different themes dominate the early epic *chansons* concerned with the matter of France: the wars of the Carolingians against the heathens on the one hand, and stories of revolt and vendetta among the Carolingian nobility on the other. Nevertheless, the similarities of attitude expressed in the poems which centre round these themes are much more striking than any contrasts, doubtless because the narrators in both cases moulded their matter to fit the conditions of the world with which they were familiar. The way in which Raoul de Cambrai is depicted in one of the most famous of the vendetta stories and the portrait of Ganelon the traitor in the *Song of Roland* give us different insights, it is true, into what the eleventh century saw as the ill qualities of a knight, just as the 'sage and valiant' Charlemagne of the Roland epic and the unjust and ungrateful Pepin of *Garin le Loherain* show good and bad qualities in a royal lord. But that is only because different poems raise different issues of honour and dishonour; the broad setting remains the same.

The world to which the poems introduce us is a tough masculine world, whose interests centre very definitely round the camp rather than the court. Their heroes are cavaliers, skilled in the new art of fighting in the saddle with the couched lance; their swords and their horses are treasured, personified possessions – like Roland's blade Durendaal, or Ogier's charger Bierefort. Off the field of battle, they are revealed as men who understand and are interested in the niceties of the customary law that governs their often violent relations with one another; and who feel sharply the full weight in honour of their obligations to their lords and to their kinsmen. Obligations in honour and in law are indeed quintessentially of the same class, almost identical for them. This often gives the poems a strongly legalistic flavour, which is as apparent in some of those that concern the wars against the heathen as in those that concern feud and revolt (witness for instance the account of Ganelon's trial in the *Chanson de Roland*).[3] The professional interest in law that the poems here reveal is worthy of the age that produced the secular jurisprudence of Eicke von Repgow and of the author of the *Leges Henrici Primi*, and is a sign of the growing sophistication of secular learning in an independent sphere of its own. Above all, through all the poems alike there rings the same grimly exultant joy of battle. The chivalrous cult of war and the cult of honour are enshrined in them together, and unassailably linked to one another.

If one subtracts from the *chansons* what is immediate to the age and area of their composition – the manner of fighting, the details of customary legal procedure, the familiar geography of northern France, of the border between France and the Empire, and of the Spanish border where Franks meet Saracens – one is left, it is true, with a scale of values that is not very different from that of earlier, heroic poetry. Martial prowess, liberality, and pride in loyal service are the hallmarks of the hero not only in the Carolingian epics but also in the older Germanic epic literature, in *Beowulf* and the *Hildebrandslied*. That these values were already traditional at the time when the *chansons* were composed does not detract from the interest for our purpose of these poems, however. We see them now transposed into a new context, a social world which is that of the eleventh- and twelfth-century aristocracy, and can observe that in the process they have acquired fresh nuances and a more refined precision. They are now the values of a society of cavaliers, for whom the possession of a war horse and a knowledge of how to handle it are marks of social identity; and legal interests have given the achievement of justice a much greater sharpness in their framework of value. Most important of all, the constant reiteration in them of such epithets as *preux, hardi, loial* and *franc* are demonstrably paving the way toward a definite pattern of knightly values, amenable to systematisation and to symbolisation, two of the principal means whereby medieval people sought to arrange and clarify their attitudes to the world around them.

The epics also helped, through the detail of their narrative, to define in a reference of value a series of stock reactions to stock situations, for instance to the claims of kinsmen, to the right of the wrongfully dispossessed and the unjustly accused, as well as to the various recurrent emergencies of war. So powerful was their impact in this respect, that when later authors wished to treat chivalrously of situations that were similar but which had a different context in place and time, they simply transposed into them these same reactions and the value judgements associated with them, with only the slightest modification. Thus in the *Romance of Alexander* the refusal of the companions of Eumenides of Arcady to call Alexander to their aid when they are surprised by the enemy in overwhelming numbers[4] is recounted in a manner reminiscent of the account of Roland's refusal to sound his horn and summon Charlemagne's succour at Roncesvalles; the outcome of the affair is different, it is true (Alexander, when finally summoned, arrived in time, whereas Charlemagne did not), but the overtones of the situation and their implications are the same. Similarly, in the Arthurian cycle of stories, the scenes of trial by combat echo similar situations in the earlier *chansons*, and the great vendetta between the kinsmen of Lancelot and those of Gawain carries us back into a world which has more in common with that of Garin le Loherain and of his titanic struggles with the kin of Fromond of Flanders than it has with the delicately drawn courtly world of Chrétien de Troyes's romances. Not only did the subject matter of the Carolingian epics remain popular; their way of looking at martial and social relations also continued to seem relevant long after the twelfth century. There was indeed a notable revival of interest in them in the last century of the middle ages at the court of Burgundy, where authors like David Aubert and Jean Wauquelin retold in prose the stories of such heroes as Gilles de Chin, Girart de Roussillon and Garin.[5] They did not have to modify the stories very much, or to alter significantly the values that they encapsulated, in order to make them relevant to the age of Charles the Bold and Louis XI. The now traditional stories and the values that they expressed seemed just as meaningful as they had done in the twelfth century.

As the popularity of the epic stories began, quite early in the twelfth century, to spread beyond the French soil of their birth, the process commenced through which chivalry came to acquire its private pantheon of heroes: Charlemagne the loyal ruler and champion of Christendom, Roland the brave, Oliver the wise, the heroic Ogier. The signs of the establishment of what can only be called cults appear. The care with which the twelfth-century Pseudo-Turpin *Chronicle* of Charlemagne lists the places where the heroes of Roncesvalles are buried is one indication of this.[6] Churches soon began to vie with one another in their claims to possess their relics.[7] Another sign of the development of a cult is the beginning of a history of the iconography of the Carolingian legend; thus we find the Roland story preserved in stone in the twelfth-century sculptures of the cathedral at Verona, and the miracle of the lances that burst into leaf overnight outside the heroes' tents on the eve of Charlemagne's great battles in Spain is recorded in the stained glass of Chartres[8] (the burgeoning lances were those of the knights who would achieve their martyrdom in the coming engagement).

It seems here significant that the basis for the iconography of the Carolingian legends is very often not the poems about them but the pseudo-historical Latin chronicles which were substantially based on the poetic accounts. This is indicative of an interest in the legends which is better described as historical than as literary. The provision of examples illustrative of perennial values and of the working of divine providence was, in the medieval eye, one of the prime functions of history. In this context of historical interest we thus see the lives, the personal qualities and the actions of the epic heroes of the new cult coming to be envisaged more clearly as an object lesson to knighthood.[9] In a similar way, iconographically they are presented as a visible expression of its values. They also offer a yardstick whereby chivalrous society may measure its contemporary achievement. Whence it comes about that in the vernacular verse chronicles which were becoming a popular form of historical writing in the late twelfth century, the story of Charlemagne becomes almost the stock foil to the history of the more recent past. Ambroise's celebration of the *prouesse* that Geoffrey de Lusignan displayed before Acre is a typical example: 'chivalry has not won so much praise', he says, 'since the time of Roland and Oliver'.[10] The foundations of what can justifiably be called an historical mythology of chivalry are here beginning to be visible.

The most eloquent early iconographical witness to the development of the cult of the Carolingian heroes are the sculptures and glass of churches, and great French churches like the abbey of St Denis played an important part in the dissemination of the legends as history.[11] This reminds us of the emphatically Christian tone of the principal stories that form the matter of France, and so of the profound impact of Christianity upon the secular martial society of the early middle ages. It is one of the features of these stories that marks them off most sharply as distinct in spirit from earlier heroic tales. Although the knightly piety that informs them had its roots not so much in the crusades as in the experience of the earlier European wars against the heathen, it was natural in the twelfth century to relate contemporary events such as the crusade to that past history, to view each in terms of the other. That is why, in the Pseudo-Turpin chronicle and its derivatives, the rather peculiar (and sometimes frankly risible) events recorded in the poem Le Pélérinage Charlemagne (which tells of Charlemagne's visit to the Holy Land) have been re-presented in a more orthodox crusading shape. It is again the reason why, in the early thirteenth century, we find the great Dominican Humbert de Romans recommending those charged with the preaching of the crusade to draw examples from that same chronicle in order to bring home their message to knights.[12] And the militant, conquistador side to the ideal of crusade rings plain, in the Old French version of Turpin's chronicle, in the words in which Charlemagne explains to Agolant the Moor the reasons for his war with him: 'Our Lord Jesus Christ, who created Heaven and earth, chose out our Christian nation and established it to rule over all the other peoples of the earth.'[13] Here the example of the old story is used to carry a highly relevant contemporary message: that the Franks have a God-given conquering destiny. Indeed, the mythology of chivalry is beginning to be drawn into a context wider than that of the crusade and its Carolingian precedents, into the Christian providential history of the working out of God's purposes for His world – a history to which the crusade was relevant, but to which much else was relevant as well.

★

One reason why the stories of Charlemagne and his peers made such a powerful impact upon the knighthood of the twelfth and succeeding centuries was because it was so easy for men to relate the preoccupations of the Carolingian world and the events of Charles's career, as they came to know them, to the preoccupations and events of their own time, especially, perhaps, to their crusading preoccupations. The stories that formed the matter of Rome the Great, of the sieges of Troy and Thebes and of the wars of Alexander and Caesar, concerned a world much more remote from the twelfth century and pagan to boot. Nevertheless, the same concerns with the relation of contemporary society to its past, and with the martial tradition that had found its contemporary climax in the crusade, have much to do with the popularity which romances based upon classical stories achieved, from the middle of the twelfth century onward.

The new interest in stories drawn from the classical past, to which the immediate popularity of the Romances of Troy and of Alexander bears witness, obviously owed much to the revived interest in antiquity in the twelfth-century schools.[14] Plantagenet court circles, where Henry II of England and Anjou extended his patronage to such scholars as John of Salisbury and Peter of Blois and to Latin *littérateurs* like Walter Map and Gerald of Wales, seem to have played an important part in setting the new literary fashion in the middle of the century.[15] In the court in which such men moved, Benoit de Ste Maure's virtuoso introduction to the *Romance of Troy*, explaining that he had relied upon the most reputable sources for his narrative of the great siege, was sure to have an impact. (Benoit's source was of course not really reputable at all, but there is no reason to doubt that he quite sincerely believed that Dares Phrygius, who in fact wrote in the fifth century AD, had been an eye witness of the siege whose evidence was for that reason preferable to Homer's.)[16] From the point of view of the knightly element in the audience, however, the fashions of the schools were probably less important in winning appreciation for the classical stories than the way in which the crusade, and a better knowledge generally of the oriental world, had opened men's eyes to wider horizons, and that not only in geographical terms. A better knowledge of the east, which had been the scene of so much in classical history, provoked all sorts of mental reactions. Some were greedy and materialistic: the crusaders' first glimpses of the wealth of Constantinople stirred their acquisitive instincts almost immediately. But the sight of the city stirred other responses too, some of which come across in the wide-eyed wonder of Geoffrey de Villehardouin when he and his fellow crusaders came there in 1203: 'I can assure you that all those who had never seen Constantinople before gazed very intently at the city, having never imagined that there could be so fine a place in all the world. They noted the high walls and lofty towers encircling it, and its rich palaces and tall churches, of which there were so many that no one would have believed it to be true if he had not seen it with his own eyes, and viewed the length and breadth of that city which rules supreme above all others.'[17]

In the east, the western knights found a world on which the imprint of the glories of the classical past, as a visible heritage, was infinitely sharper than anywhere in their homelands.[18] They also found magnificence and riches, not just in *specie* but in buildings, mosaics, statuary, and silks and damasks, on a scale which the imagination of their feudal forbears could scarcely have compassed. This richness was the backdrop to the rigours, so physically severe and so often fatal, of the early crusaders' campaigns. In the circumstances, it is easy to understand the appeal for their generation of the classical stories, which told of titanic military struggles, comparable with their own and fought against this imposing background. The lands over which Alexander and the ancient Trojans and Romans had campaigned were the same lands that the crusaders fought over. The legend of the Trojan origin of the Franks, which had enjoyed currency since Merovingian times, no doubt also helped them to relate to this ancient history: it was the history of the struggles of their remote ancestors in a richer, more cultivated, if pre-Christian past.

The instinct to relate the ancient world to the contemporary medieval one, which was no doubt largely subconscious, comes out in all sorts of small ways in the romances that tell of the 'matter of Rome the Great'. Benoit de Ste Maure was clearly at some pains to give his account of the blazoning of the shields of the Greek and Trojan heroes of his Troy book a coherence in contemporary heraldic terms. To the author of the *Romance of Thebes* it seemed natural to compare the priest Amphiaras with Archbishop Turpin and the warrior Tydeus with Roland. In a similar way the thirteenth-century author of the *Hystoire de Jules Cesar* turned Cleopatra into a western beauty, a dazzling blonde in robes lined with ermine.[19] This is reminiscent of the way in which Carolingian heroes, in the epic *chansons*, are portrayed in a social world recognisable as that of the eleventh, not the eighth century. More importantly, we can see running all through the *Romance of Alexander* a kind of analogy with the crusade. It is not just that so much of the fighting is over the same Syrian terrain: Alexander's enemies are 'Turks' and 'felon Bedouin', and the lord of Babylon is an *emir*, whom we hear swearing by his God 'Mahound'.[20] As for the heroes, you would take them for natural Frenchmen – the poet says so in so many words.[21] In a real sense, Alexander's history is told as a story 'prefiguring' the crusade.

Similarly, the chivalry of Alexander and his twelve peers (the number is the same as that of Charlemagne's paladins) prefigures medieval chivalry, and again there is more to this than the story's medieval accoutrements of hauberks and emblazoned shields and its picture of the relation between the war horse Bucephalus and his master. The real significance of the analogy is seen rather in such passages as that which describes Alexander and his young companions bathing to purify themselves before taking knighthood, or the passage which lists Alexander's knightly qualities, his largesse, his *hardiesse* in battle, his protection of the orphan and the widow.[22] Eumenides of Arcady, of whom we are told that all his joy was in arms and the tourney and the love of fair-haired girls,[23] might almost be the model for some such *tiro* of the late twelfth century as the young Arnold of Ardres of whom the chronicler Lambert wrote. Even that interdependence upon one another of *clergie* and *chevalerie*, which Chrétien de Troyes praised and which was so often vaunted after his time, is to be found here foreshadowed in the classical age, in the romance account of Alexander's attention to the guidance of his philosopher–tutor Aristotle.[24] It is of no little significance that we should thus see the ethic of chivalry carried back into the age before the Church, into pre-Christian antiquity. A very important contact has been here established for knighthood with an intellectual tradition independent of ecclesiasticism.

The battle scenes of the *Romance of Alexander* have all the ferocity of those of the *chansons de geste*, which are their literary model, but it has set them in a world of marvels just a little stranger than those of the average traveller's tale, carrying us beyond Syria and Mesopotamia to the banks of rivers that flow down from the earthly paradise, and into the desert where Alexander spoke to the trees of the Sun and Moon which cannot lie. The romances of Troy and Thebes and of Aeneas do not contain material quite comparable to this, but they tell of a world grander and richer than that of the contemporary medieval west, largely for the simple reason that the worlds that Dares, Statius and Virgil had known had been, by comparison with the west in the twelfth century, of Byzantine opulence. The writers of the romances transposed this opulence from their sources into their own works. They thus helped to develop the natural taste of their audience for luxury and display (and indeed for books and learning), and this in an age when the quickening pulse of trade between Europe and the east, greatly stimulated by the crusades, was making luxury goods more readily available in the west itself, and which witnessed too new experiments in architecture and new advances of learning. A greater love of colour, a fascination with rich robes, grandiose castles and in general with the decorative trappings of a courtly world, introduced into literature something that was notably lacking in the epic *chansons*, and fostered a taste that proved abiding, both in aristocratic literature and in aristocratic, courtly life.

The world of the matter of Rome was also a much less exclusively masculine one than that of the matter of France, again because the world of the classical authors from whom its stories were derived was less so. It was thus that the amorous ethic of the troubadours began to find its way into narrative literature (for it was as natural to the twelfth century to interpret in terms of contemporary attitudes the love of Achilles for Polixena, or of Atys for Ismene, as it was to armour classical heroes in hauberks of mail and to set them upon war horses). So we find Aeneas drawing strength in his single combat with Turnus from his thoughts of Lavinia, and Cleopatra confiding that it was Caesar's renown for *prouesse* that first won her heart.[25] The attitudes thus exemplified are not those of the classical age, but are medieval; and they become typical in all manner of romances of the later twelfth and thirteenth centuries, not just those dealing with the classical past.

If the laymen of the twelfth century pictured the classical past in terms of contemporary conditions, that does not mean that they were unaware of the great space of time that divided them from it, or that it was essentially part of history. Those who listened to the romances concerning the matter of Rome thought of them as essentially historical, whence the anxiety of authors such as Benoit to reassure their audiences about the reliability of their sources – his emphasis on the point that Dares had been a lettered knight who had actually taken part in the Trojan war. Out of the popularity of the romances, an interest in the classical past that was more strictly and recognisably historical soon began to develop. The evidence of it is the growing popularity in the thirteenth century of works somewhat different from the romances, vernacular histories of antiquity in verse or prose, and their multiplication. The *Fait des Romains*, translated from Lucan and from Caesar's commentaries and dealing mainly with Julius Caesar's own career, was probably put together between 1211 and 1215, and became very popular:[26] it was used by Philip Mouskés in his chronicle and by Brunetto Latini in his *Livre du trésor* – to quote two popular authors – and by many others. Calendres's *Histoire des Empereurs de Rome*, drawn largely from Orosius, was written a few years later, and from about the same time we have a *Histoire ancienne jusques à Céar*, largely taken from Dares. Benoit's Troy book in a revamped prose version became popular, and Jean de Flixecourt produced an unromanticised translation of Dares in 1262. The fashion thus set for translation continued, and so the range of the works dealing with the classical past that were within the compass of the layman's comprehension steadily widened.[27] The Valois Kings of France of the fourteenth century were generous patrons of translators, and at their court were commissioned translations of Livy, of Valerius Maximus, of Cicero's *Amicitia* and *de Senectute*, and of the *Ethics* and the *Politics* of Aristotle. In the fifteenth century, as the influence of humanism began to spread beyond Italy, the tide of translation swelled further, naturally. The vernacular translators of the age of Charles the Bold of Burgundy were of course infinitely more polished, more learned and more critical than those of the thirteenth century, but there was nothing new about the eagerness of the

later period for a better knowledge of classical antiquity. Indeed, its eagerness for it probably owed as much to the example of the French past as it did
to contemporary Italian humanism.

The matter of Rome, the *Chanson des Saines* says, teaches sound lessons; it
was the avowed object of the early translators to teach by example. The
practical utility of a knowledge of the classical past was a point often
laboured: 'Considering that the Roman people, among all others, by the
virtues of constancy and prudence and by their chivalrous deeds . . . knew
how to achieve so much that by their wisdom and labour they conquered the
whole world, we may see that every ruler may take example from their
wonderful deeds' – so runs the introduction to the fourteenth-century
translation of Livy.[28] It is in the perspective of this sort of comment that we
should appreciate the popularity of translations of Vegetius's treatise on
tactics: men read it because they knew the Romans conquered the world
and wanted to know how they did it. Vegetius's book, significantly, was in
translation entitled a *Livre de chevalerie*.[29] Also described as books of
chivalry were such works as those of Honoré Bonet and Christine de Pisan,
which presented in translation the comments of such great medieval
lawyers as Bartolus and John of Legnano on those parts of Roman Law
which dealt with war and the duties of the soldier.[30] This was an important
influence, reminding the world of knighthood that antiquity's example
taught that the soldier must regard his trade in the light of defined obligations, and the business of war was governed by general principles upon
which an orderly framework of inter-state relations depended. Classical
mythology, by a broadly similar process, came to be regarded as a quarry of
examples of chivalry. Christine de Pisan's *Letter of Othea to Hector* is a kind of
encyclopaedia of its didactic interpretations for knights. Thus Perseus's
rescue of Andromeda teaches that 'all knights should succour women that
have need of their succour', and his winged horse Pegasus signifies 'that his
[the knight's] good name should be born in all countries'; Ceres 'that gave
increase in corn, taking from none' stands for *largesse* in chivalry; 'in the
same way should a good knight be abundant to all persons and to give his
help and comfort after his power' – and so on.[31]

From classical history and from such works as that of Vegetius chivalry
was reminded of lessons that neither epic nor romance – nor mythology for
that matter – could teach so effectively. Here men found a new emphasis on
discipline and on training: on the need for the martial *tiro* to keep his
physique in trim, and for the soldier in the field to obey implicitly the orders
of his commander. So once again we find a new dimension of value being
grafted into the ethic of chivalry. For an illustration of the grafting process at
work as good an example as any is the fulsome commendation of his hero's
virtues by the author of the life of the great French marshal, Jean de
Boucicaut (written in the early fifteenth century, when the plethora of

translation had begun to leave a powerful mark). As a knight inspired by love of his lady, Boucicaut is compared in good traditional fashion to Tristram and Lancelot. But then another side of him is presented, his passion for physical training, which has strong echoes of Vegetius. He did exercises regularly (with special attention to breathing), in order to keep fit; and there is a splendid list of his assault course feats – he could turn a somersault in full armour, could vault armed onto his horse, and could climb up the reverse side of a ladder in armour using his hands only, feet hanging free. As a captain we are told that he was a stern disciplinarian, upon the Roman model: following Scipio's example he would have no loose women about the camp, deplored drunkenness, and would have been ready if need be to punish his own children for disobeying orders. Having heard about Demosthenes (somewhat vaguely, I presume) he understood the need for a commander to be eloquent, in order to rouse his men to action and so as to be able to explain himself to subject peoples.[32] Boucicaut, as portrayed, does not come over to the modern reader as a very attractive character. Nevertheless his portrayal does give a vivid impression of the new slant upon chivalrous duty that antiquity's example could give, with its emphasis upon disciplined service and training, on a dedicated professionalism that was coming to be expected of any captain of note. These emphases may seem alien to the individualistic chivalrous conception of the knight errant; they became notwithstanding a part, and an important part, of the image of what chivalry, at its best, ought to be.

Of the literary influences upon chivalry, that which drew upon antiquity for its models of knighthood, which made room for Hector and Alexander, Scipio and Caesar as cult figures in the chivalrous pantheon, was the one with the greatest capacity for growth over the long term. A medieval literary audience did not, on the whole, look for creative originality in narrative literature, but rather for skill, eloquence, and ingenious or decorative elaboration upon a traditional theme. Once the outlines of the Carolingian and Arthurian stories had begun to set firmly, there was a limit, therefore, to their capacity to offer new examples or to suggest new conceptions. This was not the case with the matter of Rome, for the simple reason that it had its basis in a much richer vein of literary and historical material, whose tremendous range was only gradually unfolded as new classical works and new stories were translated or rediscovered. Its history was related, moreover, to a body of legal and ethical thought and philosophical opinion recorded in non-narrative classical works, whose riches similarly were only tapped in stages by the learned medieval world, and were passed on in vernacular translation, once again by stages, to secular aristocratic society. Classical ethics, classical jurisprudence and classical philosophy, though by no means irreconcilable with Christian thought and exercising a powerful influence upon it, belonged to a pre-Christian tradition. Chivalry was thus reminded, forcefully, of the separation of the origins of its institutions from those of the priesthood, and of the original independence of its function – within the broad framework of divine providence – from the priestly one.

★

Few, in the middle ages, doubted the basic historicity of Arthur, the central figure of the third 'matter' of the *Chanson des Saisnes*, the matter of Britain. Those who wrote about him took the same sort of pains to suggest that their stories were based upon reputable authority as Benoit de Ste Maure did when writing of the Trojan war. Geoffrey of Monmouth claimed to have had before him, when he wrote his history of the Kings of Britain, a 'very ancient' book in the British language.[33] The standard account of the Quest for the Holy Grail was supposed to have been put together by Walter Map on the basis of the record compiled by Arthur's own clerks from Sir Bohort's personal testimony.[34] In 1191 more tangible evidence that Arthur was a real historical figure was provided, when his grave and that of Queen Guinevere were 'discovered' at Glastonbury, and their bones disinterred and reburied (it seems clear that the whole affair was a pious fraud, organised by the monks of Glastonbury in order to encourage a profitable cult, but it passed off successfully as a genuine find).[35] In due course, after the Arthurian story had achieved its definitive shape, we find its detail being subjected to what can only be called positively historical research. Diligent clerks in the fifteenth century extracted from the by then numerous romances the complete list of Arthur's knights, found blazons of arms for each of them, and supplied potted biographies.[36] They also used the romances to establish what they thought to have been the rules of the tournament in the days of King Uther Pendragon, and the terms of the oaths which newly made knights of the Round Table had been obliged to swear on admission to the society. Some of the details of the last have a faintly comic ring, as the reminder in parenthesis that in Arthur's day the Kingdom of Logres (Britain) had been 'well garnished with giants', and the promise, which each knight had to make, that if a lady or damsel should fall into his hands in the course of war, he would not deflower her 'unless she take pleasure in it and is consenting thereto'.[37] This rather absurd sort of solemnity is a testimony to the seriousness of the historical interest in the Arthurian story; it is the absurd solemnity that is all too often the accompaniment of pedagogic erudition.

We should not of course conclude from this historical interest in he Arthurian story that men were prepared to accept as veracious history the whole gamut of fantastic tales that were woven into it. The author of the *Chanson des Saisnes*, who recommended the stories of Charlemagne because they were true and of the Romans because they were instructive commented on the matter of Britain that it was 'vain and pleasing' – implying clearly that there was a good deal of fiction in it.[38] Philippe de Mézières, advising the young Charles VI of France about his reading in the late fourteenth century, was even more plain spoken: he told him to read of the great deeds of the Christian emperors and especially those of 'your great predecessor, the blessed Charlemagne', but to be careful of paying too much attention to the stories of Arthur, 'great as was his worldly valour', because they were too full of empty fables.[39] No one is likely to challenge de Mézières' comment on that score, and it was abundantly clear that in this respect of historicity there was an ultimate contrast between the matter of Rome and the matter of Britain. In the former case, quickening interest in the classical past led forward to a better knowledge of what really had happened in it, but this could not happen in the case of the matter of Britain because there was no comparable canon of true historical information underlying it. But if the Arthurian story had less historicity – indeed because it had – this meant that the authors who treated of it enjoyed for a time a great freedom to develop their matter as they chose, without too many limitations being imposed by sources. They found themselves able to alter and elaborate upon old stories, and to bring forward new ones in the effort to please and instruct in novel and interesting ways.

Of course few of them chose to fabricate wholly new stories: that was not expected of them. We have seen that they liked to suggest that they had good sources, and they nearly always had sources of some sort, though not such good ones as they claimed. Geoffrey of Monmouth, whose history supplied the basic outline of Arthur's personal story, was no mean scholar: he had used many quite reputable early authorities, such as Bede, Gildas and Nennius; for his Arthurian matter, where these failed him, he drew largely on Welsh legends, some at least of which he probably knew from written texts. Celtic mythology was the great quarry for the fictions that were refashioned and worked into the corpus of Arthurian romance. Breton versions of them were probably the chief source upon which the French authors drew. Breton legends were certainly the source of two famous *lais* of Marie de France, which tell of Tristram's love and of the faery mistress of Arthur's knight Lanval. Wace remarks of the Round Table (which is one of his few additions to Geoffrey of Monmouth's story) that the Bretons told many tales of it.[40] The influence of forgotten Breton *conteurs* almost certainly also accounts for the early knowledge of the Arthurian legend in those lands in which their Norman neighbours fought. The remarkable Arthurian sculpture on the archivolt of the Cathedral at Modena,[41] depicting Arthur and his Knights (Gawain and Kay among them) coming to the rescue of Queen Guinevere, is almost certainly marginally older than Geoffrey of Monmouth's book. In oral versions, and probably also in written versions which have not survived, the legend of Arthur was already very widely known in the early twelfth century, and the romance writers, whether they lived near the Celtic lands or far from them, had plenty to draw on.

The question of which particular Celtic myths underlie which Arthurian stories is one of tremendous complication: much ink has been spilled over the problem of the relations, for instance, of the story of the Fisher King with that of the Welsh Branwen, and of the Grail with the cup with which, in Irish legend, the damsel served King Conn in the palace of the phantom horseman Lug.[42] For our purpose questions such as these, fascinating as they are, are not important. What is important is the way in which the romance writers, in the twelfth and thirteenth centuries, refashioned the earlier stories. When we begin to look at things from this angle, it becomes clear that we need to be chary of overemphasising the significance of the Celtic element in the tales (important though it was in locating them geographically and in time, in Britain in the sixth century). What we have learned from the contemporary treatment of the matter of Rome is often more relevant, as once again we see antique heroes appear in twelfth-century armour, in a world whose elements of magic and faery are, it is true, borrowed from Celtic myth, but whose magnificence is modelled on what the twelfth century imagined to be the opulence of the East and of the classical past. Geoffrey of Monmouth's book is full of Virgilian echoes, and he took care to link his British matter with Rome by presenting Brutus, the first king of the Britain that would later be Arthur's, as the great-nephew of Aeneas. Arthur's capital Caerleon is to him the City of the Legions, and he stresses that at their great feasts the Britons of Arthur's time still followed the customs of Troy.[43] Chrétien de Troyes, for his romance of *Cligès*, chose a Byzantine setting: the hero is the son of the Emperor of Greece. The East, where the Baruch of Baghdad reigns over two-thirds of the earth or more, is the scene of the extravagant adventures, amorous and martial, of Gahmuret, Parzival's father, at the beginning of Wolfram von Eschenbach's romance; and we are told that there he won such riches that he could 'lavish gifts by way of rewards as if gold grew on trees'.[44] All this magnificence is interwoven into stories whose recurrent theme is good fighting, described (as it is also in the matter of Rome stories) in a manner which owes much to the epic *chansons* of the Carolingian cycle. Antique opulence and contemporary joy in knightly combat form in the Arthurian stories a thick overlay upon the substratum of Celtic legend and dark age history, and turn these into something utterly different from what they originally were. They turn them into a history which had a compelling interest for a knightly audience, because it seemed to catch the very essence of chivalry, to offer a reflection of themselves and their world not quite as it was but as they would have had it be in terms of prowess and riches, and spiced with magic and magnificence to add to the excitement.

The Arthurian stories put the finishing touches upon the ideal picture of the knight errant, and gave the tourney its rightful place as a test of prowess in the exemplary literature of chivalry. The absence of inhibitions imposed by a need to keep relatively close to their sources gave those who wrote of Arthur the opportunity also to enlarge upon other, still more important themes. We have seen how those who wrote of the matter of Rome were able to rework the amorous episodes that they found in their sources so as to present them in a courtly mould. In the old Celtic stories, as in the classical ones, women had a larger part to play than they had in the stories of Charlemagne or (as far as the surviving fragments enable us to make out) in the German heroic epics. The Arthurian writers seized the opportunity thus offered to develop the narrative potential of the eroticism of troubadour lyric to an infinitely greater degree than any of their predecessors had. Chrétien de Troyes, who knew the Provençal writings well and who was also well steeped in Ovid[45] (who among the classical authors was the most powerful single literary influence upon the medieval view of love), led the way here. Chrétien had the individuality of touch of a truly great master, and few who followed him had his interest or his insight in the exploration of love, of the inner feelings of their heroes and heroines. What they could and did understand, however, was something with more important potential for influencing the actual, active world of knighthood: that is to say, the potency of love as a force that urges a man to seek to test himself, to prove his worthiness of his mistress. Adoration and inspiration were the central focus of the troubadour ideal of courtly love, not consummation. In this context, there was little difference, it should be noted, between the capacities of adulterous love, such as that of Tristram and Iseult or of Lancelot and Guinevere (with the handling of which Chrétien himself does not seem to have been happy) and the regulated love that hopes ultimately to make a bride of an adored woman. Both equally could be a source of inspiration to higher flights of martial endeavour. Both alike, therefore, permitted the interweaving of martial adventure and amorous dedication as twinned themes of narrative; and these two recurrent and twinned themes do in fact dominate a very large part of the literature that treats of the matter of Britain.

Arthurian romance became in consequence a chief vehicle of that teaching which harnesses to the idea of chivalrous adventure the erotic force of sexual love, to act as the motor of endeavour for the knightly hero. It held up countless models to support Geoffrey de Charny's precept, that it is good for a man at arms to be in love *par amours*, because this will teach him to seek higher renown in order to do honour to his lady.[46] We have seen already what a powerful influence this combination of ideas exercised in real life upon the martial play of tournaments, whose mock war was often so staged as to link reality with literary models. It is much harder to assess its

26. The company of the Round Table: the presentation of Galahad (Bibliothèque Nationale). See pp. 60, 113ff, 118.

27 (below). Arthurian legend and courtly love: the Round Table knights as
devotees of Venus, by the Master of San Martino (Louvre). See p. 116.

28. The Nine Worthies: illustration from Thomas of Saluzzo's *Chevalier Errant* (Bibliothèque Nationale). See p. 121.

29. The Nine Heroines: illustration from Thomas of Saluzzo's *Chevalier Errant* (Bibliothèque Nationale).
See p. 121.

30. Enamel on the tomb of Geoffrey the Fair, showing his shield painted with 'lioncels' (Musée d'Histoire, Le Mans). See p. 126.

31 (facing page). Soldiers bearing the same blazon as their leader: Diepold von Schweinspunt and his knights, from Peter of Eboli's *Carmen de Bello Siculo* (Bürgerbibliothek, Berne). See pp. 127–8.

diopuldꝯ

diopuldꝯ

32. Thirteenth-century shields, from the *Chronicle* of Matthew Paris (British Library). See pp. 129–30.

33. Arms of France, and of the French royal princes, with helms and war-crests, from Gelre's *Armorial* (Bibliothèque Royale Albert 1er, Brussels). See p. 140.

34. The herald Gelre: self-portrait from his *Armorial* (Bibliothèque Royale Albert 1er, Brussels). See p. 140.

influence in a wider context, in the grimmer worlds of war and of politics, in which play had to be laid aside and in which marriages were so often arranged not on the basis of love (as in romance) but of dynastic considerations. The sources do, however, tell us just enough to suggest that it would be very unwise to write off the influence of this courtly, amorous ideal as trivial or negligible, or as a mere literary convention. The chronicles and chivalrous biographies offer us glimpses of its impact as a real emotion upon particular individuals, and are consistent in their treatment of this impact. As in romance, it is the classic spur to endeavour. 'If it is true', writes the author of the life of the Spanish hero Don Pero Niño, describing the passages of love between Pero and the lady at whose castle he was entertained in France, 'that men in love are more valiant and are better men for the love of their sweethearts, what must he have been who had such a sweetheart as Jeanette de Bellengues, Madame de Serifontaine!'[47] Boucicaut's biographer speaks with the same voice: 'We can see how love prompts men to high deeds from the stories of Lancelot and Tristram, and we can see the same from those noble men whom the service of love has inspired to valour in France in our own day, as Sir Othon de Grandson and the Good Constable Louis de Sancerre, and many others too.'[48] The story in the *Chronique des quatre premiers Valois* of how Joan of Kent vamped the Black Prince – to put it crudely – has a positively literary quality in its irony, as she, sighing, explains that her love is pledged to a knight whose prowess knows no peer, and he seeks to wring out of her the name of this paragon, which is, of course, his own.[49] This tale may be apocryphal: there is no reason, on the other hand, to question Froissart's story of the English knights at Valenciennes who wore a patch over one eye because of the vow that they had taken, each to see with only one eye until he had performed some deed of arms worthy of his lady, or Thomas Gray's story of Sir William Marmion, whose mistress had given him a gold helmet, bidding him to make it known amid glorious dangers – and who nearly lost his life outside Norham Castle while fulfilling her command.[50] In these glimpses from real life we are no doubt a long way from the psychological subtleties of the internal dialogue of Chrétien de Troyes's knights and ladies. The emphasis is here heavily on the male party and his external achievements. That however does not detract from the real significance of love and of amorous conventions in knightly life, which passages such as these that I have quoted allow us to glimpse from time to time. Most males do like their life style and achievement to catch the feminine eye. The courtly, amorous theme in chivalrous literature linked the martial scale of values to the terrific force of love, with all its potential for influencing the lives, actions and attitudes of those caught up in its meshes.

In sharp contrast to the matter of Rome (which, as we have seen, also played a part in the grafting together of the ethic of courtly love with the ideology of chivalry) Arthur's world was a world emphatically of Christian knighthood. Geoffrey of Monmouth, the founding father of Arthurian legend, tells a story deeply coloured by the tradition of Christianity's martial struggle against paganism, like so many of the Carolingian epics. There are overtones both of *Heidenkrieg* and of crusading ideology in the passage in which he describes the great battle at Bath against the Saxons, 'whose very name is an insult to heaven'. 'You who have been marked with the cross of the Christian faith, be mindful of the loyalty that you owe to your fatherland and to your fellow-countrymen,' cried Archbishop Dubricius. 'Whoever suffers death for the sake of his brothers offers himself as a living sacrifice to God and follows with firm footsteps behind Christ himself . . . it follows that if any one of you shall suffer death in this war, that death shall be as a penance and absolution for all his sins.'[51] And in the later Grail romances, of course, the idea of the crusade is never far away. The Grail castle of Munsalvesche in Wolfram's *Parzival* is guarded by Templars:[52] at the climax of *Perlesvaus* the hero finally storms the Grail castle by main force to rescue it from the power of the King of Castle Mortal who has forced the people of the land to abandon Christ's faith.[53] The story of the knights of the Round Table, is, quintessentially, the story of the greatest company of Christian knights that the world has ever known: and that, above all other things, is what sets the 'matter of Britain' apart from the 'matter of Rome'.

We see here another way in which the absence of a defined canon permitted the authors of Arthurian romance to open up new themes, in this case historical and religious ones. The Grail story not only made it possible for chivalrous romance to become a vehicle for eucharistic mysticism: it was also, as we have seen in an earlier chapter, the medium through which the chivalrous story of Arthur and his knights was linked into the sacred history of Christianity, as recounted in the Bible. The story of how the 'good knight' Joseph of Arimathea obtained from Pilate the cup from which Christ had drunk at the last supper, and caught in it the last drops of His blood as he was brought down from the Cross, and of how the risen saviour visited him in prison and entrusted the cup to his care, links the story of the Round Table and its highest quest directly to the climax of the Gospel story, the Passion and the Resurrection. The trinity of tables – that at which the Last Supper was eaten, the Grail table that Joseph set up in the desert, and the Round Table – symbolises the connections. Galahad, who came of the line of David as well as that of Joseph, links the story, typically and significantly through knightly lineage, with the Old Testament past, which prepared for and foreshadowed Christ's coming, as well as with the New Law. The whole story encapsulates the outline of an explanation of chivalry's independent origin and standing as a Christian order.

The way in which the Arthurian stories linked the traditions and conventions of the medieval knightly world with those of biblical and classical chivalry is well illustrated by the contents of one very unusual Arthurian manuscript, written up in the later thirteenth century.[54] The text of the Bodmer MS is based upon the standard or Vulgate version of the *Queste del Graal* and the *Merlin*. Into their text its scribe has,with some skill, interpolated passages from other works. On the one hand he has woven in substantial extracts from a version of the *Romance of Troy* and from the *Fait des Romains*, so as to enable his reader to set the achievements of Arthurian and of antique knighthood alongside one another. A hint of a connection between their historical roles is provided by the story (which had become an established part of the Grail history) of how the Emperor Vespasian, inspired by St Veronica, came to Jerusalem to avenge Christ's death and released Joseph of Arimathea from prison. Thus antique chivalry set young Christian chivalry upon its feet. The other principal source of the interpolations in the Bodmer text is the Bible. Much is taken from the New Testament – as we should expect, given that it is with the New Testament that the story of Joseph of Arimathea and his line connects the Round Table. But there are also substantial interpolations which are taken from the Old Testament, and from books that are from our point of view very significant: the books of Judges, of Kings, and of the Maccabees. These are the books which describe how the chivalry of Israel conquered and defended the Holy Land in the days of the Old Law. That that history was naturally conceived in chivalrous terms, the illuminations of countless biblical texts remind us. It begins to be clear that we shall not grasp the full significance of the historical mythology of chivalry if we confine ourselves to the three great matters of the *Chanson des Saisnes*: there was a fourth and greater matter too. Beside the examples of chivalry offered to us by the stories of Charlemagne, of the Greek and Roman heroes and of Arthur's knights, we need to set the example of the biblical chivalry of King David and Judas Maccabaeus, for their achievement was as much part of the historical mythology of chivalry as anything else was.

★

The Old Testament leaders had been constantly held up as an example to Christian warriors for a long time – since before the word chivalry was coined, indeed. The early rites for the blessing of banners and of the warrior's sword invoked the examples of Abraham and Gideon, David and Judas Maccabaeus.[55] So it is no surprise, for instance, to find Charlemagne in the Pseudo-Turpin chronicle lamenting Roland as the peer in prowess of Judas, and giving twelve thousand ounces of gold and as many of silver for the repose of the souls of those slain at Roncesvalles 'and in remembrance of the Maccabees'.[56] The Lady of the Lake had the same example in mind when Lancelot asked her if there had ever been a knight who had in him all the virtuous points of chivalry which she had rehearsed to him. 'Yes,' said she, 'and that before Christ suffered. In the time when the people of Israel served God faithfully and fought against the Philistines and other infidels to uphold and spread His law there were many: and among them were John the Ircanian and Judas Maccabaeus the good knight . . . and there were his brothers, and David the King, and others whom I shall pass over for the moment.'[57] She passed them over, in fact, in order to go straight on to Joseph of Arimathea and his line. There is no sharp break in the succession of the Lord's warriors as we pass from the age of the Old Testament into that of the New, not at any rate in the eyes of the Lady of the Lake.

In the age of faith in which the romance of Lancelot was written, the Bible stories were of course very familiar, in their outline anyway, in knightly circles, as in others. All the same it is interesting to find that in the same age in which, as we have seen, the knighthood's knowledge of classical history was enlarged by the beginnings of a great exercise in the translation of Latin histories into the vernacular, a parallel exercise in the translation of the Bible was being undertaken. The thirteenth century saw a complete trans-lation of the Bible into French which appears in three interrelated versions (it was from the earliest of these that the interpolations in the Bodmer Arthurian text were copied), and Guiart de Moulins also translated Peter Comestor's bible-based *Historia scholastica*.[58] It is not quite clear what sort of reader these biblical translations initially had in mind: lay folk who had associated themselves with the mendicant orders and had taken vows as Tertiaries of the Dominican and perhaps also the Franciscan order have been suggested.[59] In the fourteenth century it becomes easier to find out about those who owned copies of vernacular bibles, and there was then a fair sprinkling of the lesser nobility among them – of the chivalrous, that is to say, including captains known to us for their achievements in the Anglo-French wars, like the English knight Sir Matthew Gournay.[60] Earlier some at least of those who had shown interest in these translations also belonged to the chivalrous world, rather than to that of the pious of the cities, among whom association with the mendicant orders was most popu-lar. The magnificent Acre bible[61] seems to have been commissioned by St Louis, King and Crusader. There were, moreover, a number of translations of individual books of the Bible in circulation earlier still, in the late twelfth and early thirteenth centuries, and among the earliest books translated were those, significantly, of the Judges, the Kings, and the Maccabees. One twelfth-century translation of the book of Judges was, we know, prepared for the Knights Templar, and its introduction states specifically that through it man may learn of the 'chivalry' of the time of the Judges, and see thereby 'what honour it is thus to serve God and how He rewards his own'.[62] Clearly the rendering of the Scriptures into the vernacular was considered to be relevant – among other things – to the instruction of chivalry, and from the start. Indeed, the Old Testament stories had a particular and specific relevance to this end, especially in a crusading context. It is no accident that the Lady of the Lake, when talking of the enemies of Israel, takes care to describe them as *mescreans* – unbelievers – the same word that was used over and again to describe the Saracen infidel in vernacular texts. The stories of the conquest of the Holy Land by Joshua, and of its defence by David and Judas Maccabaeus were a clear foreshadowing, to the knightly mind of the twelfth and thirteenth centuries, of the contemporary crusade, and helped to define crusading as the highest expression of chivalrous activity.

Joshua, David and Judas Maccabaeus are a significant trio. The triad that the *Chanson des Saisnes* presents – the matter of France, the matter of Britain, and the matter of Rome the Great – is neat: neater still is the series of three matching triads which make up the tally of nine supreme heroes, to which Jean de Longuyon introduces us in his *Voeux du Paon*[63] (a new interpolation into his early fourteenth-century version of the *Romance of Alexander*). There are three champions of chivalry of the Old Law, he says, Joshua, David and Judas; three champions of the pagan law, Hector, Alexander and Julius Caesar; and three champions of the new Christian Law, Arthur, Charlemagne and Godfrey de Bouillon. This is the first appearance in chivalrous literature of the Nine Worthies (or the *Neuf Preux*), alongside whom, in due course, were to be ranged Nine Heroines (but the symmetry is not perfect; in most versions of the list they are all antique, and do not represent, as the male champions do, the three different Laws).[64] This conception was a very powerful one. Its symmetry, at once striking and symbolic, lent itself directly to iconographic representation, in painting, sculpture and illumination. There are two exquisite portrayals of the Heroes and the Heroines in the illuminated manuscript of Thomas of Saluzzo's *Chevalier errant*, and the Marquis had them painted by Jean de Yvaine on the walls of his castle at Saluzzo. We meet them again in the painted chambers of the castle of Runkelstein; in the stained glass windows of the town hall of Luneburg; in a famous tapestry commissioned by Jean de Berry; and again and again in accounts of the ephemeral pageantry of great chivalrous occasions. Verses hailing the Worthies were composed, and books recording the history of their high deeds put together. Their associated reputations established rapidly their right to occupy the first circle of what we have called the chivalrous pantheon.

There was nothing haphazard about Jean de Longuyon's triads: indeed his conception was in no sense really new. Earlier texts often throw a selection of his heroes together as examples of chivalry, and Philip Mouskés, in his mid thirteenth-century rhyming chronicle, anticipated the idea by representing the three laws with three heroes – his choices were Hector, Judas, and Ogier, the heroic Dane of Carolinigan legend.[65] Jean

simply introduced a new tidiness and symmetry. But this in itself was very
impressive. His triads symbolise beautifully the three principal 'chapters' in
chivalrous history, and clarify thereby its place in the broad framework of
Christian providential world-history, as that was interpreted in Jean's time.
The three Jewish heroes remind us that the Old Testament is the story of
God's chosen nation, which was the spiritual vessel of His purpose for
mankind, and through whose service of the one true God the way was made
ready for the coming of Christ. Christ's mission, though, was not to the Jews
only, and the pagans had a part too in preparing the way for the New Law.
Christ came as the Prince of Peace at that point in time when the Romans
had conquered the world and established their peace in it (are we not told in
the Gospel that the edict went out from Caesar Augustus that *all the world*
should be enrolled?) It was the Roman peace, built on the achievement of
pagan chivalry – Trojan, Greek, and Roman – that made possible the
journeys of the apostles, their evangelisation of the gentiles, and the establishment of the Christian Church. This is the strand in chivalrous history
that Hector, Alexander and Caesar remind us about, and its story does not
stop short with the last of them. It was Vespasian and his Roman knights
who took vengeance for Christ's death, and with the conversion of Constantine the Roman Empire and Christendom became co-terminous. Christian
chivalry is thus the fruit of the marriage of the two older traditions, the
pagan knighthood that God ordained to rule the world and to uphold peace
in it, and the biblical knighthood that He ordained to guard the holy places
and defend the religion of His chosen people. The three Christian heroes
represent the armed force of His new chosen people, the Christian nation,
whose mission derives from the earlier traditions; it being to uphold His
Peace, to spread His Law, and to guard His Holy Places. They take their
place as the three leading cult figures of Christian chivalry, the order whose
terrestrial function mirrors more sharply and precisely than either of the
earlier traditions the perennial and universal struggle of God and His
angels against the forces of darkness, of turbulence and of sacrilege.

The juxtaposition of the three biblical champions and the three classical
heroes with the principal figures of the 'matters' of France and of Britain
thus brings chivalry's role and pedigree into perspective in world history as
that was understood at the time. But there is a third figure in the last triad
alongside Charlemagne and Arthur, and a word needs to be said of him
too: Godfrey de Bouillon the conqueror of Jerusalem. Something has been
said in an earlier chapter of the way in which his legend developed, and of
how it bound together the historical events of the first crusade and its
remarkable victories with a tale of faery and of courtly love, whose marvellous events were interpreted as an indication of the divine mission of
Godfrey's lineage.[66] This was a story which in an obvious way paralleled that
other miraculous history, of the divine mission of the lineage of the

Grail keepers, to which Joseph of Arimathea, the Fisher King, Perceval and Galahad all belonged. In the framework of the universal mission of chivalry, which at every point could be assimilated to the ideal of the crusade, Godfrey had thus a clear right to his place alongside the other two Christian champions. His place in their company was important for another reason too. In terms of the early fourteenth century, when Jean de Longuyon was writing, Godfrey was by far the most recent recruit into the circle of the Nine Worthies. He, more effectively than any of the others, symbolised the fact that the story of chivalry's divine mission in the world was still in process, that that mission was an urgent and contemporary one, and that there was no reason why, with the nine, all the 'sieges' of the first circle of chivalrous honour should be regarded as occupied.

The cult of the Nine Worthies thus had a very direct message for the chivalrous world. It is here significant that the cyclic manuscripts of Godfrey's epic history, of the *Chevalier au Cygne*, do not all stop at the conquest of Jerusalem. In some an attempt has been made to carry the crusading story on to the middle of the thirteenth century. As far as the crusade to Jerusalem was concerned, the story had to stop there: the tale of the collapse of the crusader Kingdom could hardly produce any more Worthies. Other histories, on the other hand, could. In France the great constable Du Guesclin was hailed as the Tenth Worthy.[67] The Scots claimed the same honour for Robert the Bruce.[68] The author of the *Chemin de vaillance* threw into the company of the Nine not only a series of other ancient heroes (Hercules, Achilles, Jason, Scipio) but also a little group of great contemporaries, including again Du Guesclin, and alongside him Louis de Sancerre and Hugh Calverley of England.[69] For Joan of Arc it was claimed by her admirers that she had a right to be compared with the nine antique heroines.[70] The Nine Worthies symbolised the significance of a story that was emphatically unconcluded, reminding men at once of the example of the past and that the history of chivalry was still a-making.

Each group of figures and each figure of the nine had something particular to teach, and a particular relevance. Thus Hector, for instance, was the foremost warrior of the Trojan line from whom the Frankish warriors claimed ultimate descent, and Alexander was the special exemplar of *largesse*. Charlemagne was the champion whose history revealed the role of the Franks as God's new chosen host, which role was fulfilled in the achievement of Godfrey. The total effect of the cult of the Nine was to exemplify, in a very striking way, the coherence of the historical mythology of chivalry, and to exemplify at the same time the importance of what Chrétien de Troyes had to say about chivalry and learning, how pre-eminence in them must go together. The figures of the Nine Worthies, caught in stone or tapestry or stained glass, could indeed flash a message, but, for a full understanding of all that message implied, an acquaintance was required with a vast ranging and interconnected literature, religious, courtly and historical: *clergie* (learning) was required, that is to say, as well as chivalry. Representations of the great knights of the past could be made recognisable by their depiction in familiar situations or by the blazonry of their shields and banners, but to get the full flavour of all that such representation exemplified implied a knowledge not just of their stories but of the values and shades of value that their stories expressed. Once again, *clergie* was necessary. Through the establishment of its own independent historical mythology, chivalry became in its own right not just a literary but also a learned culture. To sustain itself as such, it required not only the swords of knights but the pens of clerks too, of theoretical experts in chivalry. A knight, even if lettered, could not hope to compass a full knowledge of the foundation and function of his order: he needed professional interpreters. Thus the way was made ready for the rise of a class of men who were technical experts in chivalry, a priesthood of its secular cult. We shall see in the next chapter how the heralds came, in part at least, to discharge just that role. We shall see also something of how the richness and range of the erudition with which they had to work helped to make chivalry, in its outward forms, its rituals and ceremonies, progressively more ornate and elaborate – an elaboration reflecting the complexity and sophistication of the literary heritage that it had built up already, before the heralds came into their own.

CHAPTER VII

Heraldry and Heralds

The beginnings of heraldry and the early history of the heralds are initially distinct subjects. Heraldry, which we may define as the systematic use of hereditary insignia on the shield of a knight or nobleman, was beginning to follow established rules by the end of the twelfth century. But although there are a few scattered references to heralds of arms in twelfth-century texts, it is not at that stage by any means clear that heraldry in this sense was as yet a principal concern of theirs. Their position and functions remain hard to pin down until the end of the thirteenth century, and we do not really get a clear picture of them until the fourteenth. Then, however, heraldry did come to be a first concern of theirs. For this reason a consideration of the origin and purposes of heraldry is a necessary prelude to the examination of the significance of the activities of the heralds in the history of chivalry.

Military forces have, from the earliest times, used insignia of one sort or another for purposes of recognition in the field. Heraldry seems to have originated in response to a particular medieval need in this regard. When in the history of the development of medieval personal armour the point was reached where a mounted warrior was encased from head to foot in mail and wore a helmet over his mail coif which completely concealed his features, the problem of recognition, especially of individuals in a *mêlée*, became newly acute. From a chivalrous point of view, it was particularly acute in a particular kind of *mêlée*, that of the tournament, at which it was specially important to know who it was that one had unhorsed and might hope to take prisoner – and at which a special significance was attached to the individual performance in the field of particular knights, whom judges and spectators must therefore be able to recognise. Hence paintings on shields which in the past had served merely decorative purpose came to serve as marks of recognition. Chrétien de Troyes provides a vivid picture of the knights who were not engaged in the great tournament between Noauz and Pomelegloi pointing out the combatants for the Queen and her ladies:

'Do you see that knight yonder with a golden band across his red shield? That is Governauz of Roberdic. And do you see that other one, who has an eagle and a dragon painted side by side on his shield? That is the son of the King of Aragon, who has come to this land in search of glory and renown. And do you see that other one beside him, who thrusts and jousts so well, bearing a shield with a leopard painted on a green ground on one part, on the other azure blue? That is Ignaures the well-beloved, a lover himself and jovial. And he who bears the shield with the pheasants portrayed beak to beak is Coguillanz de Mautirec.'[1]

As this eloquent passage testifies, the needs of the tournament, very particularly, fostered the use of known individual devices as marks of recognition.

At first depicted on the shield, heraldic devices came soon to be displayed also on the surcoats of knights and on their horses' trappings, as also on their seals, and on their tombs and effigies. They also came to be accepted as more than just individual marks of recognition. In true heraldry, devices painted on shields are not merely individual marks of recognition, they are hereditary to particular families; and there are besides certain well defined rules about their presentation on the shield. So, although the shields of the Norman warriors in the Bayeux tapestry are decorated with geometric and animal designs, these cannot properly speaking be called heraldic, since there is no reason to believe that they represent hereditary insignia.[2] Early twelfth-century evidence suggests that shields were at that time often already decorated when they were acquired by the future user. John of Marmoutier's description of the knighting of Geoffrey the Fair seems therefore to show that by 1128 matters were beginning to be a little less haphazard, and so marks an important step forward. A blue shield, painted with golden lioncels, was hung about Geoffrey's neck, we are told.[3] On the enamel plate which was placed on Geoffrey's tomb in 1152 we find those same lioncels – six of them on a blue shield. His son William bore a single lion, and his bastard grandson William of Salisbury bore the same device as Geoffrey, six lioncels on a blue shield. The lion thus seems to be becoming a recognisable Angevin family emblem, something like a device heraldically employed in the true sense.

The use of armorial devices upon seals in this same period, the mid twelfth century, illustrates still more clearly the same tendency, towards the hereditary employment of particular devices. The checky arms of Meulan appear on a seal of Count Waleran of Meulan which is datable to $c.1136$; they appear also on two seals of his maternal uncle, Ralph of Vermandois

(? *c.*1135 and 1146), and checky arms were borne by the descendants of both houses, of Vermandois and Meulan. Garbs (wheatsheafs) are depicted on a seal of Count Enguerand of Candavène (between 1141 and 1150); on the shield and trapper of the equestrian figure of Anselme de Candavène on his seal in 1162; and on the seal of Hugh of Candavène (1223) – five of them arranged in the form of a cross. The Guelf lion appears on the seal of Henry the Lion of Saxony in 1144, and on that of his kinsman Welf of Tuscany in 1152.[4] What we see at this stage in the twelfth century is only the beginning of a trend, it is true; many families then and later, in the thirteenth century, can be shown to have habitually used more than one device, or to have changed their arms at their own will (sometimes this was the mark of the inheritance of a new fee or of a new connection established by marriage, but often there seems to have been no more than whim behind it). Nevertheless, the trend has been set; from somewhere around 1140 on we are moving into a world of heraldic usage in the strict sense.

The earliest examples of the use of armorial bearings bring us into contact only with a limited sector of the nobility, with the great families whose wealth and wide possessions set them apart from the ordinary knighthood. Early references indeed suggest that there was a direct connection between the right to arms and the ancestral possessions of fiefs and castles, and that in battle only those endowed with a fief and leading a contingent bore individually distinctive arms.[5] The first rolls of arms (the French and English thirteenth-century rolls and the German *Clipearius Teutonicorum*) record the arms only of the greater noblemen and of knights, not of any nobility inferior to that rank.[6] A shift in practice becomes observable however in the course of the thirteenth century. The use of armorial seals by esquires and by men who though of knightly family had not themselves been dubbed, becomes much commoner. In Germany, at the end of the century, the great Manasseh codex, with its marvellous illustrations of the poets and *Minnesinger* in their blazoned surcoats and with their war crests on their helms shows many men armorially clad who, in terms of their wealth and fiefs, were of relatively humble knightly or ministerial rank.[7] The Zurich roll (*c.*1335) also blazons many ministerial coats;[8] and it is clear that by the time that it was produced, esquires in England and France were coming to be accepted as armigerous. The Manasseh codex, moreover, does more than just record the arms of the poets: it shows them at their favourite pastimes, arming for the tourney, receiving the prize of the contest, in the company of the mistresses of whose beauty they sang. Its illuminations are a record not just of the arms of individuals, but also of the culture and aspirations of the noble society in which they moved.

Behind this chronological development we can see a reflection of that process observed earlier which, from the later twelfth century onward, was drawing together those at the poles of aristocratic society, the great nobility and the simple knighthood, and was forging bonds between them founded upon ideals of patronage on the one hand and of loyal service on the other. Armoury indeed on occasion offers symbolic evidence of the closeness of these bonds and their nature. Thus in Germany we find again and again that the arms of ministerial families are derived from those of the lordship to whose ministeriality their bearers' families originally belonged. The episcopal arms of Strasbourg, for instance, were *gules a bend argent*: the von Blumenau, the Reimboldelin and the Rumelnheim, all *ministeriales* of the bishopric, bore the same arms with respectively the additions (to distinguish these family arms from those of the bishopric) of a tourneying collar *azur*, a *lilienhaspel or*, and a tourneying collar *or*.[9] Similarly in England we find a series of Kentish families, all tenants of the family of Kyriell of Kent, bearing arms which are all variant derivatives of the arms of Kyriell; and the case is much the same with some of the tenants of the honour of Clare.[10] Significantly, the point in time – a little after 1200 – when we begin to find evidence that lesser knightly families were establishing their armorial right is also the point at which we find them beginning to adopt the title of *messire*, and to imitate, on a miniature scale and with decorative intent, the architecture of the castle in the design of their manor houses.[11] This is of course also much the same point in time at which the literary culture of chivalry, focussing around the courts of the greater nobles whose glamour brought high and low in the secular martial society together, was beginning to take a definitive shape.

Heraldry, in other words, from being originally the preserve of the greater aristocracy, came in time to be emblematic of the pride of birth, station and culture of the nobility in its broadest range. Indeed, as in the later middle ages the ranks of the nobility were extended to embrace others besides knights – esquires, mere gentlemen, men at arms, the German *Rittermassigkeit* and even the urban patriciates – the title to bear arms came ultimately to displace the taking of knighthood as the key to admission into the charmed circle of the chivalrous. Wherever romances of knighthood and of courtly love were read or recited, wherever crowds gathered to witness jousts and tournaments, wherever families looked back over their record of honourable achievement and association, heraldry was in consequence a significant science. This encouraged its practitioners to infuse all sorts of symbolic meaning into its colours and devices and to read back its history into the chivalrous past as they knew it, and so to make of it the erudite branch of secular learning that, in the late medieval heyday of the heralds, it was ultimately to become.

Heraldry was capable of developing into a branch of erudition because its art of 'blazon' became systematic early. If one distinguishing feature of heraldry in the true sense was the heritability of coats of arms, the other was the way in which the arrangement and description of heraldic devices on a shield came to be regulated by well defined rules (which in heraldic doctrine still hold). Thus the 'tinctures' used in heraldry came to be limited to the five colours: *azur* (blue), *gules* (red), *vert* (green), *sable* (black), and *purpur* (purple); to the two metals, *or* (gold) and *argent* (silver); and to the two furs, *ermine* and *vair*. The French of these technical terms is yet another sign of the predominant influence of French fashion, in the early age of chivalry. There were soon more rules, too: as that which declares that colour must not be laid upon colour, nor metal upon metal. The ordinaries – the geometric patterns depicted on the shield, such as *chief, fess, chevron, bend* and *bar* – came to be defined and limited in number; so also did the birds and beasts that were accepted as properly heraldic, and the objects commonly used in heraldry, as *garbs* (wheatsheafs), or the *manche* (the lady's sleeve, with its overtones of the world of courtly love). Not only these 'charges' but also the manner of describing them (blazoning) became in time regular: the colour of the field must be mentioned first, then the principal charge, then any additional charges, and finally differences, such as marks of cadency (for example the label of three points which is the mark in arms of the eldest heir of the family). Thus one would for instance 'blazon' Geoffrey the Fair's shield thus, *azur, six lioncels or*. These rules of blazon appear quite early. They are already carefully followed in the earliest English roll of arms, Glover's Roll (? 1255), and in the French Bigot Roll (? 1254).[12] Their regulations are explained in detail in the earliest surviving treatise on heraldry, the anonymous *De Heraudie* which may have been written as early as the end of the thirteenth century.[13] This tract presents the heraldic language of blazon fully developed; but we can see signs of its beginnings much earlier. Already around 1160 Benoit de Ste Maure in his *Roman de Troye* was confining himself to the heraldic colours and charges of the future in his descriptions of the shields of the heroes of the Trojan war; thus Troilus bears *lioncels azur* on a shield *or*, and Cicilianor his bastard brother bears *d'or bende azur*. And on the Greek side, significantly, we meet Pyrrhus in arms that are said to be like those of his father Achilles.[14] It would thus seem that rules of blazon began to develop not much after the time that arms began to be regarded as hereditary. The two developments together were what made heraldry scientific, capable of the sort of learned exposition that we encounter in *De Heraudie*.

One might have expected that the right to assume arms would also have been one of the matters to become early a subject of authoritative regulation, but this was not so. In general, the right to arms seems throughout the middle ages to have been regarded as analogous to the laws of tenure which governed the descent of fiefs, but clear rules only developed late. The *Boke of St Albans* (1486) mentions four grounds on which a man may claim title to arms: because he has inherited them; or on account of the tenure of a

particular fee or office; or on the ground that he has been granted them by
some lord or prince; or, finally, because he has captured them from an
enemy in battle.[15] Of the fourth category there seem to be very few
medieval examples, and all late – the earliest that I know is the fifteenth-
century claim for the Black Prince that he was entitled to bear the arms of
France because he had captured King John of France in battle at Poitiers.[16]
What seems to be the earliest princely grant is also later than might have
been expected, being a grant made by the Emperor Lewis of Bavaria in
1338; such grants however began to be common before the end of the
fourteenth century.[17] Yet even as late as the fifteenth century it is clear that
many assumed arms of their own will, without the permission of any
superior authority, and that this was not necessarily frowned on: 'In these
days,' wrote the English legist Nicholas Upton, 'we see openly how many
poor men through their service in the French wars have become noble . . .
and many of these have upon their own authority taken arms to be borne by
themselves and their heirs.'[18]

Upton was here following the doctrine of the great Italian lawyer Bartolus, which he saw no reason to query. In a famous treatise, his *De insigniis
et armis*, Bartolus had written (*c.*1350) that men were as free to take arms to
distinguish themselves and their families as they were to take names (with
the proviso that the title of a man who has his arms by the grant of a prince
should always be preferred to that of one who has assumed them on his own
authority, even if the latter can show longer use).[19] The very early appearance in heraldry of canting arms – in which the charge upon the shield
makes play with the family name of the bearer – confirms the sureness of
Bartolus's insight in comparing the right to arms and the right to a name.
Thus the luce appears on the twelfth-century seal of Richard de Lucy
(between 1135 and 1154) and the butler's cups on the shield of Sir John le
Botiler in the thirteenth century.[20] Early German heraldry is full of canting
arms: thus in the Zurich Roll (*c.*1335) we find that Helmshoven bears a
helm *or* on a field *gules*, that Affenstein's *argent* shield is charged with an ape
(affe) gules breaking a stone *(stein)*, and that Ot a den Rand bears on his *sable*
shield a turnip *(Rande)*, a rare, perhaps unique use of this unglamorous
vegetable as a heraldic charge.[21] Devices such as these were clearly chosen
by the families that bore them because they fitted the name that was the
symbol of the unity of their house.

Canting arms make play with a name; but the charge on a shield could
carry more recondite, symbolic meaning, and here we see erudition beginning to find its way into heraldry, as it found its way also into so many other
aspects of knightly custom and observance. Both wit and learning could be
applied to fit a coat and its charges to their bearer. Thus Upton reveals the
secret behind the three partridges which the Earl of Salisbury gave to 'a
certain gentleman' (he is discreet about the name) after he had been

ennobled for valour in the field. Salisbury or his adviser (almost certainly Upton himself) had culled from the Bestiary the story that the partridge was a bird of aberrant and abhorrent sexual habits, the male being known to mount the male, whence 'to bear partridges in arms betokens the first bearer to be a great liar or a sodomite'.[22] The colours as well as the charges on a shield could also bear symbolic or allegorical meaning. In the fifteenth century, learned heralds explained a schematic relationship between the colours of heraldry and the chivalric virtues: thus *or* denotes *noblesse*; *gules*, *prouesse*; *azur*, *loyaulté*; and *purpur*, *largesse*.[23] This system, with its parallel relation of the colours to precious stones, planets, and the days of the week, is a late development. But there were those who were already feeling their way towards it as early as the thirteenth century, as we can see from Huon de Méry's descriptions of arms in his allegorical *Tournoi d'Antechrist* (*c.*1230), where we meet for instance Ywain bearing a shield 'party of love and of *franchise*, a lioncel of *prouesse* with open hands of *largesse*'.[24] The instinct to make of arms more than a mere mark of recognition, to make them convey messages of pride in loyal service, martial achievement and family connection, and to exemplify special virtues, was at work from the beginning.

Arms could also be made to recall a story, or a part of one. Thus the breach of the rules of blazon in the arms of the Kings of Jerusalem, which charged metal upon metal (laying a cross *potenté* and four crosslets *or* on a field *argent*) was supposed in later times to be deliberate: these arms were given to Godfrey de Bouillon by his companions when he was chosen to be the first King of Jerusalem, it was alleged, so that if anyone afterwards should inquire the reason for the incorrect blazoning, they could be reminded of the great triumph of Christian chivalry in the conquest of the Holy City in 1099[25] (there were, of course, no clear rules of blazon in 1099 and the whole story is a later invention). The chains in the arms of a group of Navarrese families – the Zunigas, the Muños, the Arricavales – were similarly supposed to commemorate the part that their ancestors had played in the great victory of Sancho the Strong over the Muslims at Las Navas de Tolosa, where the Navarrese were the first to break through the chains surrounding the enemy camp.[26] The family of Coucy, who long remembered with pride the part that their ancestor Thomas of Marle had played on the first crusade, told the story that their arms of *vair* and *gules* commemorated the red furred cloak which on that expedition the 'Ber de Marle' had cut in pieces and given to his companions for a device when they were surprised by the Turk without their surcoats of arms.[27] Jacques de Hemricourt's book, *Le Miroir des nobles de Hesbaye* is a great repertory of stories rather like these, and probably for the most part less apocryphal (concerning as they do lesser families whose history was not so easily glamourised into myth): of how for instance Wary de Rochefort took new arms after he had received knighthood at the Holy Sepulchure, or of how the family of Heys de Flemalle and its descendants acquired their party shield when the Count of Loos gave one Macair for good service his own arms to part with those he had inherited.[28] We can see here how the marshalling of heraldry upon a tomb, or a monumental brass, or in an armorial book could come to record, for one sufficiently versed, not merely the identity of an individual and his descent in blood, but a whole associated history of ancestral chivalrous achievement.

Two points need to be emphasised in order that we may appreciate to the full the heroic flavour and chivalrous significance of heraldry in its medieval heyday. As this brief exploration of its development has made apparent, it very rapidly came to be much more than a systematic aid to the recognition of combatants in the field. It was infused early with powerful overtones of pride of lineage and esteem for martial achievement. Recognition in the field had in itself implications beyond the merely practical level, with giving courage its due meed. That is why Jacques de Hemricourt lamented the passing of the good old days when men wore full surcoats of arms and bore their shields in battle, for then 'none dared be a coward, for one could tell the good men from the bad by their blazons'.[29] 'On the day of battle', wrote Diego de Valera, 'every noble knight and esquire should wear his coat of arms . . . and the purpose of this is that those who are noble should be known among the common soldiery, and that they should be reminded that it is their duty not to bring disgrace upon themselves and their ancestors.'[30] The coat of arms, the honour, and the lineage of the noble family were all intimately associated with one another. 'Sir,' said the Countess of Norfolk to Sir Hugh Hastings, when, during one of the lulls that Richard II's reign witnessed in the Anglo-French war, he was preparing to leave England for the East, 'I thank you entirely from my heart for the honour that you have done to the arms of Hastings in the past, and now, as you are about to pass the sea into strange lands I pray that you will continue the honour that you have done to the said arms.'[31] Emphatically, the language of heraldry was the language of honour not just in its genealogical, but in its ethical sense too.

Even in the context of the use of arms on seals which were employed to authenticate legal documents, the practical purposes of heraldry cannot be entirely divorced from ethical and honourable associations. The seal set upon a document was a sign not only of authenticity, but also of honour and faith pledged. 'In the days when true chivalry flourished,' says the *Enseignement de la vraye noblesse* (following the late medieval convention of always looking back to the past for the model of noble practice),

> those who by victory, virtue and renown had conquered and proved their title to arms and insignia, they and their successors, when they wished to

promise things of great import and to vouch for their troth, swore by their faith in God, and in witness thereto set an imprint in wax of their arms after their name: and this is what nowadays we call a seal. The which faith, name, arms and seal they would keep and guard of their free will, fearing the breach of them as the perdition of soul, body and goods, for by that breach on the one hand their faith in God would stand perjured, and the other the arms would stand in reproach for false witness.[32]

The ideas underlying this statement are the same as those which underlie that rule of honour that insists that once a knight or esquire has donned his coat of arms in the hour and place of battle, 'in that noble and perilous day he cannot be disarmed without great reproach to his honour save in three cases; for victory, for being taken prisoner, or for death.'[33] In the case of the tournament (with which the origins of heraldry were so closely associated), the practical ends of military exercise and the end of celebrating the chivalrous values and virtues became in course of time indistinguishable; and in the same way in heraldry the practical ends of recognition and authentication and the chivalrous ideology of martial honour and virtue came to be inseparably interwoven with one another.

This brings us to the second point. The significance of heraldry in the medieval past is often underrated by modern historians, and one principle reason for this is that we nowadays live with a literary culture which is far less dependent on the visual than was that of the middle ages. A simple knight or his lady in the fourteenth or fifteenth century might very well be able to read 'romances of battles' and histories, and might have often heard them read or recited. But to judge by such records as wills, it was very unlikely that such a knight would have a well-stocked library. In these circumstances the sign language of heraldry had very significant potential in a role at once social, cultural, and historical. 'I can remember a time', says Anthoine de la Sale, 'when a man took leave of his lady and she might say "Commend me to the Lord (or knight or esquire) who bears or, or it may be argent, with such and such charges . . . or to my sister or my cousin or my friend whose blazon is thus and thus." And in the good old days,' he goes on, the halls and chambers of noblemen 'were painted, or decked with tapestries, depicting the battles and conquests of past heroes, and with the blazons of the kingdom's nobles, as a reminder to all of the lessons of good conduct.'[34] This is not wishful thinking about the bon temps passé. We shall soon be hearing more about how in the fourteenth century 'a certain lady' bid Gelre Herald to find the arms of those knights of her time who were 'truly without reproach' so that she might decorate her chamber with their blazons. The artist who in the early fifteenth century painted the walls of the castle of Runkelstein took care to depict Percival in the arms that Wolfram von Eschenbach had given him, and Tristan in those described by Gottfried of

Strasbourg,[35] so that the scenes and the stories could be instantly recognised and recalled. As these references indicate heraldry had become a science capable not only of recording genealogical information, but also of identifying visibly the scenes and the heroes of chivalrous history, of passing on information with cultural, ethical and ideological overtones.

It is against this background that we must set the story told by Sir Robert Laton in 1386, when he was a witness in the great armorial dispute over the right to the arms *azur a bend or*, between Sir Richard Le Scrope and Sir Robert Grosvenor. In his youth, Laton declared, his father, who had laboured long at wars and tournaments, had made him write down in a schedule all the arms of princes, dukes, earls, barons and knights that the elder Laton could remember, and then learn them by heart.[36] This was, in that time, by no means useless or esoteric knowledge. Heraldry had become one of the prime keys to a secular chivalrous erudition that was at once literate and visual, practical and ideological.

★

When the chronicler Froissart in 1394 wanted to know what arms were borne by Henry Cristed (whom he had found courteous and gracious and from whom he had learnt much concerning Richard II's visit to Ireland) he referred to March the Herald. '*Argent*, a chevron gules with three besants gules, two above the chevron and one below,' came the prompt answer to his query.[37] By this time – by the late fourteenth century – the heralds had achieved an established position and were dignified figures in the chivalrous world. They were the acknowledged experts in armoury and in all matters of secular ceremony: in the display of jousts and tournaments, in the judgement of prowess, in the panoply of coronations, knightings and funerals. They also had important functions in the field in wartime. It was their business to record promotions to knighthood on the eve of battle, to search after it among the dead and to note the names and arms of those who had shown prowess in the field.[38] Most important of all, perhaps, in practical terms, they had achieved recognised immunity from hostile action, and therefore acted in war as messengers between belligerents. If a personal defiance was to be delivered, if a city was to be summoned to surrender, if a truce was sought or if safe-conducts were required to enable negotiators to meet and discuss terms (of truce, peace, or surrender), a herald would be dispatched to carry the message or request. By the fifteenth century the great heralds, the Kings of Arms who were the leaders of their profession, had in consequence come to play a quite significant role in princely diplomacy.

This dignity of the heralds in the later middle ages had developed from small beginnings. Their position and functions in earlier days are obscure.

The earliest reference to a herald *eo nomine* that I know of is in Wace and describes him acting as a messenger in war: in a capacity, that is to say, that was to become a traditional one for heralds – but it is an isolated reference. One modern theory is that in their original role they were relatively humble officials attached to hosts in a minor staff capacity, and the picture of the heralds going round waking the warriors on the day of the battle of Las Navas de Tolosa (1212) fits well with this.[39] The rolls which late thirteenth-century heralds compiled of the bannerets and knights present in particular hosts (the French Flanders roll of 1297, for instance, and the English Falkirk roll of 1298) suggest a particular role in mustering, and as Dennys points out, the ability to identify the enemy's leaders by their coats and banners would have been a very useful expertise in any army of the time.[40] But when Simon de Montfort saw the royal host approaching at Evesham in 1265 it was not a herald but his barber Simon, 'a man expert in arms', who identified for him the enemy banners.[41] As regards musters, moreover, though the rolls make it clear that heralds did make records of those present, their precise purpose in doing so is not absolutely clear. As far as I know, there is no occasion in which it can be shown that knights were either summoned to serve in a host or paid for their service on the basis of a herald's record. Their role here seems, therefore, to be concerned rather with the establishing of precedence among the nobles at the muster, and with celebrating the martial dignity and renown of the occasion – ceremonious, in other words, rather than practical.

This seems to confirm that, whatever the precise origins of their office were, Sir Anthony Wagner is quite right to associate the heralds' rise to prominence in particular with the part that they played in the staging and ceremony of tournaments.[42] It is in this context that they appear in the great majority of early references to them. Thus in Chrétien's *Lancelot* we hear of a herald who, on the eve of a great tournament, discovers the hero in disguise, resting in a poor lodging. The herald, who has pawned his shoes and coat in a tavern, is puzzled by the shield outside the door of the lodging, which is not familiar; entering and recognising Lancelot, he then rushes out crying 'Now there has come one who will take the measure.'[43] The witness of the *Histoire de Guillaume le Maréchal* is similar: William's detractors, we are told, put about the story that his reputation had been greatly inflated by the noisy herald Henry le Norreis, who at every tourney followed him with a cry of 'God aid the Marshal!'[44] In the partly historical romance of *Fulk Fitzwarin* the heralds and *disours* are said to be the judges of the tournament (and Fulk's arms *argent and gules indented*, are said to have been 'devised' for him by the *disours*).[45] Bretel's poem on the late thirteenth-century tournament at Chauvency is of course, as we have seen, full of the heralds, who recognise the combatants by their arms, call out their names as they enter the lists to joust, and follow them in the tournament crying out the names of the valiant. Other evidence confirms the impression that the principal original role of heralds was at the tourneying field. If a number of early rolls of arms record musters, as many or more record the arms of men who gathered for particular tournaments. There is a significant correspondence also between the 'marches of arms', the localities in which the later Kings of Arms (usually the chief herald of a particular lord) exercised authority in armorial matters, and the marches which identified the allegiance of knights attending early tournaments. It is particularly striking in the case of the King of Arms of the Ruyers, the area of the Imperial Low Countries and the Rhineland whose knights usually fought together in early tournaments but in which no single lord had general territorial authority.[46] It seems virtually certain, therefore, that the secret of the rise of the heralds lay in the part that they customarily played at tournaments, though their employment as messengers in war may also have had something to do with it, and their expertise in blazon was clearly something that could be useful in all sorts of martial situations.

Tournaments brought together great assemblies of people, over and above the participants and their aristocratic companions, male and female: grooms, armourers, minstrels, jongleurs – and heralds. Indeed it is one of the complaints of the author of the tournament-romance of *Hem* that the recent embargoes on tournaments have created a serious problem of lack of employment for these hangers-on.[47] The earliest heralds are not distinguishable by dignity or even entirely by function from this riff-raff that made a living out of the perilous favourite sport of the nobility. They do not seem, in twelfth- or early thirteenth-century texts, to be attached to the service of any particular lord, but rather to be travelling from tourney to tourney in a given area in quest of *largesse* and perhaps some shaky measure of patronage. To judge from Chrétien's herald who had pawned his clothes for a drink, their life must have been pretty insecure, probably not much different from that of the lesser minstrels. They are indeed often associated with minstrels. Baudouin de Condé (*c.* 1280) complains that there are now so many overdressed heralds going about that it is difficult to find a true minstrel.[48] When we first begin to find traces of the heralds in official records, moreover, they are bracketed with minstrels: the household clerks of Edward I lumped the two together under the general heading of *Menestralli* in their account of payments made to them, and as late as 1338 we find a record of a payment to Master Conrod, King of the Heralds of Germany, and ten 'other minstrels' for making minstrelsy before King Edward III at Christmas.[49]

These entries in the records do, however, make it clear that by the end of the thirteenth century the heralds were beginning to achieve a more settled and secure position. They have now come to be more or less regularly paid, they wear the coats of arms of their masters, and they have begun to have official duties assigned to them (in for instance Edward I's *Statutum* armorum and in the ordinance for the duel of Philip IV of France).[50] It is about this same time, too, that the vocabulary of heraldic terms of art seems to have achieved firm definition, witness the early rolls of arms and the tract *De Heraudie* (whose author states specifically that he has obtained his information from heralds).[51] It is also the point at which a *cursus honorum* in the herald's profession becomes established, from pursuivant (apprentice) to herald and ultimately to King of Arms.

From this time onwards definition proceeds apace, and with it the outward and visible evidence of increased dignity. Anjou King of Arms – *le bon Calabre* as his French herald colleagues called him – told in 1408 how he could recall the coronation of 'Charlot' as King of Arms of France by King Charles V (ob: 1380), a noble and great occasion – and he added that he had heard that the King of England made even more of the crowning of his chief herald.[52] He described too rituals for the creation of pursuivants and heralds, who should be dressed in their lord's arms for the occasion, should take a solemn oath to conduct themselves loyally in their office, and who then would be 'baptised' with their new heraldic title (Bon Repos pursuivant, say, or Ougreffont herald), the pursuivant with water and the herald with wine from a gilt cup.[53] The form of the French herald's oath, as *le bon Calabre* records it, was already set in a form which it retained, substantially without change, into the seventeenth century (and is also very similar to the form of the oath that English heralds swore in the late middle ages).[54] In Calabre's time heralds had already established numerous important privileges: the right to fees and *largesse* upon various ceremonial occasions, and to broken armour at tournaments; and their coats gave them general safe conduct as messengers in war. He looks back proudly to the (mythical) foundation of the heralds' order in classical times, and reminds his French brethren of the honour in which it was held in antiquity. The herald's office as he describes it is thus quite clearly a dignified one, with a secure niche in princely or seigneurial employment. We have travelled a long way indeed from the days when Baudouin de Condé, in the late thirteenth century, recalled the old heralds roaming over hill and dale in ragged coats of arms to where tournaments might be held, suffering outdoors in heat and cold and glad of occasional *largesse*.[55]

From Calabre's letter to his French fellows, and still more clearly from the numerous fifteenth-century treatises on heraldry (among which the famous *Blason des couleurs* of Sicily Herald must take pride of place) we get a good impression of the wide range of the functions and interests of the late medieval heralds. The tournament field remains a principal interest, and here their duties have become much more professionalised: they keep careful score sheets of blows given and received; they inspect the arms and crests of all those proposing to take part; and verify from their records that all are of sufficient gentility in blood to enjoy the privilege of participating.

Their duties as messengers in war apart, development seems to be particularly significant in two areas. It is clear that from early times heralds were expected to be able to recognise coats of arms, but now a King of Arms in his march is expected to visit his province and record the insignia of all its noblemen, their names, blazons, crests, and cries of arms, and to note which families are the most ancient and what their armorial connections by marriage are. The great French armorials of Navarre Herald, compiled in the fourteenth century, and of Berry in the fifteenth are in consequence virtually *états de noblesse* (though it is not, I think, clear that they were ever used as such).[56] The requirement to conduct visitations and to record family connections illustrates the way in which the genealogical expertise of the heralds had become, in the late middle ages, much more professionalised. The other direction in which their duties can be seen to have developed strikingly is as the official registrars of deeds of prowess. 'Sir,' says Dame Prudence to the heralds in the *Débat des hérauts de France et d'Angleterre* (c. 1430) 'yours is a fair office, for by your report men judge of worldly honour . . . [as of deeds done] in arms, in assaults, battles, sieges and elsewhere, and in jousts and tournaments.'[57] This same duty of recording prowess is stressed by Calabre, Sicily Herald, and by countless other heraldic authors. Froissart makes it clear in the prologue to his chronicle that it was because of this heraldic duty to enregister and publish feats of arms and valour that he had made such extensive use of the reports of Kings of Arms and heralds in putting together his chronicle.[58] The heralds' old function, of crying out the names of the valiant at tournies, has here developed into something much more professional, and with a much wider compass, in real war as well as mock battle.

There are certain other areas in which the print of earlier times and the heralds' preoccupations in them show significantly in the late medieval period. Though heralds in the fourteenth and fifteenth centuries were created by particular lords and attached to their regular service, the oaths which they swore when they took office contained echoes of the days of wandering and of only informal patronage. Their order owed a wide and general obligation to all men of noble blood, 'to all the estates of gentillnesse that Cristen beth' as the English pursuivants' oath has it. Especially, as the oaths emphasise, heralds owe service and duty to all gentlewomen, and they should certify the names of the oppressors of widows and maidens.[59] It is a particular duty of heralds, Calabre adds, to bear the messages of honourable lovers and to keep their secrets.[60] The influence of the ethic of courtly love, which had its roots in the twelfth century and which came, as we have seen, to suffuse the whole martial ideology of chivalry with eroticism, is here apparent. We are frequently reminded, too, that the heralds of the late middle ages were still great wanderers as their forerunners had been. It is clear that their knowledge, acquired in their travels, of the honourable customs of foreign lands and of deeds of prowess done in distant places was highly prized. 'You are welcome, Carlisle,' said Edward III to his herald Carlisle when the latter returned in 1338 from journeyings that had taken him to Prussia, Spain, Barbary, and to the Holy Sepulchre: 'Now we shall hear news from beyond the seas and from the far-off lands where you have been, which we have a great desire to hear.'[61] The list of places that Carlisle is here said to have visited has strong overtones. They are the places where Christian knighthood was still, in the fourteenth century, at grips with the infidel and where, in consequence, the highest feats of prowess might have been expected to be achieved.

The heralds' role as the registrars of prowess has connections in another context with their earlier history. The notion that they were judges of martial honour generally began to develop early; we can catch a reflection of it already in the advice that the thirteenth-century poet Ralph de Houdenc gave to knights. It is not enough, he declares, to say 'I am a knight': one must know what the obligations of knighthood are. The men who will teach one about these, he says, are the heralds, the minstrels and the jongleurs, for they are the keepers of the secret touchstone (*marestank*) of honour.[62] The connection that Ralph, like so many of his contemporaries, makes here between the heralds and the minstrels is one that is very significant in the context of recording prowess. The English herald–minstrel's *Song of Caerlaverock* is a good illustration of its relevance. This little poem starts by blazoning in verse the arms of the leaders of the Scottish expedition of 1300, then goes on to describe the siege and assault of the castle of Caerlaverock, recording the names and arms of those who distinguished themselves by their courage. The author's conscious striving to present his matter in accordance with courtly and chivalrous traditions is clear: in his treatment, for instance, of the romantic secret love and marriage of Ralph de Monthemer and Joan of Acre ('for whom he suffered hardship so long'); in his evocation of the Arthurian past (never had Arthur such a present from Merlin as Anthony Bek brought with his company to King Edward); and of the crusading achievement of Roger Clifford's ancestor, the great Marshal.[63] Chandos Herald's poetic account of the Black Prince's expedition into Spain later in the fourteenth century and of his great deeds done there is a comparable effort by an English herald–minstrel.[64] Their early connection with the minstrels ensured that the heralds were literary men. Their later role as the general registrars of prowess, which called for celebration in fashionable literary mode, ensured that they remained so.

The literary efforts of these two English herald–minstrels pale into insignificance when they are set alongside those of the great German heralds of the late fourteenth century: Claes van Heynen, the famous Gelre Herald, and the Austrian Peter Suchenwirt. In Gelre we meet a herald who is a real master of the courtly literary conventions. 'A noble lady said to me, "Gelre, I have business for you. I am going to make a new chamber, and to decorate it with blazoned shields. You shall seek out the knights who are worthy that I should paint their arms in my chamber, those who are truly *sans reproche*".'[65] And so he tells how he went to seek the names of such knights: how he heard in a wood a lady lamenting the true knight of Lady Honour, Adam von Moppertingen: worms now eat the flesh of him who served so well in Prussia, and who fought for the King of England against the Scot like a very Roland. He heard too of the deeds and fame of Count Henry of Virnebourg, that great jouster, and of the Duke of Juliers who was seven times armed against the pagan in Prussia and conquered Guelders.[66] This collection of *Lobdichte* (poems of praise) associated with the lady's chamber is by no means the whole of Gelre's literary achievement: we have from him also, for instance, the lament for the men of price who fell at Staveren in 1346 (seven knights, the best men you could have: may others follow their example), and a series of brief poetic biographies of such contemporary heroes as the noble Rutger Raets and Dietrich of Elnaer.[67] Suchenwirt's work is, in a literary way, still more polished and impressive, including likewise a number of laments for heroes of the time (rounded off in each case with the poetic blazon of their arms), and a splendid verse account of Duke Albert of Austria's crusade to Prussia in 1377. In his dialogues for example Suchenwirt shows himself besides a master of the didactic art of personified allegory.[68] Here is a herald who is also, in his own manner, a professional literary figure of real standing.

The herald Gelre is less often remembered for his poems than he is for his *Wappenboek*, the great *Armorial de Gelre* which is with little doubt the finest of all the armorial books of the middle ages. With its marvellous paintings of the arms and war crests of knights from all over Europe it is a true work of art; it is also the product of a long labour of research, for Gelre had clearly been in contact with fellow heralds in nearly every European kingdom in order to bring together an authoritative illustrated record of the knighthood of his day.[69] In fact, the world of his poetry, steeped in literary convention, and that of his professional expertise as displayed in this splendid armorial book are not far apart. The literature and mythology of chivalry, which, as we saw in the last chapter, were what gave its history and values a coherent basis, were very much the concern of heralds. The legendary record of antique prowess provided the standard alongside which the record of their contemporary world must be set, and a true herald knew that in consequence it was his business to know the blazon of the (mythical) past as well as of the present. Already in the thirteenth century the English *Heralds' Roll* blazons, along with the arms of contemporary knights, those of Prester John, Roland, Gawain and Sir Bevis of Southampton.[70] The impact of literary influences is much more obvious in fifteenth-century rolls and armorials. We find them blazoning the arms of the Nine Worthies, of Charlemagne's paladins, of the peers of Alexander's Greece; and one particular group blazons the arms of all the one hundred and fifty knights of Arthur's Round Table, with a brief biography (culled from the romances) under each coat, noting its bearer's personal appearance, his feats of arms, and his amorous proclivities.[71] A fifteenth-century manuscript of the romance of *Lancelot* still survives whose illuminator has modelled the arms of each knight that he portrays in precise conformity with this text; it was executed for that great patron of chivalry and letters, Jacques d'Armagnac Duke of Nemours, who died on the scaffold in 1478.[72] It is a magnificent testimony to the sophisticated literary flavour which heraldry had achieved at the end of the middle ages.

In an age in which tournaments were staged with didactic intent in Arthurian dress, and when great court feasts and ceremonies sought to catch an echo of legendary occasions (as the Burgundian feast of the Pheasant at Lille in 1454 looked back to the story of the vows and feast of the Peacock in the romance of *Alexander*),[73] true mastery of heraldic erudition had come to demand much more than a knowledge of genealogy and blazon. Ideally it required besides a command of the whole literary and historical culture of chivalry, an understanding of the laws of nobility and inheritance, and a knowledge of the mystical properties ascribed to plants, beasts, birds and colours. All this was necessary, if the range of human history and values with which the heralds felt themselves to be concerned were to be adequately translated into the visual symbols which were the language of heraldry.

In this context we are lucky to possess an inventory of the library of an English herald, Thomas Benolt, Clarenceux King of Arms, who died in 1534.[74] Benolt left all his books to his colleague Carlisle Herald for his life, and thereafter to his own successors as Clarenceux. The list of them, as we might expect, includes a number of books of visitations and of rolls recording pedigrees, together with some accounts of ceremonies (coronations, burials and so on). But alongside these we find the *Chronicles* of Froissart and a printed *History of France*; the *Livre du trésor* of Brunetto Latini (a kind of gentleman's encyclopaedia); and a translation of Giles of Rome's *De Regimine Principum*; the *Book of the Nine Worthies*; the *History of Troy*; the *Book of Galahad;* Geoffrey de Charny's *Livre de chevalerie;* Vegetius's treatise on tactics, *De re militari;* two copies of Honoré Bonet's *Tree of Battles* (an important and popular work on the laws of war, incorporating a translation of the major parts of the lawyer Bartolus's tract *De insigniis et armis*); a French translation of the Old Testament; two *Bestiaries*, and much more besides. This is a very significant list of titles. Among the famous 'three matters' of the *Chanson des Saisnes* those of Britain and of Rome the Great are prominent; so are the Nine Worthies. These and the Biblical translation offer keys to what I called in the last chapter the historical mythology of chivalry. Geoffrey de Charny and Bonet offer guidance about the conduct befitting a knight. The bestiaries, and a number of heraldic treatises, are there to check the allegorical significance of beasts and birds in charges, and of colours and metals. Froissart and a couple of other chronicles present the more recent history of chivalry, and a work called the *Faulette d'amours* reminds us that the world of courtly love is not forgotten. The whole range of chivalrous culture has been covered. Benolt's inventory gives us an eloquent testimony to the extent and variety of the learning in which a working herald, at the end of the middle ages, needed to be versed.

At the end of the thirteenth century, long before the time of Gelre and Suchenwirt, let alone that of Benolt, chivalry boasted an extensive literature (largely, but not entirely narrative) which explained its historical and religious foundation and its social role in Christian society. As an independent way of life, it had also become, by then, amenable to systematic exposition, as such works as Ramon Lull's *Book of the Order of Chivalry* testify. By that same time or very soon afterwards, we can now see, it had also acquired, in the heralds' order, a lay priesthood for its secular cult – and an educated, literate lay priesthood to boot. Starting from small beginnings, the heralds had established themselves as acknowledged experts in the refinements and rituals of a culture at once visual and literary. Their particular expertise, in bridging the gap between the written word and its iconographical expression, gave them the opportunity to exercise a very important influence on lay society and its manners in a period in which the richness of lay culture had outstripped the accessibility, for the layman, of the inscribed page.

From the time of the heralds' rise to prominence onward, we can in consequence see the culture of chivalry becoming markedly more ornate, more concerned with symbolism, more aware of historical models and motifs, more ceremonious. Just as the church with its literate priesthood had, from the earliest times, found means to express new movements of the spirit in additions to its liturgy and ritual and to visual religious symbolism, so now chivalry could do the same, through the medium of heraldic art and knowledge. And just as in the history of religion such additions to liturgy and observance do not denote a tired spirituality but rather the continuing vigour and infinitely variable range of religious feeling, so in chivalry increasingly complex and symbolic modes of expression and observance do not denote that it has become effete: they are signs rather of its still green growth, of its inventiveness, and of a broad awareness of the richness and potential of its independent tradition.

CHAPTER VIII

The Idea of Nobility

'Arms are the adornment of nobility':[1] that is the view of the heraldic writers. The word here used, nobility, not chivalry, is an important one. Arms were family insignia, to which men were entitled because of their heredity, not because they had been dubbed knights. Their importance to the knightly world, and the growing importance of the heralds as experts in blazon, are here symptomatic of an increasingly sharp emphasis that was coming to be laid upon lineage in the chivalric world of the later middle ages – from the thirteenth century on. This is a shift of emphasis, I must stress, and not a new development: we have noted earlier abundant evidence of the importance that was already attached to lineage in the early days of chivalry. A shift of emphasis there is, though, and an important one, and it focuses a new measure of attention on the concept of nobility and its meaning.

Nobility became a subject which the late medieval writers on chivalry and the heralds felt they needed to discuss at considerable length. In order the better to understand their evident concern, something needs to be said about certain developments which helped to call their attention to it. As I have said, lineage was regarded as important in knightly circles from a very early time. Back in the eleventh century we are told of how the Abbot of Bourgeuil took pity on a poor young man and brought him up to knighthood 'because he was a knight's son, descended from a long line of nobles'.[2] One important aspect of the shift of attitudes of a later age was a tendency to lay rather less emphasis upon the ceremony of initiation into knighthood and rather more upon eligibility to take knighthood, this coming to be regarded as principally dependent upon noble lineage. No man who cannot point to knights in his ancestry should be considered eligible to be made a knight: that is the doctrine of an ordinance of Frederick II in the first half of the thirteenth century.[3] The rider is added, that only the king himself can make exceptions to his own rule. It is the doctrine likewise of Beaumanoir, in the 1280s, and he too makes the same exception in the King's favour. A story that he tells illustrates the point: it concerns three knights who, needing a fourth to form a legal quorum on a tribunal, laid hold of a sturdy peasant and dubbed him with the words 'Be thou a knight.' This informal 'collée' could not make him a knight in law, and they were punished for attempting fraud.[4] The sharpening emphasis upon lineage is clear again in the thirteenth-century version of the rule of the Knights Templar. Their twelfth-century rule, which divided the brethren into two groups, the knights with their white mantles and the sergeants in homely brown, insisted only that those admitted to the higher rank should themselves be knights already. The thirteenth-century rule, in contrast, insisted that no man should be admitted to the order as a knight, unless he could show 'that he is the true son of a knight and a lady of gentle blood, and that he is descended on the father's side from a line of knights'.[5]

This hardening of the rules governing admission into the order of knighthood, limiting the privilege expressly to those who could show knights in their ancestral lines, went hand in hand with another development of the thirteenth century. During its course it becomes clear that in a growing number of localities young men of good family, especially among the lesser aristocracy, were abandoning their ancestors' custom of going through the formalities of dubbing.[6] The expense of a ceremony that was becoming increasingly elaborate and lavish, together with the escalating cost of equipping oneself with the full arms and armour of a knight, are the principal reasons that most historians advance to explain this growing reluctance to take on full knighthood. They place it in the general context of growing economic difficulties that were facing the landed aristocracy in the later middle ages, which in the opinion of some ultimately reached crisis proportions. We shall have to return later to some of the questions which these views raise. For the present it is enough to stress the fact that, for whatever reasons, fewer men were showing themselves willing to take up knighthood. A lesser nobility of men of knightly stock, who used on their seals the same arms as had their knightly ancestors but who were not themselves knights, comes into view.[7] Knighthood, it appears, was beginning to lose its significance as the common tie binding together higher and lower among the aristocracy, to be placed as such by a shared consciousness of noble descent and a common right to the hereditary insignia of nobility, armorial bearings.

In line with this development a new dignity began to be associated with the titles of rank that these lesser men were content with, titles often hitherto associated with service to knighthood or apprenticeship thereto, such as esquire or *damoiseau* (in England and France) or *Edelknecht* (in Germany). We find new collective words being coined, as *esquierie*, a kind of diminutive of chivalry. 'You see here gathered the flower of the *escuierie* of Brittany,' Beaumanoir told Brambourg before the Combat of the Thirty in 1350.[8] In Spain *hidalguia* becomes the general term used to distinguish a nobility of blood marked out by the capacity to receive knighthood. In Germany *rittermassig* becomes the term used to describe the nobles of lowest rank in the *Heerschild:* 'men with the name and character of nobility but who are not knights'.[9] Complementarily, there is a shift in the implication of the title knight, or *chevalier*: it begins to denote one of two things of him who has taken knighthood: that he comes from a family of high rank which has kept up the old custom of formally taking knighthood and whose sons are rich enough to sustain it, or that he is one who has either proved his worth on the field of battle or rendered valued service to his prince in council and government.

A third and related shift of usage is still more significant for our purposes. Henceforward, necessarily, there is a greater ambiguity about the word chivalry. It continues to be used, and quite frequently, in a narrow sense, to describe those collectively who had formally and ceremonially taken up knighthood. But it also comes to be used to describe the obligations, estate and style of life of those entitled, on account of their birth, to aspire to knighthood, but who may or may not be knights in fact. Thus we find esquires being admitted to the chivalrous sport of the tourney; we find that the statutes of secular orders of chivalry – such as René of Anjou's Order of the Croissant – open their membership to knights and esquires equally, insisting only that all candidates shall be able to trace four lines of noble descent; and we find Geoffrey de Charny, in his *Livre de chevalerie*, describing the way of life, the values and the Christian obligations not of knights only, but of men-at-arms generally, of all those who can aspire to an honourable position in the 'noble calling' of arms.[10] The words *chevalerie* and *noblesse* have begun to be capable of bearing complementary meaning: they will mean different things in some contexts, but very much the same thing in others. As a gloss on the *Grand Coutumier* of Normandy puts it, 'in the division of the estates, the estate of nobility is called the estate of chivalry'.[11]

At the end of the thirteenth century, just at the time when the shift of emphasis away from knighthood toward the hereditary capacity to receive knighthood is becoming clearly and generally apparent, we begin for the first time to come across a new kind of document, the royal or princely letter which confers nobility on one who is not noble by descent.[12] Rare at first, these grants or patents of nobility become gradually more and more common. They ennoble not only the individual concerned, but all his descent in the future. As a rule they are specific in mentioning, as one of the privileges of noble status, the capacity to take knighthood. Not infrequently the patent includes a grant of arms, with details of its blazon; conversely, princely grants of arms prove often, in effect, to be patents of nobility as well. When arms were thus granted by letters patent, the right of the bearer to display them in battle, at tournaments and on other martial occasions was usually mentioned.[13] Patents of nobility, in the medieval period, were not as yet granted in sufficient numbers to frighten the old nobility of blood into seeking, as they later did, to draw a sharp distinction between themselves and the *anoblis*, the newcomers (though there was a good deal of hostility toward *parvenus*, as we shall see shortly). The patent of nobility thus did serve, at this stage and in the majority of cases, as an effective entry pass into the charmed circle of the chivalrous. In that sense, it began to usurp one very important function that the ceremony of dubbing to knighthood had hitherto discharged.

Here is another significant shift of emphasis. There is an important difference between being made a noble and being made a knight. Peter de Vinea, Frederick II's chancellor wrote that 'nobility is passed on to those in the line of descent, but the dignity of knighthood is not',[14] and his words point up the significance of the distinction elegantly. The ceremony of dubbing, with its elaborate ritual whose each movement was imbued with symbolical meaning, initiated a man into an order or estate defined by function, what the German historians call a *Berufstand*. Nobility boasted no right of initiation beyond the childbirth pangs of a noblewoman: the helpless infant was born into an order defined by blood, a *Geburtstand*. As Duby has put it, 'from now on the aristocracy saw itself as the nobility – as a caste closed to all who could not claim good breeding'.[15] Lineage has here taken a long stride towards taking pride of place over vocation, on which the dubbing rite had laid such powerful emphasis.

The hardening of hereditary class barriers which is implicit here was by no means a development confined to the secular world. The chapter or cloister which imposed on those seeking to enter it armorial restrictions, such as that they must prove their right to arms or that they must be able to show four or more lines of noble descent, was a common feature of the late middle ages: in Germany before the Reformation this exclusiveness had reduced the population of many collegiate churches to a perilously low level.[16] Class jealousy clearly had much to do with this closing of the noble ranks. Many noble families were, from the thirteenth century on, beginning to feel sharply the cold wind of economic competition from prospering peasants and prospering townsmen. Their reaction was to seek to set themselves apart, to protect their pride and their privileges by erecting barriers against the entry of *parvenus* into their order. That is what lies behind the rules of the customary law books of the age that define nobility and its privileges[17] – such as the right of noblemen to levy private war, to be judged only by their peers, to bear distinctive arms and dress. Chivalrous romances and courtesy books, from the beginning of the thirteenth century and even a little before, echo and indeed anticipate the exclusiveness of the law books. So Darius, in the *Romance of Alexander*, is held up to obloquy as one who has promoted commoners and passed over the true nobles;[18] and Satan, in the *Tournoiement d'Antechrist* is portrayed as a lord who has given away his riches to sergeants, villeins and usurers, and made knights of them with his own hand. Ramon Lull, and Robert of Blois in his *Enseignement des Princes,* stress that princes should look for their councillors among the knights and nobles.[19] The French Capetian kings of the twelfth and thirteenth centuries were in historical fact a good deal criticised for their willingness to advance non-nobles, and it has been plausibly argued that this was one reason why the literary cult of chivalry, in Capetian France, tended to centre not on the royal court but on the courts of the great princely houses which were so often at odds with the monarchy, such as those of Flanders and Champagne and above all, in the early days, of Anjou.[20]

With passing time new privileges, such as the very general privilege of exemption from princely taxation, made the nobles still more jealous concerning the rights of their order. Even so, they were never very successful in preserving its purity in terms of descent. They themselves too often had an interest in the breach of the very rules whose enforcement they at other times applauded. A marriage with a rich *roturier* or *roturière* could be the saving of a family fortune that had been undermined by unthinking *largesse* or a costly lust for adventure. Whether he entered upon a noble estate by marriage or by purchasing it from one who had fallen on hard times, the pull of the noble way of life was strong upon the newcomer to noble property, and stronger still upon his descendants. They had the money – for the time being anyway – to sustain a noble style, and they found themselves called upon to meet the obligations of the noble, to serve in the wars. The rules of customary law, that nobility must follow the paternal line, and that the stain of common descent was not purged until the third generation, were in the circumstances easily forgotten. It was not even seen always as necessary that the townsman who acquired noble fiefs should quit his old urban *milieu*. In the Imperial free cities, and in such great towns as Lille and Toulouse in the late middle ages we come across an urban nobility, distinguished by the possession of estates as well as town property and by family traditions of martial as well as civic service.[21] In Italy, of course, the nobility had long been city dwellers, in many areas. The town air of Lombardy and Tuscany did not make their nobles any less proud and quarrelsome than the rural nobility of other lands, but it did open the ranks of the nobility, even more easily than elsewhere, to those who, though they lacked aristocratic origins in the *contado*, had prospered in urban life and commerce. For all the exclusiveness of the law books, the nobility of the later middle ages was in fact being constantly refreshed with new blood.

Though the traditional regard for lineage had hardened into legal doctrine, the barriers that the law erected proved very far from insurmountable. Marriage, good service, the acquisition of wealth and princely ennoblement all carried men who had no lineal claim into the ranks of the nobility, and in substantial numbers. The way was not really less open to the challenge of talent than it had been in the past. What the tighter and better defined rules did do, however, in combination with the observable fact that they were so commonly breached, was to focus attention more sharply than before on the question, what the real essence of nobility was.

Even the rules of customary law were not entirely clear in their implication here. Their usual justification for the noble privilege of exemption from taxation, that the noble discharged his public obligation by martial service, preserved the traditional emphasis on function as well as blood. So did many of the rules concering *dérogeance*, the manner in which nobility might be lost.[22] True, a noblewoman could lose her nobility by marrying a commoner, and here the emphasis was on blood: but more importantly a nobleman might lose his by falling into poverty, or taking to an ignoble profession such as commerce. Besides, the fact that the word noble carried ethical as well as social implications could not be simply ignored. What then was the real essence of nobility? The question was important, to the heralds perhaps especially as the registrars of the insignia of nobility, but to the chivalrous world generally as well. A great deal of ink came to be spilt in its discussion, and the writers who considered it drew on all the resources of their erudition. Since, in this age, chivalry and nobility were so often equated, we must take a careful look at what they had to say, to see how far it amounts to a coherent view of the matter.

We may start by setting alongside one another the views on this question of nobility of two late medieval authorities of a very different character. The first shall be Bartolus of Sassoferrato, the great Italian law professor of the fourteenth century who was also the author of the much copied treatise *De insigniis et armis*, the first truly learned discussion of heraldry. What he had to say about nobility in his commentry on the twelfth book of Justinian's *Codex* also achieved wide circulation.[23] We find his views quoted by the Castilian knight errant Diego de Valera; by the English cleric and heraldic authority, Nicholas Upton; by the *Songe du vergier*; by the German Felix Hemmerlein in his *De rusticitate et nobilitate*; and by many others.[24] So his views are clearly relevant. Bartolus was a man of the schools, an intellectual; by contrast Oliver de la Marche, who shall be our second authority, was a lettered knight. He had served the Dukes of Burgundy well in their wars, was a companion of the Order of the Golden Fleece, had acted as *maître d'hôtel* to Charles the Bold and was deeply versed in heraldic lore. Though he did know Bartolus's views, his is a very different brand of testimony.

Bartolus in his commentary distinguishes three kinds of nobility. First of all there is what he calls theological nobility: this is what separates those by God's grace elect to everlasting bliss from those predestined to damnation. Mere men, says Bartolus, cannot tell who is in this sense noble. So, from a lawyer's point of view, this category is the least important. Secondly, there is natural nobility. This Bartolus defines by reference to Aristotle, who in his *Politics* explains how some are marked out for freedom by their virtues (and specifically by their capacity to rule), and are so distinguished from those whose talents fit them only for a servile role. (Freedom, it should be noted, was a word often equated with nobility in the middle ages, hence the chivalrous value *franchise*.) Those free men whose virtues thus fit them to rule Bartolus defines as the natural nobility. The third kind of nobility he calls civil nobility. Here he reverts to his purely formal and legal standard, which accepts as noble all those whom the law and the prince as lawgiver accept to be so. From the practical point of view of the lawyer this is for him the most important kind of nobility.

These three types of nobility, Bartolus goes on to explain, are not unrelated. The prince's earthly dominion is a human reflection of the universal dominion of God; and the civil nobility represents those elected by the prince for their human virtues, just as the theological nobility represents those elected to salvation by God through His grace. There is no formal rule of positive human law, Bartolus admits, that can prevent a prince from promoting or accepting as noble those who are vicious, but it is his duty to make his dominion a true mirror of God's own by advancing those who are naturally noble. There is thus in Bartolus's scheme a clear connection between the three types of nobility, but the distinctions too are important. With regard to natural nobility, he applauded Dante's argument in his *Convivio*, that nobility does not, as the Emperor Frederick had claimed, derive from ancient riches adorned with fine manners, but is the meed of individual virtue. But this is not necessarily the case, he goes on to say, with regard to civil nobility, and with regard to that Dante's argument is unsound: for here all rests on princely recognition of the claim to nobility, which may well in fact amount to recognising ancient riches adorned with fine manners as sufficient warrant. Bartolus thus presents a definition of nobility in which virtue plays an important part, but which ultimately rests on princely recognition and customary practice (which will usually mean heredity).[25]

Oliver de la Marche starts his discussion of nobility from this very point of princely recognition, for he wrote to explain to the young master of his old age, Philip the Handsome, precisely whom he should accept as of sufficient nobility to fight a judicial duel. His statement of his views is much briefer than that of Bartolus, and is such a classic of its kind that it is worth quoting in full:

And so, my lord, it is needful both in this regard and others that you should know who they are whom you should hold for gentlemen *(gentils hommes)*, who for nobles, and who for non-nobles . . . The gentleman is he who from of old springs from gentlemen and gentlewomen, and such men and their posterity by marriage are gentle. And with regard to nobility, which is the beginning of gentility, it is acquired, firstly, by those who hold great office under the prince, and by this means they are ennobled and their posterity after them. And the heirs of such, who come after, may, by maintaining the free condition and leading the honourable life of the nobleman, call themselves gentlemen. Thirdly, when a servant of the prince or any other has led an honourable existence, and the prince has made him a knight, he thus ennobles him and his posterity . . . Fourthly, to follow the profession of arms in the rank of man-at-arms and to serve the prince valorously and long at war, this too ennobles a man. And fifthly, when a prince wishes to ennoble a man, he may do so and may give him letters to make him noble, for his good or for his virtuous living, or for his riches. And although it is true that to be ennobled by letters (patent) is the least well authorised manner of ennoblement, yet it is apparent enough that ancient nobility comes from ancient riches. And he is the happier, and is to be the more esteemed, who commences his nobility in virtue, than he who brings his to an end in vice.[26]

This summary of his views from Oliver looks superficially rather different from what Bartolus said, and less coherent, but there is in fact much common ground between them. The latter lays much more emphasis on the authority of the prince, whom he describes as the fount of all honours. Here his view is in tune with that emphasis laid by the French customary lawyers on the royal monopoly of the right to make knights from among those who are non-noble (it should be noted that both Bartolus and Oliver regard knighthood as normally conferring nobility automatically). Oliver, however, also recognises princely authority as a source of nobility, and specifically notes the authority of princely letters patent to create new nobles; and both stress how often new nobility is the reward for good service of the prince. Oliver in his turn lays sharper emphasis on the claims of descent in blood than Bartolus does, and here refines the vocabulary of the issue: a newcomer to nobility may call himself *noble*, but *gentility*, Oliver says, is something more than that, that can only be claimed in virtue of descent. Bartolus, though, allows for the claims of blood too. If the customary laws, whose validity the prince recognises, accept as noble those born of noble stock (as in most places they did in his day), then, he says, such persons are civilly noble; and he is careful to note that the taint of ignoble blood is only purged after four descents. Both writers are at one in believing that, in civil terms, ancestral nobility must derive from some original *civil* convention (otherwise, Bartolus points out, all the descendants of Adam and Eve would have to be either noble or non-noble, which would make a nonsense of the whole argument).[27] Both authors agree that a certain measure of wealth and a certain style of living are needful qualifications for nobility (*largesse*, Bartolus says, is a virtue apposite to nobility, and you cannot give *largesse* without riches). Both are agreed, once again, in their emphasis on personal virtues as necessary to nobility, though Bartolus qualifies this with regard to its civil standing; and the two do stress slightly different virtues, Bartolus emphasising the capacity to rule, La Marche valour and loyal service.

Despite their widely differing standpoint and background and despite variations in the shade of emphasis, a considerable measure of agreement between these two very different authorities thus remains. Both focus the social role of the nobility around the service of secular authority. Both offer, if in very different tones, a similar composite of qualifications for the acquisition or inheritance of nobility. They are princely recognition, vocation, wealth and style of life, virtue, and descent in blood. On these five points not only they but a host of other late medieval writers who explored the meaning of nobility concentrated their attention. In their efforts to assess the relative significance of each of them they drew on all the resources of what I have called chivalrous erudition, legal, ethical, and above all historical. What they add to what Bartolus, La Marche and others have already told us is most enlightening.

★

About princely authority and letters of nobility enough has been said, for the moment, earlier in this chapter. What the pundits have to say about vocation may therefore be examined first. The first thing to be said about this is that their writings re-emphasise another point made earlier: the way in which chivalry and nobility come to be almost complementary in meaning in the later middle ages. The historical explanations that they offer of the origins of nobility prove simply to be the same as those offered by other and earlier authors for the origin of chivalry, minimally rephrased. In the early days after the Fall of Man, quarrels and confusion drove men to choose kings, says Beaumanoir, 'and in order to defend the people against their enemies and against evil judges, they sought out those among them who were the most handsome, the strongest and the most wise, and gave them *seigneurie* over others in such a way that they should help the king to maintain peace . . . And from these men are descended those whom we call gentlemen.'[28] This is very much the same as what Lull and John of Salisbury had said about the origins of knighthood. Diego de Valera has a similar explanation of the origins of *gentility* – of nobility of blood – as originating in the measures made necessary by the confusion and strife following the fall of the Tower of Babel.[29] To judge men and to fight were the original functions of nobility. In the light of this general view, it comes as no surprise to find, for instance, Imagination in the *Enseignement de la vraye noblesse* declaring that justice is a necessary ingredient to nobility, and defining justice in the familiar chivalrous terms: 'it means the protection and safeguard of Holy Church, of widows and orphans and of the weak and simple'.[30] Similarly, the *noblesse* and the *chevalerie* are linked together in this same work as the second of the three orders, the warrior order of the familiar tripartite division of society (the men, that is to say, whose business is to uphold justice with the sword). Developing this theme in a vivid allegory, the author of *La vraye noblesse* likens the prince to the 'good carter', driving the two horses which draw the waggon of his commonwealth: the right horse signifying the clergy, the left the nobility.[31]

These theoretical views tally well with what appears to have been the accepted social attitude and practice of the later middle ages. Nobility and the martial vocation really were closely associated. When the French kings of the fourteenth century wished to raise a royal host, they summoned to their service all who were noble or held noble fiefs. When, later, in the time of Charles V and Charles VII, they began to organise their forces in standing companies, the great majority of those mustered in these companies as men at arms were nobles, and it is clear that nobles were regarded as the natural recruits in this rank.[32] In Germany, Konrad of Megenburg urged young nobles who were poor to seek wages of war in the wars of Italy, and Schäfer's analysis of the great German companies there shows how full they were of the sprigs of the lesser nobility who had followed this advice.[33] The profession of arms was moreover regarded as ennobling, in just the sense that La Marche suggested. 'We poor soldiers', wrote Jean de Buiel, 'belong to the noble estate and for the most part are noble by lineage, and those who are not noble by lineage are so by the exercise and profession of arms, which is noble in itself.'[34] Nicholas Upton tells how 'in these days we see how openly how many poor men through their service in the French wars have become noble, some by their prudence, some by their energy, some by their valour, and some by other virtues which, as I have said, ennoble men'.[35] References such as these explain how in due course it came to be one of the manners of proving nobility in France that a man could show evidence of having been mustered in the royal army as a man at arms. 'A third way [of proving nobility]', says a French sixteenth-century treatise, 'is if one of the party's ancestors, his father or his grandfather, has followed arms, for nobility is annexed to the military calling.'[36]

The shift of emphasis away from the taking of knighthood toward nobility of blood, which we observed earlier to be a feature of the late middle ages, thus clearly did not, in any significant degree, undermine the conception of the essential role of the secular aristocracy as being a martial one. In the broad sense of the word chivalry, the nobles, whether they were formally knights or not, were the *chevalerie*, the warrior order, still defined by its function.

★

Style of living, backed by adequate wealth, came to be accepted in later days, like military service, as a possible proof of nobility. Style and wealth necessarily go hand in hand, for the latter is the necessary foundation for the former. About wealth as a qualification for nobility there seems at first sight, it is true, to be some ambiguity. A host of writers emphasise how important it is that poor knights be held in honour and esteem, and to remember that riches without high qualities are nothing worth. The theme is strong both in the romances and the books of courtesy. Arthur in the prose *Lancelot* is singled out as an example of one who prized poor knights for their prowess. Alexander in romance is portrayed ordering that the poor knights who were dubbed at the same time as he should be robed before the rich.[37] Geoffrey de Charny similarly is full of praise for those whom he calls 'poor companions',[38] and the *Vraye noblesse* bids kings and captains to 'heed the words and advice of the poor companions, for there is many a man who lacks goods but who is well equipped with sense and courage for great enterprises'.[39] Along with this attitude goes an admiration for restraint in display, which has echoes of the restraint and discipline that were so admired by chivalrous writers in the martial life of classical antiquity. *La vraye noblesse* tells of the amazement of the Saracen envoy who found that pattern of chivalry, King Godfrey, sitting armed outside his tent on a straw palliasse, and of how the great Bertrand Du Guesclin took him as an example: 'he took no account of pomp and trappings, and for him it was enough that he should be mounted and armed reasonably'.[40] Machaut praises the same restraint in King John of Bohemia: 'He cared not for money: honour was the one desire of his heart. If he had a horse, and a grey coat of Frisian cloth, it was enough for him, and he would sup of rye bread, a herring or some oily soup, if good meat was lacking.'[41]

This apparent emphasis on poverty and moderation is deceptive, however. The true knight should indeed be ready to endure hardship and to take whatever fare fate offers: there is no question about that. But the brilliant descriptions in Arthurian romance of the manner in which an errant hero is welcomed when he comes to a castle – say Bercilak's welcome to Gawain at the Green Castle in *Gawain and the Green Knight* – tell us quite clearly that homeliness is not part of the style to which such a one is expected to be socially accustomed. The great virtue of the patronage of poor knights by such as Arthur and Alexander was that it made the poor richer,[42] and brought them closer to the glamorous, fur-robed and castle-dwelling world of the high nobles. Indeed we are told, and repeatedly, that it is one of the virtues of the military profession that it is an avenue to riches. Young men at arms and knights should labour to win honour and renown for their valour, writes Philip of Novara, 'and also so as to win earthly goods so that they and their children may live in honour, and do well by their friends and servants'.[43] Those who are poor and noble, we have heard Konrad of Megenburg say, should go to the wars in Lombardy and elsewhere and with their pay and winnings maintain their estate. Ghillebert de Lannoy tells his son that there are three honourable ways in which riches can be acquired: by service at court, or by a good marriage, or at the wars.[44] The implication is quite clear: wealth is necessary to maintain nobility, and the quest for it, not for its own sake but in order to maintain a noble and honourable style, is a reasonable and justifiable ambition. As one civil lawyer drily remarked, 'nobility without riches is like Faith without Works'.[45]

He was quite right. To live nobly demanded a certain quite definite style, and it was an expensive one. 'Knights and esquires should be well mounted, and they and their servants should be well equipped with arms, and bows and arrows, sharply dressed and graciously: and they should spend decently and honourably on the upkeep of their households.'[46] Even a lesser nobleman was expected to dwell in a good house, perhaps crenellated and turreted to give it something of the air of a castle:[47] to keep hawks and hounds, and to talk knowledgeably of them. Poggio's jibe, that to be noble means to live in the country and to waste all your time in the open air, hawking and hunting, is not without a certain justice.[48] The expensive leisure and rather unthinking gaiety of idle hours form a theme that comes across vividly in many descriptions of the noble life. When the Chatelain de Coucy came to dine at the castle of Favel, 'they drank their good wines freely, and all the talk was of arms and of love, of hounds and hawks and of tournaments.'[49] The lovely Vienne in the romance of *Paris de Dauphiné* was brought up to read romances and 'fair' histories, to dance and to sing, to play all sorts of instruments, and to be gracious to all.[50] Weapons and sport and hospitality were all things that cost money, and so were girls. The record of the noble life is often very alluring, but there is no doubt about its costliness.

Hospitality was also expected of the nobleman, and on a generous scale. It was high praise from Jacques de Hemricourt for the noble canon of Liège, Jean le Bel, that his board was always well spread, and that if his squires met any man of worth, be he churchman, knight or esquire, they would bid him to dine without consulting their master, because they knew all such would be welcome.[51] A nobleman was also expected to be generous in his alms-giving, in his benefactions to churches, and lavish in his instructions for the masses to be said for his soul. John de Grailly, Captal de Buch, saddled his executors with the obligation to have no less than fifty thousand masses said for his soul in the year after his death, and even a relatively poor *seigneur* might expect to provide four or five thousand for himself and his ancestors after his passing. There is a great deal of space taken up in heraldic treatises with descriptions of ceremony appropriate to noble funerals: with hatchments to be displayed, candles stamped with the arms of all the dead man's lines of nobility to be burned, and with the rules that govern the display of his arms and his effigy on his tomb.[52] If the noble way of life was expensive, so was the noble way of dying.

Thrift is a notable absentee from Lannoy's list of the ways of gaining riches honourably.[53] He thus reminds us that among the late medieval nobility we move in a social world to which any ideal of saving, let alone of capital accumulation, was alien. Riches were for redistribution, not for re-investment: *largesse* was a quality to be expected of every nobleman. True, a nobleman should take care to tailor his generosity to his pocket: prodigality was seen to be a vice, but niggardliness was a worse one.[54] Within his means it was a nobleman's business to be free with his own. It is not surprising that a good many of the lesser nobility did not find it easy to stand the pace. As Professor Duby shrewdly remarks, over-expenditure almost certainly ruined more noblemen than adverse economic conditions ever did.[55]

It is worth lingering a moment longer over the idea of the noble style of living, to try and catch something more of its quality, as well as of its expense. It is easy to exaggerate its lavishness by reference to the vivid and costly flamboyance of the great courts and the glamour of its portrait in the romances. But if the lesser nobleman could not cut quite such a figure, it is clear that he too sought and prized style, quite consciously. Let us look at the picture that Jacques de Hemricourt gives of the nobility and their manner of living in a corner of the Low Countries, in his book *Le Miroir des nobles de Hesbaye*. In this book, we are never allowed to forget that the soil is close. Libier de Warfusiez left the life of arms when his wife died, and took orders, but he kept up a certain style in his fortress manor with its famous mill which made him rich; and so was able to bring up his daughter to embroider, to play chess and to read Books of Hours and romances, accomplishments that helped her to win a husband of standing.[56] William Lord of Hemricourt loved tournaments, and very nearly lost his all at them in ransoms and re-mounts; his wife's genius for husbandry and the great flocks of sheep that her shepherds tended saved him from ruin.[57] This is a society of landowners, of wealthy squires who quarrel over claims to land and think much about good marriages for their sons and daughters. But it is also, and distinctively, a chivalrous world. All the noble families of the area had had a part to play in the local wars, and a great many had adventured

much further afield. Ottes de Warfusiez and the 'good bastard' of
Wezemale served Charles II of Anjou against the Aragonese, and were
reckoned in their day among *les trois plus preux de Hesbaye*.[58] Radout de
Colombe became a Constable of a company in Lombardy.[59] Willhelm de
Warous and Godefor de Blehen made the pilgrimage to Jerusalem and
took their knighthood at the Holy Sepulchre.[60] There is also a melancholy
tally of young hopefuls who died fighting the Saracen, in Turkey and
elsewhere beyond the sea and in Spain.[61] Tournaments and crusading and
far journeys were very much part of the life of Hesbaye's nobility, more
important to their style than milling or the keeping of sheep, though the one
had, of course, to pay for the other.

Hemricourt has certainly mixed a dash of romanticism into his picture
(and a good deal of snobbery, it should be added). All his women are lovely;
their husbands adore them for their beauty and bounty; old women recall
the young men who stirred their hearts long ago.[62] His beau-ideal is one
such as Renart de Falcomont, who wooed and married the sister of his
companion in arms Henry, Lord of Bautersem; from the two there sprang a
race of fair children, the best-renowned 'for prowess and beauty, and
gentility, and courage that you could find between the Meuse and the
Rhine'.[63] There are traces in the book of some splendid ancestral mythology, such as the story of Ameil de Lexhy, a remote forbear of one of
Jacques's favourite lineages, who, when he was going to battle one hot day
met by the water's edge the loveliest woman he had ever seen. She told him
she was a gentlewoman from a foreign land, bound on pilgrimage: after
much talk he persuaded her to come home with him, dined her and took her
to bed. In the morning she thanked him, and asked if he knew who she was.
'No,' says he. 'I am the Devil,' says she. 'The Devil?' exclaimed Ameil de
Lexhy, 'then by God's death you can tell them, when you get back to Hell,
that last night you were the best screwed devil in the wide world.' Even this
droll tale has a touch of aristocratic style, with its lovely gentlewoman and
its bold seigneur bearing her back to his manor and its hospitality, ignorant
of the dramatic nature of his baggage.[64]

★

Hemricourt's purpose in his book was not, of course, to describe style but to
trace lineages, the lineages of his own Hesbaye. Lineage and virtue are the
two qualifications for nobility that remain to be considered from the list that
we have culled from Bartolus, Oliver de La Marche, and their followers;
and they have to be considered together, since their competing claims to
decisive priority formed the theme of a long protracted debate. The essential problem round which it focussed is elegantly stated in the early thirteenth century by no less an authority than Lancelot himself in the prose

romance: 'They tell me that all peoples are descended from one man and one woman. So I do not understand how one can have more gentility in him than another . . . unless he earns it for himself by his prowess in the same way as men win lands and honours.'[65] Yet the common view of the age in which the romance of Lancelot was written was that nobility – or gentility – was a matter of birth, and the romance itself is full of emphasis on the esteem in which lineage must be held. The claims of blood and virtue competed with one another, even in the very pages of his own story and part of the point of it was to show, through his heroic career, that he was worthy of the blood that bore him.

The champions of the claims of blood and lineage rested their case more often on traditional authority than on reason. They looked back to the story in the Bible of Noah and his sons: freemen descended from Shem, it was claimed, knights from Japheth, and bondmen from Ham who dishonoured his seed by mocking his father. There was a catch in this explanation of course, as the clerk shrewdly pointed out in the *Songe du Vergier*: all three sons sprang from the same parent. That did not deter the customary lawyers, who became the busiest exponents of the claims of blood, paying careful attention to such nice points as whether the son of a commoner by a noblewoman should be regarded as noble (the answer is usually no), and to precise stipulations about the number of generations required to purge the taint of ignoble ancestry. It cannot really be said of them that they argued the point, however. Bartolus, emphasising that princely authority is the fount of all honours, and that princely recognition gives force to the hereditary rules of customary law, comes much nearer to offering a reasoned defence of the hereditary principle – but it is not, in principle, a case for the claims of blood but rather for princely authority. Even he, as we have seen, had besides made wide room for the claims of virtue alongside claims founded on particular local rules of inheritance. Apart from the legal writers, the cloud of witness is on the other side, on the side of individual virtue and achievement as the true key to nobility, rather than blood and descent.

Dante's spirited defence of individual virtue as the true basis of nobility against the claim of 'ancient riches' is sometimes thought of as foreshadowing the future humanist approach to the subject in the Renaissance period.[66] It is true that Dante put in an original and arresting way what he had distilled concerning nobility from the wisdom of the past, and gave it an extra dimension through his emphasis on the free choice of virtue as the essential quality of the noble soul. But his basic theme seems really to reflect the general view of his age, and was not novel. 'The law says that in the beginning nobility came in only from good character and manly worth and courtesy,' Andreas the Chaplain declares, writing back in the 1180s: he who gets his nobility 'only from himself' is to be preferred, he adds, to him who 'derives it as a sort of inheritance from those from whom he gets his being'.[67] 'Is he a gentleman who would claim name and praise because he has inherited nobility from others, though he has not their merit or their prowess,' asks Jeun de Meun, Dante's older contemporary, 'I say, No.'[68] Froissart, in the prologue to this chronicle, reminds his readers explicitly how many men there are who, in the recent wars, 'having risen to be knights and esquires, have advanced themselves more by their prowess than their lineage.'[69] God will mark out those who labour valorously, says Geoffrey de Charny, even though they come of little estate.[70] The more ambitious heraldic writers of the fifteenth century take the same line, and ransack all the resources of their historical erudition to prove the validity of the point. Biblical example shows clearly that nobility is not just a matter of descent: Shem, Japheth and Ham sprang from the same father, yet one was noble and the other not (here is the catch in the argument that traces heredity back to them), and David from a shepherd rose to be a king.[71] Turning to pagan antiquity, the heraldic writers pointed out that in Rome the Temples of Virtue and Honour stood side by side, and had only the one door: one could not enter the second save through the first.[72] In classical history they found a rich harvest of examples of noble men who were supposed to have risen from small beginnings: Tarquin, Hannibal, Agathocles, Marius, Cato.[73] The classical sages, such as Seneca, Cicero and Lucan, were at one in confirming the doctrine thus taught (and so were the fathers of the church), the heraldic writers claimed. Above all, Aristotle's authority was on this side. 'I have taken the advice of many noble and wise men,' wrote Gilles, King of Arms to Maximilian of Austria, 'of Kings of Arms, heralds and also of a number of notable doctors of law . . . All alike by common agreement conclude concerning the commencement and foundation of all nobility by the authority of Aristotle, who tells us that he is noble who is ennobled by his virtues.'[74]

Once settled on virtue as the prime factor, a good many chivalrous authors could not resist the opportunity offered to display their learning further by a lengthy discussion of the four cardinal virtues in their relationship to nobility. As was natural in this martial age, the one on which they laid most stress was fortitude: 'for it is generally said that nobility derives from noble courage'.[75] Magnanimity, and so largesse, were regarded as annexed to fortitude. Justice came next in order of importance with those who followed the formal categorisation of the cardinal virtues, since it defined the duty of the noble, as of the knight, to defend the poor and oppressed.[76] Other writers, abandoning this classification, simply equated the virtues of nobility with those traditionally associated with knighthood. 'Those who know that they are named as gentlemen, and wish to be held for noble, must uphold twelve virtues': that is the dictum of a little poem much quoted by the heralds, and which seems to be an abridged version of Alain

Chartier's famous *Breviaire des nobles*. When we look on to see what the twelve virtues were the list is familiar; faith, loyalty, honour, largesse, prowess, courtesy – and so on.[77]

The poem does however make it clear that there is a connection between nobility and lineage. 'You who come of noble houses, and are the heirs of gentle blood, you should be possessed of virtue and reason': those are its opening words. Virtue might be the 'foundation and commencement' of nobility, but that did not mean that lineage was unimportant. It was not as important as virtue, on that there was general agreement; but that only brought to the fore a still knottier point, what *was* the relation of virtue to lineage? For in this age in which so much went by inheritance and in which lineage was held in such high esteem there could be no doubt that there must be a link, and a close one.

The appeal to eugenics was made, though rather tentatively and less often than one might expect. The biblical example of the bad sons of Adam and of Noah stood in its way, and so did the demonstrable and freely admitted fact that virtuous parents do not always have virtuous children. Nevertheless it could be argued that this did happen more often than not.[78] Aristotle seemed to favour this view and it was true of animals, as the foals of swift horses are more often swift than others.[79] Some ingenious ideas were apparently current about human mating and were used to carry the argument further. 'It is the fact [*chose veritable*]', wrote Diego de Valera, 'that if a father is noble and is in a virtuous disposition at the time when his son is engendered, then the son will be so also, as like follows like. But a good many fathers are changed and altered in their virtuous and noble condition at the time and hour when their children are engendered, for which reason the children follow the disposition in which the father was at the time of engendering.'[80] The old captain of Crathor in Jean de Bueil's *Jouvencel* had a similar idea, but (being no doubt a chauvinist to the loins) thought it was the female partner who should take the blame for ignoble offspring. 'I shall never believe that nobles who dishonour their arms were descended from the valiant fathers whose name they bear: one must suppose that their mothers had lechers in their mind when they engendered them. Maybe indeed they were actually in bed with them.'[81] Diego's curious meticulousness in the matter of bastardy seems to derive from this same theory of moral eugenics. True bastards are those engendered by a married man upon an unmarried woman, he says, and they may be noble if their mothers be so; but children engendered upon prostitutes, or Jewesses, or Saracen women cannot be, for 'those that are engendered in vile sin should in no wise enjoy the nobility of their fathers'.[82] They are not proper bastards, he sneers, but spurious children.

Efforts to affirm direct links between virtue and the process of generation, such as these, do not seem to have carried any very profound conviction. A commoner and more sensible line, positing a looser link that was in essence environmental rather than hereditary, was much more widely followed and much more important. It is that suggested in Dante's comment: 'Therefore, let not any scion of the Uberti of Florence or of the Visconti of Milan say "I am noble", for the divine seed does not fall upon a race, that is, a stock, but on the several individuals . . . the stock does not make the individual noble, but the individuals ennoble the stock.'[83] Dante was by no means the founding father of this idea. Jean de Meun, who wrote somewhat earlier, puts very much the same point in a slightly different way: 'he who strives to come at the truth must agree that in gentility there is no good unless a man seeks to emulate the prowess of his noble ancestors. This should be the quest of everyone who would call himself gentle.'[84] This view of lineage, as the nurse and instructress of nobility, and hence of gentility, is a constantly recurrent one. Hemricourt's object in recording the lines and deeds of the Hesbaye nobility is, he says, 'so that those who are descended of such nobility may draw joy and comfort from knowing of their extraction, and strive therefore the harder toward high achievement.'[85] 'I do not know how the high deeds and fine manners of those who are dead can profit their heirs and successors,' says Imagination in *La vraye noblesse*, 'unless in this, that they take example from them.'[86] Diego de Valera sums it up well (for even he proves not to be a diehard eugenicist in the end): 'I believe and hold this to be the greatest advantage of nobility, that it constrains those who are noble and nobly born to wish to resemble their ancestors.'[87]

The medieval view of lineage and nobility is thus one which focuses not simply on birth as the determinant of caste so much as on family traditions of honour and privileged position founded in past achievement, and offering an example to future generations. Get heirs, says Philip of Novara, 'for by means of heirs who bear their father's surname, his memory and that of his ancestors shall live longer in this world.'[88] That so much attention should focus on the family – the lineage – is perfectly natural. The family was the most basic social unit that the age knew; its customary law was permeated with the idea of lineal inheritance; and the Bible with its long genealogies bore witness to the significance of lineage in the history of religion. To have sought to set the individual and his stock entirely apart would have seemed quite unnatural. Even Dante, that ardent champion of individual virtue, saw that the acts of the individual reflected upon the family: 'the individual ennobles the stock', he declares. The acts and habits of the individual members of a lineage were seen as forming those of the stock: 'you come of a noble line, *therefore* you should seek the harder to grow in virtue,' says Louis de Gavre's mother in the romance of the *Seigneurs de Gavre*.[89] Indeed this is the point of the distinction which the purists drew between nobility and gentility. For his own particular achievement a man might be ennobled, but gentility implied something more, the forming of a tradition and manner of life and conduct which had stood the test of time into a second generation.

In the late middle ages, the traditional respect for old blood of the knightly world was not so much magnified as clarified and codified, and in some measure justified. In the process of justification, the central association of nobility and virtue was never lost to sight. Louis de Gavre's mother, as we have heard, reminded him that he came of noble blood, but the moral she drew was that he must strive for virtue, 'for nobility of manners always overtops nobility of race'.[90] This advice, however, comes from romance, not from history, and for that reason leaves a question unanswered. Were not the facts, in ninety-nine cases out of a hundred, simpler than theory, and nobility and its insignia merely an inheritance, and no more? How far, if at all, was the theoretic emphasis upon virtue carried forward into the world of practice? It will take a whole chapter to try to answer even a part of this question.

CHAPTER IX

Arms, Nobility and Honour

The idea that nobility owed more to virtue than to lineage was one hammered out by learned men and explained at length in their scholarly treatises. What they taught was translated into the vernacular by lettered knights and the clerks who were their servants, and by clerks with an interest in chivalry and its lore. They reproduced what was translated in their treatises on knighthood and nobility: so we find, for instance, Diego de Valera and Nicholas Upton and Jean de Bueil all quoting views on nobility derived from those of Bartolus.[1] In a similar way, we find Jean de Bueil's clerks, in the didactic asides of his memoirs, copying out extensive passages about the laws of war from Christine de Pisan's *Livre des fais d'armes et de chevalerie* – passages which she in turn had taken from the canonist Bonet's *Tree of Battles* and from Vegetius.[2] The heralds too copied similar passages from similar works and often from the very same ones, into their commonplace books, and the fact that they also did so is important. The appearance in theoretic treatises on chivalry of words and views borrowed from an academic author is not by any means adequate evidence that such words or views were taken seriously, even when the authors of the treatises can be shown to be secular men who followed in the real world the chivalrous profession of arms. In the case of the heralds, however, there was always a concern to relate theory to practice, for their learning was their qualification for their practical profession. They were regarded, moreover, as the registrars of chivalrous value. Their science of blazon, as we have seen, offered a means of symbolising virtues and qualities in visual language. Their activities ought therefore to tell us something about how far the theoretical emphasis on virtue as the foundation of nobility had any practical relevance.

Before we start on this line of inquiry, a word of caution is needed. We must not expect too much of the heralds. Virtue is a characteristic of the inner man, of the mind or soul: external marks, such as heraldic devices, cannot be expected to take account of anything more than virtue's outward manifestation, in life and act. Heraldic blazon cannot tell us about the motives that prompted individual men to strive for honour, only about the social respect that honourable acts could earn. It could, though, be used to recognise these outward indications of an inner capacity, and so to render honour to whomsoever it seemed due, and to his lineage also.

In England, exceptionally, records survive of a considerable number of grants of arms made by heralds in the late middle ages. The following grant, made by John Smert, Garter, to Edmond Mylle in 1450, shows clearly that this King of Arms well understood the teaching that, as the adornment of nobility, arms ought to bear witness to a virtue in their bearer – and so to serve as an example to his descent and to all other men. This is its tenor:

> John Smert alias Garter King of Arms of the Kingdom of England salutes and humbly recommends himself to all present and to come who may see or hear these present letters. Equity wills and reason ordains that men of virtue and noble courage shall have the reward of renown for their merits, and that not just in their own persons in this mortal and transitory life, but in such a way that after their day the issue of their bodies shall in all places be held in honour perpetually before others by means of certain marks and insignia of honour and gentility. That is to say, by blazon, helm and crest; so that by their example others shall strive the harder to spend their days in deeds of arms and other virtuous works so as to win the fame of ancient gentility in their lineage and posterity. Now I Garter King of Arms aforesaid have been informed and advised not only by common repute but also by the report and witness of noble men worthy of belief that Edmond Mylle has long time followed the career of arms and in this and in his other affairs has borne himself so valiantly and honourably as to be fully deserving that he and his posterity shall in all places be honourably admitted, renowned, counted, numbered and received among the number and in the company of men of old gentility and noble men. Wherefore, in remembrance of this his gentility, I have devised, ordained and assigned to the said Edmond Mylle to him and his heirs the following blazon, helm and crest: to wit, a shield of six points of *sable* and *argent* charged with three bears rampant of the same chained *or* the chains thrown about them: and the crest upon the helmet a bear sable similarly chained *or* upon a torce of *or* and *gules* enmantled of the same doubled with ermine, as the picture in the margin shows: for him and his heirs to have, hold, use, possess and clothe themselves with forever. In witness whereof I Garter King of Arms aforesaid have signed with my hand and sealed with my seal these present letters, the 12th day of August, the year of Grace 1450.[3]

This grant to Edmond Mylle does not stand alone: there are a number of similarly worded English grants that survive. I do not know precisely what feats of arms Mylle had performed, and the wording is formal; so that it would not be wise to conclude that the English heralds were always careful to verify the martial virtue of those to whom they granted arms. One at least of Smert's successors as Garter seems to have been comparatively unparticular in that regard, confessedly using the scale of wealth as his measure of quality; when charged with giving arms to 'bondmen and vile persons' his reply was that he had admitted none to be nobles but men of good fame 'having lands and possessions of free tenure to the yearly value of ten pounds sterling, or in moveable goods three hundred pounds sterling'.[4] But good and proven martial service did often lie behind such promotions. That would certainly seem to have been the case for instance with John Edam, who called himself an esquire of Hertfordshire and told the Court of Chivalry in 1410 that though he was not a gentleman of ancestry he had been given arms in the presence of the Earl of Pembroke on the ill-fated expedition to La Rochelle in 1372 (he could not remember the blazon, he said, for he had not seen it for twenty-nine years).[5] And Upton records two particular occasions on which his master, the Earl of Salisbury, ennobled men for the valour they had shown in the French wars. One was the anonymous gentleman, mentioned earlier, whose homosexual tendencies earned him the supposedly sodomitical partridge as a charge in his arms. The other was a squire of Salisbury's household who distinguished himself at the battle of Verneuil, where he was wounded in the genitals. He was granted a shield of three ox's heads *sable* upon a field *argent*, for, says Upton, 'the ox is a gelded beast and therefore oxen or their heads betoken that he who first bore them was gelded or maimed in his privy parts'.[6] It looks as if the first bearer of these arms must have already fathered a son before Verneuil, for three oxes' heads *sable* on a field *argent* are the arms to this day of the family of Walrond of Devonshire.

As the phraseology of Upton and Smert indicates, English grants of arms were in effect ennoblements, the insular equivalent of the grants of nobility by letters patent which are common on the continent, especially in France. The wording of such letters often contains echoes of the views of such as Bartolus about the nature of nobility, as Smert's letter does. They are often unspecific with regard to the ground of ennoblement, referring only in the vaguest terms to the 'laudable virtues and merits' of the grantee; and the grantees prove in fact to be a very mixed bag, counting among their number town officials, clerks, physicians, and even skilled artisans. A good many letters nevertheless do testify to the good service in war specifically of those who were ennobled, or of their ancestors (this is particularly common in letters of certification of nobility, which are not strictly grants of nobility, but confirmations of a status claimed).[7] And as in England so on the continent also we come across grants whose occasion was proven and particular martial service or, sometimes, the performance of some specific deed of arms. Thus Diego de Valera recalls how the Emperor Sigismund ennobled 'one named Orsalamin' for his valour in a tournament, although it was known that he was the son of a butcher; and how Charles VII of France ennobled Jean Bureau, his master of artillery, 'for his prudence and wisdom' in arms, and made him a knight.[8] Bureau was a great man, but Charles also ennobled lesser men for notable feats of arms, as Jean Dauneau of Thiérache, who took Lord Talbot prisoner at Patay.[9] He ennobled the two soldiers, Jean Bequet of Pont de l'Arche and Etienne Guillier of Brie, who were the first to mount into the 'Tour de Friche' at Pontoise when it was taken from the English in 1441. The arms that he gave these two at the same time recalled their feat neatly: to Bequet *or*, three towers *azur*, and to Guillier *azur*, three towers *or*.[10] But the most memorable of Charles's grants was of course not to a man but to a maid. Joan of Arc's family were ennobled for her valiant deeds, and to them he gave arms which she is said to have borne upon her shield and which her pursuivant Fleur de Lys wore on his tabard, 'the which arms were *azur*, two fleurs de lys *or* and in the midst a sword of silver the point stained *gules*, the said point passing through a crown of gold in chief, signifying that at the point of the sword she had upheld the crown of France'.[11]

These particular examples of ennoblement for valour and good service involve for the most part celebrated incidents or persons: that was why they were remembered. If the heraldic treatises are anything to go by similar ennoblements for valour cannot have been by any means uncommon. The very origin of arms was associated by their authors with the idea that underlies them. 'At the great siege of noble Troy,' says one English treatise, '. . . the great lords of both parties by discreet advice drew themselves together and accorded that every man that did a great deed of arms should bear upon him a mark in token of high doughtiness . . . and if it were so that such a man had any children that they should bear the same mark as their father did, with divers differences.'[12] This is an English treatise, speaking of an ancient and mythical age, but Diego de Valera and Oliver de La Marche both speak with reference to their own time of ennoblement for valour as if it were a far from rare occurrence.[13] If, says the author of *La vraye noblesse*, the prince sees a man of low degree but of noble bearing he may promote him to nobility 'even though he be not rich or of noble lineage': the 'poor companion' who distinguishes himself for valour should, he says, be publicly rewarded.[14] Another authority adds some nice details about the involvement of the heralds on such occasions. A commoner going to the war may paint his shield with marks such as a bar or a bend at his pleasure, it says, but he must display no metal. But afterwards, if he distinguishes himself in some engagement or achieves some feat of arms beyond the ordinary, the heralds shall award him metal in his arms, and declare thus: 'Our captain and we, having consideration to your courage, nobility, and fidelity to the cause of our kingdom, propose to honour your shield and coat, and so we attribute to you (say) as the field *azur*, charged with a lion *rampant or*.'[15]

And that coat and shield, of course, the man so honoured would pass on to his children. As Garter's patent to Edmond Mylle has reminded us, his posterity shared in the reflected glory of the deeds by which their ancestor proved both his prowess and their gentility.

So far we have been considering only the ennoblement for valour of those not noble. The heralds and their patrons found no difficulty in devising means to recognise special service or distinction in valour in those who were already noble. Jacques de Hemricourt tells us how Macair de Flemalle served the Count of Loos so well that the latter granted him his arms to part with his own, so that thenceforward he bore a *party* shield, the arms of Loos impaling his own arms. The lord of Chateauvillain similarly honoured Jean de Laydier by parting with him his arms.[16] A good many grants and adoptions of this kind are recorded. In a not wholly dissimilar way the Englishman Sir Henry Guildford, who served in the wars against the infidel in Spain in the late fifteenth century, 'had his arms ennobled with a canton of Grenado by Ferdinand King of Spain, for his worthy service in that kingdom, when it was recovered from the Moors'. Another contemporary English adventurer, Wiston Browne, had his arms augmented by the same king, for similar service, with a *sable* spread-eagle facing to the *sinister*, crowned and armed *or*.[17] These two English augmentations are very reminiscent of the story of how in 1347 John Cantacuzene, the Byzantine emperor, permitted William Paujoise and John Bruidy, nobles of Metz, to change the swallows in their arms into eagles, in recognition of their good service against the Saracen.[18] We can see here a distant glimmer of the dawn of the modern method of commemorating the honourable service of a soldier by the award of a campaign medal, perhaps with clasps to testify to his presence at this or that engagement, and the award of orders or decorations for distinguished valour. Though of course there is this very important difference, that the detail of this heraldry testified to the martial record not just of an individual but of a family, and so served to mark ancestral feats and to remind the posterity of the prowess to be expected of their lineage. That was indeed one of its prime purposes.

The accolade of knighthood was another way of honouring distinguished valour in the field. As the treatises make clear, it was an acknowledged principle that those who showed themselves bold in arms might on that account be knighted in the field (though this was much less common than that other practice noted earlier, of making knights on the eve of a battle or assault, and whose object was to encourage valour, not to reward it).[19] That the principle of the treatises was no dead letter this graphic letter of Castile King of Arms will witness, and in its individuality it will also make a nice companion piece to set alongside Garter's grant to Edmond Mylle, quoted earlier:

I Castile, King of Arms of the high, mighty and excellent King of Castile, certify to all princes, knights and esquires and to my brothers in the office of arms and to all others, that Jean de Rebreviettes, nobleman and servant of my dread lord the Duke of Burgundy and of the household of Messire Anthony the Bastard, his son, being come into this land of Spain to my lord the King of Castile well furnished with arms, men and horses, in purpose to make war upon the enemies of our faith . . . was in the Kingdom of Granada armed in the King's company, and was at the taking of Ximena. Which city was taken by assault, and the said Jean was among the first at the wall and within the city, and within the city fought man to man against one of the Saracens and vanquished him; and afterwards the King sent for the said Jean and the said Jean came before him with his sword in his hand, all bloody. And when the King saw Jean, who had borne himself so valiantly, he drew his own sword and made him a knight, notwithstanding the said Jean's protesting. And I certify upon my faith and honour and by the arms I bear that I never saw, then or since, any man more honourably knighted in all Spain than the said Jean de Rebreviettes. And all this I certify for truth, witness my sign manual and my crest of arms hereon set this 10th day of July the year 1456, in the city of Seville.[20]

Jean de Rebreviettes is more usually remembered for his satirical vow at Philip the Good's Feast of the Pheasant at Lille in 1454 than for his Spanish adventures. There he swore that if he did not win his lady's favour before Philip set out for the East against the Turk (which he never did), he would on his return marry the first willing girl he should meet that should be worth twenty thousand pieces of gold.[21] In the light of Castile's certificate, what looks like the cynicism of this vow seems to be evidence rather of high spirits overlaying a real chivalrous intention. Knighthood was not the only honour that Jean de Rebreviettes won in the wars against the infidel either. Four years later a grateful King Matthias of Hungary admitted him to his Order of the Dragon of Hungary, in recognition of his service against the Turk, begging him to wear its insignia wherever he might be in memory of the great love and gratitude that the King bore him.[22] Knighthood, and admission into an exalted order of chivalry, were of course strictly individual honours: they were not hereditary. In that sense they take us one step nearer the modern system of awards, decorations for valour displayed in the profession of arms.

The accolade of knighthood was more than just a mark of distinction, for knighthood was a specific grade in the late medieval scale of aristocratic precedence, with standing immediately below the rank of baron and above that of esquire. In that sense knighthood conferred for distinguished valour had something in it of immediate promotion or the granting of a commission in the field. This aspect of the accolade of knighthood – the sense in which it raised a man to officer-status – is well brought out by Joinville's story of how he landed his men near Damietta on St Louis's crusade, back in 1249. 'When I came back to my ship [from the council of war] I put the little sloop in the charge of one of my squires, named Hugh de Vaucouleurs, whom I knighted there and then.'[23] Here clearly the accolade was a sign of Hugh's new charge, the accompaniment of his commission to command 'the little sloop'. The same idea comes out more clearly still in accounts of promotions from the rank of knight bachelor to that of knight banneret, a title which had strongly official military implications, in particular that the knight in question could muster a force of fifty lances to serve with him. Froissart gives a graphic account of the promotion of Sir John Chandos to this rank on the eve of the battle of Najera:

> Sir John advanced in front of his battalion with his banner in his hand, encased: he presented it to the Prince, saying 'My lord, here is my banner: I present it to you so that I may display it in whatever manner may be most agreeable to you: for, thanks be to God, I have now sufficient lands so to do, and to maintain the rank which it ought to hold.' The Prince, in the presence of Don Pedro, took the banner in his hands (it was blazoned with a sharp stake gules on a field argent), and having cut off the tail to make it square, he displayed it, and returning it to him by the handle, said 'Sir John, I return to you your banner. God give you strength and honour to preserve it.'[24]

The square banner of the banneret with his arms upon it was the outward and visible sign of his rank on all martial occasions, at the tourney and in war, as well as being the rallying point for his company in the field. The point of cutting off the 'tail' was that a knight bachelor was entitled only to a triangular penon, and so the alteration constituted a formal ceremony of promotion.

★

Promotion, whether to the rank of banneret or knight or simply to be noble, had to take account of the capacity of the man promoted to maintain his dignity, which was largely a matter of his wealth. It might also have to take account of the nature and degree of his merit, and this could be a nice calculation. Jean de Bueil for instance gives it as the general opinion that a non-noble who had distinguished himself in the assault of a city may be ennobled for his valour, but that he should not be knighted (as one of noble lineage might be).[25] In a field engagement it might be different, Jean says; the point is that the assault of a town is not so high a matter and does not so test courage as does fighting face to face with an enemy in the field. Here Jean introduces us to a new aspect of promotion and ennoblement for valour and virtue, to a scale of achievement which the expert must be able to judge precisely if he is to award and record honour appositely. The heraldic expert, we see, needed not only to be able to recognise deeds of prowess but also to measure them, for in practice as well as in courtesy books there were refinements, gradations of esteem for particular martial achievements.

A remarkable section in one late heraldic treatise, devoted to sepulchral monuments, offers us a glimpse of the niceties of distinction that could be involved here.[26] 'This is the manner,' it declares, 'how a man may know how a noble has lived and used his life and persevered to the end, when he is buried and his effigy is depicted upon his tomb armed.' If he has merely served in the wars as a man at arms, then he should be depicted armed, but with no coat of arms and unarmed as to his head. If he has in his time fought in the lists and acquitted himself to his honour, he may be depicted armed at all points, but with his vizor raised, with hands clasped and with his sword and spurs shown. If he has fallen in a mortal battle on the victorious side he may be depicted armed at all points with his visor closed, his drawn sword in his right hand with the point upward and his shield grasped in his left hand. If he has died of his wounds received in battle his sword should be shown sheathed and his visor detached. If he has died a prisoner, taken honourably in battle, he should be depicted all armed, but with no spurs and his scabbard empty. And in all cases, the authority adds, if he has been in mortal battle in the company of his prince he may be depicted in his coat of arms. The author of this treatise was a purist: I do not think that the rules that he adumbrated can be shown to have been followed with any precision. They are interesting nevertheless because they show that he was aware of a finely adjusted scale of chivalric values, and believed it to be authoritative.

A not wholly dissimilar range of distinctions is outlined in the statutes of the Count of Foix's Order of the Dragon. Here there is no question of burial, but of the manner in which the living companion might display his device of the order, a dragon in which 'sieges' or sockets were provided. He who had completed certain tilting courses specified in the statutes might place in the first socket a diamond. He who had fought a single foe body to body in the lists might place in the next a ruby, and a second ruby by it for fighting in the lists in a team of gentlemen. For having been present in a battle at sea he might place an emerald in another 'siege', and a second emerald by it for a pitched engagement on land. A turquoise was to signify he had been present at the assault of a city or castle. If he had been armed in the field against the Saracen he might place a sapphire in yet another siege, and finally, if he had made the pilgrimage to the Holy Sepulchre in Jerusalem he might place a second sapphire by it.[27]

These two texts give an impression of very precise distinctions being drawn between different kinds of military experience and the honour accredited to them. At this distance of time, it is no longer possible to reconstruct with detailed accuracy the refinements of the system according to which those versed in chivalrous lore accorded more or less honour to distinction in different martial acts and exercises. We would know a good deal more about the matter, no doubt, if any record had survived of the answers of the companions of King John of France's Order of the Star to the questions put to them by Geoffrey de Charny, for these fine points are the very stuff of his queries. There are said to be three different kinds of encounters in the field, he says, *rencontre, besogne,* and *bataille* (in ascending order of honour): how do you tell the difference? Which is the more honourable course for a captain, to break off a siege to meet the challenge of a relieving force at a chosen spot, or to press forward with the siege, promising battle after its completion? In what circumstances can a man at arms be taken prisoner without reproach to his honour?[28] But alas, we do not know the answers of the Knights of the Star: indeed we do not even know whether they ever gave any. The sources allow us to glimpse the broad outlines of a system. Great honour can be achieved in the tourney, greater in battle: prowess in a field engagement counts for more than prowess displayed in an assault. Special honour attaches to certain particular feats of arms, as to be first to set foot on the enemies' land from the sea, or to be first in the assault of a beleaguered strong point. or to have fought hand to hand in a mine beneath its fortifications. To take part in a crusade and to be armed against the infidel carries a special, sovereign honour. But details more precise than these remain opaque. When the Duke of Bourbon wished to know whether he could with honour break up the siege of Tunis on the terms that the Saracen offered, the Soldich de la Trau (a veteran captain and one of Froissart's heroes) advised that he might. He had achieved so much, the Soldich said, that 'as for me . . . who am but a poor knight, I hold to have been here to be equally honourable as if I had been in three great battles'.[29] Clearly, the siege had special standing because it was pressed against the enemies of the faith, but what further multipliers the Soldich would have used had it been pressed successfully I do not know, and perhaps he did not either. What seems certain, though, is that some one would have been able to give even on such a matter an informed view.

If we cannot trace the most precise gradations in honour of different sorts of engagements, we do have evidence that there were once those who felt confident that they could cast up with some accounting accuracy the measure of the honour and achievement of the champions of their time. Barbour in his *Bruce* can state with confidence that Sir Giles d'Argentine was reckoned in his time the *third* best knight in Christendom.[30] Even his enemies agreed, says Gelre the Herald, of Heinrich van Nueft, that he was the foremost of the young men of his time in the war against the Frisians.[31] In their day, Jacques de Hemricourt tells us, Waufflars de Momalle, William de Malclerre Lord of Hemricourt and the good Lord of Haneffe were reckoned to be *les trois plus preuz* of Hesbaye.[32] For Du Guesclin his French encomiasts found a special niche of honour, dubbing him the tenth *Preux*, and the Scots claimed the same place for Robert the Bruce.[33] At least one author-claimed that in a similar way Joan of Arc's valour had won for her a place alongside Penthesileia, Semiramis, Hippolyta and the rest of the nine *Preuses* of ancient time, and that the Countess of Montfort who defended Brittany when her husband was a prisoner perhaps deserved to be of their company also.[34]

We also come across clear verdicts as to who had won the 'prize' for prowess at this or that particular engagement. 'Sir Eustace,' said Edward III to the captive Eustace de Ribemont after the skirmish before Calais in 1350, 'I present you with this chaplet of pearls as being the best combatant of this day, either among those within or those from without: and I beg you to wear it for love of me.'[35] The Black Prince and his counsellors had no doubt about Sir James Audley's claim to the prize on the English side at Poitiers. 'Sir James,' the Prince told him, 'I and all the rest of us deem you the bravest knight on our side in this battle.'[36] At Loheren in 1453, the Burgundians recognised Jacques de Lalaing as having won the 'prize of the encounter'.[37] It is clear that captains, experienced knights and heralds knew how to bring the same precision of judgement that they could show at tournaments to awarding similar prizes in the grim business of real warfare. There seems little doubt that in this matter it was the experience of the tourneying field that pointed the way for their practice and its precision.

★

Perhaps, though, the most remarkable example of institutionalised prizegiving for prowess was that associated with what was called the *Eretisch* – the Table of Honour – of the Teutonic Knights. Because the wars of the Teutonic Knights against the pagans of Lithuania and Samogitia ranked as holy wars, and because the crusade – as we have seen – retained its distinct place of priority in the knightly scale of value, this was a very special chivalric occasion. In order to understand its significance, something of the background of the institution needs to be explained.

The Teutonic Knights, the German religious military order founded on the model of the Templars, had originally had two major spheres of activity, in the Holy Land and on the east European frontier of Christendom. Their conquest of Prussia was more or less complete by the end of the thirteenth century, and after the fall of Acre and the final loss to Christendom of the Holy Land, eastern Europe became the focal centre of their activity, and the castles of Konigsberg and Marienberg their headquarters. From these and other strongholds, they maintained their wars against the Lithuanians through the fourteenth century. The object of these wars was the conquest of territory from the pagans, and they reached their climax during the long Grand Mastership of Winrich von Kniprode, who ruled the Order from 1351 to 1382.[38] In these wars, the Teutonic knights relied heavily on the voluntary aid of visiting knights from other parts of Europe, and Prussia and Lithuania became, in consequence, a principal centre of crusading activity for western knighthood in the fourteenth century. The area was for most men much easier of access than the Orient, and crusaders could meet expenses on the spot by obtaining credit with the merchants of the Hanseatic towns on the strength of letters of credit obtained from merchants of their own land.[39] The names of those who came to Prussia to crusade included many of the most famous chivalric figures of the age: Henry Grosmont Duke of Lancaster, Henry Bolingbroke (the future Henry IV of England), Froissart's friend and patron Gaston-Phoebus of Foix, and Duke Albert III of Austria (of whose crusade Suchenwirt has left a vivid poetic account).[40] Nearly all of the unblemished knights whose fame the herald Gelre celebrated in his *Lobdichte* had been there; so had the 'parfit gentil knight' of Chaucer's prologue to the *Canterbury Tales*.[41] The fighting in the eastern lands was of a very different order from that which, say, Henry Grosmont or Gaston-Phoebus were otherwise used to under the sun of Languedoc, with its vines and rich towns and prospects of winning booty and ransoms. The terrain of the land that men called the Wilderness, where most of the fighting took place, was extremely difficult: it could only be traversed by cavalry in conditions of drought or deep frost, and winter was the commonest campaign season. The villages and forts of the pagans did not offer rich takings in *specie*, only in consumable goods. The knights of the Order had indeed material gains to win from the wars, because the land conquered would be theirs. But for the martial pilgrim who came to aid them the prospects of a *Reise*, as the expeditions were called, were of a different order: the dangers of death, of discomfort, and of debt incurred in consequence of the loss of horses and equipment – and glory.

In order to attract pilgrims in arms the knights of the Order took care to glamourise the accompaniment of a *Reise*. They feasted their visitors and took them hunting in the great forests where rare beasts such as bear and elk could be taken. The Table of Honour was the climax of their efforts in this direction. It was set, sometimes before, sometimes after the *Reise*, for a small number of knights, those to whom, among the pilgrims, the highest honour was judged. This was how it was described at the Council of Constance by a Polish (and hostile) witness:

Now the custom was and is, with respect to the so-called table of honour devised by the vanity of the said brothers [of the Order], that the said brothers having prepared a solemn feast for a certain number of such persons or guests, say for ten or twelve or some other small number, only those persons who were selected from among the knights by the heralds there present were assigned to places at the aforesaid table: these being such persons as had, by testimony of the heralds, traversed various parts of the world in the cause of knighthood, and had been seen by the heralds in divers regions: and according as one individual from among the knights and persons present seemed to surpass another in this respect, the places about the table were assigned and given. Those who were thus placed regarded it as a great honour to themselves, and it was so regarded by others.[42]

Alongside this general account, we may place a particular one, that given to the chronicler d'Oronville by Jean de Chastlemorand, who had been on a *Reise* in 1375.

And the Grand Master, seeing that this *Reise* had been honourably completed, on the day of Candlemas feasted the knighthood that were with him and that highly; and for the honour of the day, after Mass in his castle at Marienberg he had spread the Table of Honour, and it was his will that there should be seated at it twelve knights of the several kingdoms: and from the Kingdom of France there sat at that dais Sir Hutin de Vermeilles and Sir Tristan de Magneliers whom all called the *bon chevalier*, and from the other lands two each up to twelve, by the ordinance of the Grand Master: and they were served, for the high dignity of the day, as was their due. And thanks be to God to those twelve they explained this order of the Table and how it came to be established. And then one of the knights of that religion gave to each of them a shoulder badge on which was written in letters of gold '*Honneur vainc tout!*' And the next day the knights took their leave of the Grand Master, and returned each to his own country.[43]

Here is a prize-giving indeed! There is all the panoply of a great feast, with places assigned at a high table, a scene reminiscent (no doubt inten-

tionally) of that great table of legend, King Arthur's Round Table. Here are
the heralds and the company weighing fine judgements of honour prior to
the distribution of tokens of glory. Outside the castle and beyond stretches
another world, the wilderness land of the pagans, with its deep forests, its
bitter cold, its wild people, its sacred groves – and its hard fighting. Those
whom the Grand Master led out upon a *Reise* really did see their chivalrous
virtue tested. The regard that those who were placed at the Table of
Honour earned did not lack justification. The Teutonic knights clearly
understood that chivalry was no sham, that the lure of adventure and pride
in hard won glory were real and powerful human motives, and that by
extolling chivalrous virtue and institutionalising its reward of acclaim they
could serve their own ends. Their Table of Honour stands as testimony
both to their shrewd insight, and to the genuine ring of the metal from
which was forged chivalry's crown of glory, its meed of martial virtue.

★

So far in this chapter, the story we have been following has been that of
achievement and its recognition. It cannot be properly concluded without
some attention to the dark side of the same history. If nobility and marks or
insignia of distinction could be won by honourable prowess as well as by
birth and riches, so they could be lost by dishonourable conduct as well as by
marrying below one's station or by falling into poverty. And heraldic
science, just as it could be deployed to enregister and mark honourable
achievement, could equally be harnessed to convey by symbolic ritual the
stigma of disgrace.

   Dishonour, like honour, clearly had its gradations. The Order of the
Tiercelet, a Poitevin order of knights whose statutes provided for the
augmentation of the insignia of a member who had distinguished himself
(including a special augmentation for service on a *Reise* with the Teutonic
Knights), also provided for a diminution of the insignia of one who was
guilty of a *faute en armes*.[44] We hear similarly of technical 'reproaches' that
could entitle the heralds to exclude a knight from the tourney, such as a
suspicion of having breached his pledged faith, or of having in one way or
another done dishonour to womankind.[45] We are reminded here that the
famous phrase *chevalier sans reproche* (a qualification insisted upon as the
condition of membership of many chivalrous orders) need not necessarily
imply a truly stainless character, but simply a record clear of all technical
fault. Such technical faults were clearly not irreparable: Geoffrey de Charny
in his questions to the Knights of the Star was anxious to know by what
formal means such smirches could be repaired.

   Breach of faith could of course be a serious matter, and its treatment
illustrates neatly the way in which heraldic rituals of honour could be

reversed to show its opposite. This specific charge – breach of faith – was one that, in the fourteenth and fifteenth centuries, was raised particularly often in chivalric circles on the ground that a knight or gentleman had defaulted upon his chivalrous promise to pay a ransom (the fact that it was common practice to set prisoners free on parole to return home and raise ransom money made default relatively easy). In these circumstances, the captor could attempt to sue his prisoner, or better still those who had pledged themselves as sureties for the sum he had promised, or might challenge him to a judicial duel as a 'traitor to his pledged faith.'[46] But there was another means that a captor could resort to, and to which many did, that known as *deshonnoirement* in the French sources. What this meant was simply this: that the captor caused his defaulting captive's arms to be displayed in public places reversed, or perhaps a picture of him armed and hanging upside down or in some other degrading position. Thus the French captains Arnaut Guilhen and Thibaut des Termes displayed pictures which dishonoured the Lord of Chateauvillain, their defaulting prisoner, publicly at the gates of Berry. Their fellow captain La Hire rode on campaign with the arms of Robert de Commercy, a pledge of his defaulting prisoner Monsard d'Aisne, displayed reversed at his horse's tail.[47] The insult was a very serious one. It implied a reproach that would be universal in knightly company, and that would set the guardians of chivalrous *mores* into action – thus we learn that the companions of the Golden Fleece sat down at their chapter to discuss the case of Chateauvillain's kinsman and surety, the Seigneur de St George who was of their number, and whether his relative's dishonour extended to him as a surety.[48] Du Guesclin regarded the insult as so deadly, indeed, that he summarily hung the captain of Moncontour, who had slandered him with breach of his faith as a prisoner of the English and had reversed his arms, from his own battlements in full armour.[49] It was not a reproach that the tenth *Preux* could afford to have noised against him.

Cowardice and treason were still more serious affairs, as was to be expected in a society whose ethic was essentially martial. Gross cowardice was notionally punishable with death; lesser cowardice could involve loss of status and insignia. Sir John Fastolf was suspended from the Order of the Garter when the suggestion was voiced that he had shown cowardice at the battle of Patay.[50] The Seigneur de Montagu was expelled from the Order of the Golden Fleece when he fled after the defeat of Anthon.[51] Treason was still more dramatically treated, as one might expect, given that to betray one's lord had from the earliest days of chivalry and before been held the darkest of all the crimes with which a knight or warrior could be charged. For the traitor knight the full panoply of degradation from all honours could be brought into play, with fittingly horrific ritual. When Sir Ralph Grey, the Lancastrian captain of Bamburgh, was taken in arms resisting Edward IV, he was brought before a court martial and condemned to die a traitor's death, and to be disgraced. This is how John Tiptoft, the Constable of England, sentenced him:

> For these causes, Sir Ralph Grey, dispose thee to suffer thy penance after the law. The King hath ordained that thou shouldest have thy spurs strucken off by the hard heels with the hand of the Master Cook, the which he is here ready to do, as he promised at the time when he took off thy spurs [i.e. when Grey was knighted], and said 'an thou be not true to thy sovereign lord, I shall smite off thy spurs with this knife hard by the heels.' And so was shown the Master Cook ready to do his office, with his apron and his knife.
>
> *Item*, Sir Ralph Grey, the King hath ordained here, thou mayest see, the King of Arms and the Heralds, and thine own proper coat of arms, the which they shall tear off thy body, and so thou shouldest be degraded of thy worship, *noblesse* and arms, as of the order of knighthood; and also here is another coat of thine arms reversed, the which thou shouldest wear of thy body, going to the death-ward, for that belongeth after the law.[52]

For the notionally basest of crimes, the law provided terrifyingly condign humiliation as the accompaniment of its ultimate sanction. Ralph Grey, in fact, was in a degree lucky: King Edward pardoned him his degradation (but did not spare his life) on account of services his grandfather had once rendered the house of York and for which *he* had suffered on the scaffold. Others were not so fortunate. Andrew Harclay in 1323, condemned for intelligence with England's Scottish enemies, was stripped of his tabard and hood, had his spurs hacked from his heels and his sword broken over his head. 'Andrew,' said his judge at the conclusion of these rites, 'now art thou no knight but a knave, and for thy treason the King's will is that thou be hanged and drawn.'[53] When Philip of Hagenbach, Charles the Bold's ex-governor of Alsace, was condemned for his crimes and excesses at Brisach in 1474, there was a herald present to read out to him the formal order for his expulsion from the brotherhood of the Knights of St George's Shield, and to see to his degradation; and in order to show that he had now lost all earthly esteem, a man standing by him gave him a great buffet in contempt.[54] We have seen how the chivalrous modes of honour anticipated the award of medals and decorations in a later age: now we see its modes of dishonour anticipating the solemn sadism that has on occasion accompanied the later court martial, with nothing spared of the ritual horrors of ignominy that Kipling conjured up so vividly in his dreadful poem 'They're hanging Danny Deever in the morning.'

★

What, we must ask in conclusion, does all this record of ceremonial, of the award of badges of rank and insignia, of rituals of honour and dishonour, really tell us that is important? What it comes to is I think this. It demonstrates that the debate about the nature of nobility, and the verdict which gave priority to virtue over lineage in the definition of its ultimate essence, were not just a virtuoso literary exercise. Rather the reverse: the debate and verdict were directly related and relevant to a complicated system designed to provide for the social recognition of virtue, in practice. It was an object of that system to bring out at the same time the exemplary role that theorists assigned to public honours, privileges, and insignia. The ceremonies and rituals through which this system found expression have some things in common with those rituals that anthropologists have studied, whereby primitive peoples maintain and uphold the pecking orders of their society; but in this particular respect they are quite different from them. In contrast with primitive tribal practice the chivalric system was related to a reasoned and reasonably coherent social ideology, which had acquired a full measure of articulate literary expression. It used the same sort of methods to denote distinction of birth on the one hand and distinction in martial prowess on the other because the relation between the two (that such writers as Jean de Meun and Bartolus and the author of *La vraye noblesse* explained at length) was consciously understood. Its nice distinctions, its rituals and their symbolism were related and underpinned by an underlying social philosophy, or if philosophy seems too grand an expression, at the least by an articulate social ideology.

To be sure, that ideology had its limitations. Its conception of secular virtue, centring on courage, loyalty, perseverance and the keeping of faith, was narrowly martial. But what else should one expect of a society which interpreted the social role of the secular governing class in terms of military function – terms not so inapposite in a time when fitness to rule and the capacity to use force to uphold legal command were so often very nearly the same thing in practice? And at the least its honorific rituals gave to the notion of nobility a positive dynamism, as the accolade of virtue, that the negative force of social exclusiveness, so often stressed by historians of nobility and chivalry, could not have generated. The notion that nobility must be related to virtue modified the rigidity of class exclusiveness, and ensured the recognition of the desirability of some degree of social mobility.

The chivalrous rituals of honour also helped to maintain chivalry's relation with religion, with what the society of medieval Christendom recognised as the fount of all grace and virtue. When we hear of how John Ryther esquire lingered in Prussia to see to the placing of a glass panel of the arms of his master, Geoffrey Le Scrope, slain fighting the pagan, in the church of Konigsberg; when we read of how the Prior of Marton preserved in his treasury the coat of arms that Sir Alexander Neville had worn when he was armed at the battle of Halidon Hill;[55] when we stare at the stalls of the Garter knights in St George's Chapel at Windsor or of the Knights of the Swan of Brandenberg in the church of Ansbach, with their armorial achievements over them: we are reminded of the role of the churches great and small of Christian Europe as the mausolea of chivalry, the final resting place of its insignia and mementos of honour. There, in stone and glass and hatchment, they had their final lesson to teach, that the man who is born to the profession of arms may save his soul in the honourable discharge of his office in it: indeed that that is his duty, not only to his ancestors and descendants, but to his God as well, that he should seek to do so. That is the lesson that these mementos preach silently, and that justifies the lavish care that that heraldic author lavished on the manner in which a knight's effigy should recall how he had conducted himself in arms, for, as Jean de Bueil put it, 'we poor soldiers will save our souls in arms just as well as we might be living in contemplation upon a diet of roots'.[56] The virtue of the soldier was not the same as that of the priest, but it was virtue nevertheless, and the remembrance of that point kept chivalry and nobility in contact with values that men respected as eternal.

CHAPTER X

The Secular Orders of Chivalry

The Teutonic Knights' institution of a Table of Honour served a series of chivalrous purposes. At one and the same time it encouraged the pursuit of martial distinction and gave ritual expression to its achievement; it played upon the ideal of valour and knight errantry and to some extent exploited it; and it responded to a need on the part of chivalrous society for a measure of formal recognition of its high purposes. Very much the same might be said of the numerous secular orders of chivalry and knightly confraternities that were founded in the course of the fourteenth and fifteenth centuries. Their number is testimony to their significance, and their multiplication is one of the most remarkable developments of late medieval chivalry.

Our knowledge of these associations is very uneven: some are famous and have left substantial records; some did not last and are known, perhaps, only from their statutes; and some survive only in passing references. The most striking among them were those founded by great princes and distinguished by their lavish ceremonial and their ornate dress regulations. The oldest of these princely orders seems to be the Order of the Band, founded by Alfonso XI of Castile in about 1330. Edward III's institution of the Order of the Garter in 1348 was the next important foundation, and was followed by King John of France's Order of the Star (1351); by Louis of Naples' Order of the Knot (1352); by the Emperor Charles IV's Order of the Golden Buckle (1355); by the King of Cyprus's Order of the Sword (1359); and by the Count of Savoy's Order of the Collar (1363). Among the more memorable foundations of the next century were the Emperor Sigismund's Order of the Dragon (? 1413); Philip the Good's Order of the Golden Fleece (1431); Duke Albert Achilles of Brandenberg's Order of the Swan (1444); René of Anjou's Order of the Croissant (1448); and Louis XI of France's Order of St Michael (1469).[1] These are just a few of the more famous orders. We know much less about the confraternities of lesser knights, which were clearly quite numerous but whose history is comparatively ill documented. Their names betray their relationship with the more prestigious princely orders: among them we must number for instance the Confraternity of the Black Swan in Savoy (1352); the Order of the Tiercelet (founded by the Vicomte de Thouars in 1380); the Order of the Golden Apple (founded by the Seigneur de Listenois *c.* 1390); and the Confraternity of St George in Franche Comté (founded by Philibert de Molans *c.* 1430). The earliest that I know of is that which called itself, with a fine dash of self-mockery, the Order of Fools, founded in 1331.[2] Knightly confraternities proliferated in Germany with what seems a special vigour: there we encounter in 1362 the company or brotherhood of the Martinvogel, in the 1380s the Companies of the Lion and of St William, in 1391 the Company of the Sickle, and in 1406 hear for the first time of the Brotherhood of St George's Shield, which became famous. In consequence of particular local conditions these German brotherhoods came to play an important part in social and political life, and had an influence comparable with that of the great princely orders, though of a rather different nature.

It is natural to see a connection between these late medieval orders of chivalry and the crusading orders of an earlier period, such as those of the Temple and the Hospital, and the Spanish crusading orders – which still flourished vigorously in the later medieval age and which involved themselves deeply in the secular politics of the Spanish kingdoms. But though there is obviously some general resemblance (there are some echoes, for instance, of the rule of the Temple in the statutes of the Golden Fleece[3]), the connection between these two types of knightly association seems on closer examination to be distinctly tenuous. The crusading orders were distinguished by their commitment to Holy War; by the ascetic vows of poverty, obedience and chastity which their members swore (the rule of the Spanish Order of Santiago was unique in permitting its knightly brethren to be married); and by their judicial subjection to ecclesiastical authority. In contrast, Holy War was never the sole and seldom the principal commitment of the secular orders and confraternities: those admitted to them were ordinary secular noblemen who continued to lead ordinary secular lives; and, except with regard to their religious observances, these orders were subject to secular and not to ecclesiastical authority. It is just possible that the example of the Spanish crusading orders (and especially that of Santiago) may have helped to inspire King Alfonso's foundation of the Order of the Band, and that institution may in turn have helped to encourage Edward III toward the foundation of the Garter.[4] But it is not likely that it was a principal influence: Edward, as we shall see in due course, seems to have had a very different model in the forefront of his mind. If one is in quest of origins, it seems likely that tourneying societies, like that association of the Round Table that Ulrich von Lichtenstein founded, come closer

In this pageant is shewed howe the noble Erle Richard was made knyght of the Garter at that tyme to his greet worship And after by mavuelt act by hym ful notably and knyghtly acheved in his owne persone Did greet hono and worship to the noble ordre of knyghtes of the Garter. as by the pageant hereafter folowyng more plenyly is shewed.

35. Richard of Warwick is invested with the Order of the Garter on the field of Shrewsbury in 1403, by King Henry IV (British Library).

36. Heraldic panoply at a fifteenth-century tournament (Bibliothèque Nationale).

38. The Manasseh Codex: a knight (Rudolf von Rotenburg) and his lady (Universitätsbibliothek, Heidelberg). See p. 127.

37 (facing page, below). A tournament in which Arthurian knights are depicted with blazoned shields that follow the record in fifteenth-century armorials (Bibliothèque Nationale). Palamedes is unhorsed; for his checky arms, argent and sable, see Bibliothèque Nationale MS FR 12597 fo. 68 verso. See p. 141.

39. The Vows of the Peacock (British Library). See p. 213.

40. The shepherdess of the *pas d'armes de la Bergière*, with the shepherd knights' white and sable shields hanging from a tree (Bibliothèque Nationale). See pp. 203–4.

41. The glass name plate of Ulrich Ketzel, displaying the insignia of orders with which he was associated (Germanisches Nazionalmuseum, Nuremberg). (Another memorial plate displays further insignia.) The ape holding an apple is the charge in the Ketzel family shield. See p. 183.

43 (facing page). The Order of the Knot of Naples (Bibliothèque Nationale). The black-robed figure eating apart at the feast is a knight found guilty of a 'reproche' in arms. See pp. 192, 195–6.

42. Investiture with the order of the Band (Bibliothèque Municipale, Besançon). See pp. 185–6.

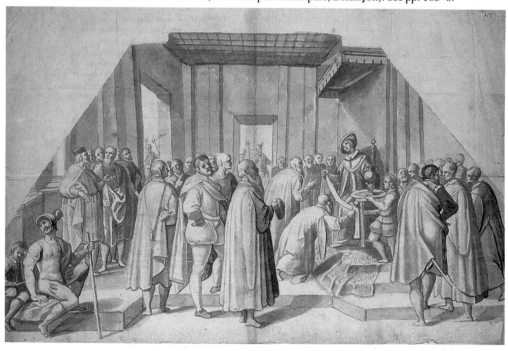

bien se aucun des dis cheualiers se trou
uoient en aucuns fains royaumes et leur
samblast que a bon eur peussent ban
niere leuer la banniere quil leueront i
doit estre dargent ou toute blanche aun
grant ray ardant ou milieu du saint
esperit et soit a leur uolonte de la leuer
especialment contre les enemis de la foy
et pour le pror et bonneur de leur natu
rel seignour maintenir en criant chascu
son cri quant vint et et apres leur cri en crieront au
droit desir.

Item se aucun cheualier auenoit chose i
quil se preist bonteusement de bataille
ou de chose ordenee la quel chose le saint
esperit ne ueulle souffrir le tour cheualier
soit tenus en toutes manieres sans mil
contredit de venir le tour de la feste au
uir chastel et doit porter robe toute noi
re si come tous les autres cheualiers la
porteront toute blanche et aussi bon
cheualier soit come le tiers tournie et
et vestir robes blanches et bien ap
partans grans et bien lisables qui i
diront lay esperance ou saint esperit de ma grant bon
te amender. Et le tour ne mangera pas auec les che
ualiers mais mangera ou milieu de la ou le prince

44. Richard Earl of Warwick entrusts his jousting challenges to his herald to carry them to the French court, from the Beauchamp Pageants (British Library). See p. 207.

to providing a prototype than the crusading orders, but the evidence concerning them is scanty. Certainly, if it is authentic, the story of the tourneying society founded in the 1290s by the Count of Holland, with the special insignia of a scallop on a livery collar, sounds very like an early forerunner of the great secular orders of the fourteenth century.[5] Among these, the Castilian Order of the Band had, as we shall see, quite specific elements of a tourneying society, which were incorporated in its statutes; and it has recently been suggested that the original seating arrangements for the companions of the Garter in St George's Chapel, with stalls on the King's and the Prince's side, were designed to reflect the selection of two well-balanced tournament teams.[6]

In constitutional terms, the closest links of the chivalric orders and confraternities of the later middle ages seem not to be with the crusading orders but with the lay confraternities, which became very numerous after the beginning of the thirteenth century. The purposes which these associations promoted were very diverse, though almost all had a pious or a charitable element in them. Religious observance (especially provision for funeral rites and the saying of masses for the dead), education, and the care of the old and sick were among their common objectives; but the craft guilds belong to the same family of institutions, and their principal *raison d'être* was the regulation of production and exchange. Very early we hear of confraternities concerned with the promotion of the crusade, by provision of funds and assistance with recruitment, and some of the Italian Guelf confraternities also had a military side to their activity.[7] The first reference to confraternities of knights in the true sense seems however to be a canon of the Council of Avignon of 1326, which refers scathingly to the disorders created by noblemen who form association upon oath: 'in the name of confraternity, and who come together once a year in some fixed spot, where they hold their chapters and conventicles, and swear together that they will uphold one another in all matters with aid, counsel and favour against all comers, their natural lords excepted: and they all dress in the same robes with particular badges or ensigns and choose a chief whom they all swear to obey.'[8] This is an excellent thumbnail description of the sort of knightly brotherhood that was soon to become very familiar.

The distinctive marks of the lay confraternities generally were, firstly, the possession of a body of statutes, regulating admission to the society; the conduct of its meetings or 'chapters'; and the manner of appointment, powers and duties of its officials. Confraternities usually adopted a patron saint, in which case the statutes would provide for the corporate celebration of his cult on his feast day. Many endowed their own chapels, or chantries in a local church, and provision was commonly made for the saying of masses for the souls of departed members. At the chapters or meetings of the association the conduct of the society and its individual members could be reviewed, breaches of regulations punished, and quarrels between one member and another might be brought to arbitration. The secular orders of chivalry conform to this pattern of organisation in every respect. They had their own statutes, which meticulously regulated admission to membership, the obligations of the companions to the order, to the officials and to one another, and the penalties for breaches of its rules. They associated themselves with particular religious cults and festivals, the Garter for instance with that of St George, the Croissant with that of St Maurice, the Knot with the Holy Spirit, the Martinvogel with St John the Baptist. Many had their own chapels, as the Garter's chapel of St George at Windsor (or the Order of the Star's chapel of Our Lady at the royal manor of St Ouen near Paris; or the chapel of the Order of the Swan in the church of Ansbach). Most provided in their statutes for regular chapter meetings, and many also made provision for the saying of masses for the souls of departed brethren. Constitutionally and judicially, lay confraternities are what the orders of chivalry were.

The possession of a body of statutes and the holding of regular chapters were important identifying marks of an order of chivalry. Oliver de La Marche, in a well known passage, makes this point very clear, and indicates in the process the confusion that could arise if it was neglected. When a prince gives a device to a number of noblemen, without limit of number and without drawing up statutes for their company, he told Philip the Handsome,

> that should not be called an order, but only a *devise*. For example, the Kings of England have their Order of the Garter . . . but besides this order they have a device which they give to knights, and to ladies, damsels and esquires, and this device, which is a rose, sometimes red and sometimes white, is given without limit of number to many persons, . . . and should be called a *devise* . . . Charles Duke of Orleans had a device, *le camail*, from which hung a porcupine, and this was borne by many worthy men, knights and esquires, but there was no limit on their number nor did they hold chapters, and so I say it was a *devise*, not an order.[9]

A society which has statutes and holds chapters but which has no limit on its membership, Oliver goes on to explain, should be called a confraternity rather than an order. The problems which were concerning him seem clear. On the one hand he wished to distinguish from other societies certain very prestigious associations, such as the Garter and more particularly the Golden Fleece, and to reserve to them the name of order. On the other, he wished to distinguish apart the insignia of orders and confraternities from what he regarded as mere badges of retinue, signs of a particular tie of loyalty binding together into an 'affinity' the followers of a particular lord.

Special badges and collars, as also livery colours, became very popular in the later middle ages, and such collars as the *camail* of Orleans actually were on occasion loosely referred to as orders.[10] The practice of certain princes encouraged such a looseness of usage. The Kings of Cyprus gave their Order of the Sword very freely to foreigners who seem thereby to have been given something like an honorary association with the Order, but who certainly were not bound by statutes and who would not have come to chapters, and the Kings of Aragon did likewise with their Order of the Stole and Jar, bestowing its badge as a mark of honour and favour to visitors to their land and court without limit of numbers.[11] Clearly such practice blurred the precise distinctions with which Oliver was concerned, and could seem very like the distribution of livery badges (which also might be given to strangers as a mark of honour and amity). The basic significance of the two kinds of insignia really was different, however. The collars of SS that John of Gaunt gave to his retainers and the *camail* that the Duke of Orleans gave to his men were signs of clientage, with chivalrous overtones indeed, but essentially emblems of alliance and allegiance.[12] The insignia that appear on – for instance – the name plate of Ulrich Ketzel in the great illustrated Ketzel family tree have quite another meaning. Here are the Sword of Cyprus, the Stole and Jar, the Dragon of Hungary, the bell which was the emblem of the confraternity of St Antony in Hainault, together with the Jerusalem crosses and the wheel of St Catherine.[13] This is testimony not to clientage, but to a career of martial errantry and of pilgrimage, in the course of which Ulrich had served in many lands and had visited the Holy Places and the monastery of Mount Sinai. It is a proud record of chivalrous achievement. Clearly, it was easy to be confused about the distinction between an order or confraternity and a *devise*: equally clearly the distinction was an important one.

Even when those fellowships that Oliver de La Marche termed *devises* and other loose forms of chivalrous associations are cleared out of the way, there still remains a considerable diversity among the knightly orders and con-fraternities of the late middle ages in terms of standing, function, and principal preoccupations. Probably the best approach to classification is that recently suggested by Dr J. D'Arcy Boulton.[14] He distinguishes three broad types of association: 'curial' orders; what he calls 'votal' orders; and 'con-fraternities'. As 'curial' he defines those orders which, besides having statutes and regular chapters, were bound together under the sovereignty of a princely founder and his hereditary successors. As votal, he defines those orders whose principal purpose was the discharge of a particular vow, usually to perform some specified feat or feats of arms. These orders were in their nature temporary, and had something in common with tourneying societies, since their vows most often involved feats that were to be accomplished within the lists. Both alike, the temporary votal orders and the standing tournament societies, had statutes which imposed rules on their companions and provided for regular meetings. As simple confraternities D'Arcy Boulton defines those knightly societies which had statutes, held chapters, and adopted common insignia, but which elected their officers (and so had no sovereign, *ex officio,* as the curial orders did). There are some difficulties with this classification scheme (it for instance relegates to the rank of a mere confraternity the Order of the Croissant which resembles a curial order in every respect except that its sovereign or 'senator' was elected);[15] nevertheless, it is probably the best that has to date been proposed. It has one great value, moreover: that it is related directly to the primary purposes behind the foundation of different kinds of orders, which is the next matter that we must examine. It will serve as a useful guide in the process.

As both the statutes and the histories of the individual 'curial' orders show, politics, propaganda and diplomacy were intimately associated in their *raison d'être*. It is clear that one of the major purposes of Edward III's institution of the Order of the Garter was to glamourise the standing of the war which he was waging against the King of France – to present the war effort in the light of a great adventure pursued by a noble and valiant company of knights against an adversary who was unjustly withholding from their sovereign his rightful inheritance. The accounts that the chronicles later give of how Henry V ceremoniously admitted the Emperor Sigismund into the Order, at the time when he was wooing Sigismund's alliance in the same war against the French, aptly illustrate the way in which association with a great curial order could be used in diplomacy.[16] The exultant reports of the English envoys at the Council of Constance, soon afterwards, that the Emperor was constantly wearing the insignia of the Order, show how significant this was seen to be as a symbol of diplomatic amity.[17] Diplomatic considerations of a rather similar kind underlay the clause in the statutes of the Burgundian Order of the Golden Fleece that forbade any companion to be a member of any other sovereign's order; this had, in this instance, a particular object, which was to forestall any attempt to bind Duke Philip to the English cause, more tightly and more chivalrously than he cared to be, by the offer of a Garter.[18] The foundation of Philip's great Burgundian Order had other and much wider political purposes as well, of course. One principal one was to bind together an elite group among the nobilities of the different provinces over which he ruled, provinces which had been brought into his dominion by a series of skilfully negotiated dynastic marriages and by the accidents of heredity but which had no unitary tradition of obedience and loyalty to a common sovereign.[19] For comparable reasons, we find a number of Neapolitan nobles being admitted to the Order of the Croissant in 1458–9, when René of Anjou was preparing for another effort to make good his claim to the Kingdom of

Naples.[20] Likewise Peter of Cyprus plainly saw in his Order of the Sword a means of glamourising his crusading projects and of attracting martial pilgrims from foreign lands into service in his expeditions.[21] As prestigious institutions, it is clear, the curial orders had great potential in the way of giving visible and evocative expression to the concepts of loyalty and of alliance, which were key concepts in the late medieval vocabulary of politics and statecraft.

As we should expect, a very heavy emphasis on the obligation of the companion to the chief or sovereign of the Order is a feature of the statutes of virtually all the curial orders. This was the point, for instance, of the rule of the Golden Fleece that a companion must on admission renounce any other order whose obligations might compete for his loyalty. In the time of Charles the Bold, the Chapter of the Order came to play an active political role in maintaining the loyalty of the Burgundian nobility: Henrik van Borselen, for instance, was forced by its ruling to resign the pension and office that he had received from Louis XI.[22] It was a clearly understood obligation on the companions of most orders that they should return the insignia in any case where natural or other obligations interfered with their loyalty to the sovereign who had granted them, and an eloquent letter survives, written by François de Surienne in 1450, explaining why he is returning his Garter to the King of England.[23] The general tone of the statutes of princely orders in this matter of loyalty is eloquently conveyed in the preamble to the statutes of the Order of the Band of Castile. Two principal objects inspired its foundation, this preamble declares: to honour chivalry and to maintain loyalty. For loyalty, it continues, 'is one of the greatest virtues that there can be in any person, and especially in a knight, who ought to keep himself loyal in many ways. But the principal ways are two: first to keep loyalty to his lord, and secondly to love truly her in whom he has placed his heart.'[24] The appeal to the ethic of courtly love makes a powerful foil here to the primary loyalty to the King that membership of the Order imposed. The general appeal of this preamble was backed up by the statutory regulations, that a companion must at all times be ready to do the King service in war, and that he must remain for ever his vassal or the vassal of one of his sons. A further regulation, common to this and many other orders, made it the duty of a companion to wear the insignia of the Order on at least one day in each week, thus making sure that the solemnity of these obligations should not be forgotten.

★

Another clause in the statutes of the Band of Castile has a somewhat different significance. It lays down that a newly elected companion must, at the next tournament to be held following his admission, run two courses against each of two fellow knights of the Band.[25] This, and the emphasis in its statutes upon the ethic of courtly love, reveals a concern with aspects of chivalrous life quite distinct from the serious businesses of war and politics – with sport and play. These became the principal concern of what D'Arcy Boulton has called the votal orders. Two particularly striking orders of this type were Marshal Boucicaut's Order of the *Dame Blanche à l'Escu Vert* and Jacques de Bourbon's Order of the *Fer de Prisonnier*.[26] The upholding of the honour of womankind was the chief avowed concern of the first of these two orders, whose companions bound themselves for five years to the service of women, especially of the defenceless and disinherited; a secondary purpose was to deliver from their vows knights and noblemen who had sworn to perform specific deeds of arms and could find no opponents to take up their jousting challenges. Jacques de Bourbon's order was more specifically concerned with the performance of feats of arms in the lists. The sixteen noblemen of name and arms who formed the Order swore together that every Sunday for two years they would each wear an emblem, the iron and chain of a prisoner fashioned in gold, until they found sixteen other gentlemen who would accept their challenge to fight on foot *à l'outrance* in harness of their choosing, on condition that they would become prisoners if vanquished. But that was by no means all that they agreed to do. They swore also to endow a chapel of Our Lady where, before her image, a candle set in a candlestick fashioned in the form of a prisoner's iron should burn perpetually through the two years, and to endow also a high and a low mass, to be celebrated in this chapel every day at nine o'clock. If they accomplished their vow they would endow the masses in perpetuity, and each would have his own coat of arms painted and hung in the chapel in remembrance of their enterprise. If any one of the original companions died within the term, the remainder would hold a service for him in the chapel, and each endow seventeen masses for the repose of his soul: and a successor would be elected by common accord. In addition to all this, Bourbon and his companions swore that for the term of their vow they would stand together in fraternal amity and each aid one another in his enterprises. Brief as was the life span envisaged for this order, there was much more to its objects, we can see, than an extravagant commitment to joust. The endowment of the chapel, the provision for funeral masses, the display of the arms of the companions and the promises of mutual fraternity and support are all features of the statutes of orders far more important than the *Fer de Prisonnier*, of those of the Garter and of the Star and of the Golden Fleece, for example, and of other 'curial' orders too.

Bourbon's order could clearly be described as a jousting society. Just how important and influential such societies could be is made clear by the example of the tourneying brotherhoods *(Turniergesellschaften)* which had a great vogue in Germany in the fourteenth and fifteenth centuries. Many

became famous, as did the Brotherhood of the Unicorn in Thuringia or that
of the Falcon and the Fish in Swabia.[27] These were no temporary associations, as Bourbon's order was, but were long lived. The obligations of the
companions were carefully defined in detailed statutes. Each brotherhood
had its officials, its 'King' and his counsellors, who presided when they held
their great court and tourney: at the end of the tournament a new king
would be elected to reign till the next 'court'. None were to be admitted to
the brotherhoods but nobles without reproach: robber knights, hardened
excommunicates and slanderers of women were all excluded – and those
who had demeaned themselves by marrying below their estate. A companion charged with dishonest or disloyal conduct might be summoned before
the 'King' and his council, and if he could not clear himself would be
excluded from the company. Any member who heard the honour of a
companion being impugned (a formal process,which might be the prelude
to complex litigation or to a feud, *Fehde*) should seek to help him to answer
the chárge. Provision was also made for the saying of masses for the souls of
departed companions.[28] The tournament brotherhoods had their own
insignia, usually hung from a collar worn about the neck, in the same
manner as the insignia of, say, the Golden Fleece: Grunenberg illustrated
the 'arms' of twelve of the most famous brotherhoods in his great armorial
book, drawn up in the 1480s.[29] With their permanent structure of government, and their carefully drafted statutes these were aristocratic societies
capable of exercising formidable influence in all sorts of quarters, even
though play was the basis of their formal objective.

The constitutions of the German confraternities of knights (*Rittergesellschaften*), which fit into D'Arcy Boulton's third category of chivalrous associations – simple confraternities – have some resemblances with those of the
tourneying brotherhoods, and many German noblemen were of course
members of both types of association. Much space in their constitutions was
for instance devoted to the same question that those of the tourneying
brotherhoods dealt with, of the duties of the members of the society in the
case where the honour of a companion was impugned. This was a matter
which should be referred to the officials of the order so that the accused
could be put to answer and either be persuaded to do right, or be upheld, in
court or in feud, by the order collectively.[30] Quarrels between members of
the society could naturally also be settled before its officials. Thus these
societies were essentially leagues of knights sworn together in friendship
and mutual loyalty, 'against all lords and all comers except our own lords
for the lands we hold of them', as the statutes of the Martinvogel put it.[31]
The members were bound to aid one another in war and feud, and in some

cases also with their ransoms or if they were injured in a tourney, in goods or body.[32] The statutes also made provision for the holding of regular chapters at specified religious feasts, at which the head of the society (the *Haupt-mann*), its marshal and its councillors would be chosen. The Chapter of the Martinvogel was to be held, for instance, at Stockheim at the feast of St John at Midsummer, that of the Sickle at Minden twice yearly, on the Sunday before Palm Sunday and the Sunday before Michaelmas.[33] These German confraternities were not however permanent institutions. Like the votal orders, they were brought together for a period of years, at the end of which the association could be (and often was) renewed. Behind the long life of the greatest of them, the Brotherhood of St George's Shield, lie a series of renewals of old bonds which in the course of the fifteenth century gave it a semi-permanent status, a chancery of its own and a powerful political influence.[34]

Specific local conditions explain the particular vigour and importance of the knightly confraternities in Germany. In southern Germany in particu-lar (and it was here that they proliferated most vigorously), the decline of the authority of the Empire after the fall of the Hohenstaufen had created a political power vacuum. Imperial cities, like those which formed the Swa-bian leagues of the fourteenth century, fought to maintain their indepen-dence, while the great princely dynasties fought to bring them and the lesser nobility under their own authority. In the resulting confusion, the con-fraternities offered to the lesser nobility a means to uphold their landed independence, their privileges and their pride in face of the hostility of cities and princes alike; and through their systems of arbitration between members they offered also a means of preventing these powerful authorities from exploiting to their own advantage the quarrels of the nobility among themselves. Thus the confraternities gave the nobility a measure of safety in corporate number; and at the same time, through their restricted aristocratic membership, their insignia, their solemn chapters, and the emphasis in their statutes upon honour and the right of feud, they bolstered the confidence of the nobles in their insecure pride of place.

Sworn brotherhoods of knights were by no means a merely German phenomenon, though it is only there that we find them playing an indepen-dent role of real political significance, forging alliances with princes and great free cities or formally declaring feud against them. There were plenty of them elsewhere, too. True, the noble leagues that disturbed the peace of France at the end of Philip the Fair's reign and in the time of his sons lacked the formal structure of the German brotherhoods, their chapter meetings and their hierarchy of elected officials (let alone their insignia); but they were hardly the true counterparts of the German associations.[35] Even in terms of political influence they compare unfavourably with them, no doubt because in France the subjection of the lesser nobility to the authority of the crown and the princes had progressed much further than in Germany (where the experience of the wars of the Investiture controversy had besides given the *ministeriales* of individual lordships sound early training in independent collective action).[36] Both in constitutional terms and in terms of the mentality that inspired their institution, the French confraternities of the age of the Hundred Years War, which in many parts of France created for substantial periods conditions of confusion comparable with those of Germany, have a much closer kinship both with the German confraternities and with the greater, curial orders. The same basic themes dominate in the statutes of, say, the Poitevin Order of the Tiercelet or the Auvergnat Order of the Golden Apple as in those of the Martinvogel or the Sickle: mutual amity, alliance against all comers with the exception of liege lords and kinsmen, arbitration in disputes between companions, assistance to companions held to ransom by enemies, and the provision for regular meetings and the election of officials.[37] It looks as if the motives that promoted the foundation of knightly confraternities in France and Germany had much in common.

At the same time, the affinities between the chivalrous confraternities of France (and of the French speaking areas bordering France proper, Savoy, Franche-Comté, and parts of the Low Countries) and the curial orders are more obvious than is the case with the German confraternities.[38] Their companions were more obviously anxious to catch something of the extravagance of these superior associations. The confraternity of St George of Rougemont in Franche-Comté was founded in the 1430s by Philibert de Morlans, an esquire of no great ancestry who never took knighthood. Nevertheless his confraternity was associated with a special chapel in the church of Rougemont, whose upkeep and services were maintained by the companions; and they held a feast on St George's day, before solemnly processing thither, robed in their insignia. There were provisions in his statutes for masses to be said for departed companions and for the display of their hatchments in the chapel.[39] The statutes of the Order of the Golden Apple in Auvergne laid down very similar regulations. So did those of the Order of the Tiercelet, and its statutes made provision also for the augmentation of its companions' badges in order to record the honourable feats of arms in which they had been involved, gilding the claws of the falcon emblem for those who had been on a *Reise* with the Teutonic Knights, or who had taken part in a royal siege, or who had fought a foe body to body in the lists.[40] Regulations such as these have very direct parallels in the statutes of curial orders, as those of the Garter (with its chapel of St George and its lavish provisions for commemorative masses), or the Croissant (with its elaborate clauses concerning the election of the 'Senator' at its chapter, and for its feast and its procession to the chapel of St Maurice in the cathedral of Angers), or of the Habsburg Order of the Eagle (with its careful regulations for the augmentation of the badge of the Order). In this way the statutes of the confraternities of the French-speaking lands offer a very useful illustration of the connections that link together all the different varieties of knightly associations – curial, votal and confraternal – connections reflected in overlapping preoccupations with a wide range of activities, devotional, sportive, social and political.

★

The goals of the chivalrous societies, as we have so far considered them, have been for the most part distinctly tangible ones: the recruitment and consolidation of political loyalty; the quest for diplomatic alliance and advantage; the maintenance of legal and social status and privilege; the promotion of activities such as tourneying which had strong tones of upper-class exclusiveness. These are none of them idealistic goals. That is no doubt the reason for the effort to add to them a flavour of romance and of honourable lustre by means of insignia and ceremonial, and to glamorise the activities of the orders by associating them with past glories and with the pursuit of idealistic goals whose honourable and ethical standing was not generally questioned. The point, that solid political and social objectives would be better served if their service could be given a more illustrious slant, was one which the more clear-headed founders of orders probably grasped quite consciously, but it does not really matter how far their understanding of it was conscious or intuitive. They certainly took pains to tap every resource of the literary mythology of chivalry to decorate and romanticise the associations that they instituted and to give them a lofty tone.

The lay confraternities offered the constitutional model for the chivalric orders; literature offered them a pseudo-historical model with a headier influence. A key passage in the *Merlin* section of the Vulgate Arthurian cycle tells how Merlin came to King Uther Pendragon and told him that he would build for him a round table, which with the table at which Christ sat at the Last Supper and the Grail Table would complete a symbolic trinity of tables. At this table there would be places for fifty-one knights.[41] The first fifty Merlin would name from the noblest and most valiant of those gathered at Arthur's court, and they would live as brothers. The fifty-first *siege* was of course reserved to the as yet unknown knight without reproach, the Grail Knight who would in due course come to the court of Uther's son Arthur. Here was a story offering an archetype for the orders of chivalry that had unnumbered resonances. An alternative (but related) archetype was offered by the story of the founding of the Order of the Free Palace in the fourteenth-century romance of *Perceforest*. In this romance, which is devoted to the adventures of Perceforest, a companion of Alexander the

Great on a mythical expedition to Britain, there is a description of the Free Palace, a miraculous round tower built by God himself: within it Perceforest and his companions found a great round table of ivory, designed to seat three hundred chosen knights.[42] The place of each knight at this table was marked by a shield of his arms on the wall behind it, and God named the first sixty-three.

The chronicles state explicitly that Edward III had the Arthurian model in mind at the time when he first decided to found an order of knighthood (though there is a good deal of confusion in their accounts, which tend to conflate the founding of the Garter and the great Round Table tournament held at Windsor a few years previously). The King, says Jean le Bel,

> in the nobility of his heart resolved that he would rebuild the castle of Windsor, which Arthur first constructed and where the Round Table was first established, on account of the prowess of the knights who were there then, who had served him so well that he held them so worthy and noble that their peers would not be found in any kingdom: and it seemed to him that he could not honour them too much, so much did he love them. And so the King proclaimed throughout his kingdom a great feast and a great court for the institution of this Round Table, and summoned from all lands ladies and damsels, knights and esquires to be present at this great feast at Windsor.[43]

Later the Garter was regarded as the almost lineal descendant of Arthur's order. 'I have read and heard', Jean Werchin of Hainault wrote to Henry IV in 1408,

> that in the time when the noble and mighty Arthur reigned over that lordship where now you reign, that there was established an order to which a number of knights belonged who called themselves the Knights of the Round Table, and in those days they excelled all in worship and chivalry . . . and now I have heard that certain kings of your kingdom in recollection of that order have instituted that which is called the Garter.[44]

John of France, whose foundation of the Order of the Star in 1350 was a kind of riposte to Edward's Garter foundation, seems to have had the Free Palace in mind. The statutes of this order of the Star follow its lead precisely in their provision for the painting of the arms and crest of each companion above his seat in the hall of the 'Noble House' of St Ouen.[45] The Order of the Knot, whose statues were in many respects modelled on those of the Star, was intended to be a company of three hundred knights, like that of the Free Palace.[46] In all three cases, the Garter, the Knot, and the Star, it seems that the literary model was invoked consciously, and for effect.

The two archetypes, of the Round Table and the Free Palace, had a particularly striking influence, but there were countless other literary associations that the statutes of various chivalrous orders sought to evoke. The growing taste for classical history and allusion was no doubt the reason why Louis of Naples, in the statutes of the Knot, ordered that those companions who had distinguished themselves should be crowned with laurel after the manner of the heroes of Roman antiquity; and he reminded them of the legendary associations of its headquarters at the Castell Dell'Ovo (the castle of the *Oeuf enchanté du merveilleux péril*, as he called it) which stood close to the cave where Virgil was in legend supposed to have worked his enchantments.[47] The *Roman de Troie* and its account of the judgement of Paris was clearly the background to the choice of their emblem by the companions of the Golden Apple, and of their motto, *La plus belle me devoit avoir*.[48] The story of Jason and his Argonauts originally inspired the choice of the Golden Fleece as the ensign of Philip the Good's great order (he had possessed a rich tapestry depicting their adventures since the beginning of his reign). But Jason's conduct was not faultless – he had broken his word to Medea – and Jean Germain, chancellor of the Order, reinterpreted the emblem as representing another fleece than that of Colchis, Gideon's fleece into which, according to the Book of Judges, the dew fell from Heaven to signify that he would overthrow Midian.[49]

The literary influences on the statutes of the orders were not limited to matters of emblems and decor. There was a more serious and a higher purpose behind, for instance, the statute of the Order of the Star which provided that at its annual feast a table of honour shall be set aside for the three princes, the three bannerets, and the three knights who by common assent had performed in the year the highest feats of arms in war.[50] The cult of the Nine Worthies clearly inspired this celebration of the virtue of valour. Similar and perhaps even more striking is the provision in the statutes of a number of orders – the Star, the Knot, the Golden Fleece and the Croissant – for the keeping of a 'book of adventures' recording the high deeds of prowess of their companions.[51] No such book has survived, but we know that René of Anjou's King of Arms began to collect material for that of the Croissant;[52] and Niccolo Acciaivoli certainly began to write about the adventures of the companions of the Knot, for Boccaccio jeered at him for it: 'he wrote in French of the deeds of the Knights of the Holy Spirit [another name for the order], in the style in which certain others in the past wrote of the Round Table. What laughable and entirely false matters were set down, he himself knows.'[53] Whether or not Niccolo exaggerated his own and his companions' glory, Boccaccio's reference to the Arthurian model is sure and true. The making of such books as these, once again in order to give valour its due, was clearly inspired by the account in the romance of *Merlin* of how, when he left Arthur's court, a knight of the Round Table had to swear that 'he would tell on his return all that had happened to him . . . be it to his honour or his shame. And by this means was made judgement of the prowess of each.'[54] The accounts of themselves given by the returning knights were set down by Arthur's clerks (or as some thought later, by his heralds); and it was generally supposed that it was from these records that Walter Map at the behest of Henry II of England had put together the history of Arthur.[55]

Literary influences were again very powerfully at work behind the foundations of votal orders. The great Pentecostal vow of the knights of the Round Table to achieve the quest of the Grail offered to such associations an ultimate model. The literary concept of courtly love is the most obvious influence, however, on many of them. It was clearly the inspiration for Boucicaut's order of the *Dame Blanche à l'Escu Vert*.[56] Boucicaut himself lived up to exaggerated standards of courtliness toward women, as his biographer is at pains to recall; when he was in Genoa and his companion told him that the two ladies whose curtsies he had returned with a salute were prostitutes, his reply was, 'Huguenin, I would rather have paid my salutations to ten harlots than have omitted them to one lady worthy of respect.'[57] The companions of the *Fer de Prisonnier* were, like those of Boucicaut's order, committed to uphold the honour of all gentlewomen and to give succour to any who asked it of them.[58] The Count of Foix gave his order of the Dragon to ladies and damsels as well as knights, and at the end of the year, if the various deeds of arms mentioned in its statutes had been achieved, they were permitted, like the knights, to decorate their dragon badges with emerald, sapphire and turquoise in memory of the companions' deeds[59] (it is worth noting here that a number of orders admitted women as well as men, as for instance that of St Anthony in Hainault: and in early days there were lady associates of the Garter who received robes of the Order).[60] It was natural that the imprint of the ethos of courtly love should have been at its sharpest with the votal orders, since so much of their activity centred round jousts and tournaments, an area in which the effort to embellish sport and martial training with colours borrowed from romance had a long history.

The romantic emphasis on the power of love and the desire for honour in the eyes of womankind, and on their capacity to inspire men to feats of valour was however taken seriously by some of the founders of more important curial orders as well. We have seen its mark acknowledged in the preamble to the statutes of the Band, which set fidelity to a beloved woman alongside fidelity to a liege lord as twin lode-stones of loyalty; Louis de Bourbon had the same theme in mind when, in the statutes of his Order of the Golden Shield he bade its companions not to suffer ill to be said of any woman, 'for, after God, a great part of the honour of the world comes from them'.[61] Stories with overtones of courtly love also circulated about the circumstances of the foundation of some curial orders, as the Garter and the Tress. The story of how Edward III, at a ball in Calais, retrieved the garter of the Countess of Salisbury and bound it on his own knee, saying 'Honi soit qui mal y pense', is certainly apocryphal, but some such rumour began to circulate quite early.[62] The emblem of the Bavarian Order of the Tress was supposed to represent the tress (in illustrations it looks more like a full grown pigtail) which was cut by the Duke who founded the order, for a keepsake from the hair of his beloved, and this story seems probably quite genuine.[63]

The literary influences, direct and indirect, on the conception of the orders of chivalry was plainly a powerful one. The long passages in the statutes of orders and confraternities (and especially in those of the more prestigious orders) which concern the ceremonial of feasts and chapters and processions and the wearing of insignia bear also the clear imprint of another erudite influence, that of the heraldic mind with its love of symbolism and its concern for ritual precision and the niceties of procedure and precedence. The manuscript books, in which the statutes of orders are recorded together with the arms and heraldic achievements of their companions are among the most decorative products of heraldic art. This heraldic influence combined with the literary one to foster that ornateness which is a particular feature of the orders of chivalry as institutions. The attention to decorative detail should not, however, be interpreted as an end in itself; it was more than that. It was a form of homage to the serious commitments of chivalry to which the companions of chivalrous orders obliged themselves.

When we come to look at what these commitments were, as the history and statutes of the orders reveal them, what is striking is their fidelity to the established pattern of chivalric ideals. At the beginning of this book we identified three themes that were woven together into the fabric of those ideals, the religious element in chivalry, the social and the martial ones. The same three themes are the very stuff of the fabric of the orders of chivalry, and this brings out forcefully how the ideal of the later middle ages remained faithful to its origins, despite the changing face of the times.

The sovereigns and patrons of the great curial orders were conscious of the need – if their purposes were to be served – of presenting their foundations as elite societies within the chivalry of their age, and saw clearly that this required due emphasis upon the Christian vocation of knighthood. That was the theme behind the religious ceremonies that preceded the chapter meetings of their orders, behind the endowment of their orders' churches and chapels, and behind the often lavish provision for masses for departed members. Their statutes also paid due attention, in many cases, to the special religious significance of Holy War. Some orders were of course not far from being secular crusading orders: Peter of Cyprus, for instance, in his foundation of the Order of the Sword was seeking to realise the potential of a chivalric association to institutionalise crusading enthusiasm in a manner very reminiscent of the Teutonic Knights with their ritual of the Table of Honour. A strong crusading flavour coloured the history too of the Spanish secular orders, especially the Aragonese Stole and Jar.[64] These are perhaps rather special cases, but the crusade was clearly prominent in the minds of other founders too. Charles of Durazzo, in the staues of his Order of the Ship, looked forward to a future reconquest of Jerusalem and provided that any companion who should be present when the Holy City was retaken should be entitled to augment his badge with a golden tiller.[65] He also provided that those companions of his order who should fight against the Saracens in other circumstances should be allowed to embellish their badges in other ways, varying according to the standing of the engagement in which they took part. The statutes of the Order of the Dragon of Foix and of the Tiercelet also permitted those who fought against the heathen to augment their insignia.[66] And there can be little doubt that the deliberately engineered shift of emphasis in the mythology of the Golden Fleece, away from the classical adventurer Jason and toward the Biblical Gideon, was associated with Philip the Good's plans for a crusade in which Burgundian knighthood, and his personal order in particular, would play a key role.

Even more striking than this concern with crusading is the emphasis in the statutes of a number of orders on the ordinary religious observances of the companions. The companions of the Croissant were expected to hear a mass once a day if they could, and if they failed to do so, to pay for a mass and to abstain from wine for a day. They were also expected to say the Hours of Our Lady daily. The companions of the Order of the Ship were to hear a mass and to say the seven penitential psalms each day; on Fridays they were to fast and to dress in black in memory of the Passion. The statutes of the Order of the Ermine of Naples reminded the companions of their duty to fast and to confess, and they were all to take communion at the High Mass on 29 September, the feast day of the Order's patron, St Michael.[69] These and similar clauses in the statutes of other orders reinforced the traditional duty of all knights to revere God and to be punctilious in their religious observance, which the first handbooks of chivalry, such as that of Ramon Lull, had stressed so strongly.

Nearly all the orders, as we have seen, provided for masses to be said for the souls of departed companions (the Garter statutes are particularly lavish in this regard).[70] In many cases, religious ceremonies were also associated with reception into an order. New admissions to the Order of the Ermine of Naples were to take place at the high mass on St Michael's day, and, during the mass, the collar of the order was taken from the altar to be hung about the neck of the new companion.[71] An elaborate liturgy was drawn up for the ceremonial admission of new companions to the Order of St Anthony in Hainault, with a long list of prayers and antiphons: its collar was solemnly blessed by the priest and sprinkled with holy water before it was handed to the head of the Order who invested the new companion. At the beginning of this church ceremony each candidate for admission had to take an oath to observe his Christian duties as a knight – to defend the church, to uphold justice, to protect widows and orphans and Christ's poor.[72] These are the old and familiar duties that the early liturgies for the dubbing of a knight had stressed. A general promise to thus uphold knighthood, and the stipulation that any known breach of these chivalric obligations rendered a candidate ineligible for admission, were a feature of the statutes of many orders.[73] In this late medieval age, when fewer and fewer noblemen were going through the formalities of being dubbed to knighthood, these solemn regulations, binding by oath the members of what were universally regarded as elite chivalric associations, were a way of keeping the high obligations of chivalry before the minds of the nobility at large. They were a partial substitute for the didactic role that the ceremony of dubbing had discharged in the past, when it was more common to take knighthood.

The founders of the great orders were careful to present them as elite societies not only in terms of virtue and religious dedication but in social terms also. Noble birth was a prerequisite for admission to virtually every curial order. Many demanded that those who sought admission should be gentlemen of name and arms, capable of proving their four lines of noble ancestry. The majority also insisted that their members should be dubbed knights, or at least that they should take knighthood within a term after their admission, though the Croissant admitted esquires and only differentiated them from knights in its sumptuary regulations.[74] The Neapolitan Order of the Ermine – it would seem uniquely – made eligible those who had been knighted for their virtue and did not come of high birth; but they had to be knights.[75] These were quintessentially aristocratic societies, as the crests and arms of the heraldic achievements of the companions, blazoned over their stalls in such a chapel as that of the Garter at Windsor, stand to remind us.

Given this all important reservation of admission to those noble by birth, the orders were, however, remarkably unhierarchical, internally. Within their ranks, the companions stood upon a par with one another, regardless of differences of wealth and title, and their statutes are emphatic to this effect. The companions of the Croissant, in their procession to the cathedral of Angers, were to walk two by two, in order of their seniority within the Order, 'without regard to their nobility, the standing of their lineages, their lordships, riches and offices, or to whether one is a knight and another an esquire'.[76] Edward III actually took pains to ensure that membership of the Garter should not be confined to the high and mighty: if a stall fell vacant, the names of three dukes or earls, of three barons and of three knights were to be selected for consideration, and the worthiest would then be chosen to fill the single vacancy.[77] Loyal brotherhood, with its strong overtones of parity, is the relationship proposed over and again as the model for those who were companions of the same order. Thus we encounter once more a theme that is familiar, especially from the literary sources, the bond of equal standing in chivalry that draws together high and low among the aristocracy and sets them on an equal footing within their own estate. There is here yet another reflection of the model of the Round Table which set the Arthurian knights, rich and poor alike, on a level of parity with one another.[78]

So far, with regard to the social ideology of the orders of chivalry, our attention has been concentrated on what the statutes of the great curial orders can tell us. The statutes of the lesser confraternities bring into sharper focus cruder aspects of noble class solidarity. The German knightly brotherhoods were not elite societies in the sense that the curial orders were. They were certainly exclusive, associations of noblemen concerned with upholding noble privilege and the preservation of the noble style of life of their members. Collective assistance to one another in war and feud, and the collective protection of privilege and independence in face of the attempted inroads of civic and princely authority: these are the themes that underlie their regulations. Their statutes reveal them as noble societies in the specifically social sense of nobility, and they also explain why it was not difficult to regard their activities as a threat to orderly government.[79] Here there is a real gulf between them and the curial orders. Nevertheless, the regulations in their statutes which reveal these aspects of the knightly brotherhoods are also to be found in the statutes of curial orders. They too imposed on their companions the obligation of mutual aid in one another's quarrels; they too provided for arbitration in the mutual disputes of members (which was one of the ways in which members of the brotherhoods sought to exclude themselves from the jurisdiction of cities and princes); they too provided for the collective support of members who had fallen on ill fortune (even, in the case of the Croissant, for the care of their children).[80] Regulations of this kind only seem less striking in the statutes of the curial orders because there is so much else there. In both contexts, curial and confraternal, they have the same basic significance, as reminders of the vital role of class pride in the social ethic of chivalry. If this was, as many have suggested, the source of most of chivalry's vices, it was also and simultaneously a vital force behind its virtues. It is no accident that the same noblemen of distinctly middling rank who sought to borrow for the French confraternities of the Tiercelet and the Golden Apple some of the gilded plumage of superior orders, were also among the crusaders of their respective *pays*.[81] The desire to embellish a little what were at root mutual protection societies and the readiness to discharge a more dangerous Christian chivalrous obligation were simply different manifestations of the same knightly pride of place.

The knight errantry of the companions of the Tiercelet and the Golden Apple brings us to the third traditional theme of chivalry, to the distinctive martial quality of the ethic that the orders sought to uphold. They were societies of fighting men. The insignia that identified them were designed to be worn or carried in battle and at the tourney. The loyalty which their statutes stressed over and again was not the corporate loyalty of nationalism, but the intimate personal loyalty of the fighting vassal or retainer to his lord, and of the companion-in-arms to his fellow. The kind of eventualities against which they sought to insure their companions were becoming the victim of a feud or being taken prisoner and set to ransom. The darkest crimes in their book were treason and cowardice, and they were meticulous about them. The Seigneur de Montjean's name was passed over the first time that he was proposed for the Order of the Croissant, because it was suspected that he had on one occasion ridden in arms against his liege lord, Charles VII of France – even though the fact was unsure and though it was in the company of the Dauphin that he had supposedly so ridden.[82] It was because the Seigneur de Montagu had fled from the battle of Anthon that the chapter of the Golden Fleece, after weighing his proven prowess on other occasions, regretfully decided that he could no longer be of their company, even though the battle was clearly lost when he fled.[83] Had Louis Robsart not been a companion of the Garter, Ghillebert de Lannoy explained to his son, he might have left the engagement in which he died, but as a companion of that order he knew that he had to stand and perish.[84] There was a very great deal of play involved in the ritual and ceremonial of the secular chivalric orders, it is true, but the men who bore them had not, for the most part, won admission to them lightly. The whole structure of the regulations of the different orders about tables of honour and augmentable badges and books of adventures were geared to a single, central end, the celebration of martial prowess.

This brings out an important point in conclusion. It is what really gives the lie to the charge that is so often brought against the secular knightly orders, that the concern with outward show and ceremony which their statutes so markedly evince is a sign of the decadence of late medieval chivalry. That is not to say that the orders were in any way above criticism: the religious obligations that their statutes imposed were no doubt often enough understood and discharged by the companions in a formal and superficial spirit, and their social snobbery was exclusive, arrogant, and potentially abusive in many circumstances. But the high price that they set upon loyalty and courage was quite genuine, and these are human values which it is not wise to undervalue in any age. The point is worth labouring, because the criticism has so often been urged against the late medieval orders that their pomp and ceremony are signs that energies that should have gone into the pursuit of idealistic ends had been diverted into the quest for elaboration and richness of decor and that over-symbolification had resulted in meaning and symbol losing touch with one another. The great Huizinga lent his authority to this view, contrasting the lavish display of the later, secular orders with the asceticism of the early Templars.[85] The comparison, though, is not really a legitimate one. Even in constitutional terms, as we have seen, the connection between the secular orders and the earlier crusading orders was a tenuous one, and in spirit the difference between them was much greater. Worldly honour and secular loyalties were pock marks on the face of such an order as the Templars' was; they were the very bone and marrow of the being of the lay orders of chivalry. The monastic rule was the model that the former adapted to a new end: with the spirit of that rule the model to which the secular orders looked back, the company of the Round Table, had nothing in common. What the Arthurian history taught was that glory – secular and visible gory – was to be associated with high courage and loyal service. The ceremony and ritual and insignia of the secular orders of chivalry were designed to uphold and teach precisely that principle.

Bartolus, discussing the relation between theological nobility on the one hand and natural and civil nobility on the other, suggested that the honours conferred by princes should be regarded as the counterpart in this world of the honours that would be conferred on the just in heaven.[86] His is a very useful analogy in the present context. Chivalry was a secular upper-class ethic which laid special emphasis on martial prowess, not an inner religion of the heart, and its system of honour positively needed external marks to clarify the working of its secular scheme of values at the human level. The rituals and robes and ceremonies of the secular orders, far from having the effect of obfuscating ideals in a fog of grandeur, were a means of giving expression to the quite genuine belief that high reputation – *bonne renommée* – was the just meed of achievement in the secular knightly world, whose professional preoccupation, in the broad framework of Christian society in this world, was seen as being with war and politics, not prayer and fasting. Knights had their Christian obligations, as all men did, and to these the orders paid due attention in their statutes, as we have seen; as specifically chivalrous societies, though, their prime concern was with affairs of this world where tangible and visible marks of distinction were appropriate.

CHAPTER XI

Pageantry, Tournies and Solemn Vows

The opulent ceremonial and the colourful robes and insignia of the secular chivalric orders are by no means the whole basis of the criticism of late medieval chivalry, that its exaggerated concern with outward forms is a symptom of loss of contact with serious values. The same trends – the elaboration of ceremony and ritual and the love of colour – are apparent elsewhere, and nowhere more plainly than in the development of the tournament and of jousting and in the extravagant vows (often associated with the performance of feats in the lists) to which knights of the late middle ages chose ceremoniously to pledge themselves. The record in both cases has been used to buttress the criticism that has been raised against the secular orders, that a more marked concern with outward forms was a sign that, in the fourteenth and fifteenth centuries, chivalry was losing touch with ideals and becoming concerned solely with externals. The object of this chapter will be to examine this charge at greater length, with particular reference to the linked topics of jousting and of knightly vows.

A recent French historian has spoken in this regard of the workings of 'un esprit de système qui formalise et tend à créer des rites'.[1] Certainly we shall encounter much evidence of such a process; we shall encounter also, in connection with the tournament in particular, evidence of a very strong streak of caste consciousness, and more generally of a concern to bring the décor of sport and of ceremony into line with the design of literary models, together with what appears to be a love of gesture for gesture's sake. As we shall also see, however, a question remains as to how far such formalism and floridity of ritual and ceremony really can be interpreted as symptomatic of a loss of contact with and confidence in serious values. For it is not necessary to regard them as signs of frivolity: one can equally well look on them as the natural by-products of the rise of heraldic science, and of chivalrous learning. If the latter be nearer the truth, formalising and imitative tendencies need no longer be interpreted as signs of loss of contact with ideals, but rather as signs of the growing consciousness of the richness of chivalry's secular tradition.

The line of development connecting the tournaments and jousts of the thirteenth century with those of the fifteenth is clear and direct. This will be seen if we set a description of one of the great staged *pas d'armes* of the later period alongside those which have already been offered, in an earlier chapter, of great engagements of the preceding period. It will also be seen how strong, at first sight, the case is which alleges that the later period sees the theatrical and decorative tendencies of the martial sport of jousting running wild and going to seed.

Let us take as an example of the late medieval joust the *pas d'armes* of the *Fontaine des Pleurs*, staged at Chalon-sur-Saône in 1450, which happens to be particularly well recorded. No account of this great *pas* would be complete without an introductory word about its central figure, the Hainault knight Jacques de Lalaing, who was the *beau ideal* of Burgundian knighthood in his generation. He came of a distinguished seigneurial family, one of whose members had served St Louis on his crusade, and could show eight lines of noble descent. Attached to the household first of the Duke of Cleves, then of Duke Philip the Good of Burgundy, he early made a name for himself as a jouster, and his friend Oliver de La Marche remembered his confidence to him, that it was his ambition to have fought thirty men within the lists by the time he was thirty.[2] Lalaing saw war service in the Burgundian conquest of Luxembourg, and later went travelling; he fought with Sir Diego de Guzman in the lists before the King of Castile, and with Sir James Douglas before the King of Scots. In a joust before the King of France he wore the tokens of the two duchesses of Orleans and Calabria (the wimple of the one and the glove of the other on his helm), having caught the fancy of both by his courage and courtesy.[3] At the *Fontaine des Pleurs* he more than completed his tally of thirty combats. He was a newly elected knight of the Golden Fleece when, a few years afterwards, he took part in the Ghent war of 1453, in which he distinguished himself at Loheren, where he was said to have won the 'prize of the encounter'.[4] His promising career was cut off a few days later, when at the siege of Pouques a cannon ball struck a gun emplacement that he was inspecting and carried off half the front of his head.

Five years before his death, in November 1448, Lalaing signed the 'chapters' of his challenge for the *pas* of the *Fontaine des Pleurs*. On the island of St Laurent on the Saône by Chalon a pavilion was to be set up, with an image of Our Lady above it. Before it was to be found a damsel, in a robe stained with tears, her hair flowing about her shoulders, tending a unicorn from whose neck hung three shields, these too tear-bestrewn (the lady and the unicorn, it is clear, were both models, not real). Here on the first day of each month a herald would be found in attendance. The unicorn's shields were of three colours, white, violet, and black: Lalaing's challengers had to touch the white shield if they wished to fight with the axe, the violet if they wished to fight with the sword, and the black for twenty-five courses with the lance. As soon as a challenger had touched a shield, his name was enrolled by the herald, who also verified that he was a gentleman of at least four lines; and a time seven days ahead was assigned for the encounter. To him among the challengers who should bear himself best with the axe was assigned as a prize an axe of gold, and a golden sword and a golden lance for the champions with the other weapons. He who was brought to the ground with the axe was to be bound to wear a bracelet of gold for a year, or until he should find the lady with the key to unlock it (there were parallel forfeits in the other two cases).[5]

The pavilion was first set up on 1 November 1449, and the *pas* closed after 1 October 1450. Before the end Lalaing had fought more than twenty-two challengers, including the Italian knight John de Boniface, who after his overthrow went off in good heart with the bracelet to find his mistress, hoping she would have the key to open it.[6] The *pas* was rounded off with a great banquet, at which Lalaing entertained those who had taken part, and at which the prizes were distributed. An elaborate model of Chalon, showing the bridge of St Laurent, the island and the pavilion, was presented as an *entremets*, to recall the detail of the occasion and to delight the guests.

If from this elaborate scene we look back to the accounts of the thirteenth-century tournaments of Hem and Chauvency,[7] which in their day looked elaborate, the connections are clear, but so are the contrasts, and they are more striking. They remain striking, moreover, even if we make allowance for the fact that the minstrels who described Hem and Chauvency wrote in verse, with the entertainment of their audience as a prime object, and that the descriptions of the fifteenth century are in prose and aim to provide a detailed and objective record. Bretel heard about the tournament at Chauvency a matter of weeks before the event; Lalaing signed the chapters of his *pas* a whole year before the pavilion was first set up on the Ile St Laurent. The tournament at Chauvency lasted a week; the elaborate drama at Chalon was a year unrolling. There were real risks of fatal injury at Chauvency; no one was badly hurt at Chalon, and no one seems to have been in much danger of it. The ritual, moreover, had become much more complex and stylised in the later events. Neither at Chauvency nor yet at Hem, for all its elaborate Arthurian setting, do we hear of anything parallel to the ceremonious process of accepting challenge by touching shields which indicate the nature of the trial to be undertaken. Nor do we hear of any comparably careful process for the verification of the noble lineage of the contestants by expert heralds (the chapters of 1448 even specified the manner of checking the arms of one who appeared as a *chevalier mesconnu*, an 'unknown knight', without damage to his assumed anonymity).[8]

The whole concept of the *pas d'armes* seems to be an extreme development of the fashion for individual jousting encounters which we saw growing at the end of the thirteenth century. It may, though, have still older origins: there is surely some anticipation of it in Anna Comnena's story of the French knight at Constantinople in 1096, who told her father that 'at the crossroads in the country where I come from there stands an old sanctuary, to which everyone who desires to fight in single combat goes ready accoutred, and there prays to God while he waits in expectation of the man who will dare to fight him. At those cross roads I have often tarried, waiting and longing for an antagonist.'[9] As the name reveals, the *pas* was a kind of re-enactment of a classic military situation (which was also, of course, a well-established literary *topos* of early epic), in which a handful of men (or even a single man) undertake to hold a confined strategic position – the 'pass' – against all comers. It has borrowed something from another source of a different kind, too, for there is a distinct echo about it of the atmosphere of the judicial duel, in which a man puts himself before judges to uphold in arms his right or his honour – or his lady's. Both these situations – the holding of a pass and a duel in which honour was involved – lent themselves readily to literary and theatrical elaboration. It is not quite clear what the story was that underlay the theatre of the *Fontaine des Pleurs*, who the damsel was, what the cause of her tears, what the part of the unicorn (though the idea of purity is plainly in some way invoked). It is clear though that she was to be understood to be comforted and upheld by the prowess of her champion. We get a half glimpse of a kind of mini-romance underlying the chapters of the *pas*, something that goes much further in the direction of theatre than the mere parade of knights in Arthurian or other romantic guise.

It is here proper to stress that Lalaing's *pas* was no isolated occasion. It was not even the most elaborate or the most extravagant of the great *pas* of the fifteenth and sixteenth centuries; it is a good example simply because its course is very fully recorded. But there were hosts of similar events: the *pas d'armes*, for instance, of the *Arbre de Charlemagne* (1443), of the *Rocher Périlleux* (1445), of *La Bergière* (1449), of *La Belle Maurienne* (1454), of the *Perron Fée* (1463), of the *Arbre d'Or* (1468) – to name only a few.[10] Their names and chapters reveal the richness and variety of their literary inspiration. For the *pas* of the *Bergière* at Tarascon in 1449, René of Anjou chose a pastoral setting. The gallery for the spectators was in the form of a thatched cottage, and in a corner of the lists was revealed a shepherdess (René's mistress, Jeanne de Laval); two 'shepherd knights' threw down the gage on her behalf, one with a sable shield of melancholy challenging those content in love, the other, with a white shield of *liesse* (happiness), challenging those amorous and dissatisfied. Anthony, bastard of Burgundy, at his *pas* of the *Femme Sauvage* in 1470 made play with notions of primitive life, and with the sort of allegory that the *Roman de la Rose* had popularised: his 'champion of the Joyous Quest' had been cured of wounds by the *Femme Sauvage* as he left the land of *Enfance* for that of *Jeunesse*, and entered the lists surrounded by a troop of her 'wild women'.[11] Arthurian and Carolingian themes were however the favourites among the patrons of the *pas*, and the tournament, as one might expect. The champions whom Duke Louis of Orleans assembled at Sandricourt in 1493 threw themselves with exuberance into the Arthurian mode, riding out into the woods near the castle (the 'Waste Forest') accompanied by their maidens to seek 'chance' encounters with challengers. Orleans herald declared that there had been no such glorious enterprise since the days of Arthur himself.[12] But some fragmentary records survive of what seems to have been a still more extravagant exercise in imitation some years earlier. The chapters of this Quest (as it is called) stipulated that each knight was to be assigned by the heralds a shield of the arms of one of Arthur's knights, that they were to be permitted to wear armour of deliberately antique design, and to take each in his company a dwarf and a maiden while seeking encounters.[13] Expense was clearly not spared to catch the colour of romance, and on this occasion at least a good deal of research seems to have gone into the staging too. The evidence of all these extravagant occasions illustrates the same accentuation of what once were only tendencies, a near-obsession with ritual gesture, an overgrown concern with imitative décor, a new scale of lavishness in expenditure. These are just the kind of developments which, as we have seen, have led historians to question the values and the validity of late medieval chivalry.

In this context, the development of the ritual element in the *pas d'armes* is worth dwelling on for a moment longer. Here the judicial duel was probably an important influence, with its very careful regulation of procedures, designed to elicit a true judgement of God. Though it was looked on as a last resort and only allowable when all the possibilities of judicial inquiry had been exhausted, the judicial duel was still permitted in the fourteenth and fifteenth centuries as a means of settling a criminal appeal in which both the parties were of noble birth. The elaborate arrangements for the construction of the lists (and of galleries for spectators and judges) for such occasions remind us of their resemblance with the joust, and treatises on the duel were much read in chivalric circles.[14] Literature, however, has left an imprint on the *pas d'armes* quite as powerful and more easily defined. A particularly striking example of its ritual influence centres round the references, which recur in the chapters of a whole series of *pas d'armes*, to a *perron* (which seems to mean an artificial mound or pillar), often placed beside a 'tree of chivalry'.[15] This *perron* was closely associated with the rites of challenge: often the shields which a challenger had to touch were hung on it. Occasionally the procedure was more complicated, but the *perron* remains central: at the *pas* of the *Perron Fée* for instance the challenger had to sound a horn that hung from it and the touching of the shields came later. This ritual has a direct literary origin. Chrétien de Troyes in his *Ywain* describes the enchanted fountain in the forest of Broceliande, shaded by the fairest tree of the world, to which first Kaleograunt and then Ywain himself were directed.[16] By this fountain was a basin fastened by a chain, and a *perron*. When the knights threw the water of the fountain from the basin onto the *perron* there was first a great tempest, then a great flock of singing birds which alighted in the tree, and then there appeared a grim knight, enraged at the disturbance that the enchantment had raised in his garden, who challenged the *chevaliers errants*. (He overthrew Kaleograunt, but Ywain overthrew him.) From Chrétien, the story of the magic challenge of the *perron* passed in different versions into a whole series of romances, and in due course became, quite plainly, the model for the ritual of the *pas*. The story of the connection is not quite complete, it is true: it is not clear for instance how the rite of touching the shields came into the picture. Nevertheless, as an example of ritual gesture based upon a literary model it is particularly telling. Especially remarkable is the fact there seems to have been no understanding of any particular signification attaching to this rite of the *perron*, beyond the general attempt to catch something of the 'other-worldly' resonance of Ywain's legend. In that sense it is the acme of gesture for gesture's sake, a truly empty rite indicative of concern with theatrical effect rather than values.

Another development, of a very different order, runs parallel with the extension of the decorative and theatrical aspects of jousting and tourneying in the later middle ages. Steadily, these sports were becoming more and more divorced from the central activity with which they were originally associated, real fighting in real war. Technical improvements and safety precautions, by reducing the danger of tourneying, reduced the resemblance with real battle. Important among these innovations was the tilt, the barrier dividing the lists which made it impossible for the horses of the combatants to collide accidentally; in engagements on foot the barrier across which the combatants struck at each other was a parallel innovation. Weapons described as arms à *plaisance* (blunted, or in the case of lances, tipped with coronals) were more and more generally used, though a certain distinction of honour lingered around the combat à *oultrance* (which meant not 'to the death', but, more simply, with weapons of war).

The use of different shields of arms in war and the tourney was a parallel development (for instance the Black Prince's shield for 'arms of war' bore the arms of England with a label of three points, but his shield for 'arms of peace' his three ostrich feathers *argent* on a *sable* field). Indeed, by the fifteenth century, shields, having dropped out of use as an item of the cavalryman's war equipment, were virtually only used in tournaments. And from the mid fourteenth century on we begin to hear steadily more in wills, accounts and inventories of special jousting armour. It was for the joust that such items of equipment as the 'frog-mouthed' helm were forged (with his head encased in this, the jouster's vision was effective only when he leant forward in the saddle in the correct position with the couched lance, and his eyes were completely protected when he straightened on impact).[17] It was only in the jousting field that such a defence as this was useful: it had no purpose in the field of war, where mobility and vision were prerequisites of good protective armour.

These technological developments are symptoms of the way in which, in the later middle ages, jousting was developing from a skill into an art (it is no longer enough to, say, unhorse an opponent: one must do so in the proper manner). From there it was a short step to the quest to present the art more artistically. There is thus a connection between the expansion of the element of theatre in the *pas d'armes* and the growing divorce between skill in joust and tourney and true military skill. Theatre and décor as it were expanded to fill the gap left by the declining relevance of chivalrous sport to martial activity. The consequences were important. As the expense of tourneying, in terms of equipment and of feasting, prizes and forfeits, rose out of all proportion, so the lists ceased to open a way forward for the indigent young champion, as they had done in the days of William the Marshal. The caste exclusiveness of tourneying society became more rigid (the increased concern with the lines of nobility of combatants reflects this). And at the same time, as we have seen, concern with ritual gesture and imitation was becoming more obsessive.

If this were the whole picture, the charge that late medieval chivalry had lost touch with true values and practical purpose would need no further sustaining, at any rate as regards its sportive activities. But it is not the whole picture. There are other aspects to it, and we must turn now to look at them.

To start with, it will be wise to remember what is easily forgotten, that the growing apart of tourneying and of martial training was a very gradual affair. Throughout the fourteenth century and into the fifteenth, the *mêlée* tournament offered useful training not only in the handling of horse and weapons, but also in fighting together as a group – as those who fought together in a tournament were very likely to do so in real war. The men who, for instance, accompanied the lords of Ghistelles and La Gruthuyse to the tournament that they had organised in the market square at Bruges in March 1393 were, as Vale has pointed out, their relatives, allies and habitual companions in war; and each divided his company into five *lignes* or groups who fought together in the *mêlée* under the banner of a knight banneret.[18] Ralph Ferrers, testifying before the English Court of Chivalry in 1386, could justifiably still describe tournaments as being 'where the study and school of arms is'.[19] Cuvelier, writing only a few years earlier, could make the Black Prince sound formidable as the opponent in war of his hero Bertrand du Guesclin by describing him as surrounded by knights hardened in the tourney.[20] His poem, and such chronicles as Froissart's, are moreover full of accounts of a particular kind of jousting, the challenges and encounters that, under cover of temporary truces, were fitted into the intervals of cpagns. Cuvelier's account of the feats of the young Du Guesclin in an encounter during the siege of Rennes belongs to this category, and so do the staged engagements between French and English knights and esquires which Froissart describes in loving detail in his account of Buckingham's expedition to France in 1380.[21] Such events were rather rarer in the fifteenth century, but the vogue was by no means dead even in the time of Bayart.[22] Engagements such as these were fought in field armour, and had a quite different scale of prizes and forfeits from those of the *pas*, usually more like those of war. If the solemnities of the *pas* had lost their relevance to real fighting, this kind of jousting clearly had not done so in the same degree; and nor had the *mêlée*.

Bayart won his fame as the *chevalier sans peur et sans reproche* in the hard fighting of the Italian wars in the early sixteenth century. He made his début in arms, though, and first attracted notice when, as a youth of eighteen, he took up the challenge of the *pas d'armes* organised by the Burgundian veteran Claude de Vauldray in 1491, and held his own with distinction against a much more experienced jouster.[23] In this combination of the two roles of genuine warrior and jousting champion, Bayart was in a large company. This fact in itself is another and a very important reason why we have to be careful not to overstress the distance between the world of the *pas d'armes* and real soldiering. The record is clear enough. Jean de Boucicaut was famous as the chief organiser of the jousts of St Inglevert near Calais in 1390 and for the prowess he showed in what was undoubtedly one of the most lavish occasions of its kind in his lifetime. In Italy too he won great fame as a jouster, as Anthoine de la Sale attests; and among those he encountered in the lists there was the *condottiero* Galeas of Mantua whom we saw hailed as a model of knighthood in the *Chevalier Errant*.[24] But Boucicaut (like Galeas) also saw much real fighting, and was present on the losing side at the two terrible battles of Nicopolis and Agincourt. The *Warwick Pageant*, commemorating the deeds of Earl Richard Beauchamp (1381-1439) has many splendid illustrations of its hero's feats in the lists, but it records also triumphs of another kind, for he had a long martial career. He was present at the battle of Shrewsbury (1403), fought all through Henry V's Norman campaigns, and as lieutenant for Henry's son commanded the English armies in Normandy from 1436 to 1439.[25] Alongside the court nobles who took part in René of Anjou's lavishly staged *Emprise du Dragon* in 1446 one will find the name of the hardy Gascon *routier* Poton de Xaintrailles, a professional soldier if ever there was one, and of his fellow captain in the field, Pierre de Brézé.[26] Their companion in arms, Jean de Bueil, has often been quoted as a critic of the chivalrous tournament in their time, and his words interpreted as a sign that jousting was no longer held in much repute among real men of arms.[27] It would seem however that he was the exception rather than the rule.

In this matter, fifteenth-century chivalric literature is a little more true to life than is sometimes recognised. Malory's picture of the *pas d'armes* of the Joyous Isle, devised by Lancelot, is a realistic description of a fifteenth-century *pas*, and it looks as if he used the rules laid down for duels by Thomas of Gloucester in the late fourteenth century as a guide for his description of the duel between Lancelot and Mador.[28] His Lancelot is nevertheless a great warrior in real battle, the greatest of King Arthur's knights in war. Anthoine de la Sale's novel, *Le petit Jehan de Saintré*, is in a different mood, but its evidence is essentially to the same effect. La Sale's fictional cartels of defiance and chapters for Saintré's jousts are precisely modelled on real cartels and chapters of his day, and are carried by heralds who really know their business. His descriptions of banquets, dances, and solemn entries into the lists are lengthy and luxuriant in their detail. But he depicts Saintré not only as the model jouster and the model squire of dames but also as the leader of a great expedition into Prussia, victor in real war as well as in mock combat.[29] The story is true to its author, who was a knight, a great traveller, an expert in heraldry and the lore of the tourney, and the bastard son of one of the most famous (or perhaps rather infamous) *routier* captains of his age, Hawkwood's great rival, Bernardino de la Sale. Time has exaggerated the distance that separates the chivalrous *pas* and tournament from the serious occupation of war in the late middle ages. In the fifteenth century, both in life and in literature, they did not seem so remote from one another: they were different but closely connected preoccupations of the aristocratic martial world.

If this seems at all surprising, it is partly because, in our amazement at the flights of imagination (and the feats of engineering) involved in the staging of a great *pas*, we easily forget that these were, comparatively, exceptional occasions. We easily fail to notice the passing but frequent references of chroniclers and memorialists to less extravagant jousts, which show them to have been a common occurrence in courtly and chivalrous life, outside periods of active war. In the same way, we easily exaggerate the caste-exclusiveness of these chivalric sports. The Burgundian dominions were a principal home of the great *pas*, but they were also the home of the bourgeois tournament. Nearly all the great cities of the Low Countries had their jousting societies, as did Bruges, Tournai, Valenciennes and above all Lille with its famous feast of the Espinette, whose champion bore away as his prize a gold sparrow hawk (an emblem with strong Arthurian connections).[30] These feasts of the Espinette were not despised or trivial occasions in the eyes of the aristocracy. Great men like Jean de Wavrin and Louis de Gruthyse and even Philip the Good himself did not disdain to joust with their bourgeois champions. A famous roll of arms, often copied, recorded the blazons of the prize-winning 'Kings' of the Espinette, and recorded how those who were not already noble had been ennobled for the prowess that they had displayed in the lists.[31] The feasts were expensive, and Duke Philip licensed, at the *echevins'* request, taxation to reimburse the 'Kings' for expenses incurred and to maintain the occasion. Though at the end – in the sixteenth century – this taxation became a burden, it is clear that it was at first imposed in response to popular demand.[32] It thus reminds us that in the fifteen century tournaments could be popular, and for material as well as for social reasons. The crowd of challengers, with their ladies, servants and hangers on, brought custom to a city, and there could be competition to host such an occasion.

The history of the tournament in Germany in the late middle ages helps to balance further the over-extravagant picture that is so easily derived from accounts of flamboyant jousts in France, Burgundy and Spain.[33] Here the organisation of tourneying was largely in the hands of the tourneying societies, and there was a dearth of lords rich enough to meet the expense that the romantic fantasy of the *pas* involved. The *mêlée* of the tournament proper also remained here more popular than in France in the fifteenth century. Though fantasy was more restrained, at least until the time of Maximilian, the German tournaments were highly ceremonious occasions, the ritual of the proceedings, from the great helm-show before the tournament to the banquet at its close, being closely supervised by the officers of the societies. The tourneying nobility was proud and jealous of its position and privileges, and there was no lack of class exclusiveness about them, but it was the class exclusiveness of noblemen much less rich, on the whole, than those who frequented the great French *pas*. Sigmund von Gebsettl's memories of some of the last of the great tournaments of the four lands, Bavaria, Swabia, Franconia and the Rhineland, bring home the contrast. 'In 1484 they held the tournament at Stuttgart in Swabia a little after . . . there were objections to my right to tourney and I had to prove my four lines: that was Gebsettl, Tettelbach, Than and Seckendorff . . . Von Winsheim lent me a white horse . . . In the same year there was a tournament at Ingolstadt in Bavaria and I was there too and tournied with my own hereditary war-crest, and Herman of Habsburg lent me a tourneying mount.'[34] This scene in which a newcomer looks about him to borrow a decent horse is indeed very different from that at Chalon-sur-Saône which we looked at at the beginning of this chapter. Sigmund's memories can be paralleled with others of the same period. Wilwolt von Schaumberg, a great tourneyer who was also a captain of great distinction, never achieved more than modest fortune in spite of all his successes.[35] As a soldier, as one of the champions of the tourneying society of the Unicorn, and as a courtly lover to boot, his career has much in common with those of Jacques de Lalaing and Boucicaut, but with the great difference, that he never had the wealth to stage a great *pas* in the way Jacques did and never found a patron ready to pay for him to do so either. Rüxner's note, in his *Turnierbuch*, of the regulations that limited the finery of noble ladies at tourneying festivities (with the explicit object of saving the poorer from embarrassment) illustrates the same point in a different way.[36] These regulations of Rüxner's were laid down by the tourneying societies. Their statutes remind us that their companions were fighting men, conscious of the need to help one another not at the tourney only but in the more serious business of war and feud too. In Germany, as in France, the history of the tournament uncovers for us plenty of evidence of class exclusiveness and of a love of gesture, but it is not so easy to say of these tastes that they have become over-flamboyant, or that they have led to a loss of contact with reality.

A matter which is dealt with at length in virtually all the surviving late medieval texts that lay down rules for the tournament is that of the 'reproaches' which disbar a man from taking part in a tournament. The one most commonly alleged in practice was inadequate hereditary qualifications. This was the charge that Sigmund von Gebsettl had to rebut in 1484 by proving his four lines of nobility. The helm-show, or the 'making of windows' (that is to say, hanging the banners, hatchments and crests of the would-be participants from the windows of the principal's lodgings), was a very important part of the preliminaries of a tournament,[37] and one which made demands on the genealogical expertise of the heralds, whose duty it was to verify the right of each man to tourney. Even at a 'tournament' arranged in an interval on campaign there might be a call for the inspection of the ancestral arms of those about to take part.[38] The matter was one to which great attention was clearly paid. Anthoine de la Sale has an entertaining account of the plight of a number of young men who, at a tournament in Lorraine in 1445, had *forgotten* how to blazon their arms and feared they would be excluded in consequence. He

He did his best for them, for he was sympathetic; the blazon of a complicated coat, as he wryly remarks, can be a bit of a mouthful.[39]

Lack of hereditary qualification, or marriage below one's estate, were the
commonest 'reproaches' against would be jousters, but there were others
too, and they are in some respects more significant. La Sale and good King
René both give lists of them in their treatises on tournies, and so does
Rüxner, and their lists are all very similar.[40] There shall not be admitted
any, however noble they may be, who are smirched with any of the following reproaches, that they are (i) violators of churches, (ii) hardened excommunicates, (iii) slanderers of womankind or men who have done ladies
dishonour, (iv) murderers of malice prepense, (v) men false to their oaths or
sealed pledges, (vi) fugitives, guilty of cowardice in the field, (vii) men who
have been discomfitted in the duel on an issue of honour, (viii) arsonists,
(ix) leaders of free companies, (x) pirates of the sea. Rüxner adds heretics to
the list and substitutes *Raubritter* (robber knights) for leaders of free companies. These are very significant lists, and offer us a new perspective on the
late medieval tournament. They may not bring its play any closer to the
serious business of war, but they do bring it into much closer relation with
genuine and ethical standards of behaviour.

It is hard to say just how seriously these lists are to be taken – what sort of
degree of verification the heralds and judges of the tournament bothered
with in respect of them. But they were certainly not just a dead letter. The
reproach of dishonouring womankind could be taken seriously, and the
'helm-show' was, among other things intended, we are told, to give the
ladies the chance to 'name' discreetly a knight who had misbehaved; the
other participants would then set on him in the lists.[41] La Sale has an ugly
tale of three Burgundian knights who had acted a farce before Duke Philip
in which they had 'covertly and in general terms cast aspersions on the
female sex'; at the next tourney, in Brussels, they were soundly beaten, and
rued their discourtesy 'many days and nights'.[42] More interesting is the
reproach of being associated with the free companies, whose pillaging laid
waste vast tracts of land in France and Italy and caused untold human
misery, or of being a robber knight. Here the rules made their dab at
tackling what we now recognise as a major social problem of the age. No
doubt their dab was not very effective towards curbing the ill – nothing was;
but it seems to have been a little more than just an empty gesture. Johannes
Roth calls the tournament the 'touchstone' of true knighthood, because the
robber knights will not dare seek to mingle there with their superiors.[43] It is
not an accident, it seems clear, that Roth's hero and patron Count Balthasar
of Thuringia was remembered both as the founder of the tourneying society
of the Unicorn and as one who fought long to curb the atrocities of the
robber knights.[44]

René of Anjou used in order to disbar the unworthy from his great order of chivalry, the Croissant, a list of reproaches very similar to that given in his treatise on tournies.[45] Like the orders of chivalry, the tournament and the *pas d'armes*, with all their glamour and ceremony and partly by means of it, could be used to remind the knightly world of the serious social and ethical responsibilities that the code of chivalry imposed. Glamour and ceremony had of course a less elevated purpose, in both cases; they were effective propaganda for the power of the patron of the *pas* or the sovereign of an order, reminding men of the attraction of his service. Both purposes however have the same moral for us as historians; that there was much more to the ceremony and ritual of late medieval chivalry than an effort to sustain an illusion of glory by aping the mode and gesture of an imaginary past.

★

We hear a good deal, in the late middle ages, of solemn vows taken in connection with tourneying, to perform this or that feat of arms in the lists (the *pas d'armes* can, indeed, be viewed as a kind of elaboration on this practice). The statutes of some of the votal orders of chivalry, discussed in the last chapter, represent a collective institutionalisation of this practice of taking vows, as in the case for instance of those of Bourbon's order of the *Fer de Prisonnier*, which bound a company of knights together in a common vow to perform specified deeds of arms in the lists within a fixed term.[46] Similar vows were also often taken by individuals, and indeed the device of a prisoner's chain, borne as the outward and visible sign of a binding vow, is one that is encountered often. In *Jehan de Saintré*, the Polish baron Loisenlech is chained hand and foot by gold fetters, on account of a vow, from which Saintré delivered him by taking up his challenge.[47] The Sicilian champion John de Boniface carried a prisoner's iron with a gold chain as an *emprise* in token of a jousting vow when he came in 1446 to Anvers, where Jacques de Lalaing delivered him.[48] Lord Scales was shackled with a slightly different but reminiscent *emprise* by the ladies of the English court in 1465, when they chose him as their champion by placing about his thigh a gold chain with a *fleur-de-souvenance* (forget-me-not) hanging therefrom.[49] The taking of vows, and the adoption against their delivery of *emprises* such as these, had become, in the late medieval period, a formal – and striking – ritual of chivalrous society.

The most celebrated and flamboyant individual vows of this kind are mostly associated with the tourney, and very often have erotic overtones. The knight's determination to do honour to his lady and make himself worthy in regard to her is the inspiration behind his vow: the chains of his *emprise* symbolise the chains of love. But if we look carefully we will also find plenty of instances of vows of a similar kind taken to perform feats of arms in real war. Thomas Gray in his *Scalacronica* has a splendid story of

45. War's horrors: a battle scene (Shrewsbury, 1403) from the Beauchamp Pageants (British Library). See pp. 208, 222.

46. A meeting of the Chapter of the Golden Fleece, from an illuminated text of the statutes (Bibliothèque Municipale, Besançon).

47. The foundation of the Order of the Star by King John the Good (Bibliothèque Nationale). See p. 190.

48. War's horrors: the warring nations of Christendom, an allegorical depiction from Honoré Bonet's *Tree of Battles* (Musée Condé, Chantilly). Fortune and her wheel are at the head of the picture. See pp. 229–30, 235.

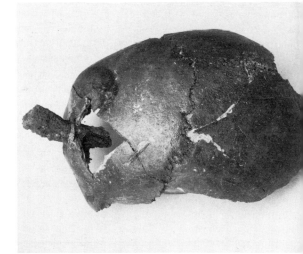

49 (top). War's horrors: burial pit of the slain at the Battle of Wisby, 1361. See p. 223.

50, 51. War's horrors: skulls from Wisby, one showing part of the mail-coif and the mark of a wound, the other pierced by an arrowhead. See p. 223.

53. The jousts of St Inglevert (British Library). See p. 207.

52 (facing page). David Aubert presents a book to Duke Philip of Burgundy in the presence of Knights of the Golden Fleece (above); the collar of the order is below (Bibliothèque Royale Albert 1er, Brussels).

54. Bertrand du Guesclin is entrusted with the Constable's sword by Charles V of France (British Library). See pp. 231–2.

IOANNES·ACVTVS·EQVES·BRITANNICVS·DVX·AETATIS·S
VAE·CAVTISSIMVS·ET·REI·MILITARIS·PERITISSIMVS·HABITVS·EST

·PAVLI·VCCELLI·OPVS·

55. Memorial plaque to John Hawkwood in the Cathedral at Florence, by Uccello. See pp. 227, 231–2.

Sir William Marmion and his gold helmet, which his mistresss had given him, charging him to bear it in arms until he should achieve a glorious feat of war. When Alexander Mowbray and his Scots appeared before Norham Castle, Gray's father, its warden, turned to Marmion with these words: 'Sir knight, you come here as a knight errant to make that helm known and it is more fitting that chivalry be accomplished on horseback . . . Mount your horse: behold, there are your enemies: spur on and do battle in the midst of them.' Marmion obeyed, and very nearly lost his life in the fray before Gray the elder rode in to rescue him.[50] Somewhat similar is Barbour's story of Sir John Weberton who had sworn to guard the castle of Lanark for a year, as a trial sufficently perilous to be worthy of her he loved (he died within the term, defending the castle against James Douglas).[51] Closer in ritual formalism to the tourneying vows are Philippe de Mézière's story of the Polish knight who had sworn that he who would not sit to eat until he had fought the infidel,[52] and Froissart's tale of the young English gentlemen whom he saw at Valenciennes, who had each covered one eye with a cloth in honour of a vow each to see only with one eye until he should achieve some feat of arms in France.[53] These notices illustrate well the close parallelism between rituals associated with the tournament and rituals associated with war, and remind us once again of the intimate association, for the chivalrous mentality, between war and the tournament, an association maintained despite the growing divergence of the skills that they put to the test.

Froissart's story of the young Englishmen who had covered their eyes in honour of a vow is a particularly interesting one. It closely echoes a story told in the poem known as the *Vows of the Heron*. This describes how, on the eve of the outbreak of the Hundred Years War, a heron was served at a court feast to Edward III and his knights, who swore by the bird to perform great deeds in France. When it came to the turn of the Earl of Salisbury, he called upon his countess, the fair Joan of Kent, to close his eye with her fingers: 'I swear now to Almighty God', he declared, 'that this eye will never be opened, for storm or for wind, for evil or for fortune, or for any let or hindrance, until I shall be in France and have lit the fires of war there.'[54] Just over thirty years before this, in 1306, a rather similar ceremony took place at the feast which Edward I held to celebrate the knighting of his eldest son. Two swans were served up, and the King and his knights swore upon them to make war upon the Scots in order to bring Bruce to heel, and afterwards to go on crusade.[55] Here is another formal chivalrous ritual, that of swearing upon a bird. It seems to have had a Lotharingian origin, and Jean de Longuyon made it famous by his mythical account, in the version of the *Romance of Alexander* that he put together for his patron Bishop Thibaut of Bar, of the vows that Alexander's champions took upon a peacock at a feast during the siege of Epheson.[56] His work (and perhaps the story of the vows of the Heron too) inspired the most famous of all vows of this kind, those of the feast of the Pheasant at Lille, in 1453, where Toison d'Or King of Arms, bearing a live pheasant with a gold collar about its neck, invoked before Duke Philip of Burgundy and his company the 'ancient custom' of 'presenting a peacock or other noble bird at a great feast before the illustrious princes, lords and nobles, to the end that they might swear expedient and binding oaths'.

The feast of the Pheasant is famous, on account of the almost incredibly extravagant theatre that was its accompaniment. The plans of Philip of Burgundy for a crusade to rescue Constantinople from the Turk provided the context for the occasion. The feast was preceded by a joust, in which Adolf of Cleves, arrayed as the Swan Knight, had challenged all comers. A great deal of complicated apparatus was devised to enhance the delight of the guests at the banquet itself, including a model of a child upon a rock, which pissed rose water. At the climax a giant, dressed after the manner of a Saracen of Granada, entered the hall leading an elephant, on which rode a weeping damsel, representing Holy Church and lamenting her oppression at the hands of the infidel. It was after she had appealed for aid to the assembled company that Toison d'Or King of Arms entered with the Pheasant, accompanied by two of Philip the Good's illegitimate daughters and two knights of the Golden Fleece, and later the vows were taken.[57] They too were very extravagant: men swore to wear no armour, not to sleep in a bed, not to sit down to eat (most of these for one day a week) until they should have accomplished some high deed of arms against the Turk. Each oath was carefully set down in a roll by Toison d'Or, and that is why the chronicler Mathieu d'Escouchy was able to preserve them for us, in all the detail of their flamboyance.[58]

It is not easy to pin down the ideas underlying the practice of taking such chivalrous vows as the knighthood of Burgundy swore at Lille in 1454, and which clearly belong to the same *genre* as those other, individual vows which we have considered, and which related sometimes to feats of arms in war, sometimes to feats of arms in the jousting lists. Imposing some deprivation, real or symbolical, to be maintained until the avowed end be achieved, they on the one hand recall religious vows of *ascesis* – to fast, recite specified prayers, to go on pilgrimage. In the statutes of some votal orders of chivalry the obligation to particular religious observances indeed form a part, though not the central part, of the undertakings imposed by a chivalrous vow.[59] The analogy frequently drawn in literary works between the trials of the chivalrous knights and the trials of the pilgrimage of life itself, remind us that the parallel is a relevant one, of which men were contemporarily conscious. Articulate Christian vows were clearly not the sole analogue of the kind of vows that we are considering, however. They have another model at the same time, in those vows of the great heroes of northern saga (and of epic *chanson*, and of romance), which were inspired not by the desire for grace but by the drink and excitement of the feast hall. The fact that so often the act of *ascesis* imposed by a chivalrous vow was purely formal or symbolical, a ritual action like the bearing of a token or a model of a prisoner's chain, is a sure sign of the relevance of this alternative analogy. The tone in which they are recorded, too, often smacks more of the determination of the saga heroes to take providence (which plays such a significant part in the campaigns of love and war) by storm, rather than of the quest for perfection in virtue. The curious ritual of swearing upon a bird, whose origins appear to be literary and legendary, seems to be another pointer in the same direction.[60] Here, indeed, we find in the world of vows a perfect analogue to the ritual and ceremonial significance of the *perron* in the *pas d'armes*, for we are never told what the precise significance of swearing on a bird was any more than we are told of any precise significance in a *perron*. A sound literary pedigree and theatrical potential seem to be the keys to ritual significance in both cases, not any coherent attempt to symbolise or signify.

Nevertheless, and in spite of their extravagance of manner, chivalrous vows cannot be divorced from serious intent. It is true that Philip the Good never went on crusade, and that the vows of the Pheasant remained in consequence unfulfilled, but they were no empty gesture. They were part of a carefully thought out attempt to give maximum *éclat* to the launching of a venture seriously intended, and were followed up by a series of less dramatic meetings elsewhere of the nobility of the Burgundian territories to gather more pledges to serve in an expedition against the Turk. Taxes were raised to meet its expenses, and detailed plans were thrashed out as to how the problems of muster, transportation and supply should be met. Changes in the European political situation were what led to their abandonment, and that only in 1456, two years after the feast.[61] About the serious intent behind the vows which Edward I and his knights swore on the swans in 1306 there is, of course, no doubt at all; and even if, as is probable, the story told of those other vows of the Heron is a fiction, it is a fiction related to very serious reality. The Earl of Salisbury certainly did light the fires of war in France. Such stories moreover as those told by Thomas Gray of Sir William Marmion or by Philippe de Mézières of the Polish knight who would not sit down to eat clearly do not concern figures of pasteboard fantasy. The making of vows may have been an extravagant gesture in itself, but the men who made them were of a kind who knew that they had to expect to face real hazards. Jean de Rebreviettes made a satirical vow upon the Pheasant at Lille, but he really did later fight for the faith in both Spain and Hungary, and risked his body to win honour in the wars there.[62]

Nostalgia for a *temps perdu*, for a past and more ideal age of chivalry, does have an important part in any account of the rituals and ceremony of late medieval chivalry. There can be no denying this, in the light of the conscious efforts to re-enact or recall romance in the staging of jousts and *pas d'armes* and of the making of vows, which we have been tracing in this chapter. But we must remember that when we use the word nostalgia with regard to the middle ages it does not carry quite the same negative implications that it does nowadays. The men of that period did not commit the modern error of confusing the march of time with progress; they were more inclined to think that things were going downhill as the world grew older. Their nostalgia had in consequence a positive force, prompting men to strive to maintain or to revivify past values. When Charles V of France, at the great banquet that he held in Paris in 1378 in honour of his visitor the Emperor Charles IV, staged elaborately a re-enaction of the story of Godfrey's capture of Jerusalem, it was not just for amusement: it was also intended to remind the company present of the example of the chivalry of the past and especially of its devotion to the cause of crusade.[63] It was in the same spirit that Philip of Burgundy sought at his feast at Lille to recall an ancient ritual when he wished to stir enthusiasm for the same crusading cause; as it was a similar instinct that inspired Pierre de Bauffremont, staging his *pas d'armes* 'in honour of our Lord Jesus Christ and of his Holy Mother and of Monsire St George', to give it a Carolingian tone and to name it the pass of the *Arbre de Charlemagne*.[64] Spectacle, at the feast and in the tourney, was not an end in itself; nor were extravagant feasts and tournaments mere attempts to escape from grim reality into illusion. There was much play, much ceremony and gesture associated with them; but the underlying purpose, of interpreting the significance and value of the 'noble calling and exercise of arms' to those born to follow it, was never quite forgotten. The nostalgic appeal to the past was not a sign of loss of seriousness, rather the opposite: it was a sign of awareness of that serious underlying purpose.

★

Late medieval chivalry was exhibitionist and extravagant – often to the point of vulgarity – in its ornate and imitative tendencies, and that has given it a bad name. From an aesthetic point of view perhaps this bad name is in part deserved, but it is not a sign of decadence. This was an age in which ritual still played a vital part in social life, was indeed still the way in which men registered some of their most important social obligations to one another: in the ceremony of doing homage, for instance, or the ceremony of coronation. It was only natural in the circumstances that, as men began to discover in semi-historical romance the richness of the secular tradition of chivalry, they should seek to express this new revelation in the forms and rituals of chivalry's favoured sports and activities. If the secular nobility, in their efforts in this direction, were sometimes over-flamboyant, it is partly because they were relative newcomers to literary erudition and were a little intoxicated by some of their discoveries. It was also partly because they sincerely wished to do justice to the dignity of a class ideal – their class ideal – which set a high price on worldly honour, the symbols of which are necessarily external.

There is an economic factor that needs to be taken into account here as well, and which also helps to render the flamboyance of later medieval chivalry, which to us can seem so bewildering, more intelligible. Within the ranks of the nobility, that sector of society to which this flamboyance made its appeal, disparities of income were widening in the late middle ages. At one extreme the higher nobility, the sort of men whose patronage paid for the extravagance of the *pas d'armes* and of chivalrous feasts, were becoming richer. They were beginning to constitute a kind of super-nobility, as Philip de Mézières perceived when he distinguished apart, among the nobles, the princes of the blood and the great lords and barons as an estate within an estate, separated from what he called the 'common run' of nobles, knights, esquires and gentlemen.[65] Men like the Dukes of Burgundy and Anjou, the Dukes of Lancaster and York in England, and the titled grandees of Castile, disposed of accumulations of wealth in land (and in jurisdictions and fiscal rights) which dwarfed by comparison the wealth of the upper feudal aristocracy of counts and barons of an earlier age. In contrast with that earlier age, however, and with other times, there were in this period few natural or automatic opportunities of ploughing back this wealth, into technical improvements or the settlement of new lands, or into new commercial or colonial enterprises. There was, on the other hand, a strong tradition that munificence and display were proper uses of noble wealth. So more was spent on them than ever before, with effects that make the products of this sort of investment look for a time frothy, exuberant, and extravagant.

At the same time things were on the whole becoming harder economically for those that de Mézières referred to as the 'common run' of the nobility. Their family revenues from land were in many cases being eroded as a result of the devastation of the countryside in wars, of the higher costs of labour and the more advantageous terms that tenants demanded in a period of demographic decline – and by extravagance in their own efforts to maintain a recognisably noble style of living. The flamboyant celebration of noble ideals was in these conditions attractive to them, because it seemed to buttress the dignity of the estate to which they belonged and whose *apartheid* was underscored by their concern over such matters as lines of noble descent. For them it was an expression of that *largesse* which the lesser aristocracy had always admired in their superiors. This in itself was a reason why flamboyance could seem a worthwhile investment to its patrons among the super-nobility. It helped to secure to their service the kind of men on whose loyal support they depended, in politics and administration and above all in war, just as their predecessors had done in earlier times.

The 'common run' of the nobility in the late middle ages was indeed becoming more than ever a nobility of service. Service, at court or in war, offered in the economic conditions prevailing much the best prop to sagging seigneurial revenues, opening the way to pensions, offices, wages of war and booty, as well as to a share in the glamour and splendour that characterised court-life and the entourages of the greater nobles. Its rewards catered for the ordinary nobility's need for reassurance simultaneously about their incomes on the one hand and their self-esteem on the other: and this was especially true of war service, because war was the traditional hereditary profession of the noble and a nobleman on the field of battle could hope to display both his insignia and his courage and to win a fortune to boot. There was thus an intimate association between the beauties and the brutalities of chivalry – the same conditions sharpened at the same time the nobility's appreciation of display and its taste for war and the chance of spoil. The tensions that were generated by pressures in these two directions will be a major theme of the next chapter.

CHAPTER XII

Chivalry and War

Huizinga viewed the chivalry of the late middle ages with its idolisation of
the aristocratic knight errant – the sort of man for whom Jacques de Lalaing
was a model – as a cultural phenomenon that was becoming more and more
divorced from what he called the 'harsh realities' of the period.[1] My argument has been that it was at once a cultural and a social phenomenon, which
retained its vigour because it remained relevant to the social and political
realities of the time. The late middle ages were no less bellicose than were
the tenth and eleventh centuries, in whose warlike circumstances chivalry
was born, and endemic warfare marked the culture of the period profoundly. Its embattled conditions, as Philippe Contamine has recently
stressed, have left their clear testimony, in the castles and citadels and town
walls which have weathered time better than any of its architecture except
for its churches, and in the great surviving collections of late medieval
armour – as also in the illuminations of late medieval manuscripts, in which
battle is the most often depicted of all secular scenes, and in the great vogue,
in the last medieval centuries, for treatises on war and translations of
classical military experts like Vegetius.[2] In this context, in which as Contamine puts it war itself has to be studied as a cultural phenomenon, it can
be no wonder that the warrior should have stood out as a figure of peculiar
significance in secular society, or that society should have sought to do
justice to its conception of his dignity through elaborate rituals.

There remain, however, important questions that need further probing,
if the suggestion that Huizinga's view needs modification is to be sustained.
How, for instance, does the cult of the knight errant, the particular type of
warrior that literature and so many of the rituals of chivalry idolised, relate
to the social and political needs of the day? As a rider to this question,
another must be added; were the risks that he ran really such as to entitle
him to the sort of acclaim that he was given? And what about those other

realities, that were harsh indeed – how did contemporaries reconcile the cult of the fighting man with their awareness of those horrors of war that bore on the non-combatant rather than the warrior, in particular the crimes and misdemeanours of soldiers, their pillaging and their brutality? To what extent did these excesses undermine their confidence in the chivalrous ethic? These are important questions, for if the cult of chivalry truly was remote from social reality, and if reality in its turn truly was calling chivalrous values into question, then Huizinga's thesis really must seem to be the one that best fits the facts.

★

Among these questions, let us first consider that of the risks of war for the fighting man, because it is the least complex in its implications. Three principal grounds have been from time to time suggested for thinking that the risks for those directly involved as combatants in knightly warfare in the late middle ages were rather less than might in principle be expected. One is that the case of armour in which the knight went to war was sufficiently proof against the sort of weapons that might be brought to bear against him to render his claim to be risking life and limb at most times a trifle exaggerated. A second is that, in any case, pitched battles were rather rare, being avoided by commanders as far as possible. The third is that, when they did meet in battle, knights took good care not to kill each other – a particular charge which leads forward to the more general one, that non-combatants were a good deal more at risk in medieval warfare than soldiers ever were.

Nothing, of course, could make a knight invulnerable, but the casing of armour in which he went to war did undoubtedly give him a very considerable measure of physical security – and no doubt a psychological sense of security as well. It is clear that a fully armoured man could, in the right position, hold at bay for quite a period a considerable number of men not so protected. The protection that armour offered to the Frankish warriors was one of the facts that, in the earlier age of the crusades, had struck observers among the Byzantines and Moslems (who never adopted full body armour) most forcibly. The Turks called the western knights 'the iron people'. 'They were armed from head to foot in a sort of armour made from a fabric of iron rings. They seemed to be an iron mass, off which blows simply glanced':[3] so wrote one Moslem writer of the Frankish knights who fought so long and furiously before their final collapse at Hattin in 1187. By the late middle ages the armourers' craft had become a highly skilled one, and new developments in design now countered new dangers: the increased range and penetrating power of long bow and crossbow, and the thrust of the long infantry pikes that were so easily fatal to horses. Plate armour began to come into general use in the later fourteenth century. Its articulated joints and the new potential for distributing the weight of the armour (which in a mail coat bore so heavily on the shoulders) were great advantages, and glancing surfaces could be presented to deflect both trajectile arrow and pike thrust. A visored bacinet replaced the great helm that in earlier times had been worn over a mail coif; it was considerably lighter and more comfortable. Improved horse armour, developed in the early fifteenth century, came to offer a more effective protection to mount as well as man.[4] Armour could not of course offer a total protection and it remained cumbersome and constricting. The man who raised his visor or who left off part of the 'gorget' protecting his throat so as to be able to move his head with more facility obtained greater ease, but at the price of greater risk.[5] The fact remains that a good suit of armour could make a knight remarkably secure.

That did not, however, solve all his problems. At the end of a strongly disputed engagement the knight, exhausted by the weight of the armour in which he had fought, was not very mobile, and the defeated could be a fairly easy prey to their conquerors. That was one of the reasons why casualties were often very heavy on the losing side. It is true that to be honourably captured implied no reproach in the eyes of chivalrous society (a flight did, notionally), but it was not a very attractive proposition. The heavy ransom that a nobleman might be expected to pay could be the ruin of his family's economic fortune, by forcing him to borrow beyond his means or to sell or mortgage his property.[6] Besides, not everyone took prisoners for ransom. The Swiss habitually gave no quarter and nor did the soldiers of the Flemish cities. After Nicopolis, Sultan Bajazeth executed most of the prisoners he had taken, reserving only those who could afford princely ransoms. And in the heat of battle at Agincourt Henry V, when he believed that a fresh French force was approaching, ordered all but the most important of his French prisoners to be killed.[7] There was remarkably little contemporary criticism of his action: much less than one might have expected, given that quarter was normally granted in the Anglo-French wars.

It is not surprising, in the light of these facts, that there were substantial periods in the late middle ages when commanders showed a very considerable reluctance to commit their forces to large-scale open conflict in the field. This second ground for putting a minimum estimate on the risks to which the late medieval knight was exposed certainly does seem to have something in it, even if the first has proved exaggerated. Sieges and intermittent skirmishes dominate the story of a good many campaigns of the late fourteenth and early fifteenth centuries. In this sort of warfare there could of course be great dangers, especially at the assault of a fortified town or castle, though they were not quite so acute for the knight or man at arms as the risks of a field engagement. Many towns however were never assaulted;

they were blockaded, and surrendered (if they did so) on terms (the most
common terms were that the garrison would evacuate if not relieved by a
given date).[8] In terms of manpower and resources, this manner of conducting a siege was economic from the point of view of both sides, and it
certainly did reduce the risks of personal injury. But that is only one aspect
of the story. A blockade could be a long drawn out affair, damaging to the
morale, and more seriously to the health of both besieged and besiegers,
especially the latter. Henry V at Agincourt was forced to fight in what
seemed to be disadvantageous circumstances with an army seriously
depleted by the flux which had broken out in his host while they were
seeking to reduce Harfleur, encamped in unhealthy conditions in the
marshlands before the town.[9] His losses as a result of disease (and deser-
tion) during his long siege of Meaux, which lasted through the bitter winter
of 1421-2, were probably even more serious, and Henry's own health began
to break down there.[10] Disease was, indeed, one of the most serious risks for
any medieval army far away from home, whether at siege or in the field, and
it was no respecter of persons. Joinville reminds us of that in his horrid
description of St Louis's sufferings in the retreat of his army from Man-
sourah: 'that night he fainted several times, and because the dysentery from
which he was suffering continually obliged him to visit the privy, they had to
cut away the lower part of his drawers'.[11] A battle was not needed in order to
put the life of a knight errant at a high level of risk.

When battle actually was joined in the field, the risks were high indeed.
This has been doubted, largely because Macchiavelli's charge against the
condottiere captains of fifteenth-century Italy, that as hired mercenaries they
were not willing to risk their lives or those of their men, and indulged
collusively in 'soft' battles where casualties were minimal in order to har-
bour their resources of manpower and maintain their influence, has been
much read and too readily believed. His picture is not really true even for
fifteenth-century Italy. At the battle of Anghiari (1440) where he claimed
that there was only one fatal casualty, there was in fact a death toll of
something of the order of 900; and comparable casualties were suffered at
other battles which he mentions as peculiarly unbloody.[12] Nevertheless, he
was right in thinking that the wars of Italy, before the French invasion of
1494, were relatively bloodless in comparison to those of other parts of
Europe. At Agincourt something of the order of 5000 to 6000 men probably fell on the French side.[13] There, as also at Poitiers (1356), some 40 per
cent of the French cavalry forces may have perished – that is to say of the
gentlemen, the knights and esquires. The casualties of the French at Cour-
trai in 1302 and of the Scots at Halidon Hill in 1333 were of a comparable
order of magnitude. Fatalities at these battles were disproportionate on the
losing side, as they were also at a number of other engagements, at Cassel
(1328), Crécy (1346), Najera (1367), Tannenburg (1410), and Flodden

(1513), for instance, and at Wisby (1361), the grim contents of whose grave pits, have provided what is at present the best evidence we have of the body armour worn by soldiers of the mid fourteenth century.[14] In the context of the grisly casualty statistics at battles such as these, the eloquence of Jean de Beaumont's contrast, in the *Vows of the Heron*, between the knight's picture in peacetime of martial glories and the realities of campaigning, leaps into life:

> When we are in the tavern drinking strong wine, and the ladies pass and look at us with those white throats and tight bodices, those sparkling eyes resplendent with smiling beauty: then nature urges us to have a desiring heart. Then we could overcome Yaumont and Agolant, and the others could conquer Oliver and Roland. But when we are on campaign on our trotting chargers, our bucklers round our necks and our lances lowered, and the great cold is congealing us together, and our limbs are crushed before and behind and our enemies are approaching us, then we would wish to be in a cellar so large that we might never be seen by any means.[15]

Personal details, in chronicles and chivalrous biographies, confirm that those who were remembered as the flower of knighthood earned their name and fame hard, in face of real and ugly dangers. At Locres Jacques de Lalaing, the Burgundian hero of the lavishly endowed jousts at Chalons, crossed and recrossed a river again and again in face of the enemy to succour his men and bring them over to safety, guarding and guiding them 'as a good shepherd watches over his sheep': he had five horses killed under him in the course of the engagement.[16] Only a few months later he was to meet his death in the field at the siege of Pouques (sieges were not always bloodless). The German knight errant Jorg von Ehingen, long remembered for the gallantry with which he despatched a Saracen champion in single combat during the Moslem siege of Ceuta in 1456, was luckier and lived long. But he was wounded seriously in 1457, fighting the Moors outside Granada, and his leg never healed: 'I was badly wounded in the shin by an arrow, and, although the wound healed, subsequently it broke out again when I returned to Swabia, and I retained into my old age a hole in the shin and a flux.'[17] The primitive surgery of the age could be hardly less physically daunting than the onrush of the enemy. Don Pero Niño the Victorious, the Castilian hero, was wounded in the leg in 1403 in a skirmish near Tunis. He was carried back to his ship, but refused to abandon his expedition, and by the time he and his men got back to Spain the wound had begun to fester. Don Pero was in a fever, his life was regarded as endangered and the doctors wished to amputate. He wanted to save the leg and insisted that they try cauterising the wound: 'They heated an iron, big as a quarrel, white hot. The surgeon feared to apply it, having pity for the pain it would cause. But Pero Niño, who was used to such work, took the glowing iron and himself moved it over his leg, from one end of his wound to the other.'[18] By great good fortune, all went well, and the wound healed, but things clearly might have gone another way, and not pleasantly.

Jacques de Lalaing, Jorg van Ehingen and Pero Niño were all knights errant, and were all great lovers of the expensive and showy sport of jousting. All three were also richly decorated: Jacques was a knight of the Golden Fleece; Jorg was admitted to the Order of La Squama by King Henry of Castile; and Pero Niño received the livery of Duke Louis of Orleans.[19] Only if one focusses exclusively on the tourneying feats of these three men can these orders be regarded as mere tokens of fashionable pre-eminence – and the facts of their biographies preclude focussing in that exclusive manner. They are not exceptional examples either: their careers conform to a pattern with which we have become familiar, that of the knight errant who was at once a devotee of the tourney, a great traveller, and a champion in the field. Their hardships, as I have recounted them, have a simple moral: that the honour that the age accorded them was a just meed in terms of the risks to which men such as they exposed body and fortune, if in no other way.

Let us turn now to a second question concerning the knight errant: in what way did the late medieval cult of errantry relate to the social and political needs of the day? This is a much more complicated problem. However, two themes in the ideal depiction of such a man will, we shall find, open a way of approach to it. One is the recurrent emphasis on his loyal service to his masters, the other the stress laid upon his outstanding individual – and individualistic – achievement. There is an apparent tension between these two themes which is significant: the reconciliation of that tension will be the key to answering our problem.

It is not surprising that so much was made of the theme of loyal service. When the late medieval man of arms came to serve his lord and his employer in war, he put more at his disposal than just his body in battle. He had to come ready armed, and the cost of his equipment was fully enough to justify setting a high price, in terms of social esteem, upon his willingness to serve. Part of the reason why he was thus expected to equip himself at his own cost was, of course, tradition. The landed vassal of an earlier period had been expected to provide his (cheaper) horses and armour from his own resources: whence, for instance, instructions such as those of the English kings of the twelfth and thirteenth centuries, detailing according to a scale of income the arms which the king's subjects were expected to keep in readiness against military summons.[20] In consequence when, in the thirteenth century, rulers began more generally to offer pay as an added inducement to service, it did not occur to anyone that the scale of pay should be adjusted to make provision for the cost of equipment: that was something that the prospective warrior ought already to possess. Indeed the contemporary view was the very opposite, as witness the *ordinamenti* regulating the *condotte* or agreements between mercenary captains in Italy and the towns and *signore* who employed them, which stipulate carefully and precisely the standard of equipment of the men whom the city or ruler expected to take into their pay.[21] Compensation for horses lost on campaign was as far as it was normal to go in making allowance in this area. Anything more would indeed have been unthinkable in a period in which the history of taxation was in its infancy, when a general tax was widely regarded as an intolerable burden, imposed by tyranny, unless it was justified by immediate emergency. Rulers simply could not have shouldered a larger proportion of the costs of war than they did, without undermining the measure of assent from their subjects which was necessary to the maintenance of their authority. Very naturally, in these circumstances, they continued to look to the traditional martial class, the nobility, to provide them with paid military service, and expected to pass on to them, as individuals, the cost of equipping themselves for that service. Pay in these conditions was rather more like a return (quite a handsome return) on an investment than wages in the modern sense. The social esteem in which nobles and knights were held on account of their readiness to serve was another part of the return on the same investment.

The additional worth of the contribution that the man at arms gave to the value of his service by equipping himself was the greater, in the late middle ages, for the fact that the cost of doing so was steadily rising. New and better armour had greater skill of workmanship behind it, had been designed and tempered to a high finish, and had often been specially tested by the discharge of crossbow bolts at point blank range.[22] So naturally it was very expensive. So were war horses which had to be strong enough to carry not only their metal and human burden but their own armour too, and which had to be specially bred and needed training. A cavalryman could not be content, moreover with just one horse; he needed remounts for himself, and less expensive mounts for his squires and other followers.[23] In 1297 Gerard de Moor, Lord of Wessegem, possessed seven horses worth together 1200 l.t. (pounds *tournois*): his principal horses, that is to say, represented an investment equal to the annual income in England of a very prosperous knight.[24] Malcolm Vale calculates that in the fifteenth century a French man-at-arms had something between six months and a year's wages wrapped up in just one war horse, and another quarter's wages, at least, in his armour.[25] This sort of investment was, in the vast majority of cases, a private one.

It was not just costs of equipment that were involved in the situation I am describing: there was also the equally important matter of training. Ramon Lull's glimpse of the potential of military colleges was, we have seen, premature: they were unheard of before the sixteenth century. The onus of training, like that of equipping oneself as a man at arms, remained to the end of the middle ages dependent on private resources. It was regarded as one of the social responsibilities of the nobility. Truly, says the author of *La vraye noblesse*, 'it is a sad business and contrary to their estate when knights and esquires who have sufficient goods do not maintain themselves well mounted and well equipped . . . and those who are so advanced in age that they cannot bear arms ought each according to his capacity, for the maintenance of nobility, to nourish and bring up in their households young gentlemen and to teach them all that belongs to *noblesse* and chivalry'.[26] What he says here brings into their proper focus of social purpose some remarks that the same author makes earlier, which could otherwise easily sound like class arrogance: 'it is more profit and honour [to a kingdom] that there should be found three or four hundred worthy knights . . . with sufficient riches to maintain their estate than a thousand or fifteen hundred others: for these four hundred knights of high enterprise and fine manners may govern, nourish, teach and lead any number of worthy squires and companions'.[27] Thus, in order to be able to call upon the service of these worthy squires and companions who could be the bulwark of his lordship in an emergency, the ruler relied on the maintenance of that style of noble living, described in an earlier chapter, which encouraged boys of good birth to take pleasure in outdoor sports that put them in the saddle, like hunting and hawking, and to prepare themselves in the tiltyard with the quintain for the trials of the jousting lists at a later age. There was equally a real social and political purpose underlying the fashion that encouraged them, in due course, to spend money on equipping themselves with horse and armour for the tournament (and so on the festivities that accompanied such occasions too), for no better way could be found of teaching them, at their own or their relatives' expense, to learn to handle horse and weapons in the full weight of armour – and with the risk of wounds and broken limbs between them and the congratulations of their fellows and the dancing with the girls. Thus the whole round of the noble style of living and its activities contributed to the value of noble service. It was worth the while both of the prince and of society to encourage and foster the social self-esteem of the nobility of which style was the outward and visible symbol.

Training, in its broad sense, did not end even at this point, however. In an army, a man who had the experience of the shocks of battle and the hardships of campaign behind him was of twice the value of one who had behind him simply an outdoor and martial aristocratic upbringing. All medieval armies, down to the mid fifteenth century, were temporary hosts of men enlisted for limited periods, and the stronger the leavening of really seasoned soldiers among them the better, from the points of view both of the commander of the army and of their fellows in it. To encourage ambitious young men of good family to seek experience of war in foreign lands and distant voyages, and to attach social cachet thereto, was in the circumstances an entirely understandable and very sensible reaction on the part of society and its rulers, besides being a traditional one. It is at this point that we begin to see clearly how the two superficially contrasting themes in the cult of knight errantry, the ideal of service and that of individualistic endeavour to meet self-imposed tests of personal enterprise and endurance, came to meet and harmonise. The needs of service demanded individualistic errantry; individual errantry in turn demanded and received recognition from those powers that required service and offered openings for it. These social facts and forces underpinned the medieval cult of the well-born warrior, and assented to his seeking justification in the eyes at once of his God, his ruler, and his beloved lady in following the profession of arms. That is why the knight who dedicated himself simultaneously to all three of these forms of service was the recurrent ideal of the rich literature of chivalry. It is the reason also why patrons were ready to encourage men to undertake distant expeditions, to Prussia and elsewhere, and to help pay for them. It made their service more valuable, and more highly reputed too.

★

We must take note, however, of a very real danger implicit in this condition of things. It was one thing to encourage individualistic errantry; it was another business, and potentially a very difficult one, to control it. Konrad of Megenberg urged young noblemen in Germany, if they were poor, to seek wages in the wars of Italy so as to maintain their estate.[28] The herald Gelre spoke of the wars of Lombardy as the 'school of arms'[29] (the same phrase, it should be noted, that was often used to describe the tourney). So far so good: here is a school for service. Errantry in Italy would prepare men to be more useful as warriors when they came home, and was therefore to be prized. But that is not how it looked from the Italian point of view: from that angle the foreign adventurers were worse than a plague. Sacchetti tells the eloquent story of how the great English *condottiero* Sir John Hawkwood was once met at the gate of Montecchio by two friars who wished him peace. 'May the lord take away your alms,' was his reply to their benediction: 'Do you not know that I live by war and that peace would be my undoing?' 'So well did he manage his affairs', the narrator adds, 'that there was little peace in his day.'[30] He and his men were a scourge to the land over which they fought and it was they and their like who prompted the indignant cry of Hawkwood's contemporary, the lawyer Bartholomew of Saliceto: 'What shall I say of those companies of men at arms who overrun the territories of our cities? I reply that there is no doubt about their position, for they are robbers . . . and as robbers they should be punished for all the crimes that they have committed.'[31] The school of arms and of errantry could, it is clear, become all too easily a school of banditry.

We are thus launched into the consideration of a further complicated question. How did contemporaries reconcile their cult of the wandering fighting man with their awareness of the horrors to which his excesses exposed civil society? The devastation and social disruption caused by the passage of armies in the late middle ages has been often written about and is hard to exaggerate. They made the ravages of war into a factor of social and economic importance at least comparable with the effect of plague. Thomas Basin's description of the state of the lands which had been fought over in the Anglo-French struggles of the fifteenth century is perhaps slightly overdrawn; but as a lugubrious vignette of the effects of war it remains worth quoting:

> I myself have seen the great plains of Champagne, of Beauce, of Brie, of the Gâtinais, of the country about Chartres and Dreux, of Maine, Perche and the Vexin. French and Norman lands alike, of the Beauvaisis, of the *pays* de Caux, from the Seine to Amiens and Abbeville, the country around Senlis, the Soissonnais and Valois as far as Laon, and even into Hainault, utterly deserted, emptied of inhabitants, overgrown with thorns and brambles, or, where trees will grow, springing into forest.[32]

Jean de Bueil, picturing himself as a young man riding through some of these same lands when the war was at its height, speaks of a countryside 'desolate and deserted', where the houses of the peasantry looked 'more like the lairs of wild beasts than the houses of men', and the nearest to noble living that one could find was an impoverished gentleman holding out in a fortified manor.[33] It was this sort of social and economic consequence of hostilities, scarring a whole countryside and its population, that stirred the imagination of Philippe de Mézières, when he sat down to draw in words an allegorical picture of Nimrod's 'horrible and perilous garden of war'. He conceived it as a barren enclosure, with an old roofless palace at its centre, and infested by blood-sucking leeches and by gigantic locusts.[34] The effect of the passing of men at arms under such leaders as Hawkwood or of the Free Companies among whom he learned the business of war, or of the *Ecorcheurs* in the fifteenth century, did resemble the passing of swarms of locusts. They stripped the land bare and human government proved powerless to restrain them.[35]

There were a number of reasons why this sort of situation was resistant to control: I will mention two principal ones. The first is related to the now familiar problem of the costs of war. Given its high cost, and given the degree to which rulers had no option but to pass on the expenses of equipment and training to the individual fighting man, it was natural that the traditional custom which allocated the spoils of war, or at least the lion's share in them, to their captors (either individually, or collectively as a company), should have been little questioned. It was seen as fair compensation for the risk they ran and for the expenses that they shouldered that they should have the advantage of the winnings of war.[36] From accepting spoil as the compensation for risks to seeking booty for its own sake was, however, a very small step and a very natural one, not least for the needy gentleman soldier who wished to maintain the class style of his living. Philippe de Mézières put his finger very surely on the dilemma of such persons, that of 'the second and third born sons and others, who have little or no portion in the inheritance of their fathers, and who by poverty are often constrained to follow wars that are unjust and tyrannical, so as to sustain their estate of nobility, since they know no other calling but arms: and therein they commit so much ill that it would be frightening to tell of all the pillaging and crimes with which they oppress poor people'.[37] For those who had no estate to keep up, the same sort of attraction was there too; for them too war could offer an occupation, and booty could open the way to temporary riches, perhaps even to lasting social advancement. The Catalan *almogarves* who under Roger Flor's leadership conquered Frankish Greece in the first years of the fourteenth century were for the most part not noble; but a number of them made themselves lords by means of their fighting quality and came to rule over the lands of noble men that they had dispossessed.[38]

The second reason why the ravages of soldiers were so hard to control is like the first, related to the problem of the costs of war, and also to the lure of booty. There was an attraction for rulers about employing companies of rootless, mercenary soldiers, in that their employer's obligations towards them ceased, at the end of a campaign, when he paid them off. For them, reciprocally, there was an attraction in service, which offered the prospects not only of pay but of loot as well, together with other less tangible benefits, a touch and perhaps more of the glamour attaching to the reputedly noble profession of arms and a chance of being able at least to dice and drink away some windfalls in style. In an age that did not question the right of all sorts of authorities – dukes, counts, noblemen, and cities as well as kings and kingdoms – to use arms to settle territorial and dynastic disputes, there was no lack of prospective employers for the mercenaries (or for the young errant in quest of experience). There were sovereign princes at one another's throats everywhere: this indeed is one of the distinctive features of the period. One party to a quarrel could hardly abstain from employing mercenaries unless it could trust the adversary to do so too, which it clearly could not. So the supply of armed men generated what one might call a kind of spurious demand; and so their numbers swelled, and their quest for continuing martial employment uprooted them from their homelands and strengthened their dependence on pillaging for survival. Roger Flor's Catalan company came into being in the war of the Vespers, in which Aragonese princes disputed with the Angevins of Naples the lordship of the island of Sicily; they moved further east in search of new employment because that war had ended and the companions needed to find a new paymaster; they ended by taking over Frankish Greece when no one would pay them enough any more. Hawkwood's famous White Company started life as a company of men at arms who, when the fighting in the Anglo-French war came to a temporary halt in 1360, left France and (after pillaging in company with others the papal Comtat Vennaissin) sought new employment in Italy. The wars of princes brought together great companies of men at arms, and in their course cast a tinsel glamour of chivalry over their activities: witness Froissart's colourful descriptions of the adventures of such ruthless freebooters as Perrot le Béarnois, Merigot Marchés, and Ramonnet de l'Épee. In the course of princely wars men like these mingled with their social superiors among their employer's vassals and familiars, and a few regularly managed to secure for themselves a permanent niche in dignified service. Princely employers expected to pay most of them off, though, at the end of the war. The trouble was that to pay them off was not the same as to disband them. They had to be left at large, still armed with equipment that was their own, beyond control; and so whole provinces were subjected to the indiscriminate pillaging of soldiery that sought to claim a share in chivalry but whose manner of living was the antithesis of what chivalry stood for, the protection of the poor, the fatherless and the widow.

It is not enough at this stage just to say that this was the antithesis of true chivalry. The idealistic chivalrous ethic, with its emphasis on the honour to be acquired by individual adventuring and on the nobility of the profession of arms, clearly itself contributed directly to the problem. The mercenary free companies were no doubt socially very heterogeneous, but it is no accident that most of their leaders came from the minor nobility; and if Schäffer's analysis of the social origins of the German companies in Italy in the fourteenth century is anything to go by, there was a very considerable leavening of men of minor noble lineage among their men at arms.[39] In any case it would be quite misleading to suggest that freebooting habits were the preserve of the professional mercenaries; an expedition like the Black Prince's great *chevauchée* across Languedoc in 1355 had among its principal objects the wasting of the countryside with fire and sword and the acquisition of booty.[40] It is true that a distinction was commonly drawn in theory between knights and gentlemen, who fought in the service of their lords

and for glory, and the mercenaries who fought for anyone who would pay
them and for loot. This was not a new distinction in the later middle ages; it
had been drawn sharply in the twelfth century, when many parts of Europe
had their first taste of large rootless companies of professional soldiers, such
as the dreaded Brabançons that Henry II of England employed in his
campaigns.[41] The distinction was, however, one that it was extraordinarily
hard to draw in practice.

The principal reason for this was that booty was no less attractive to the
'genuine' knight than it was to the mercenary. When the English antiquary
Leland wrote of Sir William Berkeley's manor at Beverstone, that it was
built out of the ransoms of the prisoners that his great-grandfather had won
at Poitiers, or of the Castle of Ampthill that it was built of the spoils that
Lord Fanhope won in France, he was describing the way in which men of
solid family had advanced their fortunes through winnings of war, not of
the rise of ex-mercenaries.[42] The agreement struck in 1421 between two
English esquires, John Winter and Nicholas Molyneux, to be brothers in
arms in the wars in France, to pool their winnings and remit them home
where they should be invested in the purchase of lands and manors, shows
us two men calculating carefully how to use to their social and economic
advantage gains won in the entirely reputable service of their native
sovereign, a cause distinctively different from mercenary service in the
usual sense, the kind of service, indeed, whose repute virtually all rulers
fostered deliberately.[43] But they could not hope to foster it for good reason
with regard to one kind of man, and to discourage it with regard to another
kind of man whose motives were comparatively degraded. The distinction
was not a real one. In terms of motivation, calculation and conduct the line
between gentleman and mercenary was simply too difficult to draw with
any precision.

At the extreme, of course, the distinction will hold. Whatever excesses
the Black Prince was responsible for on his campaigns it is pointless to call
him a mercenary. Whatever his origins (and they were noble), mercenary is
almost a flattering title for one such as Merigot Marchés, who told the Paris
court that condemned him to death for robbery and war crimes that he had
buried his treasure under the banks of the river Venves, in a spot that none
but he or his wife could find: this has the ring rather of the buccaneer's life of
a later age.[44] It was in the broad middle ground that the distinction broke
down. Take the examples, for instance, of Hawkwood and Du Guesclin.
Hawkwood is remembered as a ferocious and successful mercenary, which
he was. Du Guesclin's name lives as that of a great French warrior and
patriot, 'the tenth of the Worthies'. Hawkwood's contemporary reputation
amounted, though, to a little more than just that of a mercenary. When he
died in 1394 the grateful Florentines buried their one-time Captain General under an elaborate marble tomb in their cathedral.[45] A hundred years

later, Caxton in England quoted him as one of the knights of the past whose noble achievements in chivalry men of his own day could with profit recall as an example to themselves.[46] Conversely, in the case of Du Guesclin, it is hard indeed to dissociate the man who became the great Constable of France from the mercenary riff-raff who were so often his campaign companions. It was in his expedition to Spain in 1365–6 that he really established his reputation, leading thither some of the most bloodthirsty freebooters among the companies that were at large in France at the time, men of precisely the same stamp as those whom Hawkwood had led into Italy a few years earlier. Du Guesclin's biographer, Cuvelier, though at pains to portray him as a type of the honourable knight errant, devoted to the service of God and his country, was too acute an observer to conceal completely the true lineaments of the world in which his hero moved, and they come across in a number of wry stories of the great man and his companions. A nice example is his tale of the day that Du Guesclin sat down to dinner with a group of *routier* captains whom he hoped to persuade to join him in the expedition to Spain in the service of Henry of Trastamara, bastard aspirant to the throne of Castile. 'This is an excellent wine,' remarked Bertrand. 'How much did you pay for it?' 'I can't answer that question,' replied the principal among his hosts, 'the vendor was not alive at the time when we acquired it.'[47]

Here is the Tenth Worthy in distinctly doubtful company. From here it is all too short a step to the scene that another witness of the same times describes, of seeing the English knight Sir John Harleston and a group of captains all sitting together drinking from silver chalices, which they had looted from churches.[48] We are put firmly on our guard against the resonance of reputations, and of contemporary myth-making, and reminded that if you scratch the paint from the picture of the knight errant, you will all too often find something rather different underneath. This is the most solid basis for questioning whether the late medieval cult of chivalry was not a sham, a tinsel covering disguising the ugliness of war and political strife and permitting the nobility to glamourise the misdeeds that were the basis on which, all too often, gentlemen as well as mercenaries maintained their estate. The trouble was that there was no prospect of obtaining the loyal service of the one kind of man without promoting, or at least permitting, the outrages of the other. Since princes needed soldiers, they chose on society's behalf to do both, and for the most part to leave to God's final and unseen arbitrament the question of separating the sheep from the goats.

Thus the problem of reconciling the cult of the knight errant with an awareness of the tribulations to which the activities of wandering fighting men exposed society was very largely bypassed. It was recognised that there were some men whose careers had more of the flavour of those of the ideal knights of literature and some who resembled more those black knights who in literature usually got their deserts, but the practical difficulty of distinguishing the one from the other proved insuperable. There is nothing very surprising about this, really: it is an enduring facet of all human ideals that they create as many problems as they resolve, and to say that chivalry did this is not to condemn it but simply to speak of a permanent feature of the human situation. We all have to live with the tensions and contradictions generated by contemporary ideologies. Nevertheless, because this particular problem was recognised contemporarily, in the late middle ages, it needs to be probed further. This means that we must now go on to look carefully at what the reactions were of those who clearly recognised the difficulty for what it was, who saw quite clearly that knights and gentlemen were as often responsible for outrages as common mercenaries, and who decried the contemporary situation in which 'the man who does not know how to set places on fire, to rob churches and usurp their rights and to imprison the priests, is not fit to carry on war'.[49] Did the conditions which they witnessed with real horror undermine their confidence in the ethic of chivalry, and if not, how was it that they did not do so?

★

The critics did not mince their words. They did not merely attack the knighthood and the nobility for involvement in wholesale pillaging in war, but for a much more wholesale abandonment of what they thought had been the hardy, ascetic discipline and tradition of the chivalry of old times, for the softness of noble ways, for the extravagance of noble living, for its arrogance and vainglory, its love of luxury and its perennial quest for funds to support continuing and conspicuous waste.[50] This invective is eloquent, and has often been treated as an onslaught on the ideal of chivalry itself, as a symptom of the way in which knightly disorder led to a progressive loss of confidence in knightly values.

On closer inspection it does not seem to be quite that, however. For one thing, there is nothing new about invective of this kind at the end of the middle ages: it is as old as chivalry itself. Back in the twelfth century we find Orderic Vitalis, William of Tyre and Peter of Blois all complaining that the knights of their day have lost their vigour, unmanned by effete fashions.[51] St Bernard harps on a similar theme, contrasting secular knighthood with its gold spurs, its gaily painted shields and extravagant attire – better calculated to dazzle the eyes of women than to strike fear into the foe – with the hardy and ascetic idealism of the Templars.[52] It is not just the great clerics who make these criticisms in the early days, either. Here is Girart de Bornelh, Provençal troubador and a man of a different mould and mood, commenting eloquently in the early thirteenth century on the quest for pillage which is not worthy of the name of chivalry: 'I used to see the barons in beautiful armour, following tournaments, and I heard those who had given the best blow spoken of for many a day. Now honour lies in stealing cattle, sheep and oxen, or pillaging churches and travellers. Oh, fie upon the knight who drives off sheep, robs churches and travellers and then appears before a lady.'[53] Indeed, an underlying theme of much early chivalrous romance is the struggle of true chivalry against false knighthood, represented by those 'black knights' who are the glamorised literary versions of the robber barons of real life, and whom the champions struggle to overthrow. The critics of the late middle ages did not take up a new theme, they harped upon an old one, for chivalry had always been aware that it was at war with a distorted image of itself. That indeed was part and parcel of its ideal.

The late medieval answer to the problem of the disorders and crimes of martial men, like its diagnosis of it, was an old one, though before the end of the middle ages a new tone enters into it. It lay not in an abandonment of chivalrous values, but in a re-appeal to the traditional value of loyal and faithful service of which so much has already been said in this chapter and which had been from the very beginning at the heart of the chivalrous ethic. Thus we find the late medieval critics contrasting, in familiar vein, the abandonment and pillaging of contemporary knights and their love of luxury with the disciplined dedication of the heroes of old. Deschamps calls for a revival of jousting, as a hardy apprenticeship to arms, and urges that men should imitate antique example. Gerson appeals to the examples of St Louis, and of the Romans. Alain Chartier too looks back to antiquity as he condemns the knighthood of his own age, in terms all too familiar: 'it is not war that is being waged in this kingdom, it is robbery'.[54] Where a new tone becomes now discernible is in a sharper emphasis on the definition of true service as the service of a lawful ruler, defined as one who embodies in his authority the common weal of a people or city. This was a definition that emphatically included the Church and her war, the crusade; more importantly, it was seen more and more clearly as excluding the private war of the petty seigneur, and in due course, of all but the very greatest seigneurs. It is very clearly reflected in the writings of the great lawyers, like Bartolus and John of Legnano, who emphasise that no man has a legitimate right to take up arms in any but a just war, and exclude from that category any wars levied on the authority of one who is less than a sovereign prince.[55] It is reflected again in the writings of clerical polemists like Alvaro Pelayo, who in his great onslaught on knights, composed in the early fourteenth century, condemns them because they are ready to take up arms against their lords; because they are ready to flee from battle and to abandon their lord among his enemies, so betraying their oath to brave death in the cause of the common weal; because they fight not for God but for booty, for their private interest and not for the common one, and without the license of their superior lord.[56] We can see it reflected again in emphasis on the emerging idea that a fighting man, if he is to be entitled to the privileges of a belligerent (which included the right to a share in spoils and ransoms), ought to be on an official pay roll, or at the very least officially mustered.[57] Very significant is the corollary that the fourteenth-century canonist Bonet derives from this point in his book the *Tree of Battles*, which was much read by knights as an authority on the laws of war, that 'he [the soldier] does all that he does as the deputy of the king or of the lord in whose pay he is',[58] as the servant of the prince, that is to say. This is an idea that runs directly parallel to that teaching of Bartolus and others that was discussed in an earlier chapter, that the prince is the 'fount' of all honour, on whose recognition the title to nobility depends, and that the service of the prince and the common weal is the proper way forward for the aspirant to nobility and honour. The sphere in which errantry is to be allowed to win justifiable renown and recognition is beginning to be significantly more constricted.

In a rather similar context, we can see the same theme reflected in the increasing emphasis, in chivalrous manuals and mirrors for princes, on classical examples, in which the emphasis on service as a public obligation was clearer than in the stories of the Arthurian past, with their individualistic bent. One of the texts very commonly copied into heraldic collections in the fifteenth century was the imaginary debate between 'three chivalrous princes', Hannibal, Alexander and Scipio Africanus, who pleaded before Minos, judge of the underworld, as to which had 'by his knightly deeds surmounted all mortal men'. Minos's judgement, at the end of a long debate, went to Scipio, who, after rehearsing the knightly achievements of his youth, of his captaincies and consulates, clinched his case with this argument: 'all this that I have achieved was not in the least way in the desire to outshine others, but I set about it all in the will to maintain for ever the dignity of the name of Roman'.[59] There is a back-handed dig here at the quest for vainglory, which had inspired Hannibal and Alexander and had been their ultimate undoing, and which the critics constantly identified as one of the besetting sins of knighthood. The general moral is clear, and its emphasis is on the value of public service, whose aim is to uphold not the fame of an individual, but the honour and fortune of a people.

We must once again be on our guard, however, against interpreting this new kind of emphasis on service as being necessarily in conflict with the traditional individualism of chivalry. There is a hint of this even in this debate of the three chivalrous princes, at least in the French version that is based on the Latin original of Buonsignori of Siena; he has set these things forward, the translator says in his preface, because 'it is pleasing to praise noble enterprises and deeds of chivalry'[60] – a very individualistic way of introducing his basically anti-individualistic *exemplum*. The two themes of individualism and public service appear in combination in other contexts

too, and some of them are very significant. Jousting was often criticised as
the acme of the quest for vainglory. It could, though, be looked on in a very
different way, and by the open apologists of the claims of the public weal.
Christine de Pisan in 1412 advised that, in order to ensure that the French
nobility should be trained and prepared against the reopening of war with
their English adversaries, tournies and jousts should be proclaimed in every
diocese in France two or three times a year, and that the costs should be met
out of royal public taxation.[61] Caxton gave much the same advice to King
Richard III of England:

> that twice or thrice in a year or at the least once he would do cry jousts of
> peace to the end that every knight should have horse and harness and
> also the use and craft of a knight; and also to tourney one against one or
> two against two, and the best to have a prize, a diamond or a jewel, such as
> should please the prince. This should cause gentlemen to resort to the
> ancient customs of chivalry, to great fame and renown, and also to be
> always ready to serve their prince when he shall call them or have need.[62]

Here the diamond, the prize of individual prowess, is fitted elegantly into a
scheme whose general end is public service. There is something of the same
tone in Oliver de La Marche's classic remarks on nobility:

> It is acquired, firstly by those who hold great office under the prince . . .
> thirdly, when a servant of the prince or any other has led an honourable
> existence, and the prince has made him a knight, this ennobles him and
> his posterity . . . Fourthly, to follow the profession of arms and to serve
> the prince valorously, that ennobles a man.[63]

Here again, clearly, service and outstanding individual achievement are
presented in harmony, as part of the same scheme of things. The statutes of
some of the secular orders of chivalry make the same point with even
greater clarity. On the one hand they make provision for the augmentation
of the insignia of companions who have achieved some notable feat of arms,
and for the composition of books of adventures recording their high deeds
as knights errant; on the other, they bind them together by solemn oaths to
uphold the service of the sovereign of the order and his lineage.[64] Here we
see the very extravagance which has been condemned as dividing chivalry
from reality, and the individualism that is charged with rendering it disorderly, being so channelled as to point it anew in the right direction, towards
the obligation of service to a sovereign lord. If a new tone begins to enter
into the emphasis on service in late medieval chivalrous literature and
culture more generally, one which is related directly to the pressing social
problems that endemic war generated, it does not do so, we can now

perceive, at the expense of traditional individualism, but seeks rather to establish a harmony with it.

There is nothing surprising about this. Individual errantry had, as we have seen, real and useful purposes and retained them for as long as the need remained for rulers to pass on to the nobility part of the cost of chivalrous service and the whole of the responsibility for training themselves for it. If these rulers were to be served as they wished to be, that still implied, in the social and political circumstances of the day, the maintenance of a powerful emphasis on the significance of individual errantry (as also of ancestral example); and it also meant encouraging noblemen to cultivate skills and virtues apposite to an aristocratic martial class: liberality, courage, courtesy and good horsemanship. The perennial competition between princely courts, which were the contemporary foci of political life, promoted an extravagance in this area, within what was by now an established mode that was to the taste of the nobility whose service it sought to recruit and whose duty of service it sought to emphasise. That was why rulers were ready, sometimes even eager, to foot at least part of the bill for this extravagance.

There was no real loss of confidence in chivalrous values: the very men who decried the crimes of contemporary knights did not urge the abandonment of the chivalrous way, but appealed to the example of the chivalrous past in offering the pattern for reformation. The heralds and their patrons glamourised that same past to ram the lesson home. The revival of true and loyal chivalry, dedicated to its traditional purpose of defending the weak and the common weal, still seemed the most effective antidote to the chivalry of false values which turned the sons of poor noblemen into freebooters, and through which freebooters sought to elbow their way into the world of gentility. If the message often fell on deaf ears, that was not because people had failed to grapple with reality, but for a simpler reason. All that the critics could do with their appeal to ancient example, and all that those could do who glamourised ancient example in a didactic cult, was to encourage, in a situation where what was needed was control. In what I have called chivalry's war against its own distorted image, the uncomfortable balance between its use and abuse could not be shifted until control could keep better pace with encouragement. That did not begin to happen until after the middle of the fifteenth century, and when it did, much that had been typical at least of the trappings if not of the core of the chivalrous mode of life began very gradually to lose its significance. In a paradoxical way the very disorders to which chivalry gave rise when abused had been part of the source of its vigour. What Huizinga called the harsh realities made it purposeful and useful to hold up in contrast to them the ideal that they distorted.

CHAPTER XIII

Conclusion

At the beginning of this book I made it clear that it would concentrate on the period from, roughly, about 1100 or a little after to somewhere about 1500. At the beginning of the sixteenth century, it is true, there were not yet many signs of any abatement of the vigour of chivalric culture. Ferguson has written of the 'Indian summer' of chivalry in early Tudor England, and in France in the same period the vogue of chivalry continued similarly to flourish.[1] Francis I sought knighthood at the hands of Bayart, the *chevalier sans reproche*, and he and his contemporary, the English Henry VIII, were both great masters of the joust. In the Empire, Maximilian, the heir of Austria who married the heiress of Burgundy, in his autobiography cast himself consciously in the role of a knight errant,[2] and was an even more enthusiastic addict of the tourney than Francis or Henry. His grandson Philip II of Spain was the hero of a *pas d'armes* quite as elaborate and ingenious as any of the Burgundian 'feats' of the fifteenth century.[3] The prominent place of knightly romances and of manuals of chivalry like that of Ramon Lull among the earliest printed books, and the sixteenth-century vogue of new chivalrous romances like *Amadis of Gaul*, tell the same story of the enduring vigour, in the age of the Renaissance, of fashions set in the middle ages. Nevertheless, there are quite sound reasons for concluding a survey of chivalry somewhere round the year 1500.

For one thing, there was a lack of genuinely new departures in this time of chivalry's 'Indian summer'. It is as if the vein of fresh ore had become at last exhausted, so that the moneyers could do no more than remint old coin. New orders of chivalry (like the French King Henry III's Order of the Holy Spirit) were founded, but on the old pattern. The challengers at the tournament held at Blois in 1550 could seek to keep up with literary fashion by appearing in the guise of figures drawn from Boiardo and Ariosto, but they were not doing anything really novel in these new clothes.[4] More important than any of this, however, were changes which, in the sixteenth century, were taking place at a deeper level, and were altering the shape of the social and political structures in which chivalry had in the past flourished. What we see at the end of the middle ages is in consequence not so much the decline of chivalry, but the alteration of its appearance – which is, indeed, rather what Cervantes's indulgence in his *Don Quixote*, his appreciation of the grandeurs of chivalry as well as its follies, might lead us to expect. The forces that in the medieval past had given it life and impetus were still at work, but the outward aspects in which they found expression were changing, and the old name was losing its appositeness. Change, rather than decline, will in consequence be the theme of this closing chapter.

Chivalry is a word that came to denote the code and culture of a martial estate which regarded war as its hereditary profession: around the beginning of the sixteenth century important developments were beginning to affect radically the conduct of that martial business. On the one hand the manner of waging war was affected by major changes in tactics and by advances in military technology, on the other by the growth of public, and especially of royal fiscality. These developments have to be considered together, because they only succeeded in generating really significant effects in combination. Neither on its own would have meant so much.

The armies of the late fifteenth and early sixteenth centuries were much stronger than those of the period down to about 1450 in two arms of which little has so far been said (I hope excusably in a book about a cavaliers' code), infantry and artillery. They were also much larger than those of the preceding period. The principal element in this increase in the size of hosts was the enlargement of the infantry (itself a consequence of the development of better drills for the co-ordination of the operations of pikemen, whose long weapons could hold off cavalry, with those of archers and handgunners). At the end of the reign of Charles the Bold of Burgundy, the proportion of cavalry to infantry in the basic unit of his armies, known as the 'lance', was nine footmen (three archers, three pikemen, and three men with culverins) to one mounted man-at-arms.[5] A hundred years before, the proportion might have been one to one or even less, at most one to two. The army that the Catholic Kings of Spain led against Granada in 1489 counted 40,000 infantry to 13,000 mounted men (only a small proportion of these being equipped as men at arms: the rest were *genétaires*, light-armed Spanish cavalry).[6] In the French armies similarly the infantry arm was reinforced as the fifteenth century wore on, at first by the *francs-archers* recruited among the local communities in accordance with Charles VII's ordinance of 1448, later largely by mercenary companies of Swiss and of German *Lansknechts*. The new armies, thus constituted, looked and were different from the old hosts, witness the comment of Jean de Bueil, veteran of the Hundred Years War, on the great French army that assembled to resist the Burgundian invasion in 1471: 'War has become very different. In those days when you had eight or ten thousand men, you reckoned that a very large army: today it is quite another matter . . . As for me, I am not accustomed to see so many troops together.'[7]

It was not simply the fact that there were so many more men who expected to fight on foot that made the difference. Knights in the past had often enough dismounted to fight, and by the fifteenth century to fight chivalrously did not necessarily mean to fight on horseback. 'I saw two gentlemen of name and arms on foot,' says Oliver de La Marche, writing of the engagement at Gavre in 1453, 'the one was Messire Jacques de Foucquessoles . . . the other Messire Philibert de Jacucourt, *seigneur* of Villarnou: these two marched forward chivalrously against the enemy.'[8] What made the difference was rather the nature of the new infantry, and the changing role of the noble in the armies of which they formed part. As footmen, the Swiss and the *Lansknechts* were professionals, with a degree of training that the old communal infantry, recruited (in most European areas) largely in the towns, had never attained. The same was true of the infantry of the Spanish armies that Gonsalvo de Cordoba commanded with such skill in the early years of the Italian wars. Both the Swiss and German mercenaries, and the native infantry which were their equivalent in the Spanish armies and which in those of France came ultimately to replace them, were not for the most part recruited among the nobility. The captains who led them and who had to face the terrific problems of maintaining order among them might very likely be nobles, and an infantry command came to be considered to be a wholly acceptable and honourable office for a nobleman. Bayart and Blaise de Monluc and Gaspard de Saulx Tavannes all served for a time in the infantry. But the men of rank and file had for the most part nothing to do with the world of chivalry: that was for the officers. So the ideal of the knight errant began to blend into that of the officer and gentleman; what had been a cavaliers' code developed into the code of an officer class. Under chivalry's tutelage, the nobility had of course enjoyed before this time a long apprenticeship for this role, for the knight or man at arms did not go to war alone, and had always had command of the little troop that accompanied him and looked after his remounts and armour (and knights had often fought in medieval battles dispersed on foot among the infantry in order to strengthen their morale, essentially an officer's business). Nevertheless there was and is a difference of more than title between a knight and an officer. The latter's office has a much clearer ring of administration as well as action, of the orderly room and the need to wrestle with problems of pay and supply; and he holds his position by commission rather than by natural right. A man may be born noble and so eligible for knighthood, but an officer's commission can only be conferred by higher authority.

The only way in which the expense of the larger armies of the late fifteenth and early sixteenth centuries could be paid for was out of public taxation, levied on princely authority. There was nothing new, of course, about paying for service or about raising taxes to meet the expense of war – both dated back to the twelfth century, and indeed beyond. It was the new scale of the operations involved that made the difference at the end of the middle ages, and that put the maintenance of any effective army beyond the reach of all purses save the public, princely one. The development of artillery worked to the same effect. Guns had come into use in warfare in the mid fourteenth century, but it was not until the fifteenth that they began to be really important. In siege warfare their effect had become decisive by the latter years of the Hundred Years War. The really great stride forward came a little later, however, as the fifteenth century drew to its close, with the development of field artillery and the increasing use of handguns by foot soldiers. The number of guns that a city might require for its defence, or a prince for the siege train and artillery park of his army, now increased out of all proportion, and so did requirements in terms of powder, cannon balls and shot, and of draught beasts to haul the heavy weapons on carts or, by the end of the century, on their own carriages. Besides this, there was of course a new demand for men trained in the use of the new weapons. A new science had entered into the art of war, centring on the placing of guns, the linking of their emplacements by networks of trenches, and in course of time on the means whereby enfilade fire could be brought to bear on marching columns. It was a science that was very expensive. It was one thing, in accordance with ancient ways, to expect a man at arms to come to the host equipped with his own horses and armour, but no one, in the new conditions of war, expected a master of artillery to provide his own cannon. That kind of outgoing was way beyond the range of a private pocket.

It has been said that 'the indiscriminate death dealt out by shot and ball had ruined war as a finishing school for the knightly character.'[9] This is not quite true, at any rate as regards the late medieval period. Before the days of gunnery, English archers, at Poitiers and again at Agincourt, had dealt out indiscriminate death to the French men at arms, bringing them down 'top over turve' at a distance;[10] it was nothing new to die by an unknown hand. Chivalrous society indeed found no real difficulty in coming to terms with artillery as such. Guns came to be decorated with tracery, blazons, mottos and inscriptions, and were given names as swords once had been: they might be named after heroes of antiquity, like Louis XI's two bombards, Jason and Medea, or after great captains of recent time like some of his cannon – La Hire, Barbasan, Flavy. Noblemen adopted guns for their badges and ensigns, as did that connoisseur of chivalry, Louis de la Gruthuyse, who selected for his personal emblem a bombard with the motto

Plus en vous; captains of noble blood, like Jean de Bueil, came to regard it as part of their business to know about guns and how to use them; Jean Bureau, the great French Master of Artillery was ennobled for his 'skill and valour', and made chivalrous because of his gunnery.[11] Guns found their place too in chivalrous literature, as we hear in the fourth book of the romance of Amadis of Gaul, when the sound of cannonade begins to roll in the war of Lisuard and Perion.[12] In the long run, of course, attempts like these to accommodate chivalry to gunnery could do no more than sugar the bitter pill, but it took a long time for the full implications of the advent of 'these devilish instruments of artillery' to sink in. In the more immediate term, though, what guns did do was to help to make war more of a large-scale affair, especially in terms of money, and also a more technically specialised business. A career soldier now needed to make himself just a little more professional than he had done in the high days of errantry. In that way guns did begin to impair warfare as a finishing school for gentility; as they helped also to make it a more definitively public business, in which the directive role of the sovereign–employer of soldiers became more crucial.

The late fifteenth century saw also the appearance of what begin at last to look like national standing armies. The French led the way here, when in the 1440s Charles VII began to assert more effectively the old royal claim to monopoly of the right to muster troops, and established the *compagnies d'ordonnance*, out of which the French standing army was to grow. Charles the Bold's ordinance of 1473, laying the foundations for a Burgundian standing army, was modelled on this French example. The English too, a little earlier if only temporarily, had made their army of occupation in northern France into something that was very nearly a standing army, with permanent garrison forces and a complicated system of muster and review (after the breakdown of this experiment, to which inadequate financing substantially contributed, the English monarch became exceptional in maintaining only very small standing forces). The Italian states of the same period were likewise well aware of the need to maintain *condottiere* forces on more or less permanent call, and to have the fortresses of the *contado* garrisoned in time of peace as well as war.[13] The development was a general one, even if it proceeded at a different pace and wore a slightly different aspect in different places.

Few at first were aware of its full implications. Most of his subjects seem to have expected Charles VII to disband his army when the English war was over, and looked forward to the day too, for with the disbanding of the army there should have followed the suspension of the taxes that were needed to maintain it. But the army was not disbanded, and the *taille*, the tax which was the necessary condition of its maintenance, became permanent. In Spain similarly the Catholic kings would not have been able to maintain a permanent army in their wars in Italy but for the great overhaul of their finances which they had directed and which before the end of their reign had multiplied the receipts of royal revenue many times over. In Germany and Italy, where poorer rulers governed lands of less extent, princelings and *signore* got over the problem of resources that were inadequate to maintain substantial standing forces by making themselves 'brokers' of mercenaries and hiring their services or those of their subjects to richer princes, as did the Swiss cantons also. Thus the consequence of the appearance of larger and more permanent armies was that money, always the sinew of war, came to be needed for military purposes on an even larger scale.

It is here that the full importance of princely fiscality begins to be apparent. More efficient, more general and more permanent systems of taxation opened the way toward the solution of that problem of the control of martial forces which had dogged the governments of the middle ages. Money offered a means whereby those authorities who could bring together enough of it could begin to establish a monopoly of military force. From a 'chivalrous' point of view, the change that this implied was one of very great significance. It was no longer enough for a man to be noble and entitled to the arms that his ancestors had borne in battle for him to call himself a warrior. If a man claimed to be a soldier, he must belong to some identifiable martial unit, otherwise he was not a soldier. Where once governments' response to military emergency had been to summon for service the nobility of the threatened province and to order or induce other great noblemen to mobilise their retainers, their concern now was to ensure that garrisons and standing companies of men at arms were on a war footing, that 'lances' should be at full strength, that a sufficient force of infantry should be available and mercenaries hired if necessary. Among the visual symptoms of the change that was here taking place were the decline of the importance of the chivalrous insignia of coat-armour as a means of recognition in the field (which meant inevitably that the significance of the military role of heralds declined also), and a new insistence on the importance of uniforms as a means to distinguish one military *unit* from another. The officers commanding units or sub-units in the army and the men at arms of the elite heavy cavalry might be and very usually were men of coat-armour, but they were officers not because of their coat armour now, but because of their 'office'. Thus the conception of an estate of knighthood, with a general commission to uphold justice and protect the weak, was being pared down into the conception of the officer whose business it is to fight the King's enemies. Even though armies were larger, the path forward to military glory was thus made narrower – and became better controlled.

★

Thus more intensive and better organised revenue collection, in combination with the larger forces whose maintenance it made possible and with technical advances in military science, began to change both the aspect of war and the conception of the role of the warrior, round which the martial cult of chivalry centred. Their effect would however have been much less clear and certainly more gradual but for a third factor that from our point of view was equally important. This was what has been called the 'crisis of seigneurial revenues' of the late middle ages. Here we are brought into contact with a very long term process, one which cannot be pinned down to the period around 1500. A multiplicity of causes underlay it, and their nature, extent and significance are a matter of debate among historians. I will therefore attempt no more than a broad outline of some of the points involved.

Seigneurial revenues, especially those of the lesser nobility, had begun to come under pressure at a very early stage, by the twelfth century in some places. The revenue from land of a feudal proprietor was principally dependent on the dues of the tenants and the productivity of his domain farms, and a point came naturally when there was no further room for expansion – when the clearing of waste land and increase of population among the tenantry had gone as far as they might. At the same time, as we have noted in earlier chapters, the expense of maintaining a noble standard of life was rising. Besides, the whole period from about 1100 on was one of inflation, which, though by modern standards mild and gradual, had considerable impact. Dues, whether in kind or money, were fixed at customary rates; those in money did not keep pace with the falling value of silver currency and those in kind (where they had not been commuted for money, as happened more often than not) were less useful than of old. Expedients such as the more intensive exploitation of seigneurial monopolies (for example of milling) and the jurisdictional rights of lordship could do no more than palliate the strains which began to appear, and which are reflected in widespread indebtedness, the mortgaging and sale of manors, and the disappearance of old families from the scene. The pace and intensity of the processes should not be exaggerated: individual prodigality and sheer bad luck were no doubt the real causes of decline in many instances. But in the fourteenth and fifteenth centuries the consequences of the broad developments that I have outlined were rendered more acute by a combination of factors, in particular by the sharp demographic decline which followed the famines of 1314–17 and the series of great plagues that began with the Black Death of 1348, by the wasting of land (and especially of seigneurial domains) in the course of warfare, and by a rise in the price of labour (which had become scarce) accompanied by a relative fall in the price of agricultural produce. The prices of what we would now call industrial artefacts, and especially of the luxuries considered necessary to the noble style of living, did not, unfortunately, fall likewise. It thus became more and more difficult for the nobleman to maintain his style at a level consonant with his status, and especially for the lesser nobleman who could not hope to offset declining landed revenue by major extensions of his patrimony or by taxing his subjects and tenants, who, in fact, were driving harder bargains with him now amid his new difficulties, demanding the abolition or modification of old dues or, in other areas, a higher proportion of the profits of *metayage* (share cropping).

All this was not a strictly continuous process – there was ebb and flow as there always is in economic life – and it is not at all easy to measure the severity of the so-called 'crisis'. What is clear is that the nobility, in order to maintain their style and their social dominance, found very generally that they needed to augment the resources which they derived from their territorial patrimonies with income from other sources. The principal source of additional income to which they could look, and to which in their world of patronage and clientage they always had looked, was service – or rather the by-products of the service, martial or administrative, either of the crown or of nobles richer than themselves. Pensions, offices, wages of war and booty, in combination with the kind of patronage that might help a man towards a good marriage or his younger sons toward rich prebends, were the most obvious if not the only ways in which the gentle and impoverished might help themselves, given the social stigma so very widely associated with commerce. There was in consequence no problem about recruiting nobles into, for instance, the *compaignies d'ordonnance* that Charles VII of France organised: the men of standing who were eager for the royal pay that went with service in their ranks were legion. La Marche tells us that in 1445, when they were founded, the price of good horses rose enormously in France, because there were so many gentlemen who wanted to present themselves well equipped in the hope of being taken on to the royal musters.[14] Everywhere the magnetism of the court and of service in the 'national' armies or standing forces had become more powerful. The great force that at the end of the middle ages was bringing to birth out of the old order of knighthood what Nicholas Wright has appositely described as 'national chivalries'[15] was thus not a shift of cultural fashions or of political ideology: rather it was harsh necessity that was the midwife of the change.

All this sounds very one-sided, which it was not. The nobility – even the lesser nobility – remained rich, compared with most people, even if individual family resources were often strained; they were the only secular class that could effectively, by its collective action, resist the demands of authority (including, emphatically, its fiscal demands); and habits of independence – of violent independence – had been bred into the nobles over long generations. Their swords and their service, moreover, were equally at the disposal of the great noblemen as at that of the prince – of that 'super-nobility' of families that, starting from ample riches, had made themselves richer still by the dynastic accumulation of lands, lordships, and vice-regal offices, and who were so often at odds with their nominal overlords. They helped to make these dynasties even more powerful and ambitious, and that is why late medieval history so often appears to be dominated by the struggles of monarchs with their greater nobles, by such wars as those of the Roses in England, of Burgundians and Armagnacs in France, of the civil wars that preceded in Castile the reign of the Catholic kings, Ferdinand and Isabella. These struggles, in their turn, helped to prolong the life and the activities of the mercenary free companies in whose ranks many noblemen tarnished the reputation of their chivalry, and which contributed so much to the geneal impression of endemic disorder that the period gives. But it was not really so confused as it looks; in crude terms, it was one in which secular power tended to crystallise out around the best paymaster. This had, in most places, to be either the prince or the great nobles, and their struggles largely focussed on their respective shares of the lands, revenues and privileges which would enable them to fulfil this key role. The prince had the advantages of being nearly always a little richer than others and of disposing of a more impressive range of ancient customary rights, and being therefore nearly always secure in the backing of at least a faction among the great. In consequence royal power in most places made slow but sure headway. (The notable exception was Germany, where what I have called the process of crystallisation favoured the territorial princes rather than their nominal sovereign, the emperor, and which in consequence emerged from the middle ages with its territorial divisions sharpened, in clear contrast with the western monarchies of France, Spain and England.)

Royal power made headway, where it did, largely as a result of a compromise thrashed out behind the superficial scene of disorder and which had immense implications for the future. The parties to this compromise were central government backed by nascent bureaucracy on one hand and the nobility, the dominant secular class, on the other, and the bargain struck between them became the basis of the effective authority of most European monarchies of the early modern age. Fiscality, once again, was at the centre of this compromise, because it was in essence an understanding (to a large degree tacit) that a substantial proportion of the proceeds of taxation should be rechannelled into the pockets of the nobility, partly in the form of pay for military service in the new, larger armies, but in a whole series of other ways too (in pensions, in posts at court and in the *echelons* of administration, local and central), and should so secure their standing. Thus began a process which, in course of time swelled out of all previous proportion not only princely armies but also the size and style of princely courts and households and the personnel of royal and local administration. It also swelled significantly the level of royal expenditure on display and *largesse*.

   The beginnings of these processes are clearly visible already in the late medieval period: they are what underlie the great expansion of the royal and princely households of France in the fourteenth and fifteenth centuries, at which taxpayers so often grumbled, and the extravagance of the Burgundian court. Much of the lavish expenditure that characterised that court was laid out on chivalrous celebrations and ceremony, and this is a useful reminder that the kind of 'bargain' that I have been speaking of was much more than a mere cash settlement. It is no accident that in the later medieval *genre* of polemical treatise which takes the form of a debate between a knight and a cleric (the *Songe du vergier* is the most famous example), the former acts as spokesman both for his own secular order and for secular royal (or imperial) authority; it is a sign that the foundations were being laid for a future partnership that rested on a broader base than the financial interest alone of the secular nobility. And there was another important part of the price that central authority had to pay for a measure of successful self assertion. This was the acquiescence of that authority in the maintenance of noble social dominance and noble privilege, and its indulgence of noble aspirations, including, of course, the martial aspirations of nobility, those we can still call chivalrous.

   This last aspect of the unwritten compromise between government and nobility needs emphasis. Social precedence and honours were quite as essential to nobility as wealth was. Alongside pensions and such privileges as exemption from taxation (which outside England the nobility of the *ancien régime* secured very generally), and the monopoly or near monopoly of a whole range of offices, must be set such privileges as the nobleman's right to wear his sword and to uphold his personal honour in the duel, the protection of noble hunting rights and the limitation to the nobility of the right to heraldic insignia – in respect of all of which, for the time being at least, royal authority had to go far in meeting the wishes of the nobility. The financial price that central authority had to pay to secure a sufficient measure of acquiescence and co-operation from the secular noble class may be more calculable than this other social and psychological part of the bargain between them, but that does not render the latter less significant. It entailed for monarchy the adoption and the encouragement of a whole way of looking at the status and function of nobility, and making the nobility's standards, in substantial degree, monarchy's own. In other words, it meant giving full rein, in a national context, to those ideals of chivalry which late medieval authors had equated so often with *noblesse*. Martially, the officer and gentleman of the post-medieval period felt, and was encouraged to feel, much the same sort of pride in his service of his king as the knight had taken in the service of his natural lord and of his order. Socially, the nobleman claimed, and was permitted to claim, the same sort of precedence, imposing a similar measure of social obligation, as his knightly forbears had. This encouragement and this permission were moreover sufficiently wholehearted and express as to infect to a considerable degree with the values and attitudes of the old nobility those groups within the dominant structures of the early modern age whose influence had different origins. The most important among these were the lawyers and administrators whose background was professional, not military, and the mercantile patriciates of towns and cities. Already in the fifteenth century we can see the high financial officers of the French crown gaining patents of nobility and even knighthood, and acquiring *chatellenies* and jurisdictions, and the councillors and *gens de finances* of the Dukes of Burgundy fared equally well. As a result, the aspirations and outlook of these forerunners of the higher *noblesse de robe* of later times became infected by the chivalric mentality that dominated the courts in which they served. In a similar way, Professor D. M. Nicholas has shown,[16] we can see in late medieval Flanders the greater bourgeois of the cities marrying into noble families, acquiring patents of nobility, and taking on the values of the rural lords. Similar developments can be traced elsewhere, and in Italy, of course, the process had been at work since the twelfth century, or even before. The legacies of chivalry had an impact in consequence across a social range much wider than that of the ancient nobility of the sword.

Certain characteristic trappings of medieval chivalry did of course lose their significance with the changing conditions of the early modern period. The heralds, as we have seen, ceased to exercise important functions in armies, because it was no longer important to be able to recognise coats of arms in the field. The popularity of jousting ultimately faded as the sixteenth century wore on, because, once new techniques of war had led to the abandonment of the cavalry lance and of complete body armour, it no longer offered a training in horsemanship more relevant than that of, say, the hunting field. The old chivalrous histories of Arthur and Charlemagne lost much of their spell for associated reasons; their matter could no longer be so modified as to keep them in touch with contemporary reality. (In the fifteenth century Malory could still tailor his accounts of tourney and duel to give them a realistically contemporary flavour: a century and a half later such rehandling had become impossible, because there were no longer contemporary models to work from.) This was almost certainly as important a reason for their eclipse as a serious theme of literature as was the new vogue of the classics, for which the growing interest in antiquity in the later chivalric period had in any case prepared the way. But it was principally those aspects of chivalrous practice and culture that could not be related to the contemporary scene or to contemporary need that thus faded. The secular orders of chivalry – such as the Garter, the Golden Fleece, and the Order of St Michael – continued to flourish because they still retained their purpose of lending lustre to the personal service of a particular sovereign.

The system of promotions and of awards of honour that chivalry and the heralds had nurtured also survived, because they too had a meaningful purpose: indeed in England knighthoods are still granted to distinguished generals, and orders and decorations to valiant soldiers. The chivalric concept of nobility lost none of its force, and the notions of its essential constituents – loyalty, generosity and courage – were not much altered. Where old ways, modified as necessary, could be related to altered structures, there chivalry did not fade or decline with the coming of the Renaissance. It might parade in new dress, Castiglione's courtier might be expected to know more about the classics and less about such romantic rituals as the swearing of oaths upon a peacock than little Jehan de Saintré had; but what this denoted was a change of the chivalric courtier's wardrobe rather than a change of heart. That is why, as I said at the beginning of this chapter, the conclusion to this survey of chivalry has to be written in terms of change, not of decline.

★

The most important legacy of chivalry to later times was its conception of honour and the constituents thereof, specifically and especially in their relation to nobility. Transactions of honour, a contemporary anthropologist has said, 'provide, on the psychological side, a nexus between the ideals of society and their reproduction in the actions of individuals – honour commits men to act as they should (even if opinions differ [from society to society] as to how they should act).'[17] Chivalry's most profound influence lay in just this, in setting the seal of approbation on norms of conduct, recognised as noble when reproduced in individual act and style – and in dictating, in many respects, the mode of this approbation. It had a key impact in the fashioning of the idea of the gentleman, who was the 'type' figure of the dominant social and political estate of the *ancien régime*, and of his mode of living. It did so by enmeshing in a web of mental association his social accomplishments, his 'courtliness' (especially in regard to women) and his skills in horsemanship, the hunting field and sword play, and the social virtues to be expected of him, his courage and his generosity, his loyalty to his plighted word, his independent spirit (what the old chivalrous authors had called his *franchise*). It gave a peculiarly martial slant to noble values, through the price that it had set upon martial valour and upon martial service specifically: 'the proper, sole and essential life for one of the nobility in France is the life of a soldier,' wrote Montaigne.[18] It was likewise the influence of chivalry that made martial insignia, the crests and arms that so many families took care to engrave on their plate and to display upon their tombs, the hallmarks of later gentility. The conception that chivalry forged of a link between the winning of approbation by honourable acts and the winning of the heart of a beloved woman also proved to be both powerful and enduring; western culture has never since quite shaken itself free of it. Above all, chivalry taught the gentleman of a succeeding age to place honour at the centre of his mental and social world, as the treasure dearer to him than life – which is why gentlemen so long claimed and so tenaciously cherished the right to wear the sword and to defend personal honour in the duel.

The strong streak of individualism in chivalrous culture, which found such emotive expression in its ideal of the knight errant, also left a powerful mark on European attitudes of later times. Its influence shows in that independence of spirit that was the pride of the nobilities of the *ancien régime* (even if they often exaggerated its extent to themselves), and which preserved them from ever fully acknowledging the measure of their subservience to state authority, breeding in every generation of the old regime its minority of rebels and radicals, its natural Jacobites and *Frondeurs*. It shows, more clearly and more dramatically, in that cult of individual endeavour and endurance in distant places – of errantry in short – which needs to be put alongside technological superiority in any account of what we call the European expansion. No other civilisation has built such an articulate and sophisticated cult about the individual Odyssey of the adventurer as has that of Western Europe, and the fact that it has done so is in large part the legacy of the cult of errantry in the age of chivalry, which brought together the ideas of wandering and of honour in such a special relationship. In the early chapters of the story of the European expansion, in the days of Pizarro and Cortes, and when Lope de Aguirre could boast of how he had carried his lance to Peru in quest of *mas valer*[19] – of the same sort of individual renown that chivalrous writers christened *bonne renommée* – the lineaments of the knight errant are naturally more plainly discernible than they are in the words and careers of later explorers and empire builders who won a name for themselves (and riches too, often enough) by carrying the flag further than anyone had thought of sending it as a matter of policy. But once again a good deal of the difference is one of dress, rather than of underlying spirit. In this regard, it is worthwhile to note in passing that one particular way in which the cult of the individual adventurer has been enshrined in literature is by means of a device born of the age of chivalry, that of making his Odyssey at the same time a love-story.

The life of honour has to be lived through to the end: the final seal of approbation on it is a sepulchral monument. If one seeks the memorials of glory and renown won in war or civil office by men of good birth under the older order, one will find them in churches. In the time of the *ancien régime*, no less than in the age of chivalry proper, the church was expected to give to honour its last rites and thereby to sanctify society's view of the value of noble secular service. Here we find part of the answer to the often-levelled charge that chivalry, at the end of the middle ages, was losing touch with religion. Once again, change and modification must be my theme, rather than decline. It is true that the code of honour of the early modern period did not identify separately the religious and secular obligations of the gentleman quite so clearly as had that of chivalry with respect to the obligations of the knight. Its courtesy books do not lay the same emphasis on personal religious observances as did, say, Ramon Lull's *Book of the Order of Chivalry* or Geoffrey de Charny's treatise on knighthood. But that is, in very large degree, a reflection of the fact that in the later ages ecclesiastical and secular authority were less independent of one another than they had been in the middle ages. The church, like the nobility, had been brought more firmly under the aegis of secular authority, and the assumption, which most medieval knights had always made, that to serve the king and to serve God were usually the same thing, became in consequence even more firmly entrenched. Besides, the medieval nobleman really had been a little more independent with regard to all authorities, secular as well as ecclesiastical, than was his descendant in the early modern age, which made it necessary for the guardians of his spiritual welfare to be a little more specific about his personal responsibilities in the way of formal observance in their sphere of operations.

Something rather similar may be said with regard to the decline of the crusade after the end of the middle ages, which too has been interpreted as a sign of a growing loss of commitment to religious priorities on knighthood's part. The crusades did not fade from the horizon of politics because of a decline of holy zeal: whatever the gentlemen of early modern times may be charged with, that was not their trouble. If anything they had rather too much of it, as the history of the religious wars of the Reformation period testifies. More simply, the idea of the sort of general crusade that in the later middle ages still fired the imaginations of such as Marino Sanudo and Philippe de Mézières and even the author of the *Enseignement de la vraye noblesse* ceased to be relevant to practical politics. In consequence, princes, knights and gentlemen gradually ceased to be interested in it, though it continued to colour many hopes and fears far into the sixteenth century. The fact that there were no longer peripheral crusading areas to keep the flame of enthusiasm alive, in the way that the wars of the Teutonic knights and of the Spanish *reconquista* had done, assisted towards its demise; for the Lithuanians had been converted to Christianity in the late fourteenth century and the Moors of Granada conquered at the end of the fifteenth. Two other factors were also important in this matter. Firstly, much of the sort of energy that had once been thrown into crusading came to be thrown instead into adventure in pagan lands much further from the European homelands than Syria and Egypt, in the Americas and in India and Africa. At least in the early days of the conquest of America, the impact of the old crusading ideal upon this new kind of venture is very clear. Secondly, in the sixteenth century Christians became busier than ever fighting Christians, and if the now divided churches showed themselves quite as ready to bless that activity as the undivided church had once been to preach the crusade, that was to be expected now that Europe was sundered religiously as well as politically. Long ago, after all, the church's manner of blessing wars waged against excommunicate emperors had proved to be a formative influence upon the manner of blessing wars against infidels. More significant, really, was the fact that the churches, which were ceasing to preach the crusade, did not cease to preach that a true gentleman should be a Christian gentleman. The notion that a Christian scruple was one that a man of honour was entitled to regard as overriding all other obligations, and that even if formally illegitimate it should be accepted to be informally honourable to be governed by one, proved to be an idea that died very hard: perhaps, hopefully, it is not quite dead even today.

Through most of the heyday of chivalry the crusade had been regarded as the formal epitome of chivalrous activity; for that reason, it is an apposite theme on which to conclude finally. Peter of Dusberg, in his Prussian chronicle, has an illuminating story about the vision of a certain anchoress whose hermitage lay close to the route of march of a crusading host that rode out against the pagans in the year 1261. From her hermitage, she heard in the air the crying of demons, and asked of them what they sought: they told her they were expecting a great battle to be fought on the morrow, and she begged them to let her know its outcome when they passed on their return from it. They came back to tell of a great Christian defeat and that all who had perished were saved, but for three, whose souls were now their booty, since these three had gone into battle and on to their death not for the sake of holy zeal, but in the hope of magnifying their names in knighthood.[20]

This story offers a nice *envoi* to the history of medieval chivalry. From its beginning to its close, men going forward in the hope of magnifying their names and fortune in knighthood is the basic theme of that history. As Peter and his anchoress realised, religious priorities were very often not the driving force behind its ethic, which could confound far too easily the pursuit of wordly honour with the pursuit of spiritual merit. Even where the crusade was concerned, too frequently it was not the new approbation and the indulgences that the church reformers of the eleventh and twelfth centuries had extended to the warriors' estate that moved knights, but the glamour of martial glory and social esteem. Chivalry essentially was the secular code of honour of a martially oriented aristocracy. Its deepest roots stretched back to an origin in the social code of honour of the warrior groups of the early middle ages; it owed its strong Christian tone to the fact that those groups had operated within the setting of a Christian society, in which the Christian cult was the chief focus alike of social and religious life. It flourished, in the period between the mid-twelfth and the sixteenth century, as the ethos of the dominant secular estate of Christian Europe, and its characteristic trappings were fashioned by the social, political, and cultural conditions of those times. Its cult of the martial virtues drew strength from their disorder, its cult of individualism from the fragility of governmental controls which threw back the nobleman so heavily upon his own resources. It was able to develop into an international culture largely because in this period frontiers were less clear and less important than they later became. The rise of the secular courts, as centres of culture and as a natural meeting ground of clergy with nobility, provided the context for it to grow up from a warrior's code into a sophisticated secular ethic, with its own mythology, its own erudition, and its own rituals which gave tangible expression to its ideology of honour. As such, it not only exercised a very powerful influence on the medieval world, but also left, as we have seen, a very deep imprint on the times that followed.

Peter of Dusberg's three knights who rode into Prussia for vainglory and perished unregenerate were going through one of the rituals of chivalry's social ideology. They were seeking worldly honour through an activity recognised in its terms as glorious, not salvation. But if they – and others – aimed at something less than the true Christian spirit of dedication (whose forms of expression are not limited by constrictions of space and time, or of occupation or of class), nevertheless they were aiming at something from which it is not easy to withold respect. It seems to me that there is something to be said for the sort of worldly values that chivalry bequeathed to the dominant class of a succeeding age: indeed, if there had not been something to be said for them they would have been more easily forgotten. They were remembered for a very long time, during which time a great many people – by far the greater part of the then 'establishment' – regarded as self-evident the validity of, for instance, the price that chivalry had set upon ancestral achievement as an example to succeeding generations; of its express conflation, in its ideal of honour, of principles of personal integrity with the title to social respect; of its assumption that birthright in dignity imposes an hereditary and honourable duty to be ready to draw the sword in order to defend the weak and the oppressed. Assumptions such as these, which chivalry had nourished, underpinned the social order of the *ancien régime* (in its broadest sense), and they continued to have an immense impact, down to the end of the nineteenth century, on the 'establishments' of European society. That is why chivalry is a subject worth an historian's attention. It is only in this our twentieth century that most of them have at last been called into question; I for one am uncertain as to whether we are the richer for that – but perhaps that is just a sign that I have fallen a prey to the besetting sin of the biographer, of falling in love with his subject.

ABBREVIATIONS

AHS	*Archives Heraldiques Suisses*
Annales	*Annales, Economie, Société, Civilisation*
BEC	*Bibliothèque de l'Ecole des Chartes*
BL	British Library
BN	Bibliothèque Nationale, Paris
BR	Bibliothèque Royale, Brussels
CCM	*Cahiers de Civilisation Médiéval*
EHR	*English Historical Review*
EETS	Early English Text Society
JEH	*Journal of Ecclesistical History*
MA	*Le Moyen Age*
Mansi	G. D. Mansi, *Sacrorum conciliorum nova et amplissima collectio* (Venice, 1759 ff)
MGH	Monumenta Germaniae Historiae
PBA	*Proceedings of the British Academy*
PL	J. P. Migne, Patrologia Latina (Paris, 1844 ff)
RIS	L. A. Muratori, *Rerum Italicarum Scriptores* (Milan, 1723 ff)
RS	*Rolls Series*
TRHS	*Transactions of the Royal Historical Society*

NOTES

Notes to Chapter I

1. E. Burke, *Reflections on the Revolution in France*, in *Works of the Right Honourable Edmund Burke* (London, 1846 edn.), III, 98.
2. See J. Flori, 'La notion de chevalerie dans les chansons de geste du XIIme siècle', *MA* 81 (1975), 211 ff, 407 ff.
3. Quoted by C. E. Pickford, *L'Évolution du Roman Arthurien en prose vers la fin du moyen âge* (Paris 1966), 265; compare the introductions to the prose *Tristan*, quoted *ibid.*, 266-8.
4. See G. Mathew, *The Court of Richard II* (London 1968), 118 ff.
5. These random examples are taken from Chrétien's *Chevalier de la Charrette* (the sword bridge); from *Perlesvaus* (the glass bridge and the hermitage); and from Malory (Book IX, ch.12: the questing beast).
6. J. Huizinga, *The Waning of the Middle Ages* (London 1927), chs. 4-7.
7. See G. Duby, *Les Trois Ordres, ou l'imaginaire du féodalisme* (Paris 1978).
8. W. J. Sedgefield (ed.), *King Alfred's Old English Version of Boethius* (Oxford, 1899), 40.
9. G. Duby, 'The origins of knighthood', in *idem, The Chivalrous Society*, trans. C. Postan (London 1979), 165-6.
10. E. de Fougères, *Le Livre des manières*, ed. F. Talbert (Angers 1877), 24, 25, 26 ff.
11. Bonizo of Sutri, *Liber de vita Christiana*, ed. E. Perels (Berlin, 1930), 56, quoted by I. S. Robinson, 'Gregory VII and the soldiers of Christ', *History* 58 (1973), 190.
12. PL CLXXXII, 926.
13. Chrétien de Troyes, *Cligés*, lines 30-44.
14. John of Salisbury, *Policraticus*, ed. C. C. Webb (Oxford, 1909), II, 16.

15. *Ibid.*, II, 9; and see J. A. Wisman, 'L'*Epitoma rei militaris* de Végèce et sa fortune au moyen âge', *MA* 85 (1979), 13-31.
16. On Thomasin see D. Rocher, *Thomasin von Zerklaere: Der wälssche Gast, 1215-16* (Paris, 1977), 2 vols: a very thorough examination.
17. For the text see E. Barbazan, *Fabliaux et contes des poètes français des 11me, 12me, 13me, 14me, et 15me siècles* (Paris 1808), I, 59-82.
18. P. Meyer, 'Notice et extraits du MS 8336 de la Bibliothèque de Sir Thomas Philipps', *Romania* XIII (1884), 530; *idem.*, 'Les Manuscrits français de Cambridge', *Romania* XV (1886) 316, and XXXVI (1907) 529.
19. *Ordene de chevalier*, lines 106-27 (the bath); 128--38 (the bed); 139-63 (the cloak); 164-72 (the stockings); 181-94 (the belt); 195-209 (the spurs); 211-25 (the sword); 250-61 (the collée); 263-303 (the four commandments).
20. On Lull see E. A. Peers, *Ramon Lull* (London 1929).
21. R. Lull, *Libre de Contemplació*, ch. 104, in *Obres de Ramon Lull* (Mallorca, 1906 ff), IV, 11.
22. *A Life of Ramon Lull*, ed. and trans. E. A. Peers (London 1927), 2.
23. R. Lull, *Libre de l'ordre de cavayleria*, ed. J. Ramon de Luanco (Barcelona 1901). Caxton translated the work (from a French version) as *The Book of the Ordre of Chyvalry*, which is ed. A. T. P. Byles (EETS, London 1926). My references are to this EETS edition of the English version. For the date of composition of the original work, see Peers, *Ramon Lull*, 120-1. There is a modern edition of the French version, *Le Livre de l'Ordre de*

Chevalerie, ed. V. Minervini (Bari, 1972).
24. Lull, *Ordre of Chyvalry*, 15.
25. *Ibid.*, 22-3.
26. *Ibid.*, 24 ff.
27. *Ibid.*, 37.
28. *Ibid.*, 51.
29. *Ibid.*, 113.
30. *Ibid.*, 47 ff.
31. Gilbert of the Haye's very free Scottish version is printed in *Gilbert of the Haye's Prose MS*, vol. 2, ed. J. H. Stevenson (Edinburgh 1914); Juan Manuel translated parts of it into Castilian; Verart printed two editions of French versions, in 1504 and 1505; and Portunaris of Lyons another in 1510. There are numerous fifteenth-century MS copies of the French versions.
32. See E. Kennedy, 'Social and political ideas in the French prose Lancelot', *Medium Aevum*, 26 (1957), 103.
33. For details of Charny's career, see J. Rossbach, 'Les demandes pour la jouste, le tournoi et la guerre de Geoffroi de Charny' (thesis deposited in the BR, Brussels), 8 ff; and P. Savio in *Salesianum* I (1955), 120-41.
34. The prose *Livre de chevalerie* is printed in *Oeuvres de Froisart*, ed. K. de Lettenhove, Tome I pt. iii (Brussels 1873), 463-533. Parts of the verse *Livre* are printed by A. Piaget 'Le Livre Messire Geoffroi de Charny', *Romania* XXVI (1897), 399-410. The *Livre des questions* has not been printed; there is a transcript in Rossbach's thesis, *cit. sup.*
35. 'Qui plus fait, miex vault,' *Livre de chevalerie*, in Froissart, *Oeuvres* I, iii, 464, 465, 468, 469, 470, 471, 472.
36. *Ibid.*, 466.
37. *Ibid.*, 467-8.
38. *Ibid.*, 472.
39. *Ibid.*, 471, 475-6.
40. *Ibid.*, 483-5.
41. *Ibid.*, 508-10.
42. *Ibid.*, 511-13.
43. J. de Bueil, *Le Jouvencel*, ed. C. Favre and L. Lecestre (Paris 1887-9), II, 21.
44. Charny in *Oeuvres de Froissart*, I pt. iii, 514-15: compare *Ordene, cit. sup.*
45. See below, ch. VIII, 144.
46. On Roth, see J. Petersen, *Das Rittertum ib der Darstellung des Johannes Roth* (Strasbourg, 1909); on Roth's treatment of the knight's arms see G. Seyler, *Geschichte der Heraldik* (Nuremburg, 1885-9), I. 18.
47. Lannoy's *Instruction* is printed in *Oeuvres de G. de Lannoy*, ed. C. Potvin (Louvain 1878), 335 ff: the *Enseignement* is not printed, and survives in a number of MSS; I have taken my

references from BR 11407.
48. The original version is D. de Valera, *Espejo de Verdadera Nobleza*, ed. M. Penna, in *Prosistas Castellanos del Siglo XV* (Madrid 1959). The work circulated more widely in the French translation of Hugues de Salves, an incomplete version of which was printed in 1497; my references are to the full text of the French version in Louis de Bruges' MS, BN, MS Fr. 1280. An edition printed from a different MS (BR, MS 10979) appeared when my typescript was in an advanced state; in A. J. Vanderjagt, *Qui sa vertu anoblist* (Groningen, 1981), 237-83, I have indicated the parallel references in brackets.
49. G. Lannoy, *Oeuvres*, 450.
50. *Ibid.*, 453.

Notes to Chapter II

1. On Thomas III of Saluzzo see N. Jorga, *Thomas III, Marquis de Saluces: étude historique et littéraire* (St Denis, 1893). The *Chevalier Errant* has never been edited: my references are from BN, MS Fr. 12559. The passage quoted below has however been printed by C. Legrand d'Aussy in *Notes et Extraits des MSS de la Bibliothèque Nationale*, V (Paris, Ann. VII).
2. *Notes et Extraits, cit. sup.*, V. 576.
3. *Ibid.*, 578.
4. Lambert of Ardres, *Historia Comitum Ghisnensium* (*MGH*, SS XXIV, 557-642). Arnold's career is well studied by Duby in his 'Youth in aristocratic society', *The Chivalrous Society*, 112-22.
5. Lambert of Ardres, *cit.sup.*, 603.
6. Chrétien de Troyes, *Perceval*, Prologue, lines 7 ff.
7. Lambert of Ardres, *cit.sup.*, 603.
8. *Ibid.*, 604.
9. *Ibid.*, 604.
10. *Ibid.*, 607.
11. *L'Histoire de Guillaume le Maréchal*, ed. P. Meyer, 2 vols. (Paris, 1891); and see S. Painter, *William Marshal* (Baltimore, 1933).
12. *L'Histoire de Guillaume le Maréchal*, lines 5940-6170, 6260-84.
13. *Ibid.*, lines 7275-95.
14. *Ibid.*, lines 2875-3164.
15. Chrétien de Troyes, *Chevalier de la Charrette*, lines 1 ff (*Karrenritter*, ed. W. Foerster, Halle, 1899, 1); Andreas Capellanus, *The Art of Courtly Love*, trs. J. J. Parry (New York, 1941), 168-76.
16. *L'Histoire de Guillaume le Maréchal*, lines

3437–520.

17. *MGH* SS XX, 317; and see J. Fleckenstein, 'Friedrich Barbarossa und das Rittertum' in A. Borst (ed.), *Rittertum in Mittelalter* (Darmstadt, 1976), 392–418.

18. Quoted in E. Prestage (ed.), *Chivalry* (London, 1928), 85.

19. Orderic Vitalis, *Historiae ecclesiasticae*, Book VI, ch. 2, ed. A. Le Prevost, (Paris, 1838–55), III, 4.

20. On the stirrup see Lynn White Jr., *Medieval Technology and Social Change* (Oxford, 1962), 14–28. Lynn White also discusses the couched lance and shock combat (28 ff), but his chronology is not convincing. On shock combat see D. J. A. Ross, 'L'originalité de *Turoldus* – le maniement de la lance', *CCM*, 6 (1963), 127 ff: and R. C. Smail, *Crusading Warfare* (Cambridge, 1967), 113 ff.

21. See Smail, *cit.sup.*, 115 n.l.

22. Ross, *cit. sup.*, 133–4.

23. G. Malaterra, *Historia sicula*, Lib I. Ch. XXXIX (R.I.S., V 558).

24. Anna Comnena, *The Alexiad*, transl. E. A. S. Dawes, (London, 1928), 122–3.

25. J. F. Verbruggen, *The Art of Warfare in Western Europe during the Middle Ages*, trs. S. Willard and S. C. M. Southern (Oxford, 1977), 22–8, offers good introductory comments on these problems.

26. Quoted in P. Guilhiermoz, *Essai sur l'origine de la noblesse en France au moyen âge* (Paris, 1902), 425, 432.

27. P. Van Luyn, 'Les *milites* dans la France du XIe siècle', *MA*, 77 (1971), 5 ff, 193 ff; see especially 19 ff.

28. Duby, *The Chivalrous Society*, 127 ff, 169; and see the texts quoted by L. Huberti, *Studien zur Rechtsgeschichte der Gottesfrieden und Landesfrieden* (Ansbach, 1892), 40, 125, 157, 187, 206, 214, 304, 320.

29. Duby, *cit.sup.*, 77 ff, 84 ff, 106 ff, 159 ff, 178 ff.

30. J. Bumke, *The Concept of Knighthood in the Middle Ages*, trs. W. T. H. and E. Jackson (New York, 1982), has much of interest to say in this context: see especially 77 ff.

31. Huberti, *cit.sup.*, 37, 157, 182.

32. Adalbero de Laon, *Poème au Roi Robert*, verses 275–305 (ed. C. Carozzi, Paris 1979, 20–2).

33. Duby, *cit.sup.*, 42, 106–7.

34. On the genealogical history of the great territorial lords, see K. F. Werner, 'Untersuchungen zur Frühzeit des Französischen Fürstentums (9–10 Jahrhundert)', *Die Welt als Geschichte*, XVIII, 256–89: XIX, 146–93; XX, 87–119.

35. Suger, *Vie de Louis VI le Gros*, ed. H. Waquet (Paris, 1964), 30–2, 172–8, 250–4.

36. *La Mort de Garin*, ed. E. du Meril (Paris, 1846) 74; *Le Couronnement de Louis* lines 2254–2266 (ed. Langlois, Paris 1888, 157–8.

37, *Li Romans d'Alixandre*, ed. H. Michelant (Stuttgart, 1846), 17. The advice in the romance is of course based on that given in the letter of Aristotle to Alexander, in the widely circulated pseudo-Aristotelian *Secreta secretorum*.

38. H. O. Sommer, *The Vulgate Version of the Arthurian Romances* (Carnegie Institute, Washington, 1909 ff), III, 30.

39. *Li Romans d'Alixandre*, ed. Michelant, 250, 255; and see G. Cohen, *Histoire de le chevalerie en France* (Paris, 1949), 58; and E. Köhler, *L'Aventure chevaleresque* (Paris, 1974), 16–18.

40. William of Malmesbury, *De gestis regum anglorum*, ed. W. Stubbs (RS, 1887–9), II, 510.

41. R. Bezzola, *Les Origines et la formation de la littérature courtoise en Occident* (Paris, 1944–63), I pt. 2, 245.

42. Andreas Capellanus, I. vi, quoted by C. S. Lewis, *The Allegory of Love*, 34.

43. Quoted by Bumke, *The Concept of Knighthood in the Middle Ages*, 93.

44. E. Köhler, 'Observations historiques et sociologiques sur la poésie des troubadours', *CCM*, VII (1964), 32.

45. S. Painter, *French Chivalry* (Baltimore, 1940), 32.

46. Andreas Capellanus, *The Art of Courtly Love*, trs. Parry, 81.

47. Bezzola, *cit.sup.*, I, pt. 2, 242.

48. Chrétien de Troyes, *Erec et Enide*, lines 6734 ff.

49. *Chroniques des Comtes d'Anjou*, ed. L. Halphen and R. Poupardin (Paris, 1913), 194–6, 218.

50. PL, CLXXVIII, 114–15.

51. On family histories, see especially Duby, 'French genealogical literature', in *The Chivalrous Soicety*, 149 ff.

52. MGH, SS III, 422, 425.

53. On Lambert of Wattrelos see F. Vercauteren, 'Une parentèle dans la France du nord au XIme et XIIme siècles', *MA*, 69 (1963), 223–45; and Duby, *The Chivalrous Society*, ch.8 (138–48). For the genealogical section of Lambert's annals see MGH, SS XVI, 511–12.

54. Lambert of Ardres, MGH, SS XXIV,

566–8; *Historia pontificum et comitum engolis-mensium*, ed. J. Boussard (Paris, 1957), 11–12; *Chroniques d'Anjou*, ed. P. Marchegay and A. Salmon (Paris, 1856), I, 35, 354–5.
55. MGH, SS XVI, 512.
56. Ritter, *Ministerialité et chevalerie*, 22 ff, 32, 51–2; J. B. Freed, 'The origins of the European nobility: the problem of the ministerials', *Viator*, 7 (1976), 211–41; and see further J. Bumke, *The Concept of Knighthood in the Middle Ages*, transl. W. T. H. and E. Jackson (New York, 1982), ch. III.
57. MGH, SS XVI, 82; and see Ritter, *cit.sup.*, 87. K. J. Leyser has some very illuminating remarks on the opportunities opened to the *ministeriales* by the wars of the Investiture controversy, in his 'The German aristocracy in the early middle ages', *Past and Present*, 41 (1968), 25–53: see especially 47 ff.
58. On Werner see Ritter, *cit.sup.*, 92–3; and K. Bosl, 'Noble unfreedom: the rise of the *ministeriales* in Germany', in T. Reuter (ed.), *The Medieval Nobility* (Oxford, 1978), 291–311.
59. J. Fleckenstein, 'Die Entstehung des niederen Adels und das Rittertum', in J. Fleckenstein (ed.), *Herrschaft und Stand* (Göttingen, 1977), 22–3: J. Johrendt, '*Miles* und *milicia* im XII Jahrhundert im Deutschland', in A. Borst (ed.), *Das Rittertum im Mittelalter* (Darmstadt, 1976), 419–36.
60. Bosl, in Reuter (ed.), *The Medieval Nobility*, 302; Ritter, *cit.sup.*, 87. For an earlier instance of *ministeriales* combining to uphold their status, in 1104, see Leyser, *cit.sup.*, *Past and Present*, 41 (1968), 25 n.2.
61. MGH, SS XXIII, 432, quoted by Bosl, *cit.sup.*, 300.
62. Fleckenstein, *Herrschaft und Stand*, 30, 32–4.
63. MGH, SS 18 (Waitz), 103.
64. Wolfram von Eschenbach, *Willehalm*, ed. K. Lachmann (Berlin 1926), 229.
65. For what follows, I am deeply indebted to Professor J. Larner, whose superb lecture on chivalry in Italy in the age of Dante, delivered in 1980 at the conference in honour of Professor Denis Hay in Edinburgh, has been the source of much of what I have written. Professor Larner most kindly lent me the typescript of his paper, and most of my references come from him.
66. P. J. Jones, quoted by B. Pullan, *A History of Early Renaissance Italy* (London, 1973), 86.
67. J. Plesner, *L'Emigration de la campagne à la ville libre de Florence au XIIIᵉ siècle* (Copenhagen, 1934), quoted by J. Catto,

'Florence, Tuscany and the World of Dante', in *The World of Dante*, ed. C. Grayson (Oxford, 1980), 4.
68. G. Villani, *Cronica*, VII, 120, quoted by D. Waley, 'The army of the Florentine Republic from the twelfth to the fourteenth century', in N. Rubenstein (ed.), *Florentine Studies* (London, 1968), 93.
69. MGH, SS XX, 397.
70. Quoted by D. Waley, *The Italian City-Republics* (London, 1969), 44.
71. G. Villani, *Cronica*, VII, 89.
72. RIS, XV pt. 3, 51; IX, pt. 9, 68–9.
73. For evidence of knowledge of the *Ordene de chevalerie* in Italy, Professor Larner kindly supplied me with these references: 'Libro di Novelle e di bel parlar gentile', in *Novelline*, ed. L. di Francia (Turin, 1930), 187–92, and 'Fortunatus Siculus ossia l'Avventuroso Ciciliano', ed. G. F. Nott (Florence, 1832), III, 310–18 (in which the names of the actors are changed, from Saladin and Hugh of Tiberias to the Sultan of Babylon and Ulivo da Fontana). See also Fulgore di San Gimignano, 'Sonnetti pel cavaliere', in F. di San Gimignano, *Sonnetti*, ed. F. Neri (Turin, 1925), 65–9.
74. RIS VIII, pt. 2, 30.
75. Salimbene, *Cronica*, ed. G. Scalia (Bari, 1966), I, 85.
76. *Purgatorio*, XXVI, lines 140–7.
77. J. Catto, *cit.sup.*, in *The World of Dante*, ed. Grayson, 9.
78. *Ibid.*, 10.
79. F. di San Gimignano, *Sonnetti*, ed. Neri, 25.
80. See G. Rajna, 'Le origini delle famiglie Padovane e gli eroi dei romanzi cavallereschi', *Romania*, IV (1875), 161–83, especially 169–75.
81. L. Paterson 'Knights and the concept of knighthood in the twelfth-century Occitan epic', *Forum for Modern Language Studies*, 17 (1981), 115–30. I quote her translation of Girart, lines 4958–5009, which she presented at an Oxford seminar.

Notes to Chapter III

1. Two notable works in this context are J. A. Brundage, *Medieval Canon Law and the Crusader* (Madison, Wisconsin, 1969), and M. Villey, *La Croisade: essai sur la formation di'une théorie juridique* (Paris, 1942).
2. Much the most important work in this context is C. Erdmann, *Die Entstehung des*

Kreuzzugsgedankens (Stuttgart, 1935); there is an English translation by M. W. Baldwin and W. Goffart, *The Origin of the Idea of Crusade* (Princeton, 1977). See further F. H. Russell, *The Just War in the Middle Ages* (Cambridge, 1975), the works of Brundage and Villey, *cit.sup.*, n.1, and R. Regout, *La Doctrine de la guerre juste de St Augustin à nos jours* (Paris, 1935).

3. See F. H. Russell, *The Just War in the Middle Ages* (Cambridge, 1975), ch. I, 16 ff, and authorities there cited.

4. *Ibid.*, 31 ff.

5. Mansi, XX, 816.

6. PL CXV, 656–7; and see J. A. Brundage, *Medieval Canon Law and the Crusader* (Madison, Wisconsin, 1969), 22 ff, for further discussion of the early germs of the crusading indulgence.

7. Erdmann, *cit.sup.*, 333.

8. *Ibid.*, 330.

9. *Ibid.*, 17–19.

10. *Ibid.*, 255–60.

11. RIS V. 569.

12. On the peace movement see Erdmann, *cit.sup.*, ch. 2: Huberti, *Studien, cit. ante* (ch. 2, n. 26); Duby, *The Chivalrous Society*, ch.8; H. E. J. Cowdrey, 'The eleventh-century peace and truce of God', *Past and Present* 46 (1970), 42–67. The most authoritative modern treatment is that of H. Hoffmann, *Gottesfrieden und Treuga Dei* (Schriften der MGH, XX, 1964).

13. Huberti, *Studien*, 125, 218.

14. Mansi, XX, 816.

15. M. Villey, *La Croisade: essai sur la formation d'une théorie juridique* (Paris, 1942), 59 ff; Erdmann, *cit.sup.*, ch.2.

16. I. S. Robinson, 'Gregory VII and the soldiers of Christ, *History* 58 (1973), 169–92.

17. *Ibid.*, 187.

18. Bonizo, *Liber de vita christiana*, ed. E. Perels (Berlin, 1930), 56.

19. Erdmann, *cit.sup.*, 189–90.

20. Fulcher of Chartres, *Historia Hierosolymitana*, ed. H. Hagenmeyer (Heidelberg, 1913), 136.

21. PL CLVI, 685.

22. PL CLI, 567; Ritter, *Ministérialité et chevalerie*, 137–8.

23. PL CLXXXII, 921–7.

24. For the Templars' rule, of which there are a series of versions all deriving from the primitive Latin rule of 1128, see H. de Curzon, *La Règle du Temple* (Paris, 1886).

25. *La Chanson de Roland*, lines 2384 ff (ed. G. J. Brault, London, 1978, II, 146.)

26. *La Chanson de Guillaume*, lines 818–22 (ed. J. Wathelet-Willem, Paris 1975, II, 813).

27. *Ibid.*, lines 2035–40 (ed. Wathelet-Willem, II, 933).

28. A. Waas, *Geschichte des Kreuzzuges* (Freiburg, 1956) I, 33 ff, 41 ff.

29. Duby, *The Chivalrous Society*, 166–7; and see J. Fechter, *Cluny, Adel und Volk. Studien über das Verhaltnis des Klosters zu den Ständen* (Stuttgart, 1966).

30. PL CXLII, 682.

31. The dating of Beowulf is a much disputed question. An eighth-century date has traditionally had most support; it could be as late as the tenth. For a very full review of the problems, see C. Chase (ed.), *The dating of Beowulf* (Toronto, 1981).

32. On the Latin epics, see K. J. Leyser, 'The German aristocracy in the early middle ages', *Past and Present*, 41 (1968), 30, 42 ff.

33. J. R. R. Tolkien, 'Beowulf: the monsters and the critics', *PBA* 22 (1936), 245–94.

34. E. V. Gordon, *Anglo-Saxon Poetry* (Everyman, 1967), 99.

35. For examples see J. Flori, 'Chevalerie et liturgie', *MA* 84 (1978), 435–9.

36. Gordon, *Anglo-Saxon Poetry*, 65.

37. *La Chanson de Roland*, lines 2344 ff (ed. Brault, II, 144); and H. R. E. Davidson, *The Sword in Anglo-Saxon England* (Oxford, 1962), 212–13.

38. P. Wormald, 'Bede, Beowulf, and the conversion of the Anglo-Saxon aristocracy', *British Archaeological Reports*, 46 (1978), 32–90; on Alcuin, see 45 ff.

39. See K. Hauck, 'The literature of house and kindred', in T. Reuter (transl.), *The Medieval Nobility* (Oxford, 1978), 66 ff. On the feuds of the Liudolfings see K. J. Leyser, *Rule and Conflict in an early medieval society: Ottonian Saxony* (London, 1979), Chapter 1.

40. Bede, *Historia Ecclesiastica*, ed. C. Plummer (Oxford ,1896), I, 148.

41. J. Bédier, *Les Légendes épiques*, (Paris 1929), IV, 403 ff.

42. Gordon, *Anglo-Saxon Poetry*, 20.

43. *La Chanson de Roland*, lines 2362–3 (ed. Brault, II, 144).

44. Huizinga, *The Waning of the Middle Ages*, 59.

45. Charny, in *Oeuvres de Froissart*, I pt. iii, 510.

46. Tacitus, *Germania*, ch. 13–14.

47. G. de Villehardouin, *La Conquête de Constantinople*, ed. E. Faral (Paris, 1939), I. 20.

48. *Ibid.*, II, 169.

49. *Ibid.*, II, 73.

50. *Ibid.*, I, 67.
51. J. Bédier, *Les Chansons de Croisade* (Paris, 1909), 172.
52. *Ibid.*, 32–5, 92.
53. B. de Condé, *Le Dit dou Baceller*, in A. Jubinal (ed.), *Recueil des contes, fabliaux et autres pièces inédites* (Paris, 1839), I, 327 ff.
54. On the *Chanson d'Antioche* see S. Duparc-Quioc, 'La composition de la *Chanson d'Antioche*', *Romania* 83 (1962), 1 ff, 210 ff. See also G. Paris, 'La Chanson d'Antioche provençale et la *Gran Conquista de Ultramar*', *Romania* 17 (1888), 513–41 and 19 (1890), 562 ff; and E. Roy, 'Les poèmes français relatifs à la première croisade: le poème de 1356 et ses sources', *Romania* 55 (1929), 411–68. On the crusading cycle more generally, see S. Duparc Quioc, *Le Cycle de la Croisade* (Paris 1955), and C. Cahen 'Le premier cycle de la croisade', *MA* 63 (1957), 311–28.
55. *La Conquête de Jerusalem* ed. C. Hippeau (Paris, 1868), lines 3552 ff, 3693 ff, 4769 ff.
56. I have followed here the 'Elioxe' version, for its dramatic effect: see H. Todd (ed.), *La Naissance du chevalier* (Baltimore, 1889), and G. Paris's review in *Romania* 19 (1890), 314–40.
57. *Chanson d'Antioche*, ed. P. Paris, p.12.
58. Wolfram von Eschenbach, *Parzival*, IX sections 443–4.
59. *The High Book of the Grail* (Perlesvaus), transl. N. Bryant (Cambridge, 1978), 19, 20.
60. For an introduction to de Boron's work see P. le Genti, 'The work of Robert de Boron and the *Didot Percival*' in R. S. Loomis (ed.), *Arthurian Literature in the Middle Ages* (Oxford, 1959), ch.19.
61. *Ibid.*, chs. 19, 20; and see N. Bryant's introduction to *The High Book of the Grail*, *cit.sup.*
62. See A. Pauphilet, *Etudes sur la 'Queste del Sant Graal'* (Paris, 1921) 53–83; E. Gilson, 'La mystique de la Grâce dans la *Queste del St Graal*', *Romania* 51 (1925), 321–47.
63. J. Frappier, 'Le Graal et la chevalerie', *Romania* 75 (1954), 165–210.
64. A. de Pegulhan, quoted by S. Painter, *French Chivalry* (Baltimore, 1940), 87.

Notes to Chapter IV

1. L. Gautier, *La Chevalerie* (Paris 1884), 250, 286 ff.
2. *Chroniques des Comtes d'Anjou*, ed. Halphen and Poupardin, 179–80.

3. M. Andrieu, *Le Pontifical Roman* (*Studi e Testi* 86, Rome 1938–40), II, 579–81.
4. *Ibid.*, III, 447–50.
5. C. Erdmann, *Die Entstehung des Kreuzzugsgedankens* (Stuttgart, 1935), 330.
6. Orderic Vitalis, *Historiae ecclesiasticae*, ed. Le Prevost, II, 389.
7. *Ibid.*, II, 40.
8. Quoted by P. Guilhiermoz, *Essai sur l'origine de la noblesse en France au moyen âge* (Paris, 1902), 404.
9. *Beowulf*, lines 2864 ff (ed. Fr. Klaeber, 108); Gordon, *Anglo-Saxon Poetry*, 57.
10. Tacitus, *Germania*, cap. 13.
11. On this connection, see further J. Flori, 'Les origines de l'adoubement chevaleresque: étude des remises d'armes et du vocabulaire qui les exprime', *Traditio* 35 (1979). M. Flori's article appeared when this chapter was already fully drafted; his views of the relevant developments are more precise and better documented than mine, and have different emphases; our conclusions are nonetheless quite similar.
12. See J. Flori, 'Sémantique et société médiévale: le verbe *adouber* et son évolution au XIIᵐᵉ siècle', *Annales* 31 (1976), 915 ff. As Flori is here concerned with French vernacular texts, he does not treat the very early reference to dubbing to knighthood in the *Anglo-Saxon Chornicle* (MS E) *sub anno* 1085: 'he . . . dubbade his sunu Henric to ridere'.
13. W. Erben, 'Schwertleite und Ritterschlag', *Zeitschrift für historische Waffenkunde*, 8 (1918–20), 109 (quoting MGH, SS X, 150, 152); Guilhiermoz, *Essai sur l'origine de la noblesse en France au moyen âge*, 396, n.9.
14. MGH, SS XXI, 514.
15. Guilhiermoz, *cit.sup.*, 331–45.
16. *Le Charroi de Nîmes*, lines 637–56 (ed. D. McMillan, Paris 1972, 89).
17. See N. P. Brooks, 'Arms, status and warfare in late Saxon England', in D. Hill (ed.), *Ethelred the Unready: papers from the Millenary Conference* (Oxford, 1978), 81 ff.
18. Orderic Vitalis, *Historiae ecclesiasticae*, ed. Le Prevost, IV, 410, 422.
19. See above, ch.2 note 46.
20. Assises of Arriano, cl.19; and MGH, Const: I, 197, no. 140; 451, no. 318 (or Leg: II, 103, 185). For further discussion see E. Otto, 'Von der Abschliessung des Ritterstands' *Historische Zeitschrift*, 162 (1940), 19–39; and J. Fleckenstein, 'Zum Problem der Abschliessung des Ritterstandes', *Historische Forschungen für W. Schlesinger*, ed. H. Beumann (Cologne, 1974), 252–71, which

makes some important criticisms of Otto's work.

21. J. Boussard, 'L'origine des familles seigneuriales dans la région de la Loire moyenne', *CCM*, V (1962), 306 n.28.

22. *Renaud de Montauban*, verse 256, quoted by Guilhiermoz, *cit.sup.*, 238, n.7.

23. MGH, SS VI, 498.

24. *Recueil des historiens des Gaules et de la France*, ed. M. Bouquet (Paris, 1738...), XV, 608.

25. Ritter, *Ministérialité et chevalerie*, 11.

26. See above, note 8.

27. MGH, SS IX, 452.

28. RIS V, 643.

29. P. Bonenfant and G. Despy, 'La noblesse en Brabant au XIIᵐᵉ–XIIᵐᵉ siècles; *MA* 64, (1958), 39.

30. Chrétien de Troyes, *Perceval le Gallois*, ed. C. Potvin (Mons 1866–71), line 2824.

31. BR, MS 11407, fo 29; compare *Oeuvres de G. de Lannoy*, ed. Potvin, 403.

32. John of Salisbury, *Policraticus*, ed. Webb II, 16, 25; PL CCXII, 743–4.

33. e.g. BN, MS Fr 1280, fo 44ᵛᵒ (Diego de Valera's *Traité de noblesse*); and the oaths attributed to the Round Table knights, printed by E. Sandoz 'Tourneys in the Arthurian tradition', *Speculum* 19, (1944) 401–2.

34. Erdmann, *Entstehung des Kreuzzugsgedankens*, 330.

35. *Ibid.*, 74 n.62; and see J. Flori, 'Chevalerie et liturgie', *MA* 84 (1978), 247–78, 409–42.

36. MGH, SS I, 432; II 609, 643–4; and see Erben, *Schwertleite und Ritterschlag*, (*cit. ante.*, n. 13), 108.

37. Flori, in *Traditio* 35 (1979), *cit.sup.*, n. 11.

38. Lull, *Ordre of Chyvalry*, 28.

39. See J. L. Nelson, 'Inauguration rituals', in *Early Medieval Kingship*, ed. P. H. Sawyer and I. N. Wood (Leeds, 1977), 50 ff.

40. MGH, SS LX, 63–7.

41. Erdmann, *Entstehung des Kreuzzugsgedankens*, 76.

42. *Ibid.*, ch.7.

43. Andrieu, *Le Pontifical Romain*, I. 579–81.

44. E. H. Massmann, *Schwertleite und Ritterschlag*, (Hamburg, 1932), 164 ff; and see Guilhiermoz, *cit.sup.*, 45.

45. P. de Vaux-Cernay, *Hystoria Albigensis*, ed. P. Guébin and E. Lyon (Paris, 1930), II, 123–4.

46. *La Chanson de Roland*, lines 1116–21, 2315–37 (ed. Brault, II, 70, 142).

47. Quoted by Ritter, *Ministérialité et chevalerie*, 145.

48. *Ibid.*, 144 ff.

49. W. G. Sedgefield (ed.), *King Alfred's Old English Version of Boethius*, 40; MGH, SS XV, 513; and see J. M. Wallace-Hadrill, 'War and peace in the earlier middle ages', *TRHS*, 5ᵗʰ series, 25 (1975), 157–74.

50. See above, n.29.

51. Lull, *Ordre of Chyvalry*, 27–8.

52. Erben, *Schwertleite und Ritterschlag*, 150,

53. G. de Lannoy, *Voyages et ambassades 1390–1450* (Mons, 1840), 15.

54. *Histoire du gentil Seigneur de Bayart*, ed. M. J. Roman (Paris, 1878), 385–6.

55. E. Prestage, 'The Chivalry of Portugal', in E. Prestage (ed.), *Chivalry* (London, 1928), 143.

56. Quoted by Massmann, *Schwertleite und Ritterschlag*, 31.

57. Erben, *Schwertleite und Ritterschlag*, 155–6.

58. E.g. BL, Cotton MS Nero C IX; Buccleuch MS and MS notes in the BL copy of Caxton's own edition of the *Ordre of Chyvalry*, BL, 1 A 55071.

59. See K. Elm, 'Kanoniker und Ritter vom Heiligen Grab', in J. Fleckenstein and M. Hellmann (eds.), *Die geistlichen Ritterorden Europas* (Sigmaringen, 1980), 141 ff; F. Pietzner, *Schwertliete und Ritterschlag* (Heidelberg, 1934), 83 ff; and Erben, *cit.sup.*, 138, 151.

60. A. Schultz, *Deutsches Leben in XIV und XV Jahrhundert* (Leipzig, 1892), 547, and figs. 559–61.

61. *Chanson d'Antioche*, ed. P. Paris, I, 225; compare lines 3729 ff of *Li Bastars de Buillon*, ed. A. Scheler (Brussels, 1877), and discussion by K. Treis, *Die Formalitäten des Ritterschlags* (Berlin, 1877), 20, 25.

62. See P. Contamine, 'Points de vue sur la chevalerie en France à la fin du moyen âge', *Francia* 4 (1976), 272 ff.

63. MGH, SS IX, 644; and see Erben, *cit.sup.*, 135–6 for comparable references.

64. *Annales monastici*, ed. H. R. Luard, (RS, 1865–9) II, 357; IV, 451.

65. Orderic Vitalis, *Historiae ecclesiasticae*, ed. Le Prevost, II, 254–5.

66. Fulcher of Chartres, *Historia hierosolymitana*, ed. Hagenmeyer, 408–9; Orderic Vitalis, *Historiae ecclesiasticae*, ed. Le Prevost, IV, 245.

67. *Li Romans de Durmart le Galois*, ed. E. Stengel (Stuttgart, 1873), lines 12125 ff.

68. *Oeuvres de Froissart*, ed. K. de Lettenhove, XI, 166.

69. Sommer, *The Vulgate Cycle of Arthurian Romances*, III, 113 ff.

Notes to Chapter V

1. Sir T. Malory, *Le Morte d'Arthur*, XVII, 1.
2. *Recueil des historiens des Gaules et de la France*, ed. Bouquet, XII, 462.
3. E.g.: MGH, SS XXIV, 299; PL CLVII, 1272; PL CLXXXV, 287.
4. G. F. Warner and H. J. Ellis, *Facsimiles of Royal and other Charters in the British Museum* (London, 1903), I, no. 12.
5. Galbert of Bruges, *Histoire du meurtre de Charles le Bon*, ed. H. Pirenne (Paris, 1891), 9; MGH, SS XX, 360.
6. Mansi XXI, 439.
7. Du Cange, *Glossarium*, ed. G. A. L. Henschel, (Paris, 1887), X, 20 *(Dissertations sur l'histoire de St Louys, VI)*.
8. Nicetas Choniates, *Historia: de Manuele Comneno*, Lib III, 3 *(Corpus scriptorum historiae Byzantinae*, ed. B. G. Niebuhr, 141–3).
9. MGH, SS XXIII, 155.
10. MGH, SS XXI, 522; Rymer, *Foedera* (London, Record Commission 1816), I pt 1, 65.
11. Chrétien de Troyes, *Erec et Enide*, lines 2160–70.
12. MGH, SS XXI, 518.
13. *Ibid.*, 519.
14. M. Paris, *Chronica majora*, ed. H. R. Luard (RS, 1880), V, 17–18, 83, 265.
15. *Flores historiarum*, ed. H. R. Luard (RS, 1890), III, 30–1: W. Rishanger, *Chronica et Annales*, ed. H. T. Riley (RS, 1865) 79–80.
16. Rymer, *Foedera* (1816 edn.), I pt. 1, 65.
17. *Statutes of the Realm*, I. 230–1.
18. As far as I know, no genuine text underlies the reference to ordinances concerning tournies made by Louis VII and Philip Augustus in A. Favyn, *Le Théâtre d'honneur et de chevalerie* (Paris 1620), II, 1802–3.
19. M. Delbouille (ed.), *Jacques Bretel: Le tournoi de Chauvency* (Paris, 1932).
20. R. Coggeshall, *Chronicon Anglicanum*, ed. J. Stevenson (RS, 1875), 179.
21. MGH, SS XXIII, 595; R. Harvey, *Moriz von Craûn and the chivalric world* (Oxford, 1961), 150–1; Du Cange, *Glossarium*, X, 170.
22. *Recueil des historiens des Gaules et de la France*, XX, 512.
23. MGH, SS XXIV, 521 (different chronicles vary in their precise tally of fatal casualties; it is clear they were very heavy).
24. M. Paris, *Chronica Majora* (RS 1877), IV, 135–6.
25. R. Hoveden, *Chronica*, ed. W. Stubbs (RS, 1869), II, 166–7.
26. William of Newburgh, *Historia rerum anglicarum*, in *Chronicles of the Reigns of Stephen, Henry II and Richard I*, ed. R. Howlett (RS, 1885) II, 422–3.
27. J. de Meun, *L'Art de chevalerie*, ed. U. Robert (Paris, 1897), 14.
28. Henri de Laon, *Le Dit des hérauts*, lines 50 ff, in A. Langfors, '*Le Dit des hérauts* par Henri de Laon'. *Romania*, 43 (1914), 216 ff.
29. C. Oulmont, *Les Débats du clerc et du chevalier* (Paris, 1911), 113.
30. *L'Histoire du Guillaume le Maréchal*, lines 3381 ff.
31. *Ibid.*, lines 5941–6171, 6260–84.
32. *Le Roman du Castelain de Couci*, ed. M. Delbouille (Paris, 1936), lines 6832–99.
33. MGH, SS XXI, 534.
34. *The Legend of Fulk Fitzwarin*, ed. J. Stevenson in R. Coggeshall, *Chronicon Anglicanum* (RS), 325–6.
35. G. A. Seyler, *Geschichte der Heraldik* (Nuremberg, 1885) 48–9; *Parties inédites de l'oeuvre de Sicile Héraut*, ed. P. Roland (Mons, 1867), 98.
36. On the Espinette see L. de Rosny *L'Epervier d'Or* (Valenciennes, 1839). Dr Juliet Vale, in *Edward III and Chivalry* (Boydell, 1983), has included in chapter 2 an extremely illuminating study of civic *festes* and society in the Low Countries and Northern France', which includes the best modern discussion of the Espinette feast, and of other civic jousts recorded in the same area.
37. A. Schultz, *Das Höfische Leben zur Zeit der Minnesinger* (Leipzig, 1889), II, 117 ff.
38. E.g. BR, MS 14395 fos 39 ff; see further J. Vale, *Edward III and Chivalry* (1983), Ch. 1 and Appendix 6, for a very interesting discussion of the Espinette feast. I was privileged to see the proofs of this book before publication.
39. Geoffrey of Monmouth, *Historia regum Britaniae*, in E. Faral (ed.), *La Légende Arthurienne* (Paris, 1929), III, 246.
40. Wace, *Li Roman de Brut*, ed. Le Roux de Lincy (Rouen, 1836–8), lines 10803 ff; and see R. W. Hanning, 'The social significance of 12th-century chivalric romance', *Medievalia et Humanistica*, new series, 3 (1972), 3–29.
41. *L'Histoire de Guillaume le Maréchal*, lines 3426 ff.
42. Chrétien de Troyes, *Chevalier de la Charrette* (or *Karrenritter* in Foerster's edn.), lines

5379 ff.

43. On Ulrich see R. Harvey, *Moriz von Craûn and the Chivalric World* (Oxford, 1961); I have largely relied on her treatment.

44. Harvey, *cit.sup.*, 101.

45. For review of Ulrich's career, see the introduction to the (verse) translation of J. W. Thomas, *Ulrich von Lichtenstein's Service of Ladies* (Chapel Hill, 1969).

46. P. de Novare, *Mémoires*, ed. C. Kohler (Paris, 1913), 7, 134; and see R. S. Loomis, 'Chivalric and dramatic imitations of Arthurian romance', *Medieval Studies in memory of A. K. Porter* (Cambridge, Mass., 1939) I. 79.

47. A. Henry (ed.), *Sarrasin: Le Roman du Ham* (Paris, 1939).

48. *Ibid.*, lines 3200 ff.

49. See R. S. Loomis, 'Edward I, Arthurian Enthusiast', *Speculum*, 28 (1953), 114–27.

50. On Round Tables, see R. H. Cline, 'The influence of romances on tournaments of the middle ages', *Speculum*, 20 (1945), 204–11.

51. W. Dugdale, *Monasticon Anglicanum* (London, 1830), VI pt. 1, 350; and see J. Smyth, *Lives of the Berkeleys*, ed. J. Maclean (Gloucester, 1883), I, 147.

52. *Annales Monastici*, ed. H. R. Luard (RS 1865–9), II, 402; IV, 489.

53. *Le Roman du Ham*, ed. Henry, lines 2653 ff.

54. *Le Tournoi de Chauvency*, ed. Delbouille, lines 4305–443.

55. *Ibid.*, lines 936 ff; 2707–17.

56. C. J. Hefele and H. Leclercq, *Histoire des conciles* (Paris, 1912–13), V pt. 1, 688, 729, 825; pt. 2, 1394, 1660.

57. *Corpus juris canonici*, ed. A. Friedberg (Leipzig, 1881) II, 1215.

58. Caesarius of Heisterbach, *Dialogus miraculorum*, ed. J. Strange (Cologne, 1851), II, 327–8.

59. *Recueil des Historiens des Gaules et de la France*, ed. Bouquet, XXI, 629.

60. M. Paris, *Chronica majora*, (RS 1876), III, 143–5.

61. J. de Vitry, *Exempla* ed. T. F. Crane (London, 1890), CXLI.

62. *Oeuvres de Jacques de Hemricourt*, ed. C. de Borman and A. Bayot (Brussels, 1910) I *(Le Miroir des Nobles de Hesbaye)*, 171 ff.

63. Harvey, *Moriz von Craûn and the Chivalric World*, 148, quotes the relevant passage.

64. Henri de Laon, *Le Dit des hérauts* in *Romania* 43, *cit. ante, n. 28*.

65. See above, 47–8.

66. *Annales monastici*, (RS 1866), III, 51.

67. N. Denholm-Young, 'The tournament in the thirteenth century,' *Studies in Medieval History presented to F. M. Powicke*, ed. R. W. Hunt, W. A. Pantin and R. W. Southern (Oxford, 1948), 240–68, esp. 245–8; *idem, Richard of Cornwall* (Oxford, 1947), 56.

68. *Vita Edwardi Secundi*, ed. N. Denholm-Young (London, 1957) 23; and see J. Maddicott, *Thomas of Lancaster* (Oxford, 1970), 99–102.

69. Denholm-Young, 'The tournament in the thirteenth century', *cit.sup.*, n.67, 267–8.

70. Du Cange, *Glossarium*, ed. Henschel, X, 23.

71. Hefele and Leclercq, *Histoire des conciles*, V pt. 2, 1394, 1660; Du Cange, *Glossarium*, ed. Henschel, X, 22.

72. G. Villehardouin, *La Conquête de Constantinople*, ed. Faral, I, 3–7.

73. Cline, 'The influence of romances on tournaments of the middle ages', *Speculum*, 20 (1945), 205.

74. MGH, SS XXV, 543.

75. *Roman du Ham*, ed. Henry, lines 183 ff.

76. B. de Condé, *Le Dit dou Baceller*, in A. Jubinal (ed.), *Recueil des contes, dits, fabliaux et autres pieces inédites*, 340–1.

77. *Le Roman du Castelain de Couci*, ed. Delbouille, lines 7308 ff, 7444 ff.

78. Caesarius of Heisterbach, *Dialogus miraculorum*, ed. Strange, II, 49 ff.

79. Huon de Méry, *Le Tournoiement de L'Antechrist* (Rheims, 1851), 17, 38, 41 f, 49 f, 59 ff.

80. *Roman du Ham*, ed. Henry, lines 322 ff.

81. *Le Tournoi de Chauvency*, ed. Delbouille, lines 426 ff.

82. N. H. Nicolas, *The Controversy between Sir Richard Scrope and Sir Robert Grosvenor in the Court of Chivalry* (London, 1832), I, 155.

83. *Perceforest* I, fo 23 r.

84. *Le Tournoi de Chauvency*, ed. Delbouille, lines 2617–24.

85. B. de Condé, *Le Dit dou Bacellor*, in Jubinal, *Recueil des contes . . ., cit. sup.*, 341; G. de Charny in *Oeuvres de Froissart*, ed. K. de Letternhove, I pt. iii, 464–72.

Notes to Chapter VI

1. *La Chanson des Saisnes*, ed. F. Michel (Paris, 1832), I, 1–2.

2. Bédier, *Les Légendes épiques*, IV, 452 ff.

3. *La Chanson de Roland*, laisses 271–89 (ed. Brault, II, 228–42).

4. *Li Romans d'Alixandre*, ed. Michelant, 99

ff.

5. On this revival of interest in the *chanson* material, see G. Doutrepont, *La Littérature française à la cour des Ducs de Bourgogne* (Paris, 1909), esp. ch.1; and *idem.*, 'Les Mises en prose des épopées et des romans chevaleresques', *Mémoires d l'Académie Royale de Belgique*, Lettres, tome 40 (Brussels, 1939).

6. R. N. Walpole (ed.), *The Old French 'Johannes' translation of the Pseudo Turpin Chronicle* (California, 1976), 174.

7. Bédier, *Les Légendes épiques*, IV, 403 ff.

8. R. Lejeune and J. Stiennon, *La Légende de Roland dans l'art du moyen âge* (Brussels, 1966), I, 61 ff, and II, plates 35–40 (Verona); and I, 192 ff and plates VII-XVIII (Chartres).

9. In this context Walpole's analysis of lay patrons who commissioned translations of the Pseudo-Turpin is interesting: R. N. Walpole, 'Philip Mouskés and the Pseudo-Turpin Chronicle,' *University of California Publications in Modern Philology* (1947), 364 ff.

10. Ambroise, *L'Estoire de la Guerre Sainte*, ed. G. Paris (Paris, 1897), lines 4665–6; and see M. Keen, 'Chivalry, heralds, and history', *The Writing of History in the Middle Ages: essays presented to R. W. Southern*, ed. R. H. C. Davis and J. M. Wallace-Hadrill (Oxford, 1981), 393–414.

11. For an introduction to the role of St Denis as a centre of historical writing, see G. M. Spiegel, *The Chronicle Tradition of St Denis: a Survey* (Brookline, Mass, 1978); see also R. N. Walpole, 'The Pèlerinage de Charlemagne: poem, legend and problem', *Romance Philology*, VIII (1954), 173–86; and A. de Mandach, *La Naissance et développement de la chanson de geste en Europe*, I (Paris, 1961), 83 ff, and II (Geneva, 1963) intro.

12. Humbert de Romans, *Tractatus solemnis de praedicatione sanctae crucis*, chs. 16, 36, 37, in T. Kaeffele, *Scriptores ordinis praedicantium medii aevi*, II (Rome, 1975), 288 ff.

13. *The Old French 'Johannes' translation of the Pseudo-Turpin Chronicle*, ed. Walpole, 146–7.

14. See E. Köhler, *Les Aventures chevaleresques: idéal et réalité dans le roman courtois* (Paris, 1974), ch.2.

15. See J. Frappier, 'Remarques sur la peinture de la vie des héros antiques dans la littérature française du XIIme et XIIIme siècles', in A. Fourrier (ed.), *L'Humanisme médiéval dans les littératures romanes du XIIme au XIVme siècles* (Paris, 1964), 13–54. I owe much to this illuminating study.

16. B. de Ste Maure, *Roman de Thébes*, lines

97–100.

17. Villehardouin, *La Conquête de Constantinople*, ed. Faral, I, 130.

18. For discussion of this point, see Frappier (*cit.sup.*, n.13), 19 ff.

19. Frappier, *cit.sup.*, 34 (quoting *Roman de Thébes*, lines 4789–90), 44.

20. *Li Romans d'Alixandre*, ed. Michelant, 114, 115, 416.

21. *Ibid.*, 138.

22. *Ibid.*, 489.

23. *Ibid.*, 186.

24. *Ibid.*, 8, 17, 251.

25. Frappier, *cit.sup.*, (n.15), 46; and see for further discussion of the general point Hanning, 'The social significance of 12th-century chivalric romances', *Medievalia et Humanistica*, New Series 3 (1972), 3–29.

26. On the *Fait des Romains* see L. F. Flutre, *'Li Fait des Romans' dans les littératures françaises et italiennes du XIIIme au XVIme siècle* (Paris, 1932).

27. See on above J. Monfrin, 'Humanisme et traductions au moyen âge', in Fourrier, *L'Humanisme médiéval . . . (cit.sup.*, n.15), 217 ff. In a second study in the same volume, 246–62 ('Les traducteurs et leur public en France au moyen âge'), Monfrin examines the patrons who commissioned translations, and their readers.

28. Quoted by Monfrin, *cit.sup.*, 228–9.

29. On translations of Vegetius and their popularity, see J. A. Wisman 'L'Epitoma Rei Militaris de Végèce et sa fortune au moyen âge', *MA*, 85 (1979), 13–31.

30. On Bonet, Christine and their translations from the lawyers see G. W. Coopland's introduction to H. Bonet, *The Tree of Battles* (Liverpool, 1949); see also M. H. Keen, *The Laws of War in the Late Middle Ages* (London, 1965), ch.2.

31. S. Scrope's translation (for Sir John Fastolf) of C. de Pisan, *The Epistle of Othea*, ed. C. F. Bühler, (EETS, Oxford, 1970), 15, 36.

32. *Le Livre des faictz du bon Messire Jehan Le Maingre, dit Boucicaut*, ed. M. Petitot in his *Collection des mémoires rélatifs à l'histoire de France*, VI (Paris 1825) 390–1, 393.

33. Geoffrey of Monmouth, in Faral (ed.), *La Légende Arthurienne*, III, 71.

34. Sommer, *The Vulgate Version of the Arthurian Romances*, VI, 198–9; and see R. Howard Bloch, *Medieval French Litrature and Law* (California, 1977), 203–6.

35. See A. Gransden, 'The growth of the Glastonbury traditions and legends', *JEH*, 27 (1976) 337–358 (esp. 352 ff).

36. See E. Sandoz, 'Tourneys in the Arthurian tradition', *Speculum*, 19 (1944) 389–420. Sandoz does not print the full text, which occurs in a series of other MSS besides those that he mentions, including Bibliotheque Municipale de Lille, MS 329 and BN, MS Fr. 12.597, which I have consulted.

37. Bib. Municipale de Lille, MS 329, fo 74 (the text in this MS here differs slightly from that printed by Sandoz.)

38. *La Chanson des Saisnes*, ed. Michel, I, 1–2.

39. P. de Mézières, *Le Songe du vieil pèlerin*, ed. G. W. Coopland (Cambridge, 1969), II, 222.

40. See R. S. Loomis, 'The oral diffusion of the Arthurian legend', in Loomis (ed.), *The Arthurian Legend in the Middle Ages*, 52–63, and literature there cited.

41. See plate. 2 in Loomis (ed.), *Arthurian Literature in the Middle Ages*.

42. For references see Loomis (ed.), *The Arthurian Legend in the Middle Ages*, ch. 21.

43. Geoffrey of Monmouth, in Faral (ed.), *La Légende Arthurienne*, III, 245; and see Frappier in Fourrier (ed.), *L'Humanisme médiéval . . .*, 25 ff.

44. Wolfram von Eschenbach, *Parzival* § 53.

45. Two Ovidian translations, *Les Commandemenz Ovide* and *L'Art d'amours*, were apparently among Chrétien's earliest works (see *Cligés*, verse 1); see further F. E. Guyer, 'The influence of Ovid on Chrétien de Troyes', *Romanic Review*, 11 (1921), 97–134, 216–47.

46. G. de Charny in *Oeuvres de Froissart* ed K. de Lettenhove. I pt. iii, 483–6.

47. G. Diaz de Gamez, *The Unconquered Knight: a chronicle of the deeds of Don Pero Niño*, trans. J. Evans (London, 1928), 149.

48. *Le livre des faicts du Marechal de Boucicaut*, ed. M. Petitot in *Collection complète de des mémoires rélatifs à l'histoire de France*, 6 (Paris, 1825), 393.

49. *Chronique des quatre premiers Valois*, ed. S. Luce (Paris, 1872), 123–5.

50. Sir T. Gray, *Scalacronica* ed. J. Stevenson (Edinburgh, 1836), 145 ff.

51. Geoffrey of Monmouth, in *La Légende Arthurienne* ed. Faral, III, 232–3.

52. Wolfram von Eschenbach, *Parzival*, §§444, 445.

53. *The High Book of the Grail*, trs. Bryant, 168–173.

54. F. Vielliard, 'Un texte interpolé du cycle du *Graal* (Bibliothèque Bodmer MS 147)' *Revue d'histoire des textes*, 4 (1974), 289–337.

55. See above, Ch.3. n.34.

56. *The Old French 'Johannes' translation of the Pseudo Turpin Chronicle*, ed. Walpole, 174.

57. Sommer, *The Vulgate Version of the Arthurian Romances*, III, 116–17.

58. On the French bible translations see S. Berger, *La Bible française au moyen âge* (Paris, 1884); and C. A. Robson, 'Vernacular Scriptures in France', *The Cambridge History of the Bible*, ed. G. W. H. Lampe (Cambridge, 1969), II, 436–52, 528–32. I have also found most helpful C. R. Sneddon's introduction to his 'Critical Edition of the Four Gospels in the 13th-century Old French translation of the Bible' (Oxford D.Phil. thesis, Bodleian MS D.Phil. C 2737–8).

59. Sneddon, *cit.sup.*, I. 46.

60. Gournay owned the copy that is now BL, MS Royal 19 D iv-v; see Sneddon, *cit.sup.*, 44.

61. Robson, *cit.sup.*, in the *Cambridge History of the Bible*, II, 443; and see H. Buchtal, *Miniature painting in the Latin Kingdom of Jerusalem* (Oxford, 1957), 54–8.

62. Le Marquis d'Albon (ed.), *Le Livre des juges* (Lyons, 1913). This translation was prepared for Richard Hastings and Otho de St Omer, Templars, and is dateable to between 1151 and 1171.

63. For the text, see R. L. Graeme Ritchie (ed.), *The Buik of Alexander* (Cambridge 1925), III, lines 3910 ff.

64. On the Nine Worthie see K. J. Hölgen, 'Die "Nine Worthies" ', *Anglia*, 77 (1959), 279–309; and on their iconography R. L. Wyss, 'Die Neun Helden', *Zeitschrift für Schweizerische Archäologie und Kunstgeschichte*, 17 (1957), 73–106. For an interesting treatment of the Nine Heroines, see M. Warner, *Joan of Arc* (London, 1981), 205 ff.

65. See passage quoted by I. Gollancz (ed.), *The Parlement of the Thre Ages*, (Roxburghe Club, 1897), 120.

66. See above, Ch. III, 58–61.

67. Cuvelier, *Chronique de Bertrand du Guesclin*, ed. E. Charrière (Paris, 1839), I. line 9875.

68. 'Ane ballet of the Nine Nobles' in *The Parlement of the Thre ages*, ed. Gollancz, 134.

69. BL, MS Royal 14 E II, fo 9vo. On the *Chemin* and its author, Jean de Courcy, see A. Piaget in *Romania*, 27 (1898), 582–607 (unfortunately he is principally concerned with the poem's language).

70. Chrstine de Pisan, *Ditié de Jehanne d'Arc*, ed. A. J. Kennedy and K. Varty (Oxford, 1977), lines 217–24, 285–7.

Notes to Chapter VII

1. Chrétien de Troyes, *Chevalier de la Charrette* (*Karrenritter*), lines 5793–812.
2. For a *caveat*, see A. R. Wagner, *Heralds and Heraldry in the Middle Ages* (Oxford, 1956), 12.
3. *Chroniques des Comtes d'Anjou*, ed. Halphen and Poupardin, 179–80.
4. Wagner, *Heralds and Heraldry*, 14–15; D. L. Galbreath, *Manuel de blason* (Lausanne, 1942), 34–9; L. Bouly de Lesdain, 'Etudes héraldiques sur le XIIme siècle,' *Annuaire du conseil héraldique de France*, XX (1907), 208 ff.
5. Galbreath, *Manuel de blason*, 38. The followers might bear the arms or insignia of their leader; for an example, see E. von Berchen, D. L. Galbreath, and O. Hupp, *Die Wappenbücher des Deutsches Mittelalters* (1939), Fig. 1 (from Peter of Eboli, *Carmen de motibus siculis*).
6. For early French and English rolls of arms see A. R. Wagner, *A Catalogue of English Mediaeval Rolls of Arms* (Oxford, 1950), and P. Adam Even, *Catalogue des armoriaux français imprimés* (1946); the *Clipearius Teutonicorum* is described in von Berchen, Galbreath and Hupp, *cit.sup.*, no. 71 (91–2).
7. Von Berchen, Galbreath and Hupp, *cit.sup.*, no.3 (4–6).
8. *Ibid.*, no.9 (p.10–11).
9. F. Hauptmann, *Das Wappenrecht* (Bonn 1896), 242.
10. *Medieval England: a new edition of Barnard's Companion to English History*, ed. H. W. C. Davis (Oxford, 1924) 221; and M. Maclagan, 'The heraldry of the House of Clare', *Papers of the XIII international congress of genealogical and heraldic sciences* (1982), 3–11.
11. See C. Coulson, 'Structural symbolism in medieval castle architecture', *Journal of the British Archaeological Association*, cxxxii (1979), 74–7.
12. Wagner, *A Catalogue of English Medieval Rolls of Arms*, 3; P. Adam Even, 'Un armorial français, du XIIIme siècle – le role Bigot, 1254', *AHS* 63 (1949), 15–22, 68–75, 115–21.
13. R. J. Dean, 'An early treatise on heraldry in Anglo-Norman', *Romance Studies in memory of Edward Billings Ham* (California, 1967), 21–9; and see further R. Dennys, *The Heraldic Imagination* (London, 1975), 60–1. G. J. Brault, *Early Blazon* (Oxford, 1972) dates the development of what he calls 'classic' blazon to the mid-thirteenth century.
14. Benoit de Ste Maure *Le Roman de Troie*,

ed. L. Constans (Paris 1904–12), lines 7715, 7756–7, 23889; and see P. Adam Even, 'Les usages héraldiques au milieu du XIIme siècle', *Archivum Heraldicum*, LXXVII (1963), 18–29.
15. *Book of St Albans*, ed. Wynkyn de Worde, d., VII–VIII.
16. BL, MS Harl. 2259, fo 21. Diego de Valera only accepts that arms may be 'captured' in this way if the prisoner is taken in flight, or has lost his lordship as well as his freedom (BN, MS Fr. 1280, fo 54).
17. Wagner, *Heralds and Heraldry*, 65, 122.
18. N. Upton, *De studio militari*, ed. E. Bysshe (London, 1654), 257–8.
19. Bartolus, *De insigniis et armies tractatus*, ed. in E. Jones, *Medieval Heraldry* (Cardiff, 1943) 228–9, 234–5.
20. Galbreath, *Manuel de blason*, 34; and see Duby, *The Chivalrous Society*, 138–40.
21. E. E. Dorling, 'Canting arms in the Zurich Roll', *The Ancestor*, XII (1905), 18–41.
22. Upton, *De studio militari*, 200; and Dennys, *The Heraldic Imagination*, 50.
23. See e.g.: BN, MS Fr 5242, fo 23; compare BN, MS Fr 1953, fos 46, 54; and see Sicily Herald, *Le Blason des couleurs*, ed. H. Cocheris (Paris, 1860), 54–67.
24. H. de Méry, *Le Tournoiement del' Antechrist* (Rheims, 1851), 59; and see Brault, *Early Blazon*, 49; and, on the heraldic language of de Méry, M. Prinet, 'Le language héraldique dans le Tournoiement Antechrist', *BEC*, 83 (1922), 43–53.
25. BN, MS Fr 5936, fos 18–18vo.
26. C. F. Menestrier, *Le Veritable Art du blason* (Lyons, 1672), 250.
27. BN, MS Fr 16988, fos 167–168vo (the account of the incident appears in fact in numerous heraldic MSS).
28. Hemricourt, *Oeuvres*, I, 131, 258.
29. *Ibid.*, III, 39.
30. BN, MS Fr 1280, fo 54vo, (Vanderjagt, 270).
31. Coll. of Arms MS, *Processus in curia marescalli*, I, 462–3.
32. BR, MS 11407, fos 32vo-33; G. de Lannoy, *Oeuvres*, ed. Potvin, 410.
33. BN, MS Fr 1997, p.11; B. Prost, *Traités du duel judiciaire* (Paris, 1872), 202.
34. BN, MS Fr. 1997, p.6; Prost, *cit.sup.*, 197.
35. R. S. and L. R. Loomis, *Arthurian Legends in Medieval Art* (Oxford, 1938), 48–50, and Figs. 61 and 62.
36. Nicholas, *The Scrope and Grosvenor Controversy*, I, 111.

37. Froissart, *Oeuvres*, ed. K. de Lettenhove, XV, 181.

38. *Parties inédites de l'oeuvre de Sicile héraut d'Alphonse v Roi d'Aragon*, ed. P. Roland (Mons, 1867), 42–6.

39. C. Bullock-Davies, *Menestrellorum Multitudo* (Cardiff, 1978), 42, quoting Wace, *Le Roman de Rou*, lines 11949–50; Wagner, *Heralds and Heraldry*, 46–7 quoting Chrétien de Troyes, *Le Chevalier de la Charette*, lines 5553–65; P. Adam Even, 'Les fonctions militaires des hérauts d'armes', *AHS*, lxxi (1957), 2–33, discusses the references to heralds at Las Navas de Tolosa. Dennys, *Heraldic Imagination*, 33, suggests that the parallel account of a *preco* waking soldiers in 1098 in the *Anonymi Gesta Francorum*, ed. R. Hill (London, 1962), is the first authentic reference to a herald; this is plausible.

40. Dennys, *cit. sup.*, 36.

41. *The Chronicle of Walter of Guisborough*, ed. H. Rothwell (Camden Soc. vol. lxxxix, 1957), 200.

42. Wagner, *Heralds and Heraldry*, 25ff.

43. Chrétien de Troyes, *Chevalier de la Charette (Karrenritter)*, lines 5555–84.

44. *L'Histoire de Guillaume le Maréchal*, lines 5222 ff.

45. Wagner, *Heralds and Heraldry*, 134–5.

46. P. Adam Even, 'Les fonctions militaires des hérauts d'armes', *AHS* lxxi (1957), 22–4.

47. *Roman du Ham*, ed. Henry, lines 100ff.

48. Wagner, *Heralds and Heraldry*, 30–1, 133–4.

49. Bullock-Davies, *Menestrellorum Multitudo*, 38–44; Wagner, *Heralds and Heraldry*, 26–7; N. Denholm-Young, *History and Heraldry* (Oxford, 1965), 54–60.

50. *Statutes of the Realm*, I, 231; *Ordonnances des Roys de France*, I (Paris, 1723), 435–41.

51. Dennys, *Heraldic Imagination*, 61.

52. Bodley, Rawlinson MS C 399, fos 78–78vo.

53. *Ibid.*, fos 77–77vo.

54. *Ibid.*, fo 77vo; Wagner, *Heralds and Heraldry*, 56.

55. Wagner, *cit.sup.*, 133.

56. *Ibid.*, 53–4; Adam Even, 'Les fonctions militaires des hérauts d'armes', *AHS*, lxxi, 26–33.

57. *Le Débat des hérauts d'armes de France et d'Angleterre*, ed. L. Pannier and P. Meyer (Paris, 1877), 1.

58. Froissart, *Oeuvres*, ed. K. de Lettenhove, II, 11.

59. *The Black Book of the Admiralty*, ed. T. Twiss (RS 1871), I 297, 298.

60. Bodley, Rawlinson MS C 399, fo 76vo.

61. Froissart, *Oeuvres*, ed. Kervyn de Lettenhove, II, 394–5.

62. R. de Houdenc, *Les Ailes de prouesse*, quoted by G. Cohen, *Histoire de la chevalerie en France* (Paris, 1949), 146ff.

63. *The Roll of Caerlaverock*, ed. T. Wright (London, 1864), 11–12, 21, 22–3; and see N. Denholm-Young, 'The *Song of Carlaverock* and the Parliamentary Roll of Arms', *PBA*, 47 (1961), 251–62.

64. Chandos Herald, *Life of the Black Prince*, ed. M. K. Pope and E. C. Lodge (Oxford, 1910); and see Mathew, *The Court of Richard II*, 118–24.

65. *Wapenboek ou Armorial de 1334 a 1372 ... par Gelre Héraut d'Armes*, ed. V. Bouton (Paris, 1881) I, 67ff.

66. *Ibid.*, 90, 97.

67. *Ibid.*, 7ff. (Staveren); 41 (Rutger Raets); 49 (Dietrich of Elnaer).

68. P. Suchenwirt, *Werke*, ed. A. Primisser (Vienna, 1827); see for examples of the qualities mentioned, IV, VII, VIII, XXIV.

69. See P. Adam Even's introduction to his edition of 'L'armorial universel du Hérault Gelre, Claes Haenen, Roi des Armes des Ruyers', *AHS*, 75 (1961). Adam Even shows that Haenen was at work on his armorial for some twenty-five years (c. 1370–c. 1395), and that the sections on different nations give indications as to when he obtained his information about them (French arms are e.g. dateable to 1359–75; English to 1382–5; Breton are post-1384 etc.). He seems to have been first in the service of Jean de Chatillon, later of the Bishop of Utrecht (who probably made him Gelre Herald), of the Wittelsbachs of Hainault and Holland, and finally of Albert and William VI of Bavaria. He died c. 1415.

70. Denholm-Young, *History and Heraldry*, 52.

71. E.g. Besançon, Bibl. Municipale, Coll. Chifflet MS 186 (copy of a late 14th/15th-century roll of arms), 114–15 (arms of Charlemagne and his paladins); 115 (Arthur and selected knights); 116 (Alexander and paladins of Greece). Among the MSS blazoning the arms of all Round Table knights, with biographical details, are Lille, Bibl. Municipale MS 329, and BN, MS Fr 12597; others are listed by Sandoz, *Speculum* 19 (1944). R. L. Wyss gives a list of rolls and armorials that blazon the arms of the Nine Worthies, in *Zeitschrft für Schweizerische Archaeologie und Kunstgeschichte*, XVII

)1957), 98–102.

72. BN, MS Fr 112: and see C. Pickford, *L'Evolution du Roman Arthurien en prose vers la fin du moyen âge, d'aprés le MS 112 du fonds française de la Bibliothèque Nationale* (Paris 1966).

73. See below p. 213.

74. Wagner, *Heralds and Heraldry*, Appx. F, 150ff.

Notes to Chapter VIII

1. BN, MS Fr. 1280, fo 54 vo (in Vanderjagt's edition, 270, this passage is differently worded).

2. J. Boussard, 'L'origine des familles seigneuriales dans la région de la Loire moyenne', *CCM*, V (1962), 306 n. 28.

3. Seyler, *Geschichte der Heraldik*, 9.

4. P. de Beaumanoir, *Les Coutumes du Beauvoisis*, ed. le comte Beugnot (Paris, 1842), II 54–5; and see *Ibid.*, 223, 232–3.

5. *La Règle du temple*, ed. Curzon, 22, 25–6, 66–7, 343.

6. Duby, *The Chivalrous Soicety*, 183; and see R. Fossier, 'La noblesse picarde au temps de Philippe le Bel', in P. Contamine (ed.), *La Noblesse au moyen âge* (Paris, 1976) 105–27, esp. 118 ff.

7. P. Adam Even, 'Les scéaux d'écuyers au XIIIᵐᵉ siecle', *AHS*, LXV (1951), 19–29.

8. J. A. Buchon (ed.), *Collection des chroniques françaises – du XIIIᵐᵉ au XIVᵐᵉ siecle* (Paris, 1826), tome 23, 312.

9. Seyler, *Geschichte der Heraldik*, 8 (quoting a charter of the Count of Kiburg of 1256).

10. N. Denholm-Young, *The Country Gentry in the Fourteenth Century* (Oxford, 1969), 141 n.2 (for early references to esquires tourneying); Vulson de la Colombière, *Le Vray Théâtre d'honneur et de chevalerie*, 104, 119 (for esquires in the order of the Croissant); Charny, *Livre de chevalerie* in *Oeuvres de Froissart*, ed. K. de Lettenhove, I pt. iii, *passim* (for men-at-arms generally being chivalrous).

11. BN, MS Fr. 2765, fo 45; quoted by Guilhiermoz, *L'Origine de la noblesse en France au moyen âge*, 374, n.18.

12. On patents of nobility see R. H. Lucas, 'Ennoblement in late medieval France', *Medieval Studies*, 39 (1977), 239–60, especially 247 ff; A. de Barthélemy 'Etude sur les lettres d'annoblissement', *Revue Historique Nobiliaire*, 7 (1869), 193–208, 241–52; and P. Contamine, 'The French Nobility and the war' in K. Fowler (ed.), *The Hundred Years*

War (London, 1971), 135–62, especially 143 ff.

13. Wagner, *Heralds and Heraldry in the Middle Ages*, 65, 122–3.

14. Seyler, *Geschichte der Heraldik*, 189.

15. Duby, *The Chivalrous Society*, 183.

16. A. Murray, *Reason and Soicety in the Middle Ages* (Oxford, 1978), 320–1; and see further A. Shulte, *Der Adel und die deutsche Kirche im Mittelalter* (Darmstadt, 1922).

17. For an excellent discussion of the ideas of nobility in the *coutumiers*, see Ritter, *Ministerialité et chevalerie*, chapter V.

18. *Li Romans d'Alixandre*, ed. Michelant, 251, 254.

19. Köhler, *Les Aventures chevaleresques*, 16–17.

20. *Ibid.*, 19, 22–7.

21. P. Wolff has contributed a specially illuminating study of 'La Noblewse Toulousaine: essai sur son histoire médiévale' to Contamine (ed.), *La Noblesse au moyen âge*, 153–74. On Flanders see D. M. Nicholas, *Town and Countryside: Social, Economic and Political Tensions in Fourteenth-Century Flanders* (Bruges, 1971), 250–66.

22. On *dérogeance* see E. Dravasa, 'Vivre noblement: recherches sur la dérogeance de noblesse du XIVᵉ au XVIᵉ siècles', *Revue juridique et économique du Sud Ouest, série juridique*, XVI (1965), 23–119, and XVII (1966), 187–237.

23. Bartolus, *Comment in Cod.* 12, 1.1 (in the Basle 1562 edition of Bartolus's commentaries, 941 ff).

24. BN, MS Fr. 1280, fos 38 vo ff (Vanderjagt, 257, and see 241–3); *Le Songe du vergier*, I, ch. 150; N. Upton, *De studio militari*, ed. Bysshe, 64 ff; F. Hemmerlein *De rusticitate et nobilitate* (Strasbourg, ?1490), fo 28–9.

25. See Bartolus's comment (Basle 1562 edition, 943): 'ex predictis sequitur quod dignitas seu nobilitas cadit quandocumque in ignorantem, quod patet, quia ut dictum est, nobilitas consistit in acceptatione ejus, qui dignitatem confert – ut apparet expresse in puero nato ex nobili, quia statim est nobilis, licet nihil intelligat'.

26. B. Prost (ed.), *Traités du duel judiciaire etc.* (Paris, 1872), 45–6.

27, Bartolus, *cit.sup.*, (Basle 1562 edition, 941).

28. Beaumanoir, *Les Coutumes du Beauvoisis*, ed. Beugnot, II, 234; and see E. Kennedy, 'Social and political ideas in the French prose *Lancelot*', *Medium Aevum*, 26 (1957), 90–106, especially 102–3.

29. BN, MS Fr. 1280, fo 23–4 (Vanderjagt, 247).

30. BR, MS 11407, fo 10 vo.

31. *Ibid.*, fo 39 ff.

32. P. Contamine, *Guerre, état et société: études sur les armées des rois de France 1337–1494* (Paris, 1972), 174 ff, 471 ff.

33. S. Krüger, 'Das Rittertum in den Schriften des Konrad von Megenberg', in J. Fleckenstein (ed.), *Herrschaft und Stand* (Göttingen, 1977), 312; K. H. Schäfer, *Deutsche Ritter und Edelknechte in Italien* (4 vols., Paderborn 1911–40), especially I, 110 ff.

34. J. de Bueil, *Le Jouvencel*, ed. C. Favre and L. Lecestre (Paris 1889), II, 80.

35. N. Upton, *De studio militari*, ed. Bysshe, 257–8.

36. Besançon, Bib. Municipale, Coll. Chifflet MS 81, fo 93ᵛᵒ–94; and compare A. de la Rocque, *Traité de la noblesse* (Rouen 1735), 192.

37. Sommer, *The Vulgate Version of the Arthurian Romances*, III, 30; *Li Romans d'Alixandre*, ed. Michelant, 14, 16.

38. Charny, *Livre de chevalerie* in *Oeuvres de Froissart*, ed. K. de Lettenhove, I. pt. iii, 475.

39. BR, MS 11407, fo 76.

40. *Ibid.*, fo 73.

41. G. de Machaut, *Le Confort d'Ami*, lines 2950 ff (in *Oeuvres de G. de Machaut*, ed. E. Hoepffner (Paris 1921), III, 104–5).

42. See the pasages quoted above, note 37, which are quite specific on this point.

43. P. de Novara, *Les Quatre Ages de l'homme*, ed. M. Fréville (Paris, 1888), 39 (§.66).

44. G. de Lannoy, *Les Enseignements paternels*, in *Oeuvres de G. de Lannoy*, ed. C. Potvin (Louvain, 1878), 470–1.

45. Zilletus, *Tractatus juris universi* (Vienna, 1584), XVI, 19 (Boni de Curtili Brixiensis, *De nobilitate*).

46. BR, MS 11407, fo 81 vo.

47. See C. Coulson, 'Structural symbolism in medieval castle architecture', *Journal of the British Archaeological Association*, cxxxii (1979), 74–7.

48. Poggio, *Opera* (Basle, 1538), II, 67.

49. *Le Roman du Castelain de Couci*, ed. Delbouille, lines 460 ff.

50. BR, MS 9632, fo 2vo.

51. J. de Hemricourt, *Oeuvres*, I, 226–8.

52. R. Boutruche, *La Crise d'une société: seigneurs et paysans en Bordelais pendant la Guerre de Cent Ans* (Paris, 1947), 273 ff; M. Vale, *War and Chivalry* (London, 1981), 88–94.

53. G. de Lannoy, *Oeuvres*, ed. Potvin, 465 ff.

54. BR, MS 11407 fos 67vo – 68; and compare BL, Egerton MS 3149 (Italian MS treatise on chivalry), fo 32ᵛᵒ.

55. Duby, *The Chivalrous Society*, 184.

56. J. de Hemricourt, *Oeuvres*, I, 6–9.

57. *Ibid.*, I, 170–2.

58. *Ibid.*, I, 13–14.

59. *Ibid.*, I, 255.

60. *Ibid.*, I, 46, 51.

61. *Ibid.*, I, 76, 131, 204, 206, 228.

62. *Ibid.*, I, 430.

63. *Ibid.*, I, 159.

64. *Ibid.*, I, 198.

65. Sommer, *The Vulgate Version of the Arthurian Romances*, III, 89; E. Kennedy 'Social and political ideas in the French prose Lancelot', *Medium Aevum*, 26 (1957) 102–4.

66. Dante, *Convivio*, Trattato IV, xix–xxi.

67. Andreas Capellanus, *The Art of Courtly Love*, trs. Parry, 38.

68. Jean de Meun, *Le Roman de la Rose*, Lines 18755–8.

69. *Oeuvres de Froissart*, ed. K. de Lettenhove, II, 8.

70. Charny, *Livre de chevalerie*, in *Oeuvres de Froissart*, ed. K. de Lettenhove I, pt. iii, 494, 495.

71. BR, MS 11407, fo 12 vo; BN, MS Fr. 1280, fos 3–4 vo.

72. BN, MS Fr. 1280, fo 26 (Vanderjagt, 243).

73. *Ibid.*, fo 24 vo; compre BR, MS 10497 fo 114: 'je repute ceulx estre digne de . . . incomparable memoire et loenge lesquelz de petit estat sont parvenu a puissance et a haulte seigneuries'.

74. BN, MS Fr. 1280, fo 1vo.

75. *La Fleur des batailles*, quoted by C. C. Willard, 'The concept of true nobility at the Burgundian court', *Studies in the Renaissance*, XIV (1967), 43 n.28.

76. BR, MS 11407 fos 10vo, 11vo.

77. I have quoted from BR, MS 21552, fos 19–21vo. The poem is clearly closely related to A. Chartier's *Breviaire de nobles* (see J. C. Laidlaw, ed., *The Poetical Works of Alain Chartier*, Cambridge 1974, 395–409); the abridged version seems to have appealed especially to the makers of heraldic commonplace books.

78. Cf. BR, MS 11407, fo 14 vo: 'se ainsi estoit que vertus . . . puissent succeder de pere aux enfans comme font tenemans et richesses les saiges auroient tousjours saiges enfans . . . mais on voit journelement le contraire . . . (mais) on voit tres souvent et le plus que ceulx qui sont yssus de noble lignie sont

plus enclins a vertu que autres'.
79. BN, MS Fr 1280, fo 37 (Diego invoking Aristotle); Upton, *De studio militari*, ed. Bysshe, 66 (animal eugenics).
80. BN, MS Fr. 1280, fo 39 (Vanderjagt, 258).
81. J. de Bueil, *Le Jouvencel*, ed. Favre and Lecestre, II, 82.
82. BN, MS Fr. 1280, fos 40–1 (Vanderjagt, 259–60).
83. Dante, *Convivio*, Trattato IV, xx.
84. J. de Meun, *Le Roman de la Rose*, lines 18792–99.
85. J. de Hemricourt, *Oeuvres* I, 2.
86. BR, MS 11407, fo 14vo.
87. BN, MS Fr. 1280, fo 39 vo (Vanderjagt, 258).
88. P. de Novara, *Les Quatre Ages de l'Homme*, ed. Fréville, 45–6 (§.79).
89. BR, MS 10238, fo 8; and compare Guillaume de Lalaing's advice to his son, in G. Chastellain, *Chronique de Jacques de Lalaing*, ed. J. A. C. Buchon (Paris, 1836), 607.
90. *Ibid.*

Notes to Chapter IX

1. BN, MS Fr. 1280, fos 16 vo ff, 38 vo ff (Diego); N. Upton, *De studio militari,* ed. Bysshe, 64 ff: J. de Bueil, *Le Jouvencel*, ed. Favre and Lecestre, II, 68 ff.
2. G. W. Goopland, '*Le Jouvencel* (revisited)', *Symposium*, V (1951), 137–86.
3. Wagner, *Heralds and Heraldry in the Middle Ages*, 77, 125–6.
4. *Ibid.*, 79.
5. Coll. of Arms MS, *Processus in curia marescalli*, I. 280.
6. N. Upton, *De studio militari*, ed. Bysshe, 154, 200; and see Dennys, *The Heraldic Imagination*, 50, 77.
7. See R. H. Lucas, 'Ennoblement in late medieval France', *Medieval Studies*, 39 (1977), 239–60.
8. BN, MS Fr 1280, fo 53 (Vanderjagt, 269: the MS from which he has published the text omits the reference to Jean Bureau).
9. A. de la Rocque, *Traité de Noblesse*, 166–7.
10. *Ibid.*, 65.
11. BR, MS 21552, fos 23–23ᵛᵒ: Menestrier, *Le Véritable Art du blason*, 246; and see Warner, *Joan of Arc*, 165, 186–7.
12. BL, MS Harl. 2259, fo 11.
13. BN, MS Fr. 1280, fo 53 and vo (Vanderjagt, 269): La Marche in Prost (ed.) *Traités du duel judiciaire*, 45.
14. BR, MS 11407, fos 55, 76.
15. BL, MS Harl. 2259, fo 70 vo.
16. Hemricourt, *Oeuvres*, I, 41, 258.
17. Dennys, *The Heraldic Imagination*, 30, 31.
18. J. Schneider, 'Sire Nicole Louve: citain de Metz', in Contamine (ed.), *La Noblesse au moyen âge*, 183 n.2.
19. See above, ch.IV, 79–80.
20. Besançon, Bibl. Municipale, Collection Chifflet MS 83, fo 58. For another heralds' report of the making of a knight in the field, see BN, MS Fr 5242, fo 91.
21. *Chronique de Mathieu d'Escouchy*, ed. G. Du Fresne de Beaucourt, II (Paris, 1863), 220.
22. Besançon, Bibl. Municipale, Coll. Chifflet MS 90, fo 9.
23. J. de Joinville, *Histoire de St. Louis*, ed. M. Natalis de Wailly (Paris, 1868), 55.
24. *Oeuvres de Froissart* ed. K. de Lettenhove, VII, 195–6; compare La Marche's account of the promotion of Louis de la Viévile in 1452, which is strikingly similar: *Mémoires*, ed. J. A. C. Buchon (Paris, 1836), 468.
25. J. de Bueil, *Le Jouvencel*, ed. Favre and Lecestre, II, 113.
26. BR, MS 21552, fos 27–8.
27. P. S. Lewis, 'Une Devise de chevalerie inconnue, créée par un comte de Foix: *le Dragon*', *Annales du Midi*, 76 (1964), 77–84.
28. BR, MS 11125, fos 54 vo, 59–60, 77 vo; and see further J. Rossbach, *Les Demandes pour la jouste, le tournoi et la guerre de Geoffroi de Charny* (typescript thesis deposited in the Salle des MSS of the Bibliothèque Royale, Brussels).
29. D'Orronville, *Chronique du Bon Duc Loys de Bourbon*, ed. A-M. Chazaud (Paris, 1876), 248.
30. J. Barbour, *The Bruce* ed. W. W. Skeat (EETS, London, 1870) II, 318.
31. *Wapenboek*, ed. Bouton, I. 34.
32. Hemricourt, *Oeuvres*, I, 13–14.
33. Cuvelier, *Chronique de Bertrand du Guesclin*, ed. Charrière, line 9875; 'Ane ballet of the Nine Nobles' in *The Parlement of the Thre Ages* ed. Gollancz, 134.
34. See above, ch.VI, 121.
35. *Oeuvres de Froissart*, ed. K. de Lettenhove, XVII, 269–70. For a substantially earlier reference to the award of the 'prize' of an engagement, see *Li Romans d'Alixandre*, ed. Michelant, 89.
36. *Oeuvres de Froissart*, ed. K. de Lettenhove, V, 457.
37. O. de La Marche, *Mémoires*, ed. Buchon, 463.
38. E. Christiansen, *The Northern Crusades*

(London, 1980), provides an excellent survey of the wars in this area; see especially ch.6. See also F. R. H. Du Boulay, 'Henry of Derby's Expeditions to Prussia, 1390–1 and 1392', in F. R. H. Du Boulay and C. M. Barron (eds), *The Reign of Richard II* (London, 1971) 153–72; W. Paravicini, 'Die Preussenreisen des Europäischen Adels', *Historische Zeitschrift*, 232(1981), 25–38; and E. Mashke, 'Burgund und der preussische Ordenstaat. Ein Beitragen zur Einheit der ritterlichen Kultur Europas im späteren Mittelalter', *Syntagma Friburgense* (Constance, 1956), 147–72.

39. C. Higounet, 'De La Rochelle à Torun: aventure de barons en Prusse et relations économiques', *MA*, 69 (1963), 529–40.

40. Suchenwirt, *Werke*, ed. Primisser, IV.

41. I have discussed Chaucer's knight and his part in the crusade in a contribution to *English Court Culture in the Late Middle Ages*, ed. V. J. Scattergood and J. W. Sherborne (London, 1983), 45–61.

42. A. S. Cooke, 'Beginning the Board in Prussia', *Journal of English and German Philology*, XIV (1915), 376, n.3.

43. D'Orronville, *Chronique du Bon Duc Loys de Bourbon*, ed. Chazaud, 65–6.

44. M. Vale, 'A fourteenth-century order of chivalry: the "*Tiercelet*" ' *EHR*, 82 (1967), 340–1.

45. BN, MS Fr. 1997, p.19.

46. Keen, *The Laws of War in the late Middle Ages*, Ch.III. For a good description of a duel fought to establish a right over a prisoner, see the account of the duel fought at Rodez between Jacques Breton and Louis de Cera, BN, Collection Doat 203, fos 267 ff.

47. Keen, *The Laws of War in the late Middle Ages*, 173; and Arch. Nat. X^{iA}74, fo 91; X^{i}A 84, fo 225.

48. *Régistres de la Toison d'Or*, I, fos 15vo, 25vo (I am grateful to Mr C. A. J. Armstrong for permitting me to use his microfilm of the MS, which is in the Vienna Hofbibliotek).

49. D'Orronville, *Chronique du Bon Duc Loys de Bourbon*, ed. Chazaud, 89.

50. E. de Monstrelet, *Chronique*, ed. L. Douët d'Arcq (Paris 1857–62), IV, 331–2.

51. *Régistres de la Toison d'Or*, I, fo 2 vo.

52. J. Warkworth, *A Chronicle of the first thirteen Years of the Reign of King Edward IV*, ed. J. O. Halliwell (Camden Soc., 1839), 39.

53. *The Burt*, ed. F. W. D. Brie (EETS, London, 1906), I, 227–8.

54. J. F. Kirk, *History of Charles the Bold* (London, 1863), II, 439.

55. Nicolas, *The Scrope and Grosvenor Controversy*, I, 139, 146.

56. J. de Bueil, *Le Jouvencel*, ed. Favre and Lecestre, II,21.

Notes to Chapter X

1. The most important recent work on the orders of chivalry is unfortunately not yet published: it is D'A. J. Boulton, 'The origin and development of the curial orders of Chivalry' (Oxford D.Phil Thesis, 1975). M. Vale *War and Chivalry*, ch.2, discusses their fifteenth-century role most perceptively. Two older works are very important, Vulson de la Colombière, *Le Vray Theatre d'honneur et de chevalerie*, and F. von Biedenfeld *Geschichte und Verfassung aller geistlichen und weltlichen, erloschenen und blühenden Ritterorden* (Weimar, 1841), 2 vols. On individual orders, mentioned above, see, besides works quoted below, (i) on the Garter, E. Ashmole, *The Institutions, Laws and Ceremonies of the Most Noble Order of the Garter* (London, 1672); and N. H. Nicolas, *A History of the Orders of Knighthood of the British Empire* (London, 1842); (ii) on the Star, L. Pannier, *La Noble Maison St Ouen, la Villa Clipiacum et l'Ordre de l'Etoile* (Paris, 1878); (iii) on the Knot, E. Léonard *Histoire de Jeanne Ire Reine de Naples* (Paris, 1937), Pt II of Ch.1, 12–25; (iv) on the order of the Collar, and the confraternity of the Black Swan, E. L. Cox, *The Green Count of Savoy* (Princeton, 1967); (v) on the Golden Fleece, H. de Reiffenberg, *Histoire de l'Ordre de la Toison d'Or* (Brussels, 1830); L. Hommel, *L'Histoire du Noble Ordre de la Toison d'Or* (Brussels, 1947); (vi) on the Swan, R. G. Stillfried, *Der Schwanenorden* (Halle, 1845); (vii) on St Michael, P. Contamine, 'Sur l'ordre de St. Michel au temps de Louis XI et Charles VIII', *Bulletin de la Société Nationale des Antiquaires de France* (1976), 212–36.

2. For the order of Fools, see von Biedenfeld, *cit.sup.*, I, 109.

3. Vale, *War and Chivalry*, 38, 41.

4. R. Barber, *The Knight and Chivalry* (2nd edn., 1974), 342–4.

5. J. Reygersbergh, *Dye Cronijke van Zeelandt* (Antwerp, 1551), XXIX. Chifflet says he found more information on this in an ancient *Tornoyboek* of the Counts of Holland (Besançon, Coll. Chifflet MS 83, fos 151 ff.).

6. See below, 185 (the Band); and J. Vale, *Edward III and Chivalry* (Boydell, 1983), 86 ff.

7. G. Monti, *Le Confraternite Medievali* (Venice, 1927) I, 7–9; see also N. J. Houseley, 'Politics and Heretics in Italy: Anti-Heretical Crusades, Orders and Confratenities, 1200–1500; *JEH*, 33 (1982), 193–208.

8. Mansi, *Concilia*, XXV, 763–4.

9. *Mémoires d'Olivier de La Marche*, ed. H. Beaune and J. D'Arbaumont, IV (Paris, 1888), 161–2.

10. D'A. J. Boulton, D.Phil. Thesis, *cit.sup.*, 19; and see *anon*, 'Lettres du Duc d'Orléans, qui confèrent l'ordre du Camail', *Revue Historique Nobiliare* (1886), 13.

11. Schultz, *Deutsches Leben in XIV und XV Jahrhundert*, 544; and see *Ibid.*, figs. 551, 552, 558, 561.

12. A. Hartshorne, 'Notes on collars of SS', *Archaeological Journal*, XXXIX (1882), 376–83. The lists of those to whom the Duke of Orleans gave the Camail, in BN, MS Clairembault 1241, make it quite clear that it was essentially a livery collar; see also further C. d'Orlac, 'Les chevaliers du Porc Epic ou du Camail', *Revue Historique Nobiliaire*, 3 (1867), 337–50

13. T. Aign, *Die Ketzel: ein Nuremburger Handelsherren und Jersualempilgergeschlecht* (Neustadt, 1961), 82 ff.

14. D'A. J. Boulton, D.Phil. Thesis, *cit.sup.*, introduction, 2–5.

15. See the statutes of the Order in M. Vulson de la Colombière, *Le Vray Théâtre de l'honneur et de chevalerie* (Paris, 1648), I, 113. The case of the Order of the Golden Buckle, founded by the Emperor Charles IV, is similar to that of the Croissant: it had statutes, regular chapter meeting, and a limited membership of twenty-six, but elected its own *Hauptmann*; see von Biedenfeld, *Geschichte und Verfassung aller . . . Ritterorden*, I, 226.

16. *Gesta Henrici Quinti*, ed. B. Williams (London, 1850), 78; *St Albans Chronicle*, ed. V. H. Galbriath (Oxford, 1937), 100.

17. Rymer, *Foedera*, IX, 435.

18. *Chronique de Jean Le Fèvre, Seigneur de St. Remy*, ed. F. Morand (Paris, 1881), II, 212.

19. C. A. J. Armstrong, 'Had the Burgundian government a policy for the nobility?' in J. S. Bromley and E. H. Kossmann (eds.), *Britain and the Netherlands* (Groningen, 1964), II, 9–32, especially 25 ff.

20. M. Vale, *War and Chivalry* (London, 1981), 62; A. Lecoy de la Marche, *Le Roi René* (Paris, 1875), I, 161.

21. G. Machaut, *La Prise d'Alexandrie*, ed. M. L. de Las-Matrie (Geneva, 1877), lines 349 ff.

22. Vale, *War and Chivalry*, 49–51.

23. J. Stevenson, *Letters and Papers Illustrative of the Wars of the English in France* (RS 1861–4), I, 295–8. Besançon, Bib. Municipale, Coll. Chifflet MS 87, fo 80, gives a copy of the letter of four Italian nobles who returned Collars of St Michael to Louis XII in 1512.

24. BN, MS Esp. 33. The statutes of the Band are printed from this earliest MS in G. Daumet, 'L'ordre Castillan de l'Écharpe (Banda)', *Bulletin Hispanique*, XXV (1923), 21–32; D'A. J. Boulton offers an excellent analysis, with a translation of the prologue, D.Phil. Thesis, 49–57.

25. For this regulation see the second version of the statutes in L. T. Villanueva, 'Memoria sobre la orden de caballeria de la Banda de Castilla', *Boletin de la Real Academia de la Historia* LXXII (1918), 561.

26. For the statutes of the *Fer de Prisonnier* see L. Douët d'Arcq, *Choix de pièces inédites relatives au règne de Charles VI* (Paris, 1863), I, 370–4; for those of the *Dame Blanche à l'Escu Vert* see *Livre des Faits du Maréchal de Boucicaut*, ed. M. Petitot (Collection complète des mémoires rélatifs à l'histoire de France, vol.6), 507–12.

27. Schultz, *Deutsches Leben in XIV und XV Jahrhundert*, 487 ff. 549 ff.

28. I am here following the statutes of the bortherhood of the Falcon and the Fish, in J. C. Lünig, *Teutschen Reichs Archiv* (Leipzig, 1710), Pars Special. I, Cont.I, 2, 66–70.

29. Schultz, *cit.sup.*, 549.

30. H. Obenaus, *Recht und Verfassung der Gesellschaften mit St Jorgen Schild in Schwaben* (Gottingen, 1961), 79 ff; and see Landau, *cit.inf.*

31. G. Landau, *Die Ritter Gesellschaften in Hessen* (Cassel, 1840: supplement to Band I of *Zeitschrift des Vereins für hessische Geschichte und Landeskunde*, 1840), 98.

32. *Ibid.*, 99, 192.

33. *Ibid.*, 98, 191.

34. Obenaus, *cit.sup.*, n.25.

35. On these leagues see A. Artonne, *Le Mouvement de 1314 et les chartes provinciales de 1315* (Paris, 1912).

36. See above, ch. 2, 35.

37. On the *Tiercelet* see M. Vale, 'A fourteenth-century order of chivalry: the "*Tiercelet*"', *EHR*, 82 (1967), 332–41; on the *Pomme d'Or* see A. Bossuat, 'Un ordre de chevalerie Auvergnat: l'ordre de la Pomme d'Or', *Bulletin Historique et Scientifique de l'Auvergne*, 64 (1944), 83 ff. The statutes are printed in A. Jacotin, *Preuves de la Maison de*

Polignac (Paris, 1898–1906), II, 172 (no.283). See also M. Keen, 'brotherhood in arms', *History*, 47 (1962), 1–17.

38. The contrast here implied is of course superficial. If the statutes of the German confraternities are compared not with those of the well-known French orders but with for example those of the Golden Buckle (von Biedenfeld, *Geschichte und Verfassung aller ... Ritterorden*, I, 226) their similarity to those of a curial order becomes more striking.

39. L. Gollut, *Mémoires historiques de la republique séquanoise et des princes de la Franche Comté*, ed. C. Dauvernoy (Arbois 1846), cols 1439–42.

40. Vale, *cit.sup.*, *EHR*, 82 (1967), 340–1.

41. *Merlin*, ed. G. Paris and J. Ulrich (Paris, 1886) I, 94–8.

42. Y. Renouard, 'L'ordre de la Jarretière et l'ordre de l'Etoile', *MA*, 55 (1949), 281–300 especially 282, n.3; 294, n.23.

43. *Chronique de Jean le Bel*, ed. J. Viard and E. Déprez (Paris, 1905), II, 26–7. T. Gray, *Scalacronica*, ed. J. Stevenson (Edinburgh, 1836), seems completely to conflate the story of the Round Table tournament and the foundation of the Garter.

44. BL, Add.MS 21370, fo 1.

45. For the statutes see von Biedenfeld, *Geschichte und Verfassung aller ... Ritterorden*, I. 103.

46. Preamble to the statutes in BN, MS Fr. 4274, fo 3. The statutes are also printed by the Abbé le Febvre, *Mémoire pour servir à l'histoire de France du XIVme siècle, contenant les statuts de l'ordre du St Esprit* (Paris 1764).

47. Le Febvre, *cit.sup.*, 28–9.

48. Bossuat, *cit.sup.*, n.32.

49. R. Vaughan, *Philip the Good* (London, 1970), 152, 162, 334; and V. Tourneur 'Origine et symbolique de la Toison d'Or', *Bulletin de l'Académie Royale de Belgique*, Lettres, série 5, XLII (1956), 300–23. Jean Germain, chancellor of the Fleece and a crusading enthusiast, had much to do with promoting its association with Gideon: on his activities see Y. Lacaze, 'Un réprésentat de la politique anti-mussulmane du XVme, Jean Germain', *Positions des Thèses: École de Chartes* (1958), 67–75.

50. Von Biedenfeld, *Geschichte und Verfassung aller ... Ritterorden*, I, 103.

51. *Chronique de Jean le Bel*, ed. Viard, II, 205 (Star); BN, MS Fr 4274 and Le Febvre, *cit.ante* (Knot); *Chronique de Jean Le Févre, Seigneur de St Remy*, ed. Morand, II, 249, 250 (Golden Fleece); Vulson de la Colombière,

Le Vray Théâtre de l'honneur et de chevalier, I, 111, 116, 117 (Croissant).

52. BM, MS Clairembault 1241, 920.

53. F. Corazini, *La Lettere edite e inedite di Messer Giovanni Boccacio* (Florence, 1877), 161 (quoted by D'A. J. Boulton, to whom I owe the reference.)

54. *Merlin*, ed. Paris and Ulrich, II, 98.

55. R. Howard Bloch, *Medieval French Literature and Law* (Berkeley, California, 1977), 202 ff; compare Lydgate's *Fall of Princes*, VIII, line 2780 ff where pursuivants are described as chronicling the affairs of Arthur's court.

56. *Livre des faicts du Marechal de Boucicaut*, ed. Petitot (Collection des mémoires, vol. 6), 504 ff.

57. Quoted by Huizinga, *The Waning of the Middle Ages* (1927 edn.), 63.

58. Douët d'Arcq, *Choix de pièces inédites relatives au règne de Charles VI, I*, 373.

59. P. S. Lewis, 'Une devise de chevalerie inconnue, créée par un Comte de Foix?: le *Dragon*', *Annales du Midi*, 76 (1964), 77–84.

60. BR, MS Goethals 707, fo 33 vo (regulations concerning the device to be worn by knights, squires and ladies of the Order of St Anthony), and fo 39 ff (names, and in some cases the arms of knights, squires and ladies of the Order); and for the Garter, G. F. Beltz, *Memorials of the most noble Order of the Garter* (London, 1841), CCXXI–IV, 10.

61. D'Orronville, *Chronique du Bon Duc Loys de Bourbon*, ed. Chazaud, 12–13.

62. M. Galway, 'Joan of Kent and the Order of the Garter', *University of Birmingham Historical Journal*, I (1947), 13–50. Miss Galway's attempt to show that the story is not just early, but authentic too, is not entirely convincing.

63. Von Biedenfeld, *Geschichte und Verfassung aller ... Ritterorden*, I, 229–31; M. Letts, *The Diary of Jorg von Ehingen* (London, 1929), 13.

64. For the crusading associations of the Sword, see G. Machaut, *La Prise d'Alexandrie*, ed. Mas-Latrie, lines 349–50; for the Stole and Jar, see the account of its formation and crusading association in BR, MS 19132, fo 8–9.

65. The statutes are unpublished: the only text known is University of Pennsylvania MS Fr. 83, of which D'A. J. Boulton gives a summary (D.Phil. Thesis, 224–59), which I have followed.

66. See above, nn.37 and 59.

67. Vulson de la Colombière, *Le Vray Théâtre d'honneur et de chevalerie*, I, 108.

68. D'A. J. Boulton, D.Phil. Thesis, 235.
69. BL, Add. MS 28628, fo 2vo, 3-3vo. I know of no study of this order (whose statutes are recorded in this MS) it is said to have been founded by Ferdinand of Naples in 1465. For a brief notice of the celebration of its feast on 29 September 1497, see Besançon, Bib. Municipale, Coll. Chifflet MS 83, fo 109.
70. J. Anstis, *Register of the Most Noble Order of the Garter* (London 1724), I. 44 (cl.16).
71. BL, Add. MS 28628, fo 4vo-5.
72. Besançon, Bib. Municipale, Coll. Chifflet MS 90, fo 12 ff. This is an extremely interesting and detailed liturgy, which deserves further study.
73. See e.g. statutes of the Croissant, Vulson de la Colombière, *Le Vray Théâtre d'honneur et de chevalerie*, I. 107, 110. The statutes of the Confraternity of St Anthony in Barbefosse stipulate (Besancon, Bib. Municipale, Coll. Chifflet MS 90, fo 15) that a candidate for admission must swear 'quod non sit captor puellarum, oppressor viduarum et pupillorum, incendiator ecclesiarum et sanctorum locum, interfector clericorum . . . nec praedo publicorum viarum aut honoris et nobilitatis prophanator'.
74. *Chronique de Jean Le Fèvre, Seigneur de St Remy*, ed. Morand, 211 (Golden Fleece); Vulson de la Colombière, *Le Vray Théâtre d'honneur et de chevalerie* I, 107 (Croissant); Besançon, Bib. Municipale, Coll. Chifflet MS 90, fo 14vo (St Anthony in Barbefosse).
75. BL, Add. MS 28628, fo 10vo: 'decernimus hunc ordinem eis qui viri clari et nobiles fuerunt non in innobilibus et minus claris esse conferendum: sive nobilitate a majoribus accepta sive a se labore et industria potita'.
76. Vulson de la Colombière, *Le Vray Théâtre d'honneur et de chevalerie*, I, 119.
77. J. Anstis, *The Register of the Most Noble Order of the Garter*, I, 44 (cl.17).
78. See above, ch.2: and also Keen, 'Brotherhood in arms', *History*, 47 (1962), 1–17, for the idea of loyal brotherhood.
79. See the texts quoted in Von Biedenfeld, *Geschichte und Verfassung aller . . . Ritterorden*, I, 130–2, concerning the excesses committed by the Companions of the Brotherhoods of the Horn, the Star, the Falcon, and the *Alte Minne*.
80. Vulson de la Colombière, *Le Vray Théâtre d'honneur et de chevalerie*, I, 112.
81. Bossuat and Vale in their articles, *cit.sup.*, n.37, examine the careers of the companions of these two orders, which illus-

trate their chivalrous reputations and interests, including crusading experience.
82. BN, MS Clairembault 1241, p.907.
83. *Régistres de la Toison d'Or*, I, fo 2vo.
84. G. de Lannoy, *Oeuvres* ed. Potvin, 457–9.
85. Huizinga, *The Waning of the Middle Ages*, 66, 80.
86. See above, chapter 8, 149.

Notes to Chapter XI

1. A. Planche, 'Du tournoi au théâtre en Bourgogne: le *Pas de la Fontaine des Pleurs* à Chalon-sur-Saône, 1449–50', *MA*, 81 (1975), 117.
2. O. de la Marche, *Mémoires*, ed. Buchon, 433.
3. *Le Livre des faits de Jacques de Lalaing*, in *Oeuvres de G. Chastellain*, ed. K. de Lettenhove, VIII (Brussels), 1866), 48–55.
4. O. de la Marche, *Mémoires*, ed. Buchon, 463.
5. For the full text of the chapters of the *pas*, see *Oeuvres de Chastellain*, ed. K. de Lettenhove, VIII, 189–197.
6. *Ibid.*, 214.
7. See above, ch. 5, 93–94.
8. *Oeuvres de Chastellain*, VIII, 190.
9. Anna Comnena, *The Alexiad*, X, 10.
10. For the *Arbre de Charlemagne*, see O. de la Marche, *Mémoires*, ed. Buchon, 378ff, and BN, MS Fr. 16988 to 213vo–217vo for the chapters; for the *Rocher Périlleux*, G. Du Fresne de Beaucourt, *Histoire de Charles VII*, IV (Paris, 1888) 183–4; for *La Bergière*, *Oeuvres complètes du Roi René*, ed. le comte de Quatrebarbes (Angers, 1844), II, 49–83; for *La Belle Maurienne*, BN, MS Fr. 16988, fos 197 ff; for the *Perron Fée*, see *Le Pas du Perron Fée*, ed. F. Brassart (Douai, 1874); and for the *Arbre d'Or*, O. de la Marche, *Mémoires*, ed. Beaune and D'Arbaumont, III, 123ff, and S. Bentley, *Excerpta Historica* (London, 1833), 238ff.
11. Planche, *art. cit.*, *MA*, 81 (1975), 102. nn. 27, 28.
12. Vulson de la Colombière, *Le Vray Théâtre d'honneur et de chevalerie*, I, 147–58.
13. BN, MS Fr 1997 p. 81 ff: this MS is damaged, but the full text can be followed from a later copy, BN MS Fr. 5241, from fo 105vo.
14. See Prost *Traités du duel judiciaire . . . :* see also *The Black Book of the Admiralty* (RS) I, 300 ff, 330 ff (ordinances for the duel of

Thomas of Woodstock, Constable of England, and of Philip IV, King of France, both texts frequently copied into heraldic MSS).

15. This subject has been most interestingly explored by S. Anglo, 'L'arbre de chevalerie et le perron dans les tournois', *Les Fêtes de la Renaissance*, ed. J. Jacquot and E. Konigson, III (Paris 1975), 283–98. I am much indebted to this illuminating and learned study.

16. Chrétien de Troyes, *Le Chevalier au Lion* (*Löwenritter* in Foerster's edn.), lines 410 ff, 800 ff.

17. C. Blair, *European Armour, c.1066–c.1700* (London, 1958), ch. 7; for frog-mouthed helms, see 157–8.

18. Vale, *War and Chivalry*, 84.

19. Nicolas, *The Scrope and Grosvenor Controversy*, I, 155.

20. Cuvelier, *Chronique de Bertrand du Guesclin* ed. Charrière, I, lines 11070 ff.

21. *Ibid.*, lines 1670 ff; *Oeuvres de Froissart*, ed. K. de Lettenhove IX, 248, 275–7, 281, 323–30.

22. *Histoire du gentil Seigneur de Bayart*, ed. Roman, 110 ff.

23. *Ibid.*, 24–38.

24. *Oeuvres de Froissart*, ed. K. de Lettenhove, XIV, 105–51 (for St Inglevert); and for Boucicaut in Italy, A. de la Sale, *Histoire du petit Jehan de Saintré*, chs. 55 and 56, trs. I. Gray (London 1931), 210–14.

25. *Pageant of the Birth, Life and Death of Richard Beauchamp Earl of Warwick*, ed. Viscount Dillon and W. H. St. John Hope (London 1914), eg Plates XIV, XXII, X-XIX–XXXi (tournies); VI, VII, XXXVI–VIII, XL (war scenes).

26. Vulson de la Colombière, *Le Vray Théâtre d'honneur et de chevalerie*, I, 89, 90.

27. J. de Bueil, *Le Jouvencel*, ed. Favre and Lecestre, II, 99 ff; and see R. L. Kilgour, *The Decline of Chivalry* (Cambridge, Mass. 1937), 330; and Huizinga, *The Waning of the Middle Ages*, ch. 4.

28. L. D. Benson, *Malory's 'Morte Darthur'* (Cambridge, Mass. 1976), 182–4.

29. A. de la Sale, *Histoire du petit Jehan de Saintré*, chapters 21, 29, 50, 54, 65 (jousting); 58–62 (war in Prussia); in Gray's translation, pp. 115, 132, 186, 202 ff, 246 ff; and 216–41.

30. L. de Rosny, *L'Epervier d'Or* (Paris, 1839), especially 27–45; and F. H. Cripps-Day, *The History of the Tournament in France and England* (London, 1918), 21–2. A new and more detailed survey of civic tournaments, including the *Espinette*, is offered by J. Vale in her *Edward III and Chivalry* (1983),

ch. 2. I am most grateful for having been allowed to see the proofs of this most interesting book.

31. BR, MS 14935, 39 ff; and see J. Vale, *cit. sup.*, for a comprehensive list of MSS containing this roll.

32. De Rosny, *L'Epervier d'Or*, 46–56.

33. For a fine example of a lavish Spanish joust, see the account of the jousts held at Valladolid in 1434, where the chief judge was accoutred as the God of Love, in R. Boase, *Troubadour Revival* (London, 1978), 145–7.

34. Seyler, *Geschichte der Heraldik*, 49.

35. *Die Geschichte und Taten Wilwolts von Schaumburg*, ed. A. von Keller (Stuttgart, 1859) gives a graphic amount of his career, on which the account by Mrs H. Cust in *Gentlemen Errant* (London, 1909), 123–240 is based.

36. G. Rüxner, *Turnierbuch* (Frankfurt, 1566), CLXXXIII vo, CCXXVII.

37. BN, MS Fr. 1997, p. 16; Prost, *Traités du duel judiciaire*, 206.

38. *The Alliterative Morte Arthur*, line 1688.

39. BN, MS Fr. 1997, 34–5; Prost, *Traités du duel judiciaire*, 216–17.

40. BN, MS Fr. 1997, 18–19; Vulson de la Colombière *Le Vray Théâtre d'honneur et de chevalerie*, I, 64 ff; Rüxner, *Turnierbuch*, XI–XV, CLXXXIV vo, CCII vo. I have followed La Sale's list, the first of these.

41. BN, MS Fr. 1997, 16–17. This passage, and those quoted in the preceding and succeeding notes, are not in the text as printed by Prost. He printed from an autograph MS of La Sale, so these must be additions, or matter omitted in a final draft.

42. *Ibid.*

43. J. Petersen, *Der Rittertum in der Darstellung des Johannes Rod* (Strasbourg, 1909), 169, quoting Roth, *Der Ritterspiegel*, verse 963 ff.

44. *Ibid.*, 39.

45. Vulson de la Colombière, *Le Vray Théâtre d'honneur et de chevalerie*, I, 110.

46. See above, ch. X.

47. A. de la Sale, *Histoire du petit Jehade Saintré*, ch. 48 (Gray's translation, 174).

48. *Oeuvres de G. Chastellain*, ed. K. de Lettenhove, VIII, 70 ff.

49. Bentley, *Excerpta historica*, 178.

50. T. Gray, *Scalacronica*, ed. J. Stevenson (Edinburgh, 1836), 145 ff.

51. J. Barbour, *The Bruce*, book VIII, lines 488 ff.

52. Arsenal MS 2251, fo 13. The knight's name is given as Albert Pachost.

53. *Oeuvres de Froissart,* ed. K. de Lettenhove, II, 372.
54. T. Wright, *Political Poems and Songs* (RS, 1859), I, 10–12; and see B. J. Whiting, 'The Vows of the Heron', *Speculum,* 20 (1945), 261–78. I am not entirely happy with the suggestion there made that the whole poem is satirical in intent.
55. *N. Triveti Annales,* ed. T. Hog (London, 1845), 408–9; *Flores historiarum,* ed. Luard (RS), III, 131–2. See further N. Denholm-Young, 'The Song of Carlaverock and the Parliamentary Roll of Arms', *PBA,* 47 (1961), 251–62; and C. Bullock-Davies, *Menestrellorum Multitudo* (Cardiff, 1978).
56. *The Buik of Alexander,* ed. R. L. Graeme-Ritchie (Edinburgh, 1921–9), I, xxxvi–xlvii.
57. O. de la Marche, *Mémoires,* ed. Buchon, 488, 490, 494–504.
58. *Chronique de Mathieu d'Escouchy,* ed. G. Du Fresne de Beaucourt (Paris 1863), II, 165–222.
59. See above, ch. X, 186.
60. I have tried in vain to pinpoint an origin, literary or historical, for the practice of swearing oaths on a bird. It is natural to connect it with the story of the challenge of the Knight of the Sparrow Hawk, which appears in several Arthurian romances (especially given the reference, which Graeme Ritchie notes, to the Vows of the Sparrow Hawk in 1315). But all precision has eluded me.
61. R. Vaughan, *Philip the Good* (London, 1970), 360 ff; and see G. Doutrepont, 'La croisade projetée par Philippe le Bon contre les Turcs', *Notes et Extraits de la Bibliothèque Nationale,* 41 (1923), 1–28.
62. See above, ch. IX, 167.
63. D. A. Bullough, 'Games people played: drama and ritual as propaganda in medieval Europe', *TRHS,* 5th series, 24 (1974), 97–122.
64. BN, MS Fr. 16988 fo 213vo and ff.
65. P. de Mézières, *Le Songe du vieil pèlerin,* ed. G. W. Coopland (Cambridge, 1969), I, 507.

Notes to Chapter XII

1. On Huizinga's treatment of chivalry, see Vale, *War and Chivalry,* 1–12, a very perceptive discussion; see also Keen, 'Huizinga, Kilgour and the decline of chivalry', *Medievalia et Humanistica,* New Series, 8 (1977), 1–20.

2. P. Contamine, *La Guerre au moyen âge* (Paris, 1980) 232–41. These eloquent pages, annotated with a very substantial array of references, need to be read carefully; I have gained much from them.
3. H. Delpech, *La Tactique au XIIIme Siècle* (Paris, 1886), I, 374, nn. 1 and 3; Verbruggen, *The Art of Warfare in Western Europe during the Middle Ages,* trs. Willard and Southern, 62–4.
4. M. Vale, *War and Chivalry* (London, 1981), 105–14, and refs. there cited, in particular C. J. Ffoulks, *The Armourer and his craft from the XIth to the XVIth Century* (London, 1912).
5. Vale, *cit. sup.,* 119. Cornelius, Bastard of Burgundy, was killed at Rupelmonde in 1452 in consequence of leaving off a piece of armour, the 'bevor' at his throat; and Charles the Bold was wounded at Monthléry in 1465 for the same reason.
6. A. Boussuat published two detailed and illuminating studies of the economic implications of ransoms for individual families: 'La rançon de Guillaume de Chateauvillain', *Annales de Bourgogne* (1951); and 'La rançon de Jean, Seigneur de Rodemack', *Annales de l'Est* (1951), 145 ff.
7. J. H. Wylie and W. T. Waugh, *The Reign of Henry V* (Cambridge, 1914–29), II, 171 ff. An almost exactly parallel incident took place at Aljubarotta in 1385, when the Portuguese killed their prisoners in an emergency on the orders of King James, see *Oeuvres de Froissart,* ed. K. de Lettenhove, XI, 179–81. The chroniclers record both incidents very calmly.
8. Keen, *The Laws of War in the Late Middle Ages,* 127 ff.
9. Wylie and Waugh, *The Reign of Henry V,* II, 66–73.
10. Wylie and Waugh, *The Reign of Henry V,* III, 337–357; and see K. B. McFarlane, *Lancastrian Kings and Lollard Knights* (Oxford, 1972), 127.
11. Joinville, *Histoire de St. Louis,* ed. Natalis de Wailly, 108.
12. Contamine, *La Guerre au moyen âge,* 417.
13. On the Agincourt casualties, see Wylie and Waugh, *The Reign of Henry V,* II, 217–29, especially 225 ff.
14. See B. Thordeman, *Armour from the battle of Wisby 1361* (Stockholm, 1939), 2 vols.
15. *Political Songs,* ed. T. Wright (RS), I, 21.
16. O. de la Marche, *Mémoires,* ed. Buchon, 463.
17. *The Diary of Jorg von Ehingen,* ed. Letts,

38.

18. G. Diaz de Gamez, *The Unconquered Knight: a Chronicle of the Deeds of Don Pero Niño*, trs. J. Evans (London, 1928), 99–100.

19. G. de Chastellain, *Oeuvres*, ed. K. de Lettenhove, VIII, 249; *The Diary of Jorg von Ehingen*, ed. Letts, 67; G. Diaz de Gamez, *The Unconquered Knight*, 141–2.

20. See M. Powicke, *Military Obligation in Medieval England* (Oxford, 1962), 54–6, 82–3, 85, 87.

21. Contamine, *La Guerre au moyen âge* 285–91; D. Waley, 'The army of the Florentine republic from the 12th to the 14th century', in N. Rubenstein, *Florentine Studies* (London, 1968), 83 ff; and see for later times and texts A. da Mosto, *Ordinamenti Militari delle soldatesche dello stato Romano dal 1430 al 1470* (Rome, 1903).

22. Vale, *War and Chivalry*, 113.

23. P. Contamine, *Guerre, état et société* (Paris, 1972), 17–21; Vale, *War and Chivalry*, 122–8; V. Chomel 'Chevaux de bataille et ronçins en Dauphiné au XIVme siècle', *Cahiers de l'histoire*, VII (1962), 5–23.

24. Verbruggen, *The Art of Warfare in Western Europe during the Middle Ages*, trs. Willard and Southern, 26–7.

25. Vale, *War and Chivalry*, 126.

26. BR, MS 11407, fo 82.

27. *Ibid.*, fo 35.

28. S. Krüger, 'Das Rittertum in den Schriften des Konrad von Megenberg', in J. Fleckenstein (ed.), *Herrschaft und Stand*, 312.

29. Gelre, *Wappenboek*, ed. Bouton I, 203 (he is recounting how Daniel de la Werde went to Lombardy 'dair die scool van weypen leyt').

30. F. Saccheti, *Novelle* (Milan 1804–5), III, 91–3.

31. Bartholomew de Saliceto, *Super VIII Cod.* Tit 51, l. 12.

32. T. Basin, *Histoire de Charles VII*, ed. C. Samaran (rev. ed., Paris, 1964), I, 86.

33. J. de Bueil, *Le Jouvencel*, ed. Favre and Lecestre, I, 19.

34. P. de Mézières, *Letter to King Richard II*, ed. and transl. G. W. Coopland (Liverpool, 1975), 57–9.

35. On the effects of war see further H. Denifle, *La Guerre de Cent Ans et la Désolation des églises, monastères et hôpitaux en France*, 2 vols. (Paris, 1899); and R. Boutruche, *La Crise d'une société: seigneurs et paysans du Bordelais pendant la Guerre de Cent Ans* (Paris, 1947).

36. Keen, *The Laws of War in the Late Middle Ages*, 146 ff.

37. Bodleian, MS Ashmole 865, fo 423.

38. The activities of the Catalans are brilliantly described in Muntaner's *Chronicle*, trs. Lady Goodenough (London, 1920–1).

39. Schäfer, *Deutsche Ritter und Edelknechte in Italien*, I, 110 ff.

40. See H. J. Hewitt, *The Black Prince's Expedition of 1355–7* (Manchester, 1958), especially 10 ff and ch. VII.

41. Contamine, *La Guerre au moyen âge*, 396–404; and see J. Boussard, 'Les mercenaires au XIIme siècle: Henri II Plantegenet et les origines de l'armée du métier', *BEC* 106 (1945–6), 189–224.

42. *The Itinerary of John Leland*, ed. L. Toulmin-Smith (London, 1907–10), I, 102–3 (Ampthill), IV, 133 (Beverstone); and see K. B. McFarlane, 'The investment of Sir John Falstolf's profits of war', *TRHS*, 5th series, 7 (1957), 91–116.

43. K. B. McFarlane, 'A business-partnership in war and administration, 1421–45', *EHR* 78 (1963), 290–310.

44. H. Duplés-Agier (ed.), *Régistre Criminel du Chatelet de Paris 1389–92* (Paris, 1861–64), II, 210.

45. On Hawkwood's career, see J. Temple-Leader and G. Marcotti, *Sir John Hawkwood* (London, 1889).

46. Caxton, *Book of the Ordre of Chyvalry*, 123. Compare Thomas of Saluzzo's *Chevalier Errant* where it is said of Hawkwood that 'en Ytale ne fu cent ans devant plus vaillant capitain ne plus sage de lui' (BN, MS Fr. 12559, fo. 150vo). Hawkwood here is one of two captains who occupy special seats in Fortune's Palace – the other is Bertrand Du Guesclin!

47. Cuvelier, *Chronique de Bertrand du Guesclin*, I, 261–2.

48. M. Fréville, 'Les grandes compagnies au XIVme siecle', *BEC* V (1843–4), 246.

49. H. Bonet, *The Tree of Battles*, trs. Coopland, 189.

50. The fullest discussion of this criticism is given by R. L. Kilgour, *The Decline of Chivalry* (Cambridge, Mass., 1937), which I have found immensely helpful, even though I question some of the interpretation.

51. Keen, 'Huizinga, Kilgour and the decline of chivalry', *Medievalia et Humanistica*, New Series, 8 (1977), 5–6.

52. Bernard, *Opera*, ed. J. Leclercq and H. M. Rochais, III (Rome, 1963), 216–17.

53. Girart de Bornelh, quoted by Kilgour, *The Decline of Chivalry*, 5–6.

54. Kilgour, *cit. sup.*, chs. III–IV. Among the

references that he quotes, see in particular E. Deschamps, *Oeuvres,* ed. Le Marquis de Queux de St.-Hilaire and G. Raynaud (Paris, 1878–1903), II, 214–26; III 141–2; Gersob, *Opera,* ed. E. Dupin (Antwerp, 1706), I, 457–67; IV, 607–11. The remark of A. Chartier which I have quoted is discussed by Kilgour, p. 206.

55. N. A. R. Wright, 'The *Tree of Battles* of Honoré Bouvet and the Laws of War', in C. T. Allmand (ed.), *War, Literature, and Politics in the late Middle Ages* (Liverpool, 1976), 12–31; and see Keen, *The Laws of War in the Late Middle Ages,* 69–81.

56. Alvarez Pelayo, *De Planctu Ecclesiae* (Lyons, 1517) art. 31, quoted by Contamine, *La Guerre au moyen âge,* 440–1.

57. See e.g. *Ordonnances des Roys des Frances,* V, 657–661; XIII, 306–13.

58. Bonet, *The Tree of Battles,* ed. Coopland, 135.

59. BR, MS 10497, fo 120vo.

60. *Ibid.,* fo 111.

61. C. de Pisan, *The 'Livre de la Paix',* ed. C. C. Willard (The Hague, 1958), 134; quoted by Vale, *War and Chivalry,* 63.

62. Caxton, *Book of the Ordre of Chyvalry,* ed. Byles, 124.

63. La Marche, *cit. sup.,* ch. VIII, 150.

64. See above, ch. X.

Notes to Chapter XIII

1. A. B. Ferguson, *The Indian Summer of English Chivalry* (Durham, N. Carolina, 1960); E. Bourciez, *Les Moeurs polies et la littérature de cour sous Henri II* (Paris, 1886).

2. See J. Strobl, *Kaiser Mazimilians I Anteil am Teuerdank* (Innsbruck, 1907).

3. D. Devoto, 'Folklore et politique au château ténébreux', *Les Fêtes de la Renais-sance,* ed. J. Jacquot, II (Paris, 1960), 311–28.

4. Bourciez, *cit. sup.,* 20.

5. Contamine, *La Guerre au moyen âge,* 254.

6. *Ibid.*

7. J. de Bueil, *Le Jouvencel,* ed. Favre and Lecestre, I, cclxxxi, quoted by Vale, *War and Chivalry,* 148–9.

8. La Marche, *Mémoires,* ed. Buchon, 484.

9. J. Hale, 'War and public opinion in the fifteenth and sixteenth centuries', *Past and Present,* 22 (1962), 23.

10. *The Brut,* ed. F. W. D. Brie, II (London, 1908), 378.

11. On artillery and chivalry, see Vale, *War and Chivalry,* 143–6.

12. Bourciez, *Les Moeurs polies et la littérature de cour sous Henri II,* 81.

13. Contamine, *La Guerre au moyen âge,* 305–6.

14. La Marche, *Mémoires,* ed. Buchon, 407–8.

15. N. A. R. Wright, 'The *Tree of Battles* of Honoré Bouvet and the Laws of War', in C. T. Allmand (ed.), *War, Literature, and Politics in the Late Middle Ages* (Liverpool, 1976), 31.

16. D. M. Nicholas, *Town and Countryside: Social, Economic and Political Tensions in Fourteenth-Century Flanders* (Bruges, 1971), 250–66.

17. J. Pitt-Rivers, 'Honour and social status', in J. G. Peristiany (ed.), *Honour and Shame* (London, 1965), 38.

18. M. de Montaigne, *Essais,* II, 7.

19. Quoted by J. C. Baroza, 'Honour and shame: a historical account of several conflicts', in Peristiany, *cit. sup.,* 95.

20. Peter of Dusburg, *Chronicon terrae Prussiae,* ed. M. Töppen (*Scriptores rerum Prussicarum,* I, 101). quoted and discussed by W. Paravicini, 'Die Preussenreisen des europäischen Adels', *Historische Zeitschrift,* 232 (1981), 28 ff.

BIBLIOGRAPHY

I. Manuscript Sources

BESANÇON, Bibliothèque Municipale
Collection Chifflet, MSS 81, 83, 86, 90, 91

BRUSSELS, Bibliothèque Royale
MSS 9632, 10238, 10497, 11124–6,
11407, 14395, 21522
MS Goethals 707

EPINAL, Bibliothèque Municipale
MS 217

LILLE, Bibliothèque Municipale
MS 329

LONDON, British Library
Cotton MSS, Nero C IX, D VI
Egerton MS 3149
Harleian MS 2259
Royal MS 14 E II
Additional MSS 21370, 28628

LONDON, College of Arms
Processus in Curia Marescalli, I and II

OXFORD, Bodleian Library
Ashmole MS 865
Rawlinson MS C 399

PARIS, Archives Nationales
X1a 74, 84

PARIS, Bibliothèque de l'Arsenal
MS 2251

PARIS, Bibliothèque Nationale
MSS Français 112, 1280, 1953, 1997,
2765, 4274, 5241–2, 5936, 12559, 12597,
16988
MSS Français, Nouvelles Acquisitions
1075
MS Espagnol 33
MS Clairembault 1241
Collection Doat 203

II. Printed Primary Sources

Adalbero de Laon, *Poème au Roi Robert,* ed.
C. Carozzi (Paris, 1979).

Alexander, *Li Romans d'Alixandre,* ed. H.
Michelant (Stuttgart, 1846).

Alexander, *The Buik of Alexander,* ed. R. L.
Graeme Ritchie (Edinburgh, 1925–29).

Alfred, *King Alfred's Old English Version of
Boethius,* ed. W. J. Sedgefield (Oxford, 1899).

Ambroise, *L'Estoire de la Guerre Sainte,* ed. G.
Paris (Paris, 1897).

Andreas Capellanus, *The Art of Courtly Love,*
trans. J. J. Parry (New York, 1941).

Anna Comnena, *The Alexiad,* trans. E. A. S.
Dawes (London, 1928).

Annales monastici, ed. H. R. Luard (RS,
1865–69).

Anonymi gesta francorum, ed. R. Hill (London,
1962).

Anstis, J., *Register of the Most Noble Order of the
Garter* (London, 1724).

Antioch: *La Chanson d'Antioche,* ed. P. Paris
(Paris, 1848).

Barbour, J., *The Bruce,* ed. W. W. Skeat
(London, 1870).

Bartolus of Sassoferrato, *De insigniis et armis,*
ed. in E. Jones, *Medieval Heraldry* (Cardiff,
1943).

Bartolus of Sassoferrato, *Comment. in cod.*
(Basle, 1562).

Basin, T., *Histoire de Charles VII,* ed. C. Samaran (Paris, 1964).

Bayart: *Historie du Gentil Seigneur de Bayart,*
ed. M. J. Roman (Paris, 1878).

Beaumanoir, *Les Coutumes du Beauvaisis,* ed.
le Comte de Beugnot (Paris, 1842).

Bentley, S., *Excerpta historica* (London, 1831).

Black Book of the Admiralty, ed. T. Twiss (RS, 1871–76).

Bonet, H., *The Tree of Battles*, ed. and trans. G. W. Coopland (Liverpool, 1949).

Bonizo, of Sutri, *Liber de vita Christiana*, ed. E. Perels (Berlin, 1930).

Boucicaut: *Le Livre des faictz du bon Messire Jehan le Maingre, dit Boucicaut*, ed. M. Petitot, in *Collection des Memoires relatifs a l'histoire de France* (Paris, 1825), VI and VII.

Bretel, J., *Jacques Bretel: Le Tournoi de Cauvency*, ed. M. Delbouille (Paris, 1932).

Brut, The, ed. F. W. D. Brie (EETS, London, 1906).

Bueil, Jean de, *Le Jouvencel*, ed. C. Favre and L. Lecestre (Paris, 1887–89).

Caesarius of Heisterbach, *Dialogus miraculorum*, ed. J. Strange (Cologne, 1851).

Chandos Herald, *Life of the Black Prince*, ed. M. K. Pope and E. C. Lodge (Oxford, 1910).

Charny, Geoffroi de, *Livre de chevalerie*, in *Oeuvres de Froissart*, ed. K. de Lettenhove, tome I, pt. iii (Brussels, 1873).

Charroi de Nîmes, Le, ed. D. MacMillan (Paris, 1972).

Chartier, A., *The Poetical Works of Alain Chartier*, ed. J. C. Laidlaw (Cambridge, 1974).

Chrétien de Troyes, *Erec und Enide*, ed. W. Foerster (Halle, 1896).

Chrétien de Troyes, *Der Karrenritter (Chevalier de la Charrette)*, ed. W. Foerster (Halle, 1899).

Chrétien de Troyes, *Cligès*, ed. W. Foerster (Halle, 1884).

Chrétien de Troyes, *Perceval le Gallois*, ed. C. Potvin (Mons, 1866–71).

Chrétien de Troyes, *Der Löwenritter (Yvain)*, ed. W. Foerster (Halle, 1887).

Christine de Pisan, *Le Ditié de Jeanne d'Arc*, ed. A. J. Kennedy and K. Varty (Oxford, 1977).

Christine de Pisan, *The Epistle of Othea to Hector* (S. Scrope's translation for Sir J. Fastolf), ed. C. F. Buhler (Oxford, 1970).

Christine de Pisan, *Le livre de la paix*, ed. C. C. Willard (The Hague, 1958).

Chronicon W. Rishanger, ed. H. T. Riley (RS, 1885).

Chronique des quatre premiers Valois, ed. S. Luce (Paris, 1872).

Chroniques d'Anjou, ed. P. Machegay and P. Salmon (Paris, 1856).

Chroniques des Comtes d'Anjou, ed. L. Halphen

and R. Poupardin (Paris, 1913).

Coggeshall, R., *Chronicon Anglicanum*, ed. J. Stevenson (RS, 1875).

Condé, B. de, *Le Dit dou Baceller*, in A. Jubinal (ed.), *Recueil des contes, fabliaux et autres pieces inédites* (Paris, 1839), Vol. I.

Couci: *Le Roman du Castelain de Couci*, ed. M. Delbouille (Paris, 1936).

Couronnement Louis, Le, ed. E. Langlois (Paris, 1888).

Cuvelier, *Chronique de Bertrand du Guesclin*, ed. E. Charrière (Paris, 1839).

Dante, *Le Opere di Danti Alighieri*, ed. E. Moore and P. Toynbee (Oxford, 1924).

Débat des hérauts d'armes de France et d'Angleterre, ed. L. Pannier and P. Meyer (Paris, 1872).

Deschamps, E., *Oeuvres*, ed. Le Marquis de Queux de St Hilaire and G. Raynaud (Paris, 1878–1903).

Diaz da Gamez, G., *The Unconquered Knight: a chronicle of the deeds of Don Pero Nino*, trans. J. Evans (London, 1928).

Douet d'Arcq, L., *Choix des pièces inédites rélatives au règne de Charles VI* (Paris, 1863).

D'Orronville, *Chronique du Bon Duc Loys de Bourbon*, ed. A.-M. Chazaud (Paris, 1876).

Du Cange, *Glossarium*, ed. G. A. L. Henschel, X (Paris, 1887).

Dugdale, W., *Monasticon Anglicanum* (London, 1830).

Duplès-Agier, H. (ed.), *Régistre criminel du Chatelet de Paris, 1389–92* (Paris, 1861–64).

Durmart: *Li Romans de Durmart le Galois*, ed. E. Stengel (Stuttgart, 1873).

Ehingen, J. von, *The Diary of Jorg von Ehingen*, ed. M. Letts (London, 1929).

Escouchy, M. de, *Chronique de Mathieu d'Escouchy*, ed. G. Du Fresne de Beaucourt (Paris, 1863).

Fitzwarin: *The Legend of Fulk Fitzwarin*, in R. Coggeshall, *Chronicon Anglicanum*, ed. J. Stevenson (RS, 1875).

Flores Historiarum, ed. H. R. Luard (RS, 1890).

Fougères, Etienne de, *Livre des Manières*, ed. F. Talbert (Angers, 1877).

Fulcher of Chartres, *Historia Hierosolymitana*, ed. H. Hagenmeyer (Heidelberg, 1913).

Fulgore di San Gimignano, *Sonnetti*, ed. F. Neri (Turin, 1925).

Galbert of Bruges, *Histoire du meutre de Charles le Bon*, ed. H. Pirenne (Paris, 1891).

Garin, La Mort de, ed. E. du Meril (Paris, 1846).

Gelre Herald, *Wapenboek ou Armorial du 1334 a 1372 . . . par Gelre Héraut d'Armes*, ed. V. Bouton (Paris, 1881).

Geoffrey of Monmouth, *Historia regum Brittaniae*, in E. Faral (ed.), *La Légende Arthurienne* (Paris, 1929).

Gerson, J., *Opera*, ed. E. Dupin (Antwerp, 1706).

Gesta Henrici Quinti, ed. B. Williams (London, 1850).

Ghislbert of Mons, *Chronicon Hanoniense* (MGH, SS XXI).

Gilbert of the Haye's Prose MS, ed. J. H. Stevenson (Edinburgh, 1914).

Gollancz, I., (ed.), *Parlement of the Thre Ages* (Roxburgh Club, London, 1897).

Gray, Sir T., *Scalacronica*, ed. J. Stevenson (Edinburgh, 1836).

Héfele, C. J., and Leclercq, H., *Histoire des conciles*, V (Paris, 1913).

Hemmerlein, F., *De rusticitate et nobilitate* (Strasbourg, ? 1490).

Hemricourt: *Oeuvres de Jacques de Hemricourt*, ed. C. de Borman and A. Bayot (Brussels, 1910).

Histoire de Guillaume le Maréchal, ed. P. Meyer (Paris, 1891).

Historia Pontificum et Comitum Engolismensium, ed. J. Boussard (Paris, 1957).

Hoveden, R., *Chronica*, ed. W. Stubbs (RS, 1869).

Humbert de Romans, *Tractatus solemnis de praedicatione sanctae crucis*, in T. Kaeffele (ed.), *Scriptores Ordinis Praedicantium Medii Aevi*, II (Rome, 1975).

Huon de Méry, *Le Tournoiement d'Antechrist* (Rheims, 1851).

Jacotin, A., *Preuves de la Maison de Polignac* (Paris, 1898–1906).

Jacques de Vitry, *Exempla*, ed. T. Crane (London, 1891).

Jerusalem: *La Conquête de Jerusalem*, ed. C. Hippeau (Paris, 1868).

John of Salisbury, *Policraticus*, ed. C. C. Webb (Oxford, 1909).

Joinville, J. de, *Histoire de St. Louis*, ed. M. Natalis de Wailly (Paris, 1868).

Juges: *Le Livre des Juges*, ed. d'Albon, le Marquis de (Lyons, 1913).

La Marche, O. de, *Mémoires*, ed. J. A. C. Buchon (Paris, 1836).

La Sale, A. de, *L'Histoire du petit Jehan de Saintré* (trans. I. Gray, London, 1931).

Lalaing, J., *Le Livre des faits de Jacques de Lalaing*, in *Oeuvres de G. Chastellain*, ed. K. de Lettenhove (Brussels, 1866).

Lambert of Ardres, *Historia Comitum Ghisnensium* (MGH, SS XXIV).

Lambert of Wattrelos, *Annales Cameracenses* (MGH, SS XVI).

Lannoy, Ghillebert de, *Oeuvres de G. de Lannoy*, ed. C. Potvin (Louvain, 1878).

Le Bel, J., *Chronique de Jean le Bel*, ed. J. Viard and E. Deprez (Paris, 1905).

Le Fébvre, Abbé, *Memoire pour servir a l'histoire de France du XIVe-siecle, contenant les statuts de l'ordre du St. Esprit* (Paris, 1764).

Le Févre, J., *Chronique de Jean Le Févre, Seigneur de St. Remy*, ed. F. Morand (Paris, 1881).

Leland, J., *The Itinerary of John Leland*, ed. L. Toulmin-Smith (London, 1907–10).

Lull, R.: Peers, E. A., (ed.), *A Life of Ramon Lull* (London, 1929).

Lull, R., *The Book of the Ordre of Chyvalry*, ed. A. T. P. Byles (EETS, 1926).

Lunig, J. C., *Teutschen Reichs Archiv* (Leipzig, 1710).

Machaut, G., *Oeuvres de G. de Machaut*, ed. E. Hoepffner (Paris, 1921).

Machaut, G., *La Prise d'Alexandrie*, ed. M. L. de Las-Matrie (Geneva, 1877).

Malaterra, G., *Historia Sicula* (RIS, V).

Malory, Sir T., *The Works of Sir Thomas Malory*, ed. E. Vinaver (Oxford, 1947).

Merlin, ed. G. Paris and J. Ulrich (Paris, 1866).

Méry, H. d, *see* Huon de Méry.

Meun, J. de, *L'Art de chevalerie*, ed. U. Robert (Paris, 1897).

Meun, J. de, *Le Roman de la Rose*, ed. E. Langlois (Paris, 1914–24).

Mézières, P. de, *Le Songe du vieil pèlerin*, ed. G. W. Coopland (Cambridge, 1969).

Mézières, P. de, *Letter to King Richard II*, ed. and trans. G. W. Coopland (Liverpool, 1975).

Monstrelet, F. de, *Chronique*, ed. L. Douet d'Arcq (Paris, 1857–62).

Nicolas, N. H., *The Controversy between Sir Richard Scrope and Sir Robert Grosvenor in the Court of Chivalry* (London, 1832).

Novara, P. de, *Mémoires*, ed. C. Kohler (Paris, 1913).

Novara, P. de, *Les Quatre Ages de l'homme*, ed. M. Fréville (Paris, 1888).

Ordene de chevalerie, in E. Barbazan (ed.), *Fabliaux et contes des poètes francais des 11e-, 12e-, 13e-, 14e- et 15e-siècles* (Paris, 1808), Vol. I.

Orderic Vitalis, *Historiae ecclesiasticae*, ed. A. Le Prevost (Paris, 1838–55).

Ordonnances des Roys de France de la Troisième

Race (Paris, 1723–1849).

Otto of Freising, *Gesta Frederici Imperatoris* (MGH, SS XX).

Oulmont, C., *Les Débats du Clerc et du Chevalier* (Paris, 1911).

Paris, Matthew, *Chronica Majora*, ed. H. R. Luard (RS, 1877).

Perlesvaus: *The High Book of the Grail*, trans. N. Bryant (Cambridge, 1978).

Pero Nino, *see* Diaz da Gamez, G.

Pisan, C. de, *see* Christine de Pisan.

Pontificals: M. Andrieu, *Le Pontifical Romain* (*Studi e Testi*, 86, Rome, 1938–40).

Prost, B. (ed.), *Traités du duel judiciare, relations de pas d'armes et tournois: par O. de la Marche, J. de Villiers, H. de la Jaille, A. de la Sale* (Paris, 1878).

Roland: *La Chanson de Roland*, ed. G. J. Brault (London, 1978).

Roll of Caerlaverock, ed. T. Wright (London, 1864).

Rüxner, G., *Turnierbuch* (Frankfurt, 1566).

Rymer, T., *Foedera* (London, 1704–26).

Sacchetti, F., *Novelle* (Milan, 1804–05).

Saisnes: *La Chanson des Saisnes*, ed. F. Michel (Paris, 1832).

Sarasin: *Sarasin: Le Roman du Ham*, ed. A. Henry (Paris, 1939).

Schaumburg, W. von, *Die Geschichten und Täten Wilwolts von Schaumburg*, ed. A. von Keller (Stuttgart, 1859).

Sicily Herald, *Le Blason des couleurs*, ed. H. Cocheris (Paris, 1860).

Sicily Herald, *Parties inédites de l'oeuvre de Sicile héraut d'Alphonse V Roi d'Aragon*, ed. P. Roland (Mons, 1867).

Sommer, H. O., *The Vulgate Version of the Arthurian Romances* (Carnegie Institute, Washington, 1909 ff).

Songe du vergier, ed. Brunet (Paris, 1731) and reprinted in *Revue du Moyen Age Latin*, XIII (1957).

Stevenson, J. (ed.), *Letters and Papers illustrative of the Wars of the English in France* (RS, 1861–64).

St. Albans Chronicle, ed. V. H. Galbraith (Oxford, 1937).

St. Albans: *Book of St. Albans*, ed. Wynkyn de Worde.

Suchenwirt, P., *Werke*, ed. A. Primisser (Vienna, 1827).

Suger, *Vie de Louis VI le Gros*, ed. H. Waquet (Paris, 1929).

Temple: *La Règle du temple* ed. H. de Curzon (Paris, 1886).

Trivet: *N. Triveti Annales*, ed. T. Hogg (London, 1845).

Troyes, Chrétien de, *see* Chrétien de Troyes.

Turpin: *The Old French 'Johannes' translation of the Pseudo Turpin Chronicle*, ed. R. N. Walpole (California, 1976).

Ulrich von Lichtenstein: *Ulrich von Lichtenstein's Service of Ladies*, trans. J. W. Thomas (Chapel Hill, 1969).

Upton, N., *De studio militari*, ed. E. Bysshe (London, 1654).

Vieillard, F., 'Un texte interepolé du cycle du Graal (Bibliothèque Bodmer MS 147)', *Revue d'histoire des textes*, 4 (1974).

Villehardouin, G. de, *La Conquête de Constantinople*, ed. E. Faral (Paris, 1939).

Vita Edwardi Secundi, ed. N. Denholm-Young (London, 1957).

Vitry, J. de, *see* Jacques de Vitry.

Wace, *Li Roman de Brut*, ed. le Roux de Lincy (Rouen, 1838).

Walter of Guisborough, *The Chronicle of Walter of Guisborough*, ed. H. Rothwell (Camden Soc., 1957).

Warkworth, J., *A Chronicle of the first thirteen years of the reign of King Edward IV*, ed. J. O. Halliwell (Camden Soc., 1938).

Warwick: *Pageant of the Birth, Life and Death of Richard Beauchamp Earl of Warwick*, ed. Viscount Dillon and W. H. St. John Hope (London, 1914).

Widukind of Corvey, *Res gestae Saxonicae* (MGH, SS III).

William of Malmesbury, *De gestis regum Anglorum*, ed. W. Stubbs (RS, 1887–89).

William of Newburgh, *Historia rerum Anglicarum*, ed. R. Howlett (RS, 1885).

William of Orange: *La Chanson de Guillaume*, ed. J. Wathelet-Willem (Paris, 1975).

Wolfram von Eschenbach, *Willeham*, ed. K. Lachmann (Berlin, 1926).

Wolfram von Eschenbach, *Parzival*, ed. A. Leitzmann (Tübingen, 1961).

Wright, T. (ed.), *Political Poems and Songs* (RS, 1859).

III. Secondary Works

Adam Even, P., *see* Even, P. Adam.

Aign, T., *Die Ketzel: ein Nuremberger Handelsherren und Jerusalempilgergeschlecht* (Neustadt, 1961).

Allmand, C. T. (ed.), *War, Literature and Politics in the late Middle Ages* (Liverpool, 1976).

Anglo, S., 'L'arbre de chevalerie, et le perron dans les tournois', in *Les Fêtes de la Renais-*

sance, ed. J. Jacquot and E. Konigson, III (Paris, 1975).

Armstrong, C. A. J., 'Had the Burgundian government a policy for the nobility?, in J. S. Bromley and E. H. Kossmann (eds.), Britain and the Netherlands, II (Groningen, 1964).

Artonne, A., Le mouvement de 1314 et les chartres provinciales de 1315 (Paris, 1912).

Ashmole, E., Institution, Laws and Ceremonies of the most noble Order of the Garter (London, 1672).

Barber, R., The Knight and Chivalry (London, 1970).

Barnie, J., War in Medieval Society: Social Values and the Hundred Years War 1337–99 (London, 1974).

Barthélemy, A. de, 'Etude sur les lettres d'annoblissement', Revue Historique Nobiliaire, 7 (1869).

Bédier, J., Les Legendes épiques (Paris, 1908–13).

Bédier, J., Les Chansons de Croisade (Paris, 1909).

Beltz, G. F., Memorials of the Garter (London, 1841).

Benson, L. D., Malory's Morte d'Arthur (Cambridge, Mass., 1976).

Berger, S., La Bible française au moyen âge (Paris, 1884).

Bezzola, R., Les origines et la formation de la littérature courtoise en occident (Paris, 1944–63).

Blair, C., European Armour, c. 1066–c. 1700 (London, 1958).

Bloch, M., Feudal Society, trans. L. A. Manyon (London, 1961).

Bloch, R. Howard, Medieval French Literature and Law (Berkeley, California, 1977).

Boase, R., The Troubadour Revival (London, 1978).

Bonenfant, P., and Despy, G., 'La noblesse en Brabant (XIIe-XIIIe siécles)', MA, 64 (1958).

Borst. A., (ed.), Das Rittertum im Mittelalter (Darmstadt, 1976).

Bosl, K., 'Noble unfreedom: the rise of the ministeriales in Germany', in T. Reuter (ed.), The Medieval Nobility (Oxford, 1978).

Bossuat, A., 'Un ordre de chevalerie Auvergnat: l'ordre de la Pomme d'Or', Bulletin Historique et Scientifique de l'Auvergne, 64 (1944).

Bossuat, A., 'La rançon de Guillaume de Chateauvillain', Annales de Bourgogne (1951).

Bossuat, A., 'La rançon de Jean Seigneur de Rodemak', Annales de l'Est (1951).

Boulton, D. A. J., 'The Origin and Develop-ment of the Curial Orders of Chivalry (Oxford D. Phil. Thesis, 1975).

Bouly de Lesdain, L., 'Etudes héraldiques sur le XIIe siecle', Annuaire du Conseil Héraldique de France, XX (1907).

Bourciez, E., Les Moeurs polies et la littérature de cour sous Henri II (Paris, 1886).

Boussard, J., 'Les mercenaires au XIIe siècle: Henri II et les origines de l'armée du métier', BEC (1945–46).

Boussard, J., 'L'origine des familles seig-neuriales dans la région de la Loire moyenne', CMM, V (1962).

Boutruche, R., La Crise d'une société: seigneurs et paysans en Bordelais pendant la Guerre de Cent Ans (Paris, 1963).

Brault, G. J., Early Blazon (Oxford, 1972).

Brooks, N. P., 'Arms, status, and warfare in late Anglo-Saxon England', in D. Hill (ed.), Ethelred the Unready: Papers from the Millenary Conference (Oxford, 1978).

Brundage, J. A., Medieval Canon Law and the Crusader (Madison, Wisconsin, 1969).

Buchtal, H., Miniature Painting in the Latin Kingdom of Jerusalem (Oxford, 1957).

Bullock Davies, C., Menestrallorum multitudo (Cardiff, 1976).

Bullough, D. A., 'Games people played: drama and ritual in medieval Europe', TRHS, 5th series, 24 (1974).

Bumke, J., The Concept of Knighthood in the Middle Ages, trans. W. T. H. and E. Jackson (New York, 1982).

Cahen, C., 'Le premier cycle de la croisade', MA, 63 (1957).

Catto, J., 'Florence, Tuscany and the world of Dante', in C. Grayson (ed.), The World of Dante (Oxford, 1980).

Chase, C. (ed.), The Dating of Beowulf (Toronto, 1981).

Chomel, V., 'Chevaux de bataille et roncins en Dauphiné au XIVe siècle', Cahiers de l'Histoire, VII (1962).

Christiansen, E., The Northern Crusades (London, 1980).

Cline, R., 'The influence of romances on tournaments of the middle ages', Speculum, 20 (1945).

Cohen, G., Histoire de la chevalerie en France (Paris, 1949).

Contamine, P., Guerre, état et société: Etudes sur les armées des Rois de France, 1337–1494 (Paris, 1972).

Contamine, P., 'The French nobility and the war', in K. Fowler (ed.), The Hundred Years War (London, 1971).

Contamine, P., 'Points de vue sur la chevalerie en France en la fin du moyen âge', *Francia*, 4 (1976).

Contamine, P. (ed.), *La Noblesse au Moyen âge* (Paris, 1976).

Contamine, P., 'Sur l'Ordre de St. Michel au temps de Louis XI et Charles VIII', *Bulletin de la Société Nationale des Antiquaires de France* (1976).

Contamine, P., *La Guerre au moyen âge* (Paris, 1980).

Cook, A. S., 'Beginning the board in Prussia', *Journal of English and German Philology*, XIV (1915).

Coopland, G. W., '*Le Jouvencel* (revisited)', *Symposium*, V (1951).

Coulson, C., 'Structural symbolism in medieval castle architecture', *Journal of the British Archaeological Association*, cxxxii (1979).

Cowdrey, H. E. J., 'The eleventh-century peace and truce of God', *Past and Present*, 46 (1970).

Cox, E., *The Green Count of Savoy* (Princeton, 1967).

Cripps-Day, F. H., *The History of the Tournament in England and France* (London, 1918).

Cust, Mrs. H., *Gentlemen Errant* (London, 1909).

Daumet, G., 'L'ordre Castillan de l'Echarpe (Banda)', *Bulletin Hispanique*, XXV (1923).

Davidson, H. R. E., *The Sword in Anglo-Saxon History* (Oxford, 1962).

Dean, R. J., 'An early treatise on heraldry in Anglo Norman', in *Romance Studies in memory of Edward Billing Ham* (California, 1967).

Delpech, H., *La Tactique au XIIIe-siecle* (Paris, 1886).

Denholm-Young, N., *History and Heraldry* (Oxford, 1965).

Denholm-Young, N., 'The tournament in the thirteenth century', in *Studies in Medieval History presented to F. M. Powicke*, ed. R. W. Hunt, W. A. Patin and R. W. Southern (Oxford, 1948).

Denifle, H., *La Désolation des églises, monastères et hôpitaux en France pendant la Guerre de Cent Ans* (Paris, 1897–9).

Dennys, R., *The Heraldic Imagination* (London, 1975).

Devoto, D., 'Folklore et politique au *chateau Ténébreux*', in *Les Fêtes de la Renaissance*, ed. J. Jacquot, II (1960).

Dorling, E. E., 'Canting arms in the Zurich Roll', *The Ancestor*, XII (1905).

Douptrepont, G., *La Litterature française à la cour des ducs de Bourgogne* (Paris, 1909).

Doutrepont, G., 'La croisade projetée par Philippe le Bon contre les Turcs', *Notes et Extraits de la Bibliothèque Nationale*, 41 (1923).

Doutrepont, G., 'Les mises en prose des épopées et des romans chevaleresques', *Mémoires de l'Académie Royale de Belgique, Lettres*, 40 (1939).

Du Boulay, F. R. H., 'Henry of Derby's expeditions to Prussia', in F. R. H. Du Boulay and C. M. Barron (eds.), *The Reign of Richard II* (London, 1971).

Duby, G., *La Société aux XIe et XIIe siècles dans la région mâconnaise* (Paris, 1953).

Duby, G., *Les Trois Ordres, ou l'imaginaire du féodalisme* (Paris, 1979).

Duby, G., *The Chivalrous Society*, trans. C. Postan (London, 1979).

Du Fresne de Beaucourt, G., *Histoire de Charles VII* (Paris, 1881–91).

Duparc-Quioc, S., *Le Cycle de la Croisade* (Paris, 1955).

Duparc-Quioc, S., 'La composition de la *Chanson d'Antioche*', *Romania*, 83 (1962).

Elm, K., 'Kanoniker und Ritter von Heiligen Grab', in J. Fleckenstein and M. Hellmann (eds.), *Die Geistlicher Ritterorden Europas* (Sigmaringen, 1980).

Erben, W., 'Schwertleite und Ritterschlag', *Zeitschrft fur historische Waffenkunde*, 8, (1918–20).

Erdmann, C., *Die Enstehung des Kreuzzugsgedankens* (Stuttgart, 1935).

Even, P. Adam, *Catalogue des armoriaux français imprimés* (1946).

Even, P. Adam, 'Un armorial français du XIIIe siecle: le rôle Bigot, 1254', *AHS*, 63 (1949).

Even, P. Adam, 'Les scéaux d'écuyers au XIIIe siècle', *AHS*, 65 (1951).

Even, P. Adam, 'Les fonctions militaires des héauts d'armes', *AHS*, 71 (1957).

Even, P. Adam, 'Les usages héaldiques au XIIe siècle', *Archivum Heraldicum*, lxxvii (1963).

Even, P. Adam, 'L'armorial universel du Hérault Gelre, Claes Haenen, Roi des Armes des Ruyers', *AHS*, LXXV (1961).

Favyn, A., *Le Théâtre d'honneur et de chevalerie* (Paris, 1620).

Fechter, J., *Cluny, Adel und Volk. Studien uber das Verhältnis des Klosters zu den Standen* (Stuttgart, 1966).

Feruguson, A. B., *The Indian Summer of English Chivalry* (Durham, North Carolina, 1960).

Fleckenstein, J., 'Zum Problem der Abschliessung des Ritterstandes', in *Historische Forschungen für W. Schlesinger*, ed. H.

Beumann (Cologne, 1974).

Fleckenstein, J., 'Friedrich Barbarossa und das Rittertum', in A. Borst (ed.), *Rittertum im Mittlealter* (Darmstadt, 1976).

Fleckenstein, J., *Herrschaft und Stand* (Göttingen, 1977).

Fleckenstein, J., and Hellmann, M., (eds.), *Die Geistlicher Ritterorden Europas* (Sigmaringen, 1980).

Fleckenstein, J., 'Die Enstelung des niedner Adels und das Rittertum', in J. Fleckenstein (ed), *Herrschaft und Stand*.

Flori, J., 'La notion de chevalerie dans les chansons de geste du XIIme siècle', *MA*, 81 (1975).

Flori, J., 'Sémantique et société médiévale: la verbe *adouber* et son évolution au XIIe siècle', *Annales*, 31 (1976).

Flori, J., 'Chevalerie et liturgie', *MA*, 84 (1978).

Flori, J., 'Les origines de l'adoubement chevaleresque: étude des remises d'armes et du vocabulaire qui les exprime', *Traditio*, 35 (1979).

Flutre, L., *"Li Fait des Romains" dans les littératures françaises et italiennes du XIIe au XVIe siècle* (Paris, 1932).

Fossier, R., 'La noblesse picarde du temps de Philippe le Bel', in P. Contamine (ed.), *La Noblesse au moyen âge.* (q.v.).

Fourrier, A. (ed.), *L'Humanisme médiéval dans les littératures françaises et italiennes du XIIIe au XVIe siècle* (Paris, 1964).

Frappier, J., 'Remarques sur la peinture de la vie des héros antiques dans la littérature francaise des XIIe et XIIIe siècles', in A. Fourrier (ed.), *L'Humanisme médiéval* (q.v.).

Frappier, J., 'Le Graal et la chevalerie', *Romania*, 75 (1954).

Freed, J. B., 'The origins of the European nobility: the problem of the *ministeriales*', *Viator*, 7 (1976).

Fréville, M., 'Les grandes copmpagnies au XIVe siecle', *BEC*, V (1843–4).

Galbreath, D. L., *Manuel de blason* (Lausanne, 1942).

Galway, M., 'Joan of Kent and the Order of the Garter'. *University of Birmingham Historical Journal*, I (1947).

Gautier, L., *Le Chevalerie* (Paris, 1884).

Gilson, E., 'La mystique de la Grâce dans la Queste del St. Graal', *Romania*, 51 (1925).

Gollut, L., *Mémoires historiques de la République Sequanoise et des princes de la Franche Comté*, ed. C. Dauvernoy (Arbois, 1846).

Gransden, A., 'The growth of the Glastonbury traditions and legends', *JEH*, 27 (1976).

Guilhiermoz, P., *Essai sur l'origine de la noblesse en France au moyen âge* (Paris, 1902).

Guyer, F. E., 'The influence of Ovid on Chrétien de Troyes', *Romantic Review*, 11 (1921).

Hale, J. R., 'Fifteenth and sixteenth century public opinion and war', *Past and Present*, 22 (1962).

Hanning, R. W., 'The social significance of 12th-century chivalric romance', *Medievalia et Humanistica*, new series, 3 (1972).

Hartshorne, A., 'Notes on collars of SS', *Archaeological Journal*, XXXIX (1882).

Harvey, R., *Moriz von Craun and the Chivalric World* (Oxford, 1961).

Hauck, K., 'The literature of house and kindred', in T. Reuter (ed.), *The Medieval Nobility*, q.v.

Hauptmann, F., *Das Wappenrecht* (Bonn, 1896).

Hewitt, H. J., *The Black Prince's Expedition of 1355–7* (Manchester, 1958).

Higounet, C., 'De la Rochelle à Torun: aventure de barons en Prusse et relations économiques', *MA*, 69 (1963).

Hoffmann, H., *Gottesfrieden und Treuga Dei* (Schriften der MGH, xx, 1964).

Holtgen, K. J., 'Die "Nine Worthies"', *Anglia*, 77 (1959).

Hommel, L., *L'Histoire du noble Ordre de la Toison d'Or* (Brussels, 1947).

Houseley, N. J., 'Politics and Heretics in Italy: anti-Heretical Crusades, Orders and Confraternities, 1200–1500', *JEH*, 33 (1982).

Huberti, L., *Studien zur Rechtsgeschichte der Gottesfrieden und Landesfrieden* (Ansbach, 1892).

Huizinga, J., *The Waning of the Middle Ages* (London, 1927).

Johrendt, J., '*Miles* und *milicia* im 11 Jahrhundert in Deutschland', in A. Borst (ed.), *Das Rittertum im Mittelalter*, q.v.

Jorga, N., *Thomas III, Marquis de Saluces: études historique et littéraire* (St. Denis, 1893).

Kennedy, E., 'Social and political ideas in the French prose *Lancelot*', *Medium Aevum*, 26 (1957).

Kilgour, R. L., *The Decline of Chivalry* (Cambridge, Mass, 1937).

Kirk, J. F., *History of Charles the Bold* (London, 1863).

Köhler, E., *L'Aventure chevaleresque* (Paris, 1974).

Köhler, E., 'Observations historiques et sociologiques sur la poésie des troubadours',

CCM, VII (1964).

Kruger, S., 'Rittertum bei Konrad von Megenburg', in J. Fleckenstein (ed.), *Herrschaft und Stand*, q.v.

le Genti, P., 'The work of Robert de Boron and the *Didot Percival*', in R. S. Loomis (ed.), *Arthurian Literature in the Middle Ages*, q.v.

La Curne de Ste. Palaye, J. B., *Mémoires sur l'ancienne chevalerie* (Paris, 1759).

La Rocque, A. de, *Traité de la Noblesse* (Rouen, 7735).

Landau, G., *Die Rittergesellschaften in Hessen* (Cassell, 1840).

Langfors, A., '*Le dit des Hérauts* par Henri de Laon', *Romania*, 43 (1914).

Lecoy de la Marche, A., *Le Roi René* (Paris, 1875).

Lejeune, R., and Stiennon, J., *La Légende de Roland dans l'art du moyen âge* (Paris, 1966).

Léonard, E., *Histoire de Jeanne Ire-Reine de Naples* (Paris, 1937).

Lewis, P. S., 'Une ordre de chevalerie inconnue, créée par un comte de Foix: le *Dragon*', *Annales du Midi*, 76 (1964).

Leyser, K. J., *Rule and Conflict in an early medieval society: Ottonian Saxony* (London, 1979).

Leyser, K. J., 'The German aristocracy in the early middle ages', *Past and Present*, 41 (1968).

Loomis, R. S. (ed.), *Arthurian Literature in the Middle Ages* (Oxford, 1959).

Loomis, R. S., 'Chivalric and dramatic imitations of Arthurian romance', in *Medieval Studies in memory of R. K. Porter* (Cambridge, Mass., 1939).

Loomis, R. S. and L. R., *Arthurian Legends in Medieval Art* (Oxford, 1938).

Loomis, R. S., 'Edward I, Arthurian enthusiast', *Speculum*, 28 (1953).

Lucas, R. H., 'Ennoblement in late medieval France', *Medieval Studies*, 39 (1977).

Maclagan, M., 'The heraldry of the house of Clare', *Papers of the XIII international congress of genealogical and heraldic sciences* (1982).

Mandach, Ade, *La Naissance et développement de la chanson de geste en Europe* (Paris, 1961f).

Mashke, E., 'Burgund und der preussiche Ordenstaat. Ein Beitrage zur Einheit der ritterlichen Kultur Europas im späteren Mittelalter', *Syntagma Friburgense* (Constance, 1956).

Massmann, E. H., *Schwertleite und Ritterschlag* (Hamburg, 1932).

Mathew, G., *The Court of Richard II* (London, 1968).

McFarlane, K. B., 'The investment of Sir John Fastolf's profits of war', *TRHS*, 5th series, 7 (1957).

McFarlane, K. B., 'A business partnership in war and administration, 1421–45', *EHR*, 78 (1963).

McFarlane, K. B., *Lancastrian Kings and Lollard Knights* (Oxford, 1972).

Menestrier, C. F., *Le Véritable Art du blason* (Lyons, 1672).

Meyer, P., 'Notices et extraits du MS 8336 de la bibliothèque de Sir Thomas Phillips', *Romania* XIII (1884).

Meyer, P., 'Les manuscrits français de Cambridge', *Romania* XV (1886), and XXXVI (1907).

Monfrin, J., 'Humanisme et traductions au moyen âge', in A. Fourrier (ed.), *L'Humanisme médiéval . . .*, q.v.

Monfrin, J., 'Les transducteurs et leur public en France au moyen âge, in A. Fourrier, *L'Humanisme médiéval . . .*, q.v.

Monti, G., *Le Confraternite Medievali* (Venice, 1927).

Morris, C., '*Equestris Ordo:* chivalry as a vocation in the twelfth century', *Studies in Church History* 15 (1978). ed D. Baker, 87-96.

Nelson, J. L., 'Inauguration rituals', in *Early Medieval Kingship*, ed. P. H. Sawyer and I. N. Wood (Leeds, 1977).

Nicholas, D. M., *Town and Countryside in Fourteenth-Century Flanders* (Bruges, 1971).

Nicolas, N. H., *History of the Orders of Knighthood of the British Empire* (London, 1841–2).

Obenaus, H., *Recht und Verfassung der Gesellschaften mit St. Jorgen Schild in Schwaben* (Göttingen, 1961).

Otto, E., 'Von der Abschliessung des Ritterstands', *Historische Zeitschrift*, 162 (1940).

Painter, S., *William the Marshal* (Baltimore, 1933).

Painter, S., *French Chivalry* (Baltimore, 1940).

Pannier, L., *La Noble Maison de St. Ouen, la Villa Clipiacum et l'Ordre de l'Etoile* (Paris, 1878).

Paravicini, W., 'Die Preussenreisen des Europaischen Adels', *Historische Zeitschrift*, 232 (1981).

Paris, G., 'La *Chanson d'Antioche* et la *Gran Conquista d'Ultramare*', *Romania*, 17 (1888).

Paterson, L., 'Knights and the concept of knighthood in the twelfth century Occitan epic', *Forum for Modern Language Studies*, 17 (1981).

Pauphilet, A., *Etudes sur la 'Queste del Sant Graal'* (Paris, 1921).

Peers, E. A., *Ramon Lull* (London, 1929).

Petersen, J., *Das Rittertum in der Darstellung des Johannes Roth* (Strasbourg, 1909).

Piaget, A., 'Le *Livre* Messire Geoffroi de Charny', *Romania*, XXVI (1897).

Pickford, C. E., *L'Evolution du roman Arthurien en prose vers la fin du moyen âge* (Paris, 1966).

Pietzner, F., *Schwertleite un Ritterschlag* (Heidelberg, 1934).

Pitt-Rivers, J., 'Honour and social status', in J. G. Peristiany (ed.), *Honour and Shame* (London, 1965).

Planche, A., 'Du tournoi au théâtre en Bourgogne: le Pas de la Fontaine des Pleurs à Chalon-sur-Saône, 1449–50', *MA*, 81 (1975).

Powicke, M., *Military Obligation in Medieval England* (Oxford, 1962).

Prestage, E., *Chivalry* (London, 1928).

Prinet, M., 'Le langage héraldique dans le *Tournoiement Antechrist*', *BEC*, 83 (1922).

Rajna, G., 'Le origine delle famiglie Padovane, e gli eroi dei romanzi cavallereschi', *Romania*, IV (1875).

Regout, R., *La doctrine de la guerre juste de St. Augustin à nos jours* (Paris, 1935).

Reiffenberg, H. de, *Histoire de l'Ordre de la Toison d'Or* (Brussels, 1830).

Renouard, Y., 'L'ordre de la Jarretière et l'ordre de l'Etoile', *MA*, 55 (1949).

Reuter, T. (ed.), *The Medieval Nobility* (Oxford, 1978).

Ritchie, R. L. Graeme, *The Buik of Alexander* (Edinburgh, 1925–29).

Ritter, J., *Ministérialité et Chevalerie* (Lausanne, 1955).

Robinson, I. S., 'Gregory VII and the soldiers of Christ', *History*, 58 (1973).

Robson, C. A., 'Vernacular Scriptures in France', in G. W. H. Lampe (ed.), *The Cambridge History of the Bible*, II (Cambridge, 1969).

Rocher, D., *Thomasin von Zerclaere: der walsche Gast* (Paris, 1977).

Rosny, L. de, *L'Epervier d'Or* (Paris, 1839).

Ross, D. J. A., 'L'originalité de Turoldus – le maniement de la lance', *CCM*, 6 (1963).

Rossbach, J., Les demands pour la jouste, le tournoi et la guerre de Geoffroi de Charny' (thesis deposited in BR, Brussels).

Russell, F. H., *The Just War in the Middle Ages* (Cambridge, 1975).

Sandoz, E., 'Tourneys in the Arthurian tradition', *Speculum*, 19 (1944).

Schäfer, K. H., *Deutsche Ritter und Edelknechte in Italien* (Paderborn, 1911–40).

Schneider, J., 'Sire Nicole de Louve: citain de Metz', in P. Contamine (ed.), *La Noblesse au moyen âge*, q.v.

Schulte, A., *Der Adel und die deutsche Kirsche im Mittelalter* (Darmstadt, 1909).

Schultz, A., Das Höfische Leben zur Zeit der Minnesinger (Leipzig, 1889).

Schultz, A., *Deutsches Leben in XIV und XV Jahrhundert* (Leipzig, 1892).

Seyler, G., *Geschichte der Heraldik* (Nuremberg, 1885–89).

Smail, R. C., *Crusading Warfare* (Cambridge, 1967).

Sneddon, C. R., 'A Critical Edition of the Four Gospels in the 13th-century Old French translation of the Bible' (Oxford, D.Phil. Thesis).

Spiegel, G. M., *The Chronicle Tradition of St. Denis; a survey* (Brooklane, Mass., 1978).

Stillfried, R. A., *Der Schwanenorden* (Halle, 1845).

Temple-Leader, J. and Marcotti, G., *Sir John Hawkwood* (London, 1889).

Thomas, J. W., *Ulrich von Lichtenstein's Service of Ladies* (Chapel Hill, 1969).

Thordeman, B., *Armour from the Battle of Wisby, 1361* (Stockholm, 1939).

Tolkien, J. R. R., '*Beowulf*: the monsters and the critics', *PBA*, 22 (1936).

Tourneur, V., 'Origine et symbolique de la Toison d'Or', *Bulletin de l'Académie Royal de Belgique*, Lettres, serie 5, XLII (1956).

Treis, K., *Die Formalitäten des Ritterschlags* (Berlin, 1877).

von Berchen, E., Galbreath, D. L., and Hupp, O., *Die Wappenbucher des Deutsches Mittelalters* (1939).

von Biedenfeld, F., *Geschichte und Verfassung aller geistlichen und weltlichen, erloschenen und bluhenden Ritterorden* (Weimar, 1841).

Vale, J., *Edward III and Chivalry*, (Boydell, 1983).

Vale, M., *War and Chivalry* (London, 1981).

Vale, M., 'A fourteenth century order of chivalry: the *Tiercelet*', *EHR*, 82 (1967).

Van Luyn, P., 'Les milites dans la France du XIe siecle', *MA*, 77 (1971).

Vanderjagt, A., *Qui sa vertu anoblist* (Groningen, 1981).

Vaughan, R., *Philip the Good* (London, 1970).

Verbruggen, J. F., *The Art of Warfare in Western Europe during the Middle Ages*, trans. S. Willard and S. C. M. Southern (Oxford, 1977).

Vercauteren, F., 'Un parenté dans la France,

du nord au XIe et XIIe siecles', *MA,* 69 (1963).

Villanueva, L. T., 'Memoria sobre la orden de caballeria de la Banda de Castilla', *Boletin de la Real Academia de la Historia,* lxxii (1918).

Villey, M., *La Croisade: essai sur la formation d'une théorie juridique* (Paris, 1942).

Vulson de la Colombière, M., *Le Vray Théâtre d'honneur et de chevalerie* (Paris, 1648).

Waas, A., *Geschichte des Kreuzzuges* (Freiburg, 1956).

Wagner, A. R., *Catalogue of English Medieval Rolls of Arms* (Oxford, 1950).

Wagner, A. R., *Heralds and Heraldry in the Middle Ages* (Oxford, 1956).

Waley, D., 'The army of the Florentine Republic', in N. Rubinstein (ed.), *Florentine Studies* (London, 1968).

Waley, D., *The Italian City Republics* (London, 1969).

Wallace-Hadrill, J. M. 'War and peace in the earlier middle ages', *TRHS,* 5th series, 25 (1975).

Walpole, R. N., 'The *Pélérinage Charlemagne:* poem, legend, and problem', *Romance Philology,* VIII (1954).

Walpole, R. N., 'Philip Mouskés and the Pseudo-Turpin Chronicle', *University of California Publications in Modern Philology* (1947).

Walpole, R. N. (ed.), *The Old French 'Johannes' Translation of the Pseudo Turpin Chronicle* (California, 1976).

Warner, M., *Joan of Arc* (London, 1981).

Werner, K. F., 'Unters cuhungen zur Fruhzeit des Französischen Furstentums', *Die Welt als Geschichte,* XVIII, XIX, XX.

White, Lynn, Jr., *Medieval Technology and Social Change* (Oxford, 1962).

Whiting, B. J., 'The Vows of the Heron', *Speculum,* 20 (1945).

Willard, C. C., 'The concept of true nobility at the Burgundian Court', *Studies in the Renaissance,* XIV (1967–68).

Wisman, J. A., *L'Epitoma Rei Militaris* de Végèce et sa fortune au moyen âge', *MA,* 85 (1979).

Wolff, P., 'La noblesse Toulousaine: essai sur son histoire médiévale', in P. Contamine (ed.), *La Noblesse au Moyen âge.*

Wormald, C. P., 'Bede, Beowulf, and the conversion of the Anglo-Saxon aristocracy', *British Archaeological Reports,* 46 (1978).

Wright, N. A. R., 'The *Tree of Battles* of Honoré Bouvet and the laws of war', in C. T. Allmand (ed.), *War, Literature and Politics in the late Middle Ages',* q.v.

Wylie, J. and Waugh, W. T., *The Reign of Henry V* (Cambridge, 1914–29).

Wyss, R. L., 'Die Neun Helden', *Zeitschrift fur Schweizerishe Archaölogie und Kunstgeschichte,* 17 (1957).

INDEX